THE
SECOND-HALF ADVENTURE

DON'T JUST RETIRE—USE YOUR
TIME, SKILLS, AND RESOURCES
TO CHANGE THE WORLD

KAY MARSHALL STROM

MOODY PUBLISHERS

CHICAGO

All Scripture quotations, unless otherwise indicated, are taken from the *Holy Bible,
New International Version®*. NIV®. Copyright © 1973, 1978, 1984 by International
Bible Society. Used by permission of Zondervan. All rights reserved.

Scripture quotations marked KJV are taken from the King James Version.

Scripture quotations marked NRSV are from the *New Revised Standard Version* of
the Bible, copyright 1989, by the Division of Christian Education of the National
Council of the Churches of Christ in the USA. Used by permission. All rights reserved.

Editor: Pam Pugh
Interior Design: Ragont Design
Cover image: LeVan Fisher Design
Cover photos: © Image Source Photography, © Alex Staroseltsev/Shutterstock
    Images and © OJO Images Photography/Veer.

Library of Congress Cataloging-in-Publication Data

Strom, Kay Marshall
    The second-half adventure : don't just retire— use your time, skills, and resources
to change the world / by Kay Marshall Strom.
        p. cm.
    Includes bibliographical references.
    ISBN 978-0-8024-7875-7
    1. Retirees—Religious life. 2. Retirement—Religious aspects—Christianity.
    I. Title.
    BV4596.R47S77 2009
    248.8'5—dc22
                                                                    2009008594

All websites and phone numbers listed herein are accurate at the time of publication
but may change in the future or cease to exist. The listing of website references and
resources does not imply publisher endorsement of the site's entire contents. Groups
and organizations are listed for informational purposes, and listing does not imply
publisher endorsement of their activities.

We hope you enjoy this book from Moody Publishers. Our goal is to provide high-
quality, thought-provoking books and products that connect truth to your real needs
and challenges. For more information on other books and products written and produced from a biblical perspective, go to www.moodypublishers.com or write to:

Moody Publishers
820 N. LaSalle Boulevard
Chicago, IL 60610

1 3 5 7 9 10 8 6 4 2

Printed in the United States of America

I humbly dedicate this book to all Second-Halfers
who are stamping their adventures with eternal significance.

CONTENTS

Introduction

High in the Himalayan mountains, where Nepal edges up against China, a line of sun-worshiping laborers stare into the rising sun and pray desperately for enough sustenance to make it through another day. Just one more day.

All around the world, billions of people perform myriad rituals and offer an untold number of sacrifices before hundreds of millions of deities in desperate attempts to curry favor and win their help. In southern India, one village prepares to sacrifice a little girl to the local goddess. A seven-year-old child's life in exchange for the hope of a disaster-free year, and, should the goddess be pleased, the village's continued survival.

In countries from northern Africa to those in the Middle East to Indonesia, Muslim fanatics volunteer to blow themselves up—as well as anyone unfortunate enough to be close by—in exchange for a promise of immediate admittance into paradise.

Why?

Because people everywhere are in a frantic search for hope. Because they are desperate to find meaning in this life and the promise of something positive to come. As Christians, we know that true hope only comes through Jesus Christ. He is the one who gives meaning to this life and the promise of an eternity in the presence of God. But so many in the world have never yet heard the name of Jesus. Or if they have heard, they don't know He is the Son of God, the Savior of the world.

There was a time when we Christians plunked a couple of dollars in the offering plate on Sunday mornings and trusted that enough money would be peeled off to support the career missionaries whose job it was to make certain that the gospel was shared to the ends of the earth. But the times, they are a-changing. Missionaries and mission fields are not what they used to be. The world has changed. We have changed, too.

It used to be that the face of missions was that of a man freshly out of Bible school, prepared to take his wife and little ones to spend their lives in Africa . . . or India . . . or China . . . or some other place no typical person ever intended to see. That's no longer the case. Today, missions has a whole new face, and increasingly that face is chiseled with wrinkles and topped by graying hair. A whole new wave of unexpected missionaries is washing across the globe, and they are much different from what many of us traditionally expected. Instead of that young couple, it's the couple's parents who are boarding the plane. Or maybe their grandparents.

Welcome to the stage, baby boomers!

I grew up in the church, but I must admit that I was never much interested in missions. To me, being sent to Africa or India or China seemed a punishment God meted out to people who had displeased Him. Either that, or missionaries were far greater saints than I ever hoped to be. I dozed through more mission slide shows than I can count. But I heard enough to know I did not want to be doing what those people up in the front of the church did—troop through unlovely places trying to convert unwilling locals. I prayed fervently to be spared the fate of being "called to be a missionary."

My attitude changed after I was asked to edit a book for Partners

International. The purpose of the book was to explain the idea of Western ministries that partner with indigenous ministries in order to achieve jointly what neither Western nor indigenous could achieve alone. Ordinary people could actually use their own talents and skills to step alongside our brothers and sisters around the world and work together to grow God's kingdom—*not* to remake ourselves to fit into a premade missionary mold, but to reshape that mold to fit what God made each one of us to be. What a concept!

When I met Nelson Malwitz and he told me about Finishers Project and its focus on the baby boomer generation, I could hardly wait to go to the Finishers website and plug in my own profile. Within the month, I had an opportunity to sit in on the Mission ConneXion in Portland, Oregon, and actually meet some of Finishers' one hundred-plus ministry partners.

Without the Finishers Project, and the cooperation of founder and Chief Innovation Officer, Nelson Malwitz, and President/CEO, Don Parrott, this book would not exist. It is due to their diligence, work, and organization that the rest of us have access to so much helpful information and that so complete an array of resources is available at the touch of a few computer keystrokes.

Today, high in the Himalayan mountains, where Nepal edges up against China, a fifty-two-year-old woman sits with a clutch of women gathered around her as she teaches them to make candles. Later, she will show them how to make soap. Under the tutelage of this missionary, the village women have started a business of their own, the first ever "store" in their area. They walk miles to neighboring villages to barter for such necessities as rice and beans and oil, then they bring it all back and stock their shelves. Now they will add candles and soap to their inventory, two luxuries no one in the area has ever had before. No longer will the villagers need to worry about sustenance for tomorrow.

In southern India, a village prepares its children, but not for the goddess. Child sacrifice was recently abolished. For the first time, the village children are going to school—even the girls. The teachers are

Indian, but they were trained by retired American teachers who spent three intensive weeks demonstrating various teaching methods. "For God . . . so loved . . . the world . . . " a seven-year-old girl reads as her teacher points out the words printed on a chalkboard.

Two retired businessmen have their bags packed, but they couldn't tell me where they were going because the area in which they will spend the next three months is too sensitive. "Just say North Africa," one suggested. "That's close enough." One man is an accountant and the other has expertise in the area of marketing.

A retired paralegal is on her way to Tanzania, although she had to get out a world map to see just where Tanzania is. "They have such a backlog of social justice cases there," she said. "I will be there for a month, so I can at least get some things moving through the system."

Another woman with a simple résumé—she is a mother and grandmother—is on her way to an orphanage in South Africa where she will sit in the sun-dappled courtyard under flowering bougainvillea and cuddle AIDS babies. She has an entire repertoire of lullabies to sing to them: "What a Friend We Have in Jesus" . . . "Amazing Grace" . . . "How Great Thou Art" . . . "The Old Rugged Cross" . . . "Jesus Loves Me" . . .

Men and women in the second half of their lives, living out the love of Jesus in their actions. Through their words, pointing the way to forgiveness. Through faith in Christ, opening the door to meaning in this life and hope for the next.

"The skills, experience and passions found in the boomer are exactly the qualities needed to enter the unreached portions of our world and be the presence of Jesus to those still needing to hear of God's unconditional love and forgiveness," says Don Parrott.

Welcome to missions, twenty-first-century style.

Chapter 1

Hey, World,
Here We Are!

Baby boomers—can there possibly be anyone who has not heard about them? Heard and heard and heard some more? So much has been written on this greatest population boom ever to hit the United States. In the eighteen years after World War II—1946 to 1964—seventy-seven million babies crammed their way onto the American scene. For ten years straight, the number of births increased annually until it peaked in 1957 with more than 4.3 million children ballooning the country's population.

So many Lindas and Jims, such a crowd of Bobs and Carols and Marys and Johnnys.

So many hopes and dreams and plans and goals, such a wealth of potential.

Flower children and peaceniks, protesters and activists, social reformers and would-be world changers. It always has been a booming generation of people determined to leave the world a better place than they found it.

Always passionate, always demanding to be heard, always championing a cause—when the notoriously independent baby boomers flooded onto the American stage, they cried out for change, and their voices rocked society.

Okay, generalizations are unfair. It is especially unfair to stereotype an entire generation. The fact is, baby boomers were an unexpectedly massive age-band that was shaped by its times. An uneasy peace and a tumultuous war . . . the promises of education for everyone and unlimited opportunity for all . . . great medical strides holding forth dramatic cures for devastating illnesses. Oh, and indulgent parents who had seen far too much suffering in their own Depression- and war-era lives to be willing to allow their children to endure any sort of deprivation.

The boomers who shook up society when they roared in as babies caused a whole new quake as their generation approached adulthood. But then harsh reality struck successive blows squarely at the heart of their optimism. You would be hard-pressed to find an upper-end age range baby boomer who cannot tell you exactly where he was when President John Kennedy was shot, or precisely what she was doing when she heard that Martin Luther King Jr. had been killed. In the wake of life's harshness, idealistic determination faded into day-to-day living. The boomer generation merged into the very same American success-driven existence against which they had so fervently railed.

In C. S. Lewis's great allegory *The Screwtape Letters*, senior devil Screwtape writes to junior devil Wormwood in order to instruct him in the art of pulling human beings over the edge of temptation. Screwtape tells his young protégé that it is especially easy to catch people as they move out of the middle stage of their lives. Screwtape points out all the disappointments and frustrations that "wear out a soul"—the routine of adversity, the decay of youthful hopes and dreams, quiet despair. But, he says, if a person's life has been prosperous, it is even easier to coax that person into temptation. "Prosperity knits a man to the World," Screwtape explains. "He feels that he is 'finding his place in it,' while really it is finding its place in him. His increasing reputation, his widening circle of acquaintances, his sense of importance, the growing pressure of absorbing and agreeable work, build up in him a sense of being really at home on Earth, which is just what we want."[1]

Had Screwtape been writing today, he might have come right out and told Wormwood, "Zero in on the baby boomers."

Many boomers have indeed made a wonderfully secure and self-sufficient spot for themselves here on earth. But now, when the generation that refused to trust anyone over thirty, who promised to stay forever young and vowed never to look back at life and say, "When I was your age, I . . ." looks in the mirror, what they see looking back at them are the faces of their parents. To their amazement, they hear themselves chide the young folks, "Why, when I was your age, I . . . " The fact is, boomers are on the cusp of becoming senior citizens (though they would never use that term!). Whether aching with disappointment over the passage of time or proud of their accomplishments, every seven seconds another one turns fifty. That's 12,000 people a day. Nearly 4.5 million each year.

As boomers enter the second half of life, because of their sheer numbers, they are poised to rock society all over again. As I write this, approximately 35 million Americans are age sixty-five or older. By the year 2030 that number will have doubled to a whopping 70 million. Some who look at this burgeoning population have raised a collective gasp of alarm. "What are we going to *do* with all those old folks?" they cry. "What will happen to our society? It's only going to get more and more decrepit!"

Those people underestimate baby boomers. Boomers have never done anything in the same old way things had always been done before, so why would they start now? The fact is, they are already in the process of reinventing retirement. And without a doubt, they are the ones to do it. Not only because of who and what they are, but because they are approaching their second half healthier, more educated, and more full of vigorous years than any generation that preceded them. They may be getting older, but they definitely remain a vital force to be reckoned with.

The second half of life is a time to be valued for its gain. As the Susans and Davids on the younger end of the boomer spectrum juggle families and careers, and as the Jims and Marys on the upper end search for significant ways to spend the rest of their lives, one thing is certain: boomers are blooming.

Boomers in Bloom

Consider Steve. He and his wife, Sherry, met and married when both were career navy. When Steve retired after twenty years, he was neither gray-haired nor wrinkled. He was only thirty-eight years old. Even so, he was skilled, fully pensioned, and eager to get on with his life in a meaningful way. "I just wanted to serve the Lord," Steve said.

Chances are good that Steve will be able to do that for many years, for another thing that happened during the baby boomer generation is the advance in longevity. In 1946, when the first boomers were born, life expectancy was sixty-five. Today, it is seventy-eight and increasing. By the time the youngest of the boomers approach their centennial birthdays, cakes flaming with one hundred candles will likely be a commonplace occurrence.

But it's not just a question of living longer. The boomer generation is also living better. They are on the leading edge of a phenomenon some call "down-aging." You've likely heard of it. People say: "Today's sixty is like our parents' forty." Or, "Eighty is the new sixty." Well, in terms of vigor and well-being, it's quite true. But the thing is, this doesn't just mean an extra fifteen years or so tacked on to the end of old age. No, those added years are padded into the middle of life. What baby boomers are seeing is a new and improved "midlife." Imagine what this means to someone taking an early retirement—such as Steve!

"I wanted to go to Bible school and then start a church," Steve said. "Or maybe I'd start a radio station. I wasn't quite sure."

Entire industries rose and fell on boom generation fads. Very quickly, businesses learned just how important it was to cater to their whims and ideas. This was a generation that knew what it wanted—

at least for the moment—and they had access to the money to buy. Pleasing them pretty much guaranteed market success. Ignoring them was business suicide. Boomers made up their minds, then they threw themselves into their passions. The generation framed by Vietnam and civil rights, bookended by peace and war, has always possessed a palpable drive to create change and an abiding belief that they had the power to accomplish anything.

"Sherry and I sold our house and lived on our retirement," Steve said. "We had everything all planned out. But things didn't work out the way we thought they would. As our savings ran low, I thought: *Oh, man, I'm a lazy bum.* But I really wanted my life to matter."

Just because the first wave of boomers is reaching the traditional age of retirement doesn't mean they have given up looking for ways to change the world. Besides this fact, consider the sheer numbers of boomers that are and will be available for engaging with the world: "As some of the demands of work and family . . . recede, boomers will have the potential to become a social resource of unprecedented proportions by actively participating in the lives of their communities."[2]

Yes, and not only in their communities, but also in the entire world! For instance, by September 2008, twelve months after the Peace Corps launched an online campaign aimed at baby boomers, applicants over the age of fifty had increased by a full 50 percent.

The leading edge of the boomer generation—the first 3 million—are marching into seniorhood just as they would want to—in good health, well-educated, and still filled with ambition. (Although somehow that word "senior" just doesn't seem to fit a generation as likely to be found zipping around Singapore on a motorcycle or poring over a new computer program as it is to be seen pushed back in a recliner for an evening of television.)

A Wealth of Experience

So, baby boomers being what they are, just about every group in the country is eyeing them. What organizations see is a mass of experienced potential volunteers. They cannot wait to tap into that unprecedented reservoir of knowledge and wisdom and energy and experience at the affordable price of—well, free!

Now consider for a moment: What if boomer retirees, whose passion is for God, were to take Christ's teachings seriously? What if they were to determine to use their acquired skills and expertise to demonstrate God's love to the world in practical ways? Imagine what could happen!

"The unique values and sheer numbers of the boomer generation have not taken God by surprise," Don Parrott of Finishers noted. "I believe He has been preparing exactly the kind of workforce He would need from North America at this time in history."

When Steve decided to start a new church, he considered his passion to serve the Lord, but he didn't think to look at the skills he had gained during his career in the intelligence community. It never occurred to him that they could be of use. But when he heard a speaker from a country where it really costs something to serve Christ, where the local people were the ones growing the church but yet badly needed help and support from the West, it made him stop and think. He accepted an application from the sponsoring organization. Then, just because he had that application, he went ahead and filled it out.

Truth was, the head of the ministry had impressed Steve with his passion, and so had the others associated with him. The ministry head was himself a member of an oppressed people group, and he spoke with a zeal that moved Steve's heart. So, when Steve was contacted and asked to come in for a personal interview with the ministry leader, he went. But he was honest. He said right out that he had already made his plans. He was going to start a church in the Midwest.

"Did you know that in the United States there is one pastor for every 250 people?" the ministry leader asked Steve. "You can start another church and affect 250 people, or you can join our ministry to the unreached people, and you can change the world."

Baby boomers have spent their lives identifying with the world. They crave purpose. It's what their generation has always been about.

Changing times don't change needs and desires, they merely alter the pathways to reaching them. In fact, if we frame "retirement" correctly, it may well give us the opportunity to actually live out all those unfulfilled dreams.

Being the most well-educated, healthiest retired generation in human history sets the bar high. But if ever a generation was up to the task, it is the baby boomers.

"I knew what God wanted me to do," Steve said. "He wanted me to get on board and hang on!" And in the end, that is exactly what Steve did.

Along with their other attributes, baby boomers can be a bit of an opinionated bunch. They insist on positions where they can make a difference. Never mind those outmoded ideas about hiring consultants to do the real work, then using volunteers to file stacks of papers and stuff envelopes. That just is not going to cut it with most baby boomers. Across the country, from libraries to urban renewal groups to government institutions to mission organizations, efforts are under way to figure out just what kinds of activities will both attract boomers and serve society. It's interesting the things they have come up with. Boomers can be great English teachers, for instance, both through local tutoring programs and in countries around the world. "Anyone can do it," says Bob Savage of Partners International. "Everyone everywhere is learning English. People in other countries already know the rules; they just don't know conversational English. So if you are a friendly person, even if you aren't a leader, all you need to do is spend a couple of weeks talking to people."

Some boomers are eager to travel the world—my husband and I have enjoyed teaching writing classes in India, for example—but other people only want to go as far as their computer. That's fine. Global Media Outreach is one organization that actively looks for just such people. It needs individuals willing to be trained to answer some of the hundreds of questions that come in to their online websites daily from people around the world. Some consist of comments (*From Texas:* "*It's funny, I was looking 4 ringtones & your pages came up with 4 steps 2 God.*

I am at work. God always lets me know he's with me.") but most have questions (*From India: "I am from India. My mom is a Christian and my dad is a Hindu. My question is can I accept Jesus as my Lord and saviour?"*). Every response is answered by a volunteer armed with resources.

Baby boomers have always been a *How-do-I-find-meaning-in-this?* generation. Now, as they begin to look toward their second half of life, they find themselves reflecting more and more on the meaning of their lives. And what they are coming up with is an entirely new way to garner change. They have already affected the North American church in unprecedented ways, and they will continue to do so. "We are just now seeing the early effects of sixty-year-olds who are relating to church in ways different than they did in their child-rearing days," says Don Parrott.

Who would have thought that in the dawn of their seniorhood, baby boomers would once again burst upon society with such strength of presence? Only this time, they come armed with time, abilities, skills, and hard-won life experience. Teachers and engineers, artists and writers and doctors, nurses and lawyers and secretaries, accountants and carpenters and quilt makers, farmers and plumbers and homemakers, and many others of every imaginable description, are ready to make their presence felt. People who have lived and loved and weathered life, people who know from firsthand experience what really matters, are ready and able to make a difference in the world.

Welcome back, boomers! The time has never been better for you.

We Make Our Plans, God Sets Our Path

Steve did not start a new church in the Midwest. He took the international job. Today, in his midfifties, he still works full time for the organization. And, yes, he is using the skills he developed and honed in his twenty years in intelligence work. "We are just one tiny cog in the body of Christ," he says of the organization. "And I'm just a small part of that cog."

Perhaps. Yet Steve is living life as it is meant to be lived. And all because he was willing to explore new avenues in his second half, to test his limits and see just how far he could go, and to make use of the skills he had gathered in his first half.

"Humanity does not pass through phases as a train passes through stations," C. S. Lewis wrote in *The Allegory of Love*. "Being alive, it has the privilege of always moving yet never leaving anything behind. Whatever we have been, in some sort we still are."[3]

Everything you always were and then some. That's great news, baby boomers. You are finally in a unique position to change the world. And the world is ready and waiting for you!

Chapter 2

What's Wrong with Golf?

For nine years I was the full-time caregiver for my first husband, Larry, who suffered from a rare genetic condition. After he died, I felt lost yet desperate to reinvent my life. When my friend Christina invited me to spend a week with her in the mountains, I jumped at the chance.

It so happened that a longtime friend of Larry's and mine lived close to the area where Christina and I stayed. His wife had died several years earlier, and he offered to show Christina and me around. The day was so pleasant. We drove to beautiful scenic areas, my old friend and I in the front seat of the car reminiscing, and Christina sitting quietly in the backseat. We three had a picnic together, we visited several tourist spots, then we all went to dinner and to a concert. Back in our hotel room, I chattered on and on to Christina about how much my friend and I had in common.

"So, when you finish talking about the old days, what will you say to each other then?" Christina asked.

I couldn't think of a single answer.

Right now, the question in your mind may be, "Why would I want to reinvent retirement? It sounds pretty good just the way it is." You dream about retirement, right? Every morning as you slap at the alarm clock with its infernal ringing, you dream. Each time you grudgingly set the morning newspaper aside, mumbling that you wish that just once in your life you had time to actually complete a crossword puzzle, you dream. As you again brush a layer of dust off your unused golf clubs, you dream.

It's true that retirement can sound pretty good.

The Desperation of Retirement

Retirement sounded good to Rich, too. A launch engineer employed by the government, his schedule was hectic and stressful. Rewarding and challenging, yes, but hectic and stressful nevertheless.

Rich had a wonderful position of responsibility and acclaim that commanded both respect and a healthy paycheck. He was used to being called "Sir," and he liked it. A man of faith, Rich was active in his church and he regularly led Bible studies in his home. Even though faith was a rare commodity among his colleagues, he made no apology for his relationship with Christ.

Everything Rich did, he did with eagerness and zest. And he did everything well. When he first began to dabble with making movies of his family, for instance, he invested in the best and most up-to-date equipment. Very soon he was making documentaries that his friends and neighbors actually stayed awake to watch. Over the years, as Rich moved from creative films of his family to meatier subjects, his editing proved to be as sharp as his photographic eye.

For twenty-eight years, Rich worked on the cutting edge of the aerospace industry. But his final years were fraught with frustration as his Christianity more and more became a pathway for scorn. And then he was offered an opportunity to retire early—and profitably. At the same time he heard about a major ministry's plans to produce a documentary showcasing its work around the world. What could be more perfect? This had to be from God! Rich could retire and be financially set for life. Instead of being ridiculed for his faith, he would go to work every day where he would be surrounded by fellow believers. Even more, he would be doing what he loved—filmmaking. Why, who knows, it just might be that his documentary would be good enough to win some type of award.

Bursting with eager anticipation, Rich sold his house, and he and his wife moved across the country. But when he went to check out his new office, he discovered it was simply a table and chair in a corner of the basement. The documentary? No, no, he was told, they had hired a professional to do that. Rich's job would be to catalogue the pictures in the "media morgue."

No one ever called him "Sir." In fact, few people called him at all. Rich was just another face in a pool of volunteers.

Rich is no longer associated with the organization. But he cannot go back to his old job either. He is retired and not on his terms.

"What can I do?" Rich asked in frustration. "Serve soup at a soup kitchen? I'm not saying that is beneath me, but it certainly is not using my gifts. As a retiree, I think I'm a hopeless case."

Not hopeless. But not atypical either. For many people—especially men—their identity lies in their careers and their value in the respect they get from others. Their jobs may be hectic and stressful, but they were energized by their careers. With that gone, they slump back like Rich and ask, "Is this all there is?"

"But what's wrong with sleeping late?" you ask. "And playing golf, and doing crossword puzzles?"

Nothing. Not a thing is wrong with any of that. Do all those things after you quit work. Take a nice vacation. Take two or three vacations. Or, if you want, do absolutely nothing at all. But the time is sure to come when your own version of Christina will settle herself in the backseat of your mind and ask: "But after you do this, what will you do then?"

How many hours can you sleep? How many puzzles can you work? How many rounds of golf can you play? The problem with the blessing of endless vacation is that it has a nasty way of turning into the curse of boredom.

Experts say that among people retired two to three years, they see an increasing amount of depression. They also say that relationships between husband and wife begin to deteriorate as retirement goes on. Rich can attest to both.

Another Way . . .

You may not relish slipping into a life of boredom, but the idea of pressing on at your job indefinitely isn't what you want either. This is precisely why reinventing retirement is such an exciting concept.

Active and busy is good. But actively busy at something meaningful is a whole lot better. This is why more and more boomers at the threshold of their second half are purposely pausing to take stock of the skills they've accumulated throughout their lives, the experiences they have amassed, and the talents they have identified. "I don't want to waste all this," they say. "There has to be some way for me to put it to good use."

That is good thinking. What a waste it would be to abandon the things we do well. To walk away from all those abilities we have honed over a lifetime. Reaching a certain age doesn't mean we throw off our God-given talents or forget our passions. Just the opposite.

In a past era, retiring to lazy days of waiting for the end to come might have made sense, but not today.

Paul was a carpenter and a businessman who owned a lumberyard in Iowa. He ran the business and his wife, Colleen, ran the office. The business was successful and profitable, and Paul and Colleen were good stewards of all it brought to them. Their church was hugely supportive of missions, and while Paul and Colleen were always ready to write a check, they did have the nagging feeling that giving money and never getting their hands dirty was taking the easy way out. All that changed when a ministry called Urban Impact, which works in the inner city of New Orleans, Louisiana, purchased an old bank building in the city and sent out a call for volunteers to help renovate it.

Being in the lumber business, Paul and Colleen knew a thing or two about construction and remodeling, so they were immediately interested. In January 1996, they took their first short-term mission trip—with a group of adults from Iowa to the inner city of New Orleans. "Talk about culture shock!" Paul said. "Talk about being out of our comfort zone!"

Yet Paul and Colleen were hooked, and the next January they went back. As they left on that second trip, Paul slipped a cassette into the van's player and the strains of the first song struck his heart: "I Surrender All." "I knew what God wanted me to do," he said. "Leave the lumber business and join the staff of Urban Impact Ministries."

Maybe so, but Colleen was not the least bit impressed by Paul's decision. Still, after much discussion and even more prayer, she agreed, and they made their plans. They would sell the business and begin a new career. With so much profit, they could buy an RV and travel the country for a couple of years, visiting a whole variety of ministries. That would still leave them with plenty of money to support their ministry and carry them comfortably through their golden years.

That was the plan, but that's not what happened. The business didn't sell. For three-and-a-half years it didn't sell. Finally, at a conference together, Paul and Colleen heard a speaker talk on Luke chapter 5 where Peter said, "Let's go fishing," and then caught not one boatload of fish, but two. It was verse 11 that really hit Paul: "So they pulled their boats up on the shore, left everything and followed [Jesus]." Paul said to Colleen, "That's it! It's time to leave it all on the shore and follow Him. It's time to close up the business and liquidate everything."

Liquidating meant no hundreds of thousands of dollars of profit. But it also meant no debts. And no more waiting. They began almost immediately to set things in motion, and two weeks after their liquidation sale ended, Paul and Colleen moved to New Orleans.

An Abundant Life

Some of us hail from warm and balmy states, and others of us spend our winters digging out of the snow. Some of us drive sleek automobiles, and others of us get around in old clunkers. Some of us never worry about our bank balance and others of us live on a strict budget. Wherever we are from, whatever the discomforts of our lives, we in this country have been gifted with a comfortable life. Yes, even those of us who struggle to make ends meet, even we who have to stretch our food budget to pay the rent. Even the ones who know what it is to endure a foreclosure or have had to liquidate a business. The very fact that we have shelter from the sun and the snow, and that we know we will not have to watch our families starve, puts us among the richest people in the world.

In 2 Corinthians 5:10, we read: "For we must all appear before the judgment seat of Christ, that each one may receive what is due him for the things done while in the body, whether good or bad."

Not that golf is bad, mind you. It certainly is not. Nor should we feel guilty about relaxing and enjoying ourselves after years of hard work. Nor does reinventing retirement mean you need to launch a new career the way Paul and Colleen did. What it does mean is keeping Christ's words in Luke 12:48 firmly fixed in your mind: "From everyone who has been given much, much will be demanded; and from the one who has been entrusted with much, much more will be asked."

Each of us is urged to take our gifts and passions and skills and push them beyond the easy places of safety and control. We are challenged to take them beyond our own self-sufficiency, and to move on into the area where we can do nothing but trust God.

That's not to say you need to sell everything and move to the inner city. Certainly such a move is nothing to take lightly. But do pause between your golf games, do set your crossword puzzles aside, and do be willing to take a chance. Do something of substance that gives you a bit of a scare. If you feel that God is leading you to make a big change, talk it over with another person. Accountability is a wonderful thing. Talk also to someone who has done this before—someone like Paul and Colleen. Who better to reassure you, and to ground you in reality, than someone who has already been there?

Volunteers

We ourselves are the best answer to that rumored specter of a flood of aging baby boomers washing over the country, hands ever out for higher Social Security checks and more Medicare payments. Our lives refute the dire warning that seniors, retired to lazy days on the golf course, will suck the country dry. Vivacious boomers simply are not about to sit around and contribute nothing. Consider the results of a survey conducted by Experience Wave, which is a national campaign to provide older Americans with more opportunities to stay engaged in work and volunteering. Its survey of adults fifty or older showed some interesting results:

- A majority (53 percent) say the coming wave of retiring baby boomers will actually be an asset to society. Not only will they be a pool of skilled workers, they will have more free time to dedicate to their communities. This compares to 35 percent who say they will be a major burden on society because they will put a severe strain on programs like Medicare and Social Security.
- Seventy percent said it is very important to find ways to keep older Americans engaged in society, such as working and volunteering.
- Nearly 60 percent said they themselves plan to do volunteer work.[4]

Some boomers will want to continue working full-time. They enjoy their jobs and they like the stimulation of the workplace. Besides, they watched their friends and relatives take early retirement only to slide into disappointment and boredom, and they have no intention of doing the same. They see the scientific surveys that show that people who continue to work as they grow older live longer, healthier lives than those who don't. So why should they quit? Not everyone wants to continue to work full-time, of course. And some who don't, worry that when they retire they will really miss the action and stimulation of the workplace. Their solution is to work part-time. Others have no choice. The retirement decision is made for them when they reach a mandatory age.

In whatever category you find yourself, reinvented retirement means a fresh chapter in your life. It is a perfect time to reevaluate your priorities and set new goals, to look over options, to begin new activities.

Civil rights leader and Baptist minister Dr. Martin Luther King Jr. said, "Our lives begin to end the day we become silent about things that matter."[5] Never in their lives have baby boomers been willing to stay silent about the things that matter to them. Why should they start doing so in their second half?

"If we boomers decide to use our retirement to change the world, rather than our golf game, our dodderdom will have consequences for society every bit as profound as our youth did," wrote Nicholas D. Kristof, Op-Ed columnist for *The New York Times*, in a July 2008 column.

Yes, and if we channel that into work for God's kingdom, it will have benefits for all eternity.

Consider Your Possibilities

"The feet take a person to where one's heart is," states an Ethiopian proverb.

Of course, where the heart is isn't necessarily where the paycheck is. But for many baby boomers, money isn't the point. When people were asked in a survey conducted by Merrill Lynch what would motivate them in their choice of second-half work, 67 percent responded: *continued mental stimulation and challenge.* Only 37 percent categorized *continued earnings* as a "very important" part of the reason they intended to keep working.[6] I wonder what the responses would have been had the survey been given to Christians and one of the choices had been *finishing well with a life of eternal significance?*

The parable of the talents (Matthew 25:14–30) is one of sobering eternal consequence. It teaches us that God gives us opportunities to invest our lives for His glory. It is our responsibility to match our abilities and be faithful to whatever extent we are equipped. We dare not bury our talent. The one-talent servant is just as important as the five-talent servant. Here is the wonderful thing: God measures us against ourselves, not against each other.

"I just don't know if there is a place for me," Rich said of a worthwhile second half.

The answer is, "There most certainly is!" It may not be making documentaries. It may not be anything you expect. But there is surely a place, and you are even now being prepared for it.

Paul and Colleen were businesspeople. That's what they went to New Orleans to do, and that's what they did there—worked in an office. Until Hurricane Katrina hit, that is. Then, because they were knowledgeable and settled in the city, they were in a perfect position to be hands-on people helpers. In Iowa, they could not possibly have known what God was preparing them for. But He knew.

According to the Merrill Lynch survey, baby boomers are ten times more likely to put others than themselves first (43 percent) compared to those who put themselves first (4 percent). The more skeptical among us might say, "Well, that's how they want to see themselves." Perhaps so. But it is still a long way from the priorities of the so-called me generation.

What's wrong with golf? Nothing at all.

Not a thing.

But the very fact that you are reading this book indicates that you are not entirely convinced about golf, or any such leisure activity, being the sole choice for the rest of your life. "The feet take a person to where one's heart is." Could it be that your heart is urging you to put down the golf clubs and the crossword puzzles and ask: "Okay, Lord, what would You have me to do now"?

Chapter 3

Reweaving
a Dream

For my husband, Dan, and me, the turning point came in Indonesia. We were there a year after the great tsunami disaster to document the way donor funds had been used to aid victims. In a devastated village just outside the tsunami epicenter, where over half the population was washed away, every family had a tale of horror to tell. The area was 100 percent Muslim. Never before had the people even seen a Christian. Yet a government official who had come to dedicate the new school announced to the assembled handful of Westerners, "We know your love for God. You showed it to us when you showed your love for us."

We Americans like to think of ourselves as the global good guys. As a matter of fact, the tsunami was a time when Americans displayed themselves in a truly positive light. The Pew Research Center reported that in the wake of our response to that disaster, favorable opinions of the United States jumped from 15 percent (in 2003) to 38 percent (in 2005). But overall, we are not nearly as popular as we think we are. I have had the privilege of traveling to forty-one countries, mostly to talk with people in conjunction with writing projects,

and much of what I have seen and heard has been anything but favorable. Between some of our diplomatic strategies and the invasive
influence of American pop culture, at the time of this writing, world
opinion of America has sagged even among our allies. (It seems that
the rest of the world is as sick of chase-and-shoot movies and self-
important singers as we are!)

Perhaps this situation is already changing. One way to continue to
improve the world's perception of Americans in general—and of
American Christians in particular—is for us to actually move into
some of the places where people rely on preconceived ideas, or no
ideas at all, to form their opinions. If we settle down and live alongside
the world's poor and unreached, if we work with them and learn about
their culture rather than simply preaching to them, we will discover a
unique opportunity to demonstrate how much we really do care.

For Paul, the turning point came when he saw how much difference a team of dedicated workers can make in an American inner city.
When Hurricane Katrina roared through New Orleans and the levees
broke, he and Colleen were affected just like their neighbors. They, too,
had to be evacuated. It wasn't what they signed on for, but they were in
New Orleans "for such a time as this." And it was because they were
already there, because they were affected right along with everyone
else, that they were able to minister in ways no outsiders could. Only
in heaven will they know the full extent of their ministry.

For Tom, the turning point came when he unexpectedly found
himself between jobs with the benefit of three years' pay. He had a
prestigious background: naval officer, banking executive, associate in
a law office, upper management in business. And then, in his midfifties and with three pre–high school children, he found himself in a
sudden life gap.

"I enjoyed my business life," Tom said, "but I wanted to do something of eternal significance."

Tom considered several options, and the one that especially interested him was an opportunity to go to Uganda for a couple of years
to manage a children's home.

"I took my wife out to dinner and I told her what I had in mind," Tom said. "At first she seemed pleased, but the next day she said she didn't feel God's leading. It was the hardest time in our marriage."

Tom's wife had legitimate concerns. Their son had been injured in a bike accident and had to be rushed to the emergency room. "What if we were in Africa and this happened?" she asked. "How can we take that chance with our children?"

At Tom's suggestion, he and his wife went to the annual envisioning meeting at New Hope Children's Center in Uganda. The first thing Tom did was locate the hospital and show it to his wife. "I was certain the trip would convince her," Tom said. It did. It convinced her that she did not want to take her family to Uganda!

Finally Tom told his wife, "Okay, we won't go." When he said that, his wife answered, "Let's go." Tom suggested one year. His wife said two years. Feeling free to have a say in the matter was her turning point.

Turning points can be encouraged, and they can also be stymied. Destructive myths can delay turning points because they drain us of a sense of what is possible. But watching potential in action, seeing others model what can be done, encourages us to reach out and grasp our own turning points.

Four Myths and a Model

Perhaps because baby boomers descended upon the country in such massive numbers, their generation has attracted more than its share of labels. More than its share of those labels have stuck, too. The majority are not flattering. So where are the facts behind the most persistent of the baby boomer myths?

Myth #1: *The "Me" Generation Thinks Only of Itself.*

The "me" generation—now that is a tag that has certainly stuck. Strange, since boomers are particularly united by their social awareness and their deep concern for both this country and the world. A full 70 percent say they feel a responsibility to make the world a better place.[7]

After the attacks of September 11, 2001, I longed to hear from our Christian brothers and sisters in the hard places of the world and to tell their stories so that we in this country could better know and understand them. I already had books out through several Christian publishing houses, so I contacted each of them with a proposal. My idea was that I would travel around the world and gather challenging and inspiring stories for a book to share with American believers. But again and again, I got the same response: Sounds intriguing, but not enough of a readership. Finally the soon-to-be-retiring senior editor at one major publishing house told me flat out, "It's a great idea, Kay, and I would love to read such a book. But the fact is, no one will buy it. Americans simply don't care about anything beyond their own borders." The editor for books aimed at people in their twenties and thirties, who herself happened to be at the younger end of the baby boomer age range, happened by just at that moment. "Speak for your own generation, not ours," she said. "We care very much!"

The boomer generation has a history of recognizing social needs in this country. Just look at the progress made in the area of civil rights. Boomers have also shown that they care about the world. Look at the difference made by the Peace Corps. In ways sometimes wise and sometimes wild, baby boomers have shown that they certainly do care.

Myth #2: *Poor Old Boomers Are Technologically Challenged.*

The world has changed more quickly and more drastically during the boomers' lifetime than during any generation before them. It's hard to imagine that when the first of them were born, almost no one had a home television. It wasn't until 1948 that the most progressive families took some of their accumulated war-years savings and splurged on television sets. This being the case, the reasoning goes, how can anyone expect a generation with such ancient roots to keep up with the lightning-speed development of technical gadgets?

Expect it or not, the study respondents report that 82 percent of them use the Internet. And not simply for e-mail or quick reference, either. Many say they download movies and music, they take full advantage of digital photography, and they use a whole array of digital equipment.

For some, the Internet is a means to a ministry.

Myth #3: *Baby Boomers Are Rich, Rich, Rich.*

While it's true that boomers are the wealthiest generation in history, they are hardly rich. In fact, one quarter have no savings at all. Some are under the mistaken impression that they have more than they actually do—as many discovered when the stock market went into free fall in the latter half of 2008. And as Paul and Colleen discovered when they had to sell their business, their home, and all their possessions at liquidation prices.

Myth #4: *Baby Boomers Will Be Retiring En Masse.*

We have already done a pretty thorough job of busting this myth. According to the Merrill Lynch study cited earlier, a mere one in ten plans to stop working at retirement age. Many are already working at second careers. Others are already in volunteer positions. And an increasing number are exploring creative possibilities for serving Christ.

. . . *And a Model*

Worldwide focus . . . capable and adept . . . understanding of limitations (financial and otherwise) . . . eager to stay involved. Sound like a snapshot of you? If so, you are probably asking, "Where do I go from here?"

Our greatest marching orders come from Jesus Himself. We read them at the end of the book of Matthew: "Therefore go and make disciples of all nations, baptizing them in the name of the Father and of the Son and of the Holy Spirit, and teaching them to obey everything I have commanded you" (Matthew 28:19–20). You can do this on the golf course. You can do it in your community. You can do it at a part-time job. You can do it as you volunteer at the library.

Or you can do it in a place few other Christians go.

What Do You Want?

You, with your skills and abilities and time, are a valuable commodity. Many organizations will be vying for your time and talents. So how *should* you spend the second half of your life?

That depends on what you want. What is it you really care about?

Mike wants to see Christians more involved in governmental endeavors. Patti wants to teach children in another country. Kathy wants to show Jesus to women through the quilt she designed. Helen wants to write books and David wants to illustrate them. Tom wants to train up a new generation of globally aware Christian businessmen and women. Paul and Colleen—well, they just want to obey God.

How about you? Now is your chance to do whatever it is that has been calling you. Now is your time to catch hold of your second-half vision.

Once you know what you want to do, you can begin to make a plan for your second-half adventure.

You may find that your dream adventure calls for a long step of faith. But if you take time to do the research, if you ask the important questions and do your best to answer them honestly, you will have a much easier chance of making a smooth transition from here to there.

Change is always a challenge. Give yourself every opportunity to make it successful before you go for it!

A good way to do this might be to ease yourself into a potential new position. Is there a short-term opportunity that will give you a trial run? Can you volunteer on a temporary basis before you make a firm commitment? Can you find a natural starting point? If so, what steps will help you take the best advantage of that starting point?

We have been encouraged to think of retirement as the natural result of reaching a certain birthday. But in fact, life stages evolve. For instance, it has been less than two hundred years that we have had any concept of adolescence at all. Throughout most of history, teenagers were simply adults. Only recently has a stage between childhood and adulthood been recognized.

In the past, the years after a person's career has come to an end have generally been a time to get things in order and prepare for life's end. In fact, if you look up the word *retire* in the dictionary, you will find such stark definitions as: *To withdraw from active life* and *To depart*.

But consider this: What if your work-for-hire years have simply been prep time for the most important part of adulthood? What if the next ten or fifteen or twenty or thirty years is what you were really made for? What if your second half turns out to be your opportunity to throw all your accumulated skills and training and education and life experiences and financial resources behind a new and exciting kingdom opportunity?

For most of us, when we recognize a specific need, our perspective shifts from taking it easy to wanting to effect a real change. And more often than not, the initial recognition comes about because we have already been faithfully serving in what seemed to be a small, unimportant ministry.

Today, the main players in overseas kingdom work are not trained cross-cultural missionaries, nor are they nongovernmental organization (NGO) professionals. They are everyday folks who take their current experience and use it to serve people and point them to Christ.

Finishers Project

"Okay," you say, "here am I. So how do I know what's out there? And how do I know what fits me personally?"

If you are like most of us, your first impulse will be to let your feelings be your guide. So let's begin with a couple of warnings about going with your feelings. If you have had a successful career, but you are tired of it and feel ready to toss it aside and jump into something with significance, step back for a bit. Significance doesn't often come along that easily. If you have a hobby you really enjoy, and you have been dreaming about spending all your time on it and making that your new full-time ministry, tread slowly. What is fun and challenging as a hobby has an annoying way of turning into not-so-fun work when it becomes a full-time job. If you are great at your job but you want something new, and you figure, "Hey, if I can do one thing successfully, surely I can be just as successful doing something else," take warning. It's a common assumption, but understand that in unfamiliar territory, you will be both unknowing and an unknown.

So, if you can't go with your feelings, what are you to do?

Right here is the very reason I didn't write this book several years ago. The idea was there, and so was encouragement from both readers and the editor at Moody Publishers. But I just couldn't get past this question: *How can a person know what to do?*

It was when I bumped into a representative of Finishers Project at a mission conference several years ago that an answer began to dawn. A cooperative movement of some one hundred leading mission organizations, Finishers has put together an entire program to help people— especially baby boomers—find their second-half niche in the kingdom of God. (The name *Finishers* refers to finishing well.) In 1996, founder Nelson Malwitz, who at the time had a prestigious career as a chemical engineer in research and development for a multinational company, went to an industry meeting for missions and came away determined to get mission organizations talking to one another about receiving a wave of people who had already had marketplace careers. Then he used his cutting-edge computer skills to sketch out an approach of matching up retirees with volunteer mission projects. The first Finishers Forum conference was held two years later, in 1998. Since then, Finishers has helped over three thousand people move toward ministry-related roles, and has served over 25,000 individuals who desire to do something that really matters in the second half of their life. By presenting them with a full spectrum of opportunities—both at home and abroad, both short-term and long-term—Finishers helps interested people make an informed decision about their second-half adventure.

A year after Hurricane Katrina blew through New Orleans, Paul and Colleen sensed that the work for which God had brought them to that city had been accomplished. When a subsequent possibility in Alaska ended up with a closed door, they were left confused and floundering. "I had no idea what to do," Paul says. "I didn't know how we were going to make ends meet." It was at this lowest point that he stumbled across the Finishers Project website (http://finishers.org). "I immediately began to post my profile," he recalls, "although it did take more nudging from the Holy Spirit to get me to actually hit the 'submit' key!" A week and a half later, Paul had already gotten eight replies from interested organizations.

The areas in which many business and industry baby boomers have excelled—flexibility, creativity, focus, and organization—are the very ones many mission agencies need. But they have as much trouble locating interested and qualified individuals as interested and qualified individuals have finding them. The director of regional mobilization for Wycliffe said, "Finishers.org is the eHarmony.com of mission work. A person who is seeking a position lists all their traits and plugs in their abilities. The agencies do the same. Then the computer matches them with each other."

The Changing Face of Missions

If you still think of missionaries as folks running through the jungle seeking out people to convert, you are badly in need of an update. Even if that approach were accurate—which it definitely is not —a majority of the countries most in need of the gospel have their doors locked and bolted against those long thought of as "traditional missionaries." This includes China, India, most of the countries that end in "stan," North Africa, and the countries of the Middle East. And yet those very same doors swing wide open for computer specialists, or English teachers, or civil engineers, or doctors or nurses, or any one of a number of other skilled people. Today, the nations of the world want to know how to do business, agriculture, government—even church planting and organization. And these tasks are best taught by mature people. The main players in missions today are laypeople who take their expertise and use it to serve people in other nations. They are the ones who come alongside local Christians in other countries and enable them to do what they can do best.

An estimated 1.5 billion people have never had a chance to hear the gospel of Jesus Christ—more than a quarter of the earth's population! People are already at work on the front lines in adjoining areas, people such as Dr. B. E. Vijayam of TENT Ministries in Hyderabad, India, who is methodically training indigenous Indian Christians to go out and reach the four thousand unreached people groups of that country.

Still, millions of others live where no Christian nationals do same-culture evangelism. The best way of reaching out to them is to live among them, to work and sweat alongside them, and to help them improve their lives. When people see us caring and reaching out to help, it can give hope and soften the hearts of even the most hardened cynics. This is missions today.

Paul and Colleen now both work full time on the staff of Finishers Project. But a commitment such as theirs is by no means required.

ReachAcross, for instance, looks for short-term workers for anywhere from six months to two years who teach English in Muslim areas. Business as Mission (BAM) has opportunities for businesspeople to go abroad to consult and teach on business methods, ethics, and other topics that often end in the formation of small businesses. Mission Aviation Fellowship (MAF) has welcomed early retiree pilots willing to mentor its pilots. Global Media Outreach trains volunteers to sit at their own computers and respond to people's spiritual inquiries. Imagine that you had been the person who had the privilege of answering this message: "I want to be saved by Christ, but my whole family is Muslim and they have promised to disown me. Will you help?"

Is your old dream of profit margins and financial success wearing thin? Here is the solution: Reweave that dream with the everlasting threads of eternity.

In Psalm 31:15, the psalmist David wrote, "My times are in your hands."

You can pray that very same prayer. To understand this truth, to truly believe it, will bring equilibrium to the span of events that make up your life.

Moving on In

After a dramatically miraculous escape from slavery in Egypt, after following up that great success by forty years of wandering in the wilderness, the Israelites found themselves faced with a whole new future. Moses had died, and now Joshua was going to lead them on into the land God had promised them. Finally, their long time of preparation was over, and it was time to move on to where they were supposed to be. As they prepared to cross the Jordan River under the direction of their new leader, as they prepared for a whole new life that was going to require walking by faith, they said to Joshua: "Whatever you have commanded us we will do, and wherever you send us we will go" (Joshua 1:16).

What a great verse to claim as your own as you begin your second-half adventure!

Prep time is behind you. You have put in your years of learning, you have developed your skills, and you have honed your talents. Your best is yet to come!

Chapter 4

But I Don't Have That Much to Offer

For Christmas my husband gave me a beautiful, 16-inch globe set in an elegant cherrywood stand. As I brushed my hand over the flat deserts of Africa, I recalled my travels in that great continent, and the haunting words from the refugee camps of Sudan rang in my mind: "Does anyone know we exist? Does anyone care about us?"

I ran my hand up to Egypt and thought about the believers there who bear tattooed crosses on their wrists that forever mark them as followers of Christ. Across the Red Sea to Saudi Arabia; then to the huge, irregular land mass of China where more believers than anyone can count are tucked into its mountains and valleys and plains; then across the raised peaks of the Himalayan mountains where networks of sex traffickers entrap unsuspecting girls; and on down through the mosaic of India where so many people have become so very dear to me. From Australia, my fingers traced the deceptive smoothness of the vast Pacific Ocean. So much ocean, peppered here and there with islands I never knew existed. And finally, on the other side of the world, North America and home.

I spun the globe around and watched as a kaleidoscope of continents and countries zipped past. I felt as though I had the whole world at my fingertips.

You know what? I do! And so do you.

Right here I want you to know something about me: I have no astounding background. I have no medical training, I am not a businessperson, and I am no technology expert—not by a long shot! I use a computer, but no one would ever make the mistake of asking me for computer assistance. What I am is a writer, and in my distant past, an elementary school teacher; I spent many of my teaching years in the capacity of a substitute teacher. I am also a wife and the mother of grown children. Throughout my life I have done volunteer work in the church—mainly, whatever most needed doing. Sounds like a pretty pathetic résumé, doesn't it? Yet I went to the Finishers website and filled out all the forms and questionnaires. *Here goes nothing*, I figured as I clicked the "submit" key.

Imagine my amazement when the responses started coming in. Here is just a small sample:

From ISP (International School Project):

"Greetings from the offices of ISP! Thank you for taking the time to research mission opportunities through the Finishers Project website. They forwarded your inquiry to us as matching some of the mission opportunities that we have available.

"Between May 1991 and December 1996, ISP trained almost 42,000 public school teachers in 119 cities in Russia, Ukraine and eight other countries in the former Soviet Union and Eastern Europe to use the *JESUS* film and a Bible-based curriculum called *Foundations of Christian Ethics* in their classrooms. Most of these teachers made major changes in their belief systems, going from atheism to a solid belief in God.

"The CoMission, a unified effort of over 80 organizations and churches, was formed to send teams of 6–10 Westerners to each of these cities for at least one year to follow up and disciple those teachers. This resulted in over 1,500 workers going to 53 cities over a six-year period.

"This still left the teachers in 66 of the original Convocation cities, however, without any form of follow-up. Therefore, in 1996 ISP began a second-phase strategy to take teams of Westerners back to these remaining cities to equip teachers with additional teaching skills and to help them take the next step in their spiritual journey. The Character Development Seminar (CDS) Trips and Leadership Development Conference (LDC) Trips were designed to provide a means of follow-up and discipleship for these teachers."

From Global Media Outreach:

"A primary area of ministry interest is writers. Our preference at this point is to commit to short-term, from six months to two years. We are open to where in the world opportunities might be."

From Operation Mobilisation (OM):

"Some people do work as 'tentmakers' in more sensitive areas. With this amount of diversification, we can almost always find a place for anyone called by God to serve in missions. At the same time, we are committed to helping you in any way we can to find exactly where God would have you serve, whether it is with OM or one of the many other worthy agencies doing God's work. We, ourselves, are 'finishers' and have traveled this path of discovery."

From ReachAcross:

"The Finishers Project connected your name with us . . . Evidently some of the countries or regions which may be of interest to you are a part of the Muslim world which has been the main focus of our team for more than fifty years. "

I received over thirty responses. Imagine, so much interest for someone like me! Some responses I passed over fairly quickly, but others really intrigued me. Teaching in a venue that is changing the belief system of an entire area? What an amazing idea! And how about the Muslim world? What could I possibly do there? It would be an exciting option to explore.

Our world truly is shrinking. One nation's pain today will tomorrow become global anguish. Not everyone likes us, nor does everyone like the God we serve. But for multitudes, it has nothing to do with like or dislike; people simply do not know God. And unless they hear from someone like you and me, they never will.

Doubts and Fears

David is a professional artist, a painter, and a printmaker who has appreciated both the freedom and the frustrations of self-employment. His wife, Helen, is a writer. Since 1988, they have worked together, combining their talents to produce quality products such as their beautiful hardback picture book on Psalm 23, *The Lord is My Shepherd*.

David and Helen always supported various ministries, but in 1999, they decided they would donate books instead of money. Rather than give $1,000, for instance, they could give an organization an equal amount in books that it could turn around and sell for five times that amount. When they saw how much their books were appreciated and enjoyed by those who could afford to buy them, their hearts were moved for those who could not. So they expanded their giving to include foster kids and children in shelters. Then they reached out with books for homeless children in tent cities.

"We wanted to touch the lives of as many hurting people as we could," Helen said. "And that included those who had made bad choices and those who had given up on themselves."

So David and Helen sent copies of *The Lord is My Shepherd* to prisons, as well.

"Picture books aren't just for children," Helen says. "A book like this is filled with color and life. Every page has beautiful images, and the words are easy to read. This is important because many people in prison can hardly read. Even if they can, it is not easy to concentrate in such a place."

If you are having doubts and fears about whether you can find a second-half adventure fit, you need to meet Helen and David. Not just because neither of them fits into the medical-teacher-computer-church planter missionary box we usually think of, but because they personify the challenges of the boomer generation. Helen contracted polio from the early vaccine even as it was being touted as a cure for one of the greatest physical horrors of the time. As for David, he knows firsthand the repercussions of the Vietnam era's scourge, Agent Orange. Both still suffer effects today. Helen is legally blind and has endured bouts of profound weakness from post-polio syndrome. And yet they get up each day and go about the business of ministering in the place God has put them.

"Our physical problems have done two things," Helen says. "They have made us grateful for every day, and they have encouraged us to ask God to show us what He would have us do while we are still on earth."

David added, "Serving others in God's name takes our mind off ourselves."

Today's globalized economy has provided new areas of need, and it has created new opportunities as well. Leadership Development International, for instance, does amazing leadership work in China in the areas of education and business training with programs that combine innovative learning techniques with the principles of character and truth. They especially need people with years of business experience (just the definition of many baby boomers) who can serve as business consultants in China. In contributing to the economic health of that community, these workers also build avenues for ministry. Business As Mission (BAM) is another organization that provides a natural opening for ministry through business. People want jobs; they want to have small businesses; they want to be part of the developing world.

Doubts and fears are natural. But the fact is, by the time you reach the second half of your life, you have a lot to offer. Finishers Project has 20,000 opportunities listed. You are sure to find many options among them that will fit you and your situation. Determine to keep your mind open, and don't be too quick to sell yourself short. Oh, and prepare yourself for some amazing responses.

A Great Cloud of Everyday Witnesses

While I was speaking on the topic of finishing well at a conference in the Northwest, a woman in the back of the room raised her hand and said, "I'm not a professional in any field. I wish there was something I could do with the rest of my life, but the truth is, I am nothing special."

Nothing special? Well, that's good news! Because God delights in using everyday, nonspectacular people to accomplish His purposes. Just thumb through the Bible, and you will see that it is filled with "nothing special" people. Here are but a few examples:

- **Moses**—Born a slave and raised as a foreigner, he killed a man in anger and had to run for his life and hide out in the desert. God wanted him to be a spokesperson, but Moses couldn't even speak well!
- **Job**—Trouble and disaster—that was Job's lot in life. And despite common belief, Job *did* lose patience and ask God for an explanation.
- **Naomi**—A destitute widow living alone in enemy territory, that was Naomi. No husband, no sons to care for her, and a long way from home. Hers was about the most helpless situation imaginable in that day.
- **Peter**—Impulsive, quick to talk and slow to understand, this rough fisherman also had a strong cowardly streak.

- **Saul of Tarsus**—An effective and dedicated man to be sure, but look what he was dedicated to—ferreting out Christians and persecuting them. And he was most effective at it, too.

You probably recognize every one of these names, although the descriptions are likely not the ones that automatically pop into your mind. That's because the important element of these people's lives is not what they were, but what *God did through them*. Consider:

- **Moses**—This mumbling man stood fearlessly before the all-powerful Pharaoh and demanded that God's people—Egypt's slave workforce—be set free. That accomplished, Moses led the people through forty years in the wilderness all the way to the Promised Land. After the death of this great leader and lawgiver, these words were written: "Since then, no prophet has risen in Israel like Moses, whom the Lord knew face to face" (Deuteronomy 34:10).
- **Job**—His name is synonymous with patience, because despite his questions, he refused to deny God. "Though he slay me, yet will I trust in him" were more than words to Job (Job 13:15 KJV).
- **Naomi**—She made her way back from Moab, accompanied by her daughter-in-law Ruth whom she counseled with motherly wisdom. Naomi lived to enjoy her grandson—who became the grandfather of King David, which put him and Naomi in the direct lineage of Jesus.
- **Peter**—Peter, the rock, the dauntless leader of the early church, became a great man of strength, always ready to claim his loyalty to Christ, even to his own death by crucifixion.
- **Paul**—From chief persecutor to chief missionary of early Christianity, it was Saul, turned the apostle Paul, who took the gospel of Jesus Christ to the Gentiles.

Many of these "nothing special" people are recorded in the great hall of heroes found in Hebrews chapter 11. Of course, many, many

biblical characters could be listed alongside these few, but notice another characteristic of each of the ones selected: Each of them seems
to have improved with age. They didn't start their real work until
their faces were worn and their hair streaked with gray. And they were
not alone. Many others whose deeds are recorded in the Bible also
began their real work only after they had amassed good, hard-earned
life experience—Abraham, for instance, and Joshua and Caleb, too.

God is in the business of turning the ordinary into extraordinary.

What God did in history, He is still doing today through people
such as Paul and Colleen in New Orleans . . . and Mike in areas of the
world too sensitive to be listed . . . and Helen and David in prisons and
foster homes and shelters around the country . . . and Tim and Joan
who are right now deciding whether to take their healing skills to
Thailand, where they have gone on so many short-term trips, or to
Mexico, where they have also gone, because they can see with their
own eyes that they are making a difference for the kingdom of God
in both those places.

But Is There a Place for Me?

"I never thought my marriage would break up, but it did," Grace
said. "I never thought I'd spend years working with troubled girls, but
I did. Instead of being the stay-at-home mother I expected to be, I
spent time standing with one friend after another who went through
the death of their own spouses. Several times I helped out as caregiver. My life experiences were hard-earned by walking along beside
others."

God is still in the business of turning the ordinary into extraordinary.

In her North Carolina home church, Grace leads a divorce recovery group. The fact that she has been down that road herself certainly gives her credibility and insight, but that's not what makes her
such an effective leader. What makes her so effective is her unique
ability to listen. Because of her work with the girls, because of her
time shouldering the burdens of hurting friends, Grace has the gentle

heart and sharpened skills that come only with experience.

Whoever you are, whatever your skills, wherever your life road has taken you, whatever its bumps and jogs, you can use what you have gained to help change the world. There is work to be done, and there is a place for you.

At the conclusion of a mission conference panel discussion led by Nelson Malwitz, Luisa, a fiftyish woman with flowing black hair sprinkled with gray raised her hand and said, "I'm a high school substitute teacher. I cover everything from band to Spanish. But I've only been subbing for eight years. Most of my life I was just a mom. But now my kids are grown and they don't need me at home. My dream job would be to be in some other country doing something for Christ. But a mom who is a substitute teacher—is there any place for me?"

Suddenly everyone on that panel was talking at once. "You really can teach a variety of things?" one asked. Luisa said she not only could but she loved doing it.

"You, lady, are gold dust!" the panelist announced.

You think your particular skills can't do much to change the world? Don't be too sure. Those 20,000 opportunities Finishers Project has available include everything from mechanic to guesthouse host, from construction worker to bookkeeper, from plumber to writer.

"You may not understand," Luisa said to the panelists. "I'm not an expert in any of the subjects I teach. I only know enough of any one thing to fill in for other teachers. Just enough to stay ahead of the students."

"You don't need to worry about that," the panelist assured her. It seems that even we who are just okay in a skill here at home are experts by the standards of many countries.

"Who would have thought it?" Luisa said with a grin. "I'm going home to plan the rest of my life."

The question, then, isn't whether or not you have anything to contribute. The question is, what is the best way to go about finding the best fit for what you have? How can you know what your options are?

Short-term, part-time, or full-time? Local or national or around the world? How can you know enough to make an informed decision?

The vice president of volunteer services at Wycliffe said, "If a baby boomer wants to serve and can afford to do it, he or she can go almost anywhere and do almost anything."

Brad Benson, Wycliffe's director of regional mobilization, adds, "For every language worker, we need one or two people in a support role. This is all across the board: teachers, pilots, accountants . . . also IT (information technology) support people to work with computers, as well as with shortwave radios and satellite phones in places that have no infrastructure."

Then there are those whose skills no one even knows to ask about, such as the artist who accompanied his medical doctor wife to West Africa. Everyone was overjoyed to see her. A doctor made sense in such a place, for the clinic there had no trained medical personnel. But an artist? More than a few people snickered at the idea. But he paid them no mind. As his wife set to work in the clinic, he set up a little studio for himself in a forty-foot shipping container. For more than a year he spent his days sitting with the people of the village, drinking tea with them, working alongside them, trying to understand them. His evenings he spent in his studio. How strange it was, he thought, that the culture had no art other than the paint the villagers spread across their own bodies. After six months, the artist opened his studio door and brought out the long pieces of bark he had used as canvas. He laid his paintings in a line beside the road. There, pictured in the paintings, were the village people pieced together with biblical themes. And at each important interval of village life, there was a cross. The fascinated villagers stared at the paintings. They pointed out specific images and poured out questions to the artist. Because of the time they had spent together, the artist understood them, and his paintings conveyed the gospel in a way that spoke to them.

The couple stayed in West Africa for two years, and during that time the doctor did wonderful work healing bodies. But it was the artist, who had touched the souls of the people, who introduced God's truth to the area.

"God can use a multiplicity of skills," Brad Benson said. "Many, many roles are open. You may not be a church planter, but what you can do enables those who are church planters to do their job. We need English teachers, construction workers, vacation Bible school leaders, medical people, plumbers, child care workers. . . . Many skills can be suitably applied in different ways. For instance, some of our best recruiters are salesmen."

The question for you to ask is not, *Do I have anything to offer?* The question is, *What will I do with what God has given me?*

Chapter 5

A Solution
Waiting to Happen

Six weeks after Mike first heard of the small West African country of Ghana, he was there. For several years, he had been looking for the right place to use his abilities for the good of the kingdom, so when he saw the posting by a government agency requesting an export business development adviser, he applied. Only later did he take out a map to see where Ghana was. Of course, since Mike had already applied for many other jobs from Morocco to Afghanistan, he didn't hurry to pack his bags. Yet within days he received a call. The agency wanted someone with just his skills.

Mike had also completed a Finishers Project opportunity form, and he was getting many responses from that. One was from a business-oriented program in Ghana. Because of that contact, Mike was met at the Ghanaian airport by a Christian brother who quickly became a friend.

From Iraq to Vietnam, from Ukraine to Latin America, from the Himalayan Mountains to the Saharan Desert, people want to be part of the developing world. And from Los Angeles to Birmingham, from Portland to Houston, people want jobs . . . and homes . . . and help . . . and hope.

Baby boomers have the tools that can help them all achieve their goals. Besides the technology and business and trade skills, they have a whole gamut of experiences. They have the maturity and understanding that comes with raising children and running a home and balancing the demands of life and family. Baby boomers who are also believers can add yet another dimension to their résumés—they know what they believe and the reason for their faith from firsthand experience. Almost always they have outlived the rote platitudes of easy religion. They know what it is to live by faith.

The Nitty-Gritty How-Tos

Most of us find the journeys of others, such as Mike, thought provoking and inspirational. We recognize the questions they ask, and we identify with their scars. Yet their journeys are enough removed from our own lives that we can be a bit more objective than when we only look inward. So while reading the stories of other people helps us to clarify the bumps and avoid the boulders on our own road, vicarious adventures only take us so far. At some point we have to stop and ask: *But what about me?*

Perhaps you are considering a local volunteer opportunity, either through your church or your community, one that requires just a small commitment of time. Actually, that's a good way to start. And you can be certain that wherever you offer your services, you will find doors open and arms outstretched to welcome you. Such a commitment isn't too hard to make. Of course you will want to approach even a limited commitment with prayer and consideration. But since you are not risking too much, you can afford to move forward quickly and in confidence.

On the other hand, if you feel nudged toward a larger ministry, your decision will require more time and care. Such a multifaceted decision will affect many areas of your life. If you are married, it will also affect the life of your spouse.

Jo's first trip abroad was to Brazil, and it had nothing to do with making the world a better place. Her husband, Marko, had business meetings there and Jo tagged along. But while Marko spent his days in meetings, Jo went out to an orphanage their church helped to sponsor and volunteered her time. A communications professional, she was able to help them complete a grant proposal that had been in the works for months. She enjoyed the people there so much that she persuaded Marko to cancel the sightseeing they had planned for the final three days of their trip and spend it at the orphanage instead.

Six months after Jo's trip to Brazil, she received an invitation to spend two weeks in an untamed area of Indonesia, helping the administrator of a cluster of small schools from outlying areas write grants. Since Jo worked at home, her time was flexible. Marko said the decision was hers, but she could count him out.

"She may not mind sleeping on a hard cot with mosquitoes and bugs crawling all over her, but I'm a clean-sheets-and-hot-American-dinner kind of guy," he said. "I hate roughing it."

Marko did, however, arrange with his company to match any funds raised for Jo's trip. Then he talked to the mission committee at church on her behalf, and to several individuals as well.

Jo went to Indonesia alone. And also to Romania and India and Sudan. Every time Marko picked her up from the airport, she bubbled over with inspiring reports. "The thing is, the money is out there," she told Marko. "It's just that the people have no idea how to apply for it. There is nothing as wonderful as using what you know to empower others."

"The reason you are able to go is because I raise the money for you," Marko pointed out.

Jo had their future all planned out: Marko could retire from his job so they would be free to travel full-time. She could continue with her job, but on a slower schedule. Marko's retirement and her continued income would allow for a much-simplified lifestyle. They would be free to travel to a specific place and live there for approximately six months—a major location in Indonesia, say, or a city in sub-Saharan Africa—and people from surrounding areas could come to her for training in grant writing. Marko could use his time to help with local construction projects.

"I know you would enjoy that," she said excitedly. "You had so much fun building the addition onto our house. And the rental unit out behind . . . that was expert work!"

Marko said, "It's your vision, Jo, not mine."

"Not a vision," Jo corrected. "A calling. God has definitely called me to this ministry."

"Maybe so," Marko said, "but He didn't call me."

This is an important step in your life, and you want to proceed wisely. How do you keep from making needless stumbles?

Begin by asking yourself the following questions:

Question #1: *What skills do I have?*

Carefully analyze your skills—not just your job skills, but your people skills, as well as the skills you have gathered through your lay ministry work and your hobbies. Try to be as specific as possible. Rather than *teacher*, you might say *developed home Bible study on the books of Mark, John, and Acts. Led the studies for five years during which time I trained three others to be leaders as well.* In addition, be inclusive. This is not the time to be modest. Rather than: *business skills*, you might list *bookkeeping, accounting, excellent computer skills, and I am fluent with Excel.*

Most people don't know the difference between "learned skills" and "innate skills." For instance, the specific how-tos of grant writing are learned skills for Jo. But her ease at working with people, and her comfort in new and unfamiliar surroundings are innate skills. She applies them to working with children just as she applies them to writing grants in Indonesia. The skills of a farmer or a plumber or a bookkeeper or an English language instructor are no less valuable than Jo's more specialized skill.

Question #2: *What am I passionate about?*

What is it that really tugs at your heart? What is the thing you long to do? How does this mesh with your past experience?

A warning reminder here: Just because you were successful in one particular area doesn't automatically guarantee that you will be successful in another area. Not even if the new endeavor was your favorite pastime.

It is important that you look at your passion, because it's your passion that moves you to action. But your passion can also be something of a trap. Because you do feel so strongly about it, it can make the first year or so in a new position appear to be a good fit. But while passion moves you to action, you need know-how to carry you along. (The travel Jo finds such a challenging adventure may wear exceedingly thin before a six-month tour of duty is up.) This is where your learned skills come in. And, sure, sometimes those skills can transfer over to another line of work—sometimes, but not always. Most people operate best in a structure similar to the one in which they learned and worked. For Jo, this means working with a high degree of independence, where she can set her own schedule.

Question #3: *What is my adventure goal?*

When you think about how you will answer this question, consider all the various facets:

Is your goal humanitarian? Is it evangelistic?

What will bring you satisfaction? Do you need to be creative? Do you desire to be a decision maker, or would you prefer to play a backup position? Do you long to be in a place of action, or do you need a slower tempo?

Do you have a passion to live in a specific part of the world?

What else defines your ultimate goal? If Jo is honest, she will include something such as "cultural adventure" here.

Mike's goal included both humanitarian and evangelistic elements.

He wanted a place of action, and he was willing to consider anywhere in the world. Specifically, his goal was to help make a way for evangelicals to work alongside the government and business sectors with mutual respect and assistance. The job in Ghana was a perfect fit.

Can you state your goal as specifically as Mike did?

Question #4: *What is my ministry track record?*

In what ministry are you involved right now? What other types of ministries have you done in the past? Have you been faithful in your ministry work? Why have you chosen those particular involvements?

Not only are these important questions to help you understand your own commitment, but they are questions you will almost certainly be asked by ministries that consider working with you.

Yoshi Hanks, of Grace International Ministries, an organization that sends English teachers to Japan, said, "We ask applicants about their ministry. We like to have people who have taught Sunday school and Bible studies."

As in any endeavor, a track record says a lot about you.

Question #5: *Do I have physical limitations?*

Regardless of how willing and passionate you are, if you have health challenges, it may set some boundaries for you. This is also true of anything that limits your energy level. To some degree, you may be able to work on getting into shape, but it is vital that you be honest with yourself—as well as with any potential ministry partner—about where you are now, not where you hope to be in the future. Better to look at the options that are more realistic for you: local work, perhaps, or jobs you can do by computer.

The same considerations apply to those whose spouses have physical limitations. Rich received an offer to consult with a university at Delhi for a year, but he didn't even consider it. "My wife has health concerns," he said. "She cannot handle hot weather. It is a good opportunity for someone, but not for us."

While a physical limitation won't rule you out, it may help you define your options.

Question #6: *Do I have the support of my spouse?*

If you are married, this is an extremely important consideration. Do you and your spouse feel the same call from God? Do you share the same passions? Do you have the same adventure goals? Are you willing to go to the same places?

Marko made his concerns clear to Jo, and also the fact that he did not share her calling from God.

If you cannot answer the preceding questions with a confident *yes*, what compromises are you and your spouse willing to make? Very few ministries are willing to see a family go in two different directions.

Tom was ready to change his plans because his wife didn't feel she could support his ministry plan, but God changed her mind. Brad did abandon his first choice, because what he felt was his call, his wife did not feel was her call. Jo and Marko are still deciding. So far, she is going on one- or two-week trips alone, financed by Marko's fundraising efforts.

This, of course, is more of a challenge for believers with unbelieving spouses who cannot understand their passion to make their life count for kingdom purposes. Should this be your situation, you would do well to talk with and pray about the specific ministry in which you are interested. For some, it will matter. For others, it will not. Remember, you don't need to go to a distant country to make a difference. People are doing so every day sitting at their own computers.

Whatever your situation—alone or single, with a cooperative spouse or not, balancing all challenges—there is a job that fits you.

Question #7: *Have I thoroughly prayed about this?*

Most Christians we talk to about finding the right second-half adventure say that first and foremost they want to follow God's leading. The best way to do this is to blanket your search with prayer. Consistent and conscientious prayer "is powerful and effective" (James 5:16). Pray alone, pray with your spouse, pray with your family and close friends, and ask others to pray for you.

"Every time I call to talk to someone referred to us by Finishers, I take time to pray with them," said Pat Sheppard of SIM (Serving in Mission). "Several people have commented on how important that is to them. We know it is important to us."

Take Philippians 4:6 to heart: "Do not be anxious about anything, but in everything, by prayer and petition, with thanksgiving, present your requests to God."

"I prayed about this and Marko prayed about it," Jo said. "But because we didn't want to cause waves, we seldom prayed together. Our first big step forward is a commitment to pray together daily about this big decision."

Question #8: *Have I asked the advice of those who know me well?*

When you find yourself faced with a smorgasbord of exciting possibilities, it can be hard to be objective about what actually fits you best. Proverbs 15:22 warns that "Plans fail for lack of counsel, but with many advisers, they succeed."

This is the time to seek counsel, especially from people who know you well and love you enough to be honest with you. Not just one person, but several. Ask them their thoughts about the adventure you are considering, then listen carefully to what they have to say. Do they enthusiastically confirm your ideas? Are they hesitant? If so, ask them why. What concerns do they voice? What warnings do they offer?

In the excitement of new possibilities, it is easy to assume that your passion plus your work experience will automatically add up to a successful new venture. But that's not necessarily true. Don't be too quick to brush off friends who point out considerations you would rather not hear. Take seriously questions such as, "Has someone actually given you a job description? Do you know exactly what to expect and what will be expected of you?" Since you already put in so much time learning and training, you may simply assume you will ease right in at the top. But your assumptions may not match the organization's ideas; they may be thinking mass mailings. It's good to have someone else help you think of all the angles.

Question #9: *What is my financial situation?*

Certainly God wants us to trust Him and to walk by faith, but He also wants us to be wise. It is important that you know where you are financially before you attempt a new adventure. Many people hope to find a ministry that pays a salary, but those positions are relatively few. Are you secure enough to be self-supporting? Can you stretch your retirement money in ways that will enable you to do what you feel called to do and still have something left for your golden years? Are you willing to sell certain assets—downsize your home, for instance, or sell a vacation house? If the ministry calls for fund-raising, are you willing to do that? Do you have other ideas about finances?

Question #10: *Where can I start serving right now to prepare myself for my adventure?*

Are you already using your skills in ministry? In what way? Write out those involvements, and be specific. Also, write out your past ministry work, along with dates. For instance, you might write: *I have been using my teaching skills by teaching a first grade Sunday school class in an inner city church from 2005 until the present. I expanded on the curriculum by writing stories and adding activities more appropriate to our children. In 2008, I expanded my organizational skills by heading up vacation Bible school. I also headed up VBS the next year, and supplemented the curriculum with mission stories.*

If your list of involvements is lean, ask yourself: Where can I plug in and get to work using my skills?

Moving On

A careful reading of the ten questions above should give you a pretty fair idea of where you are right now. So you are probably already asking the next question: *Where do I go from here?* This is where the Finishers Project comes in. Its team of experts has developed an excellent web-based matching service that can move you from basic questions to where you are ready to pack your bags. I especially appreciate the way Finishers customizes the entire process. You are, after all, an individual with your own skills and gifts as well as your own challenges and concerns. No cookie-cutter approach will work.

So your next step is to check out the Finishers website at http://finishers.org. Chief Innovation Officer Nelson Malwitz has provided a vehicle to help you progress through every step of the process, from an overview of global statistics, to a listing of top ministry needs, to short-term ministry and vision trip openings complete with contact information. Then proceed to the easy walk-through of the three *Process Stages* that will enable you to determine your own second-half adventure, at your own pace. (This is a safe place to explore because you can withdraw at any time.)

- **I'm just beginning:** so where do I start?
- **I'm investigating:** starting to put the pieces together
- **I'm deciding:** what to do where

Go to the website and browse. Then pour yourself a cup of coffee, sit back in a comfortable chair, and return to the homepage. Click on the tab: *For Individuals.* Under that, click on *Process Stages.* Start with *Beginning* and work your way through *Investigating* to *Deciding.*

Unfortunately, most ministry organizations have neither the staff nor the expertise to completely match your twenty-five-plus years of experience with an exact job in their organization. This is why it is important that you provide all the information you possibly can regarding your personal strengths and skills, and that you fully define the type of job you have in mind. If you simply list your final goal as *counselor*, for instance, that is too vague. Think something more like: *I am interested in working as a counselor, preferably with young people between the ages of twelve and eighteen. I am experienced in listening and directing families to resources as I have fifteen years of experience in public school administration. I would also be interested in putting together a resource file for any area I'm in, something I did in my past job.*

To date, close to ten thousand people have completed profiles on the Finishers website. Approximately one-third of those found a connection with a ministry for which they feel God has prepared them.

After you complete your profile, you will receive a custom-prepared list of ministry organizations that match your interests, experience, and/or job skills.

Some pretty amazing matches have come out of the Finishers website. For instance, one man said, "I've done well-digging in Africa before and I'd like to do it again." Extremely specific, yet two exact matches came back.

At a mission conference panel discussion moderated by Nelson Malwitz, a petite woman in a bright red jacket raised her hand. "I'm a Home Ec teacher, and I'll be retiring next year," she said. "My husband is a civil engineer and he's ready to quit work today. Here's my question: Is it possible to place a couple with such very different skills?"

Nelson stepped back, a grin spreading across his face. He knew the answer, but he deferred to the panel. And all five of them answered as one with a resounding, "Yes, it absolutely is!"

And Then . . .

Then, your homework begins. Find out about each of the ministries that interests you. Not just where they are and where they work and what type of ministry they engage in, but get to know them. Read each website thoroughly and make a list of any questions that come to you. Then talk with a representative of each ministry and don't hesitate to ask your questions.

Finishers can help you get to know individual ministries through the Finishers Forums it sponsors (you will find them listed on the Finishers website). These weekend events provide a hands-on opportunity to connect. Finishers partner agencies send representatives to these Forum weekends, and you will be able to interact with them directly, one-on-one. A huge side benefit is that you will also be able to meet and interact with other second-halfers as well.

"But," you may be asking, "even with all of this, will I be ready to make a commitment for the rest of my life?"

Probably not. But you don't need to make a commitment for the rest of your life. Certainly not at this point. You will find short-term and long-term opportunities available to you, some at home and others abroad. As you probe the openings with organizations that make the most sense to you, as you prayerfully compare and discuss each one, ask God to guide you to the "retirement plan" that best fits you.

"Within the DNA of the boomer generation is a strong desire to make a difference in the latter years of life," says Don Parrott, president/CEO of Finishers. "There are many places to do that . . . in our families, our communities, through our churches, or perhaps in another part of the globe. God has been preparing many of us to make a difference in another culture. Combining the preparation we have received through corporate America with our passion to invest ourselves well provides opportunity for a world-class impact. What a privilege!"

Chapter 6

The Gift of Maturity

"What do an elegant Jewish lady, a girl who sells herself to men for alcohol money, three women cast aside from their home church fellowship, a nonbelieving young woman who will not make eye contact, and a doubting husband listening in at the door have in common?" Clint wrote in his ministry newsletter from Ukraine. "They have the simple love of Jesus as He sits at the well and talks straight to their hearts. He bestows a crown of beauty on each as they piece together the story of a woman of long ago, yet amazingly so like a woman of today."

Clint, an engineer, was writing from a three-week ministry trip he was on with his wife, Kathy, as she carried her Woman at the Well quilting sessions from a small sun-draped town nestled along the shore of the Black Sea to a dying village deep in the heart of Crimea. It's the same ministry that has taken them to churches in the United States, and also to several locations in Venezuela.

The Woman at the Well Quilt Project centers around a twenty-five-piece quilt block Kathy designed. Each piece represents an element of the Samaritan woman's story from John chapter 4. Women, and an occasional man, are invited to a presentation of quilting history and technique. Then, using the quilt pieces, Kathy tells the story of the Samaritan woman and shares the good news of Jesus Christ. The women hand-piece the block from a kit that is provided, complete with fabric, needle, pins, thread, and a gospel of John. When the session ends, each person leaves with a finished block as a reminder of an encounter with Christ and, for some, of a day that marks a change for all eternity.

Now Clint is not himself a quilter, and this is not the second-half adventure he had planned. A specialist in the "Theory of Constraints" approach to business, he was the one with the marketable skill. When Clint decided to join his church's short-term mission trip to Venezuela, he carefully planned out a business presentation that he could present to university students in the engineering department. At the last minute, Kathy joined the group and put together packets of her Woman at the Well quilt block. Almost apologetically, she took all of them—fifty packets.

Clint's plan didn't get off the ground. He was never given any opportunities to present his carefully prepared address. But at the airport, an entourage met the team; they wanted to see Kathy. "We've got a lot of women interested in your quilt," she was told. "We hope you have enough supplies for ninety women."

So Clint folded up his presentation notes, picked up a pair of scissors, and got busy helping Kathy. And that has become their ministry. When he isn't setting up the room, or ironing seams, or sharing the good news with a husband who came along, he grabs up his toolbox and fixes broken hinges on doors, or repairs leaky faucets, or mends sagging steps.

In one village, Clint wrote, the Woman at the Well session had sixty visitors join from a neighboring village. "We didn't bring enough patterns and kits, so June rushed back home to bring more while Kathy and Yana went through the story and the gospel. This is the largest group Kathy has had and she began the sewing portion with clear instructions that helped keep the group from chaos. 'Pin first, sew later!' Who knows the work that the Spirit wrought that day."

Here is why I love Clint and Kathy's story: It's a wonderful picture of reinventing retirement, then re-reinventing it in order to go in God's direction. No but-I'm-the-one-with-the-big-skills discussion, no prideful wavering, no my-way-or-the-highway attitude. Clint had a great idea for his second-half adventure, but seeing his plan through was not his prime goal. His prime goal was jumping on board with God's plan. Both Clint and Kathy demonstrated flexibility and grace, just two of the wonderful attributes that come with maturity.

That's not to say maturity automatically comes with age, of course. It most certainly does not. We only have to look around us to see example after example of immature gray heads and foolish wrinkled faces. Yet, by virtue of the fact that they have lived life and learned from their experience, those who reach the half-century mark are more likely to demonstrate the attributes of maturity.

Again and again, we see wonderful examples of individuals and couples whose maturity has made it possible for them to fit into the unique place God formed for them. So let's look at six characteristics of maturity and see how they bear on your own second-half adventure.

Mature Flexibility

Inside every fifty-year-old is a thirty-five-year-old asking, "Hey, what happened here?"

Baby boomers are known for their endless optimism about life. "An overwhelming 79 percent feel they will not experience serious limitations until beyond age seventy," said Dr. James Sliwa, medical director of the General Rehabilitation Program at Rehabilitation Institute of Chicago (RIC).[8]

For many boomers, that is exactly how it will be. But not for all. When limitations do intrude, what then? Suppose Helen, who was afflicted with such a myriad of problems, and David, who suffers from the Agent Orange effects, had looked at their health issues and decided it wasn't worth their time or God's to pursue a second-half adventure. How many neglected prisoners and foster children and young ones in shelters might never have heard the gentle words of the Good Shepherd? But that's not what Helen and David did. They got on with the work God had for them, and they have no intention of stopping anytime soon.

Mature boomers have cultivated contentment, a wonderful trait that allows them to be flexible. It lets them work with their spouse's quilt ministry when they had planned on teaching business models to university students. It allows them to be houseparents for missionary kids when they had hoped to find a job working in a hospital.

The apostle Paul was the model of mature flexibility. In Philippians 4:12, he wrote: "I have learned the secret of being content in any and every situation."

Mature Knowledge

Boomers have spent years honing their professional skills. They know how to use a whole array of tools of their trade—and they probably own many of those tools as well. If they don't know how to do something, they most likely know someone who does. They have access to so many resources that they can solve almost any problem and answer just about any question. Compared to most of the world, Americans are overskilled.

Mature knowledge not only can do, but it can teach others to do.

Because of your mature knowledge, you hold a lot more power than you realize. Immature knowledge says you aren't serving unless you are suffering. The fact is that you should be comfortable in your second-half adventure. It should fit you, and you should find it significant and worthy of the investment of your time, effort, and resources.

Yoshi Hanks, from Grace International Ministries, stresses that "spiritual experience and life experience are very important" in the ESL teachers she sends to Japan. This is one reason she likes mature applicants.

"Today's sixty-year-old is mature and needs far less training in living skills than his or her younger counterpart," said Wycliffe's vice president for recruitment ministries. "Traditionally, mission organizations send new missionaries in their twenties and thirties through an orientation process, like a jungle camp, so they can learn how to survive the harsh living conditions in the field. But a person in his or her fifties and above has triumphed through their productive years and already has built-in strategies for success."

That certainly is the case with Grace, who was involved in social work for so many years. She spent hours in group homes listening to the girls talk. Many times she had things she wanted to say, but she learned it was best to bide her time. She was careful to choose the best moment to speak, and when she did speak she selected her words carefully. Ever since Grace retired, much of her ministry has been framed by her unique ability to listen, to support, and to speak with care. That is mature knowledge.

Mature Insight

"If only I had been able to . . . "

Clint did not waste a minute running though the wouldas, couldas, and shouldas of his original ministry plans. He refused to squander a day on regrets for what might have been. It matters not who originated the ministry, he says, or whose skill is showcased more dominantly. What matters is accomplishing the work of the kingdom.

"We may have been seed planters or we may have been harvesters—we won't know until we get to heaven," Clint says of their time in Ukraine. "We are content to do God's will."

For every choice we make, we leave an uncountable multitude of options untried. Each untried option provides an opportunity to second-guess . . . to brood . . . to ask, "What if . . . ?" That mix of real and imagined missed opportunities can tie a person up in a web of longing for a "do over."

Reevaluation is normal as one approaches the second half of life.

And as time moves forward, there simply is more and more of a temptation to dive into introspection about life. That's not all bad, of course. There's a lot to be said for reevaluating. The problem comes when we let the what-ifs and the should-haves and the I-wish-I'ds paralyze us.

Mature insight recognizes that just because your days of wide-eyed idealism have been tempered by life doesn't mean your best opportunities are lost. On the contrary, none of us seem to learn the really deep lessons of existence without experiencing life. Just as we don't experience our most meaningful encounters with God in life's good times. It is when the storms come, it is when we have to walk over impassibly rough roads, that we learn to trust Him.

Immature insight melts when well-meaning friends look at you bent low in the hard times and, misquoting 1 Corinthians 10:13, insist that "God will never give you more than you can bear." Never mind that the verse actually reads: "No *temptation* has seized you except what is common to man. And God is faithful; he will not let you be *tempted* beyond what you can bear. But when you are *tempted*, he will also provide a way out so that you can stand up under it" (italics my own). By interpreting this verse as referring to the troubles of life rather than as a warning against yielding to sin, immature insight heaps needless guilt on top of the pain.

Mature insight pulls itself up straight and says, "God always allows us more than we can bear. If He didn't, we wouldn't need Him. What He promises is that He will be there in those rough times and that He will bear us!" Mature insight clings to 2 Corinthians 12:9: "My grace is sufficient for you, for my power is made perfect in weakness."

Mature insight knows we cannot depend on our own strength, because mature insight understands how much we need the Lord!

The Wisdom of Maturity

Yoshi Hanks says that Grace International Ministries gets 90 percent of its teachers from Finishers. "There are so many fun things for young people to do in Japan," she says. "Older people realize it is not a pleasure trip. They can see Japan, but that's not their real purpose. They understand what they are there for. Working successfully in Japan requires respect, humility, honesty, a humble heart, and it requires a person to be teachable."

In other words, it requires the wisdom of maturity.

> *Teach us to number our days aright,*
> *that we may gain a heart of wisdom.*
>
> —PSALM 90:12

Growing older is a given; gaining wisdom is an option.

The wisdom of maturity is not only displayed in your desire to serve God, but also in the way you go about preparing for your second-half adventure. Maturity pays attention to the admonition of 1 Corinthians 14:40: "But everything should be done in a fitting and orderly way." We talked about this in regard to finding the best way to use your time, resources, and skills in your second half, but it also applies to the attention you pay to your own personal affairs.

One woman who took this to heart talked of setting her financial house in order before she made her second-half adventure decision. It was something she had long put off. She took her attorney's advice and put everything, including her home and car, into a trust. She gathered all of her medical information together, and she filled out a legal medical directive. Then she gathered up her life insurance documents along with all her other important papers, and she made copies of everything. She put a complete set into each of three different folders, one for each of her children. "It's not that I think anything will happen to me," she said. "I just see this as a good time to put order in my life."

The wisdom of maturity is based on faith and trust, but it plays out in intentional actions.

The fear of the Lord is the beginning of wisdom,
and knowledge of the Holy One is understanding.

—PROVERBS 9:10

Maturity Brings Respect

Looking upon age as a period of uselessness is a Western idea. In most cultures, age is valued and revered. Years indicate experience. And a person of experience is assumed to be a person of credibility and knowledge. Such a person deserves respect, not only for his or her accomplishments, but for what he or she can pass along to the next generation.

When mature men and women go out into the world, they are often amazed to find local people eager to listen to what they have to say. Those cultures want to hear from people who have lived long enough to know what they are talking about.

An African proverb says, "Anyone skilled in his work stands before kings." This is you on your second-half adventure—skilled and worthy of royal respect.

The Grace of Maturity

A young woman we will call Karla went to Japan with GIM, eager to be an evangelist. Her job was that of an English as a Second Language (ESL) teacher, but she clung to her own agenda. The Christian church in Japan is small—fewer than 1 percent of all Japan's people even know about Jesus Christ—and the churches there use the ESL classes as an outreach. But roles in Japan are carefully defined; the pastor is the pastor, and the teachers are the teachers. Even so, Karla saw herself as an evangelist, and she refused to accept the warning to stay in her place. Although Karla was a good teacher, and although she loved Japan and truly desired to serve God, she could not stay.

"That's not how it's done in Japan," said Yoshi. "You are not going to change the culture in the church. Your job is to serve. If you come from America and point a finger and say, this is a better way, it is offensive. A missionary needs a discerning spirit."

A missionary needs the grace of maturity.

Experts tell us that older people are happier in the present. They take into account the fact that the first half of their life has already been lived, and they determine not to waste a minute of the time they have left. Perhaps this is why an expanding portion of the mission face is creased with lines of experience.

Pat Sheppard, representative for Serving in Missions (SIM), told of a retired couple who went to Bolivia. The wife taught in the local school, and the husband was a handyman who also worked in the school library. Pat said, "That man told me, 'These are the best years of our lives!'"

An Indian proverb says, "To know the road ahead, ask those coming back." Because you are in a position to look back and see the times when God demonstrated His faithfulness in your life, you can walk forward with confidence knowing He will also be faithful on the road ahead. In the second half of life, you are the perfect age to share this insight with those coming up the road behind you who question what the road ahead holds.

> "Excellence . . . cannot be had without experience and discipline, and therefore cannot be had by the very young."
>
> —C. S. Lewis
> in *An Experiment in Criticism*[9]

Chapter 7

Confronting
the Barriers

It was when Intel sent Brad to Japan on a business trip that he was introduced to the new face of missions by ESL teachers. He had a good management position with the company, but what he saw in Japan touched his heart. So Brad began to pray, "Lord, give me something meaningful to do." Years passed, but by the time his children were in high school, Brad determined that they should have some short-term experience being a part of what God is doing around the world. So as a family they went to Brazil, and for two weeks they worked construction on a children's home. "The kids in that group home came from situations too wretched to endure," Brad said. "They had all been treated horribly." As his children played with the local kids, Brad set about installing the electrical wiring on a new group home.

Those two weeks profoundly impressed Brad. Back at the sending church, he and the team gave an enthusiastic presentation on the trip. Afterward a woman approached him and said, "We have a team going to Romania. We could sure use someone with your skills. Want to come along?"

Without giving it a second thought, Brad told her, "Sign me up!"

The following year he went to Romania for three more weeks. (This time he worked in children's ministry.) Then later his home church asked him to lead a short-term group to Hungary, which he did. They spent their days putting on a vacation Bible school and sports camp for the kids, and ESL classes for the adults. In the evenings, they worked with evangelistic teams. They were invited to come back to Hungary the following year.

"We were reaching the people," Brad said. "We were actually making a difference!"

In an intensive research survey conducted in the late 1990s, the Finishers Project posed the question: *What prevents individuals from serving in missions ministry?* The following seven barriers draw from the top responses to that question.

Barrier #1: Knowing God's Will

Of those who responded to the survey, a full 97 percent indicated a genuine desire to be accountable to the Lord before they moved forward into any second-half adventure. They earnestly longed to know God's will. Every now and then someone tells of a bold, dramatic leading from God, an event almost like Saul of Tarsus experienced when he was struck blind on his way to Damascus and Jesus spoke to him from heaven (Acts 9:3–6).

Sometimes, but not usually.

More often our request for guidance is answered the way the psalmist David was answered when he implored, "Teach me your way, O Lord; lead me in a straight path" (Psalm 27:11). His answer comes in verse 14: "Wait for the Lord; be strong and take heart and wait for the Lord."

What does it mean to "wait on the Lord"? Sit and twiddle your thumbs until God does decide to knock you down with a blinding light and speak to you from heaven? Not according to the Bible. There we find waiting to be more of an attitude than an action. Waiting on the Lord means to trust Him. In times of uncertainty, it means to know for sure that He will answer. It means to continually seek His face. Psalm 27 is not a psalm about thumb twiddling. It is a psalm of trust.

None of us knows how life will unfold. But we can decide to trust God as we proceed from one step to the next. And we have God's assurance that "they that wait upon the Lord shall renew their strength" (Isaiah 40:31 KJV).

As you "wait on the Lord," be busy about the business of seeking God's will. The place to start is in His Word. Search the Scriptures and claim them for your own. Take God at His word. Start with the Great Commission in Matthew 28:19–20: "Therefore go and make disciples of all nations, baptizing them in the name of the Father and of the Son and of the Holy Spirit, and teaching them to obey everything I have commanded you. And surely I am with you always, to the very end of the age."

Expand your prayers beyond yourself. Pray for others who are already ministering, either at home or somewhere around the world. Pray for those who have shown the boldness to accept positions in the hardest places. Pray for those who reach beyond their comfort zone.

I don't mean to make this sound simplistic. It is anything but.

Brad was appropriately proactive as he waited on the Lord. When he heard that a church was offering the Perspectives Course on World Missions (www.perspectives.org), he immediately signed up for it. He also attended a Finishers Workshop at Missions Fest NW (now Mission ConneXion), which made him more certain than ever that God was leading him into missions work. But it also left him more frustrated than ever. How could he possibly leave his job and go to some distant country? Why would God call him to do something he couldn't do?

Barrier #2: Dealing with Finances

The second most commonly cited barrier was financial concerns. Only 20 percent of those who responded to the Finishers survey said they were in a position to support themselves in a ministry. So where would the money come from for the others? Did they have any hope of finding a paid mission-type position?

It is tempting to look at this whole issue of finances and decide, "Well, that's that. This just isn't going to work for me!" But many more options exist than are immediately apparent. For instance, you might need some financial support right now to pay your travel expenses and maybe to meet your monthly bills, but it is only a temporary need. Later on, when you are no longer ministering, your assets may well be enough to take care of you for the rest of your life. A partial, temporary need is a far cry from needing total support. Or you may find that you can even pay for your monthly bills, it's just your travel and ministry expenses you can't meet. Or you may find that you are able to pay for everything while you are ministering, but it's the long-term costs that concern you.

Each of these is a different situation, and each calls for an individual approach. Whatever your calling, don't give it up because of finances. Take the time to evaluate your actual position. If you aren't certain where you are or what you need, consult a financial adviser. He or she could run the basic calculations for you, then work through a sound financial planning process geared specifically for you. Ask friends and your pastor if they can refer you to a place where you can safely explore your goals and obligations without pressure and risk.

Lots of people say, "If someone gave me the money, I would . . ."

Maybe. But don't count on the big gift that will solve all your problems. It doesn't often happen that way. And when it does, it usually comes as a result of success in work you are already doing. Linda is a good example. She had finished a term teaching English in India and was home for several months before she went to do the same in Ukraine. As she sat on the patio with a longtime friend, telling about her experiences and what was happening through the work, her friend suddenly said, "I can't go and do anything like that, but I want to help support you."

Nearly seven in ten American workers plan to continue working full or part time after they retire from their main job, many for economic reasons, according to a Rutgers University study. Clint is an example. In his midfifties, he simply cannot afford to stop work, so he uses his vacation time for ministry.

There are alternatives to consider:

- **Can you partner with someone or an organization?** Dan and I used this approach with our *Give a Voice* writing seminars. Several Christian publishing companies—including Moody Publishers—along with Partners International, partnered with us so that we could instruct promising Indian Christians who desired to make their voices heard in the American marketplace.
- **What free resources are available?** Not everything has to be purchased. Once we put the word out about our *Give a Voice* seminars, for instance, people offered all kinds of suggestions for curriculum and materials. We even had computers donated for some Indian writers who needed them.
- **Is there a team of people who can help you brainstorm ideas for a particular project?** In our church, a committee of people over the age of fifty meets monthly to do just that. Perhaps your pastor —or mission pastor, if your church has one—can help you put together a similar group.

Clint is still employed full time and plans to remain so in the foreseeable future.

Tim and Joan plan to sell their house and live with one or the other of their daughters. Also, Tim plans to continue working part time.

Paul and Colleen sold assets, including their business.

Mike works on a contract basis.

Brad took advantage of financial counseling which helped him work out a plan where he could pay his own way.

Grace rents out her house on the West Coast and lives less expensively in the South.

Helen and David search out new markets where they can sell their books.

Charlie sold his business.

Linda serves with her children's encouragement. She jokes that their inheritance will come to them in heaven.

Barrier #3: Concerns about Safety, Hardship, and Comfort

Not all of them wanted to come right out and say it, but more than a few survey respondents placed a high premium on their own comfort. They wanted to serve the Lord, but not in too hard of a place. Certainly not where they had to worry about their safety.

This is a legitimate concern. Some of the destinations available do carry a degree of risk, and it would be foolish not to weigh that. You are wise to address your or your spouse's concerns, then to assess the level of discomfort with any particular place or situation.

Tom's wife had major concerns for her children's health and safety in Uganda, but she overcame them. Others may not. Tom's family came back to the United States when the children reached high school age. So did Pat and Gary. Linda delayed her leaving because of health issues with her parents.

If your concerns loom up before you, be honest about the realities of your life. You don't have to go to Africa or India or Cambodia. It is certainly possible to take a less daunting adventure and still be effective. You don't even have to go to New Orleans. Plenty needs to be done right in your own hometown. You could even work right in your own home, seated in front of your computer. Let Finishers help you discover how and where and when.

Barrier #4: Family Concerns

Brad's short-term trip to Hungary was so successful that the Christians there begged him to come back. The next team was small—only four members—but they prepared for a great city outreach complete with music, drama, skits, and preaching. Then an hour before the team was to leave, Brad got a call that his father, who had been ill for some time, had died. Brad didn't know what to do. On the one hand, none of his family were believers, and he certainly did not want to offend them. On the other hand, many people in Hungary were depending on this team, and he knew the others would not go without him.

Family considerations are a huge concern for baby boomers, and rightfully so. Most see their priorities as: God first, ministry to their families second, and ministry to others third.

"God will not lead me where my family is insecure," one respondent wrote confidently. Many others agreed with that assessment.

As for Brad, through tears and covered in prayer, he bid his father a final good-bye and boarded the plane to Hungary. Two and a half years later when his mother died, Brad was able to reach out through his deep grief and take charge of many of the arrangements for the family. That was also a time to grieve for his father.

Barrier #5: Agenda Conflicts

In his Perspectives class, Brad was asked to describe what he planned to do with the training he received. No problem. He knew the answer to that question, and he wrote it out in great detail.

Some people move into their second half with a definite dream in mind. But it sometimes happens that when they get feedback from Finishers, they are disappointed because no response is an exact match to the ideal position they pictured. Fortunately, most people are willing to step back and rethink in broader terms. "I'm making a commitment to be useful," one person said, "so I need to at least consider the whole range of possibilities open to me."

Besides, choosing a ministry doesn't have to be a one-shot deal. Linda said, "I don't really want to be committed to only one place. I like the idea of doing several things in several different places over the span of my second half."

But Brad didn't have any of these worries. He got a call from a Wycliffe recruiter who said, "I have the perfect job for you! It is a 100 percent match with your profile." The recruiter was going to Indonesia, and he needed someone to take his place as a mobilization director in Portland, Oregon. It did indeed seem to be an almost exact match to what Brad had written in his Perspectives class description.

The perfect job except for one minor detail—his wife didn't want to move their family. "Go if you want to," she told him, "but I'm staying right here."

Even a 100 percent match isn't always perfect enough. Yet because Wycliffe had a position for him, and because it was located less than an hour from his home so that he could drive back and forth, Brad was able to join the organization. God had worked out the details.

Barrier #6: Lack of Confidence

Some people tend to do an interesting thing when they make up their profiles: They focus on what they lack, such as formal training or degrees. Or they measure themselves against the top people in similar jobs and always see themselves as coming up short. The result is that they shake their heads sadly and say, "I wish I could, but . . ."

Brad's plan had been to retire by the age of fifty-five, then to work full time in a mission ministry. But to him, mission ministry automatically meant going somewhere on the other side of the world—somewhere such as Indonesia. It never occurred to him that he could actually serve God in a global way right here in the United States. It was Finishers that introduced him to that possibility. "I had no idea missions ministry was possible anywhere but overseas," Brad said.

But even when he saw that Wycliffe was a great match for him, even though his wife was in favor of him being involved in the work, even though Wycliffe was eager to have him, Brad wasn't so sure. "Is there a problem here?" he asked the recruiter. "I don't know the first thing about Bible translation!"

More than likely, you have already done the preparation for your second-half adventure. More than likely, but not certainly. You can always get extra training if you need it. In most cases, completing a few courses is all it takes. But if you come out a match as Brad did, you probably are not going to need the extra skills that are causing you worry. Brad was told that he didn't need to know how to do Bible translation. Even though that's what Wycliffe is most known for, translation would not be a part of his job.

As I sat in Finishers workshops at a mission convention, I watched as one person after another raised an anxious hand and said some version of: "We are a housewife and a plumber . . . I am a midwife . . . I am an engineer . . . We are a secretary and a farmer . . . Can God use us? Can God use me?" And every time, representatives from mission organizations assured each one that if they were willing to use their skills for God, places were available for them.

Barrier #7: Personal Needs Issues

"But . . . will I actually be able to do what the job requires? I mean, can I do what it takes?"

This is a difficult question to ask, but a fair and important one. If you are across the street or if you are across the globe, will your own needs be met? Often the question seems to arise either because of a particular issue or because someone heard of an individual who had a problem in this area. In fact, for many boomers, "What will the mission do for me?" is a deciding factor on where they will go. More and more say they want some assurance that the organization will care for them as persons and not simply treat them as someone to get a job done. They want a real fit. What they are looking for is an organization that values people over programs.

Here is today's good news: Ministries are taking member care seriously. More and more are following Wycliffe's lead and are putting someone in the position of overseeing just such a program.

There is a huge difference between joining God and taking a vacation cruise. God never promised otherwise. In his letter to the Jewish converts, the writer of the book of Hebrews penned these words: "Let us, then, go to [Jesus] outside the camp, bearing the disgrace he bore. For here we do not have an enduring city, but we are looking for the city that is to come" (Hebrews 13:13–14).

Outside the city is not a comfortable place to be. Inside the city is where the warm fire glows and hot soup bubbles and a comfortable bed awaits, sheltered from the wind and rain. Outside the city wall it is raw and lonely and frightening. As for the disgrace, we know what happened to Jesus outside the city, and it is not at all an appealing thought.

Yet outside the city is where we are called to be. Outside the city is where God is waiting to meet us.

On his way back from a business meeting in California, Brad ran into a colleague from Intel in the airport. They had both been in the company's retirement planning class together, and the other man asked, "So, have you done anything about retirement?"

Brad hadn't discussed his thoughts on this subject with anyone outside his family. The job at Wycliffe wasn't even certain, because it depended on another man being moved from the position in question to Indonesia and the local church that supported him was balking at that move. Certainly, Brad had no intention of saying anything to anyone at his company. Yet, for some reason that he couldn't explain, he found himself blurting, "As a matter of fact . . . " and then he poured out the whole story.

When Brad got to the part about the position still being in question, his colleague interrupted him and said, "Oh, yes, I know all about that. I chair the mission board at the church that's wrestling with that decision."

Within days, the church agreed to the man's appointment in Indonesia. Brad was accepted as a member of Wycliffe and offered the newly vacated job. On July 1, 2004, he retired from his job at Intel. In the morning, he cleaned out his office. In the afternoon he flew to Orlando to begin training with Wycliffe for a job a short drive from home.

Chapter 8

As Though Eternity Depended on It

Pat and Gary could be retired now. They are the right age, and they have certainly earned some kick-back-and-relax time.

Actually, I guess you could say they *are* retired, but only by their own "reinvented retirement" definition.

"Every time we talked about retiring from our jobs, we looked at each other and asked, 'But what would we do then?'" Pat said. "And the answer was always the same: 'Probably exactly what we're doing now.' Because we really love missions."

So to Pat and Gary, retirement means continuing with their jobs as recruiters for SIM (Serving in Mission). But it was a long progression of experiences and acquiring skills that led them to this point.

At the end of Gary's last year of Bible school, as he wondered what he was going to do with all his training, he sat on a bus one day reading about the five missionaries martyred by Auca Indians in the jungles of Ecuador. "I'd love to be a pilot like Nate Saint," he said to his buddy in the seat next to him. "But where could I ever get that kind of training?"

"At Moody Bible Institute," his friend answered. "I've applied there myself and I'm on my way to Chicago for their presessions."

But when his friend returned, he brought discouraging news. It was impossible to get into so demanding a school, he said. *Well, that's that*, Gary figured. *If he can't get in, I certainly can't*. Still, he had brought Gary an application, so what would it hurt to fill it out?

Out of more than three hundred applicants, twenty-four were invited for a week of aviation pretraining. Gary was one of them. Half of these were chosen to take the course. Gary's name was on that list, too. While Gary went to Moody, Pat attended nurses' training in Philadelphia, and they married the day after her graduation. Together they made plans to go to the mission field.

"Timbuktu, Mali, West Africa," a letter from their home church in New Jersey urged. "The mission board needs a pilot and a nurse to go there."

"Timbuktu?" Gary said. "That's where my mother always said she'd send me! I didn't know it was a real place." But before they could get their bags packed, the aviation program there was canceled, and they had to start their search all over again. They ended up going to Niger, a French-speaking country in West Africa. The mission there needed a pilot, but not a nurse. It did, however, need dorm parents, so that's what Pat and Gary did—they were dorm parents.

When Gary encountered some of his buddies who flew for SIM, they told him their mission needed another pilot—*right now*! If he and Pat moved to Nigeria, Gary could stay in aviation and Pat could work in the hospital there. It was a perfect match, and the two missions agreed to the switch. Then when SIM opened an aviation program for French-speaking countries, Gary was on hand to start it. He knew the language, he knew the territory, and he didn't even mind the hot, dry deserts.

Altogether, Gary and Pat spent fifteen years in West Africa—three years in Niger and twelve years in Nigeria. When their children reached high school age, they came back to the states where Gary found a secular job in aviation. But their hearts continued to be drawn to missions, and they kept on representing SIM, though not in an official capacity. They did eventually go back to Niger for a time, and for the past twenty-three years have represented SIM in the United States.

A random life story?

Absolutely not. For from their earliest adult years, Pat and Gary lived their lives as though eternity depended on it. And all that time God was laying the groundwork for their second-half adventure.

"In our mission career, we lived in the city and we lived in the bush," Pat says. "I worked in a large modern hospital, and I worked in a bush clinic. Gary flew in all sorts of conditions, and he developed an aviation program. Oh, and we were dorm parents."

The only thing they love as much as mission work is getting other people involved in missions, which is what they do today.

Imagine the great cloud of witnesses from Hebrews 11, who praise God as they bear witness to His faithfulness in Pat and Gary's lives and cheer them on as they race toward the finish line.

You may be thinking, *Well, yes, but Pat and Gary are career missionaries. That's not me.*

No matter—the same great cloud has also assembled to watch your race. They cheer you on, too, and they also bear witness to your faith and to God's faithfulness in your life. That crowd has a better view of eternity than we on earth can possibly have, because they can see what is really at stake.

So, what of your race? Are you satisfied to meander along? To go with the flow and wait to see how things turn out? Or have you determined to be proactive and run a race worthy of your calling?

A husband and wife came to Laurie Parker of World Concern, and told her about their passion to work with children in Darfur. They were not missionaries. His background was in business and hers in office work. "They wanted a paid position with us," Laurie said. "Unfortunately, World Concern doesn't have many of those."

But the couple was tenacious. They attended short-term disaster relief training and team-building sessions, and they watched the dedicated staff at work. Each one of those staff members could be making good money somewhere else, but they chose to be where they were because they wanted to be part of God's work. The couple loved every one of them. "But in the end, we had to give the couple bad news—Darfur was too dangerous for people without appropriate experience," Laurie said. "We simply could not send them." The couple had no support raised, but even so, they pleaded to be sent as volunteers—no pay, support only anticipated. "We seldom agree to this," Laurie said, "but we made an exception." The couple moved to Nairobi, Kenya, with the intention of working in Somalia.

"They really wanted to work in a conflict zone," Laurie said. "The wife longed to write, and we desperately needed her talents to keep up with newsletters and reports. They wanted to start a school, and they had set aside money to finance it themselves."

The couple's goal was to demonstrate to the area that people who had all but given up could not only survive, but they could actually thrive.

When the husband and wife arrived in Nairobi and began their work, they quickly discovered just how little they knew. Nothing happened the way they expected it to. They decided a better plan would be to take their money and start their own business (something they knew how to do), then to donate the profits to the ministry. But then they hit upon the best plan of all—take what they had already learned about sustainable income and its long-term impact, combine it with their business and office skills, then take their money and give it to the community, and let the local people start *their own* businesses. And this is what the couple did. They helped start an import business that sells locally made handcrafts.

Because of their proactive approach and strategic planning, that couple has their own thriving ministry today. They are careful stewards of what God afforded them, and they regularly put the profits of the new business into a fund to care for local orphans.

"They are not working with World Concern," Laurie said. "But what does it matter? They are working for the Lord in the same areas we're working in. We are partners together with the same kingdom goal."

I know, I know. You probably never will go to Somalia. Maybe you will never go anywhere in Africa. Perhaps you won't even leave your hometown. But it's not your destination that matters. It's the comfortable fit of your ministry.

Take John, for instance. He spent his entire life as a bread delivery truck driver in central California. He started his day at four every morning. John retired two years ago, but a lifetime routine of getting up at four in the morning isn't easily changed. So he simply switched getting up to deliver loaves of bread to getting up to share the bread of life. Every morning at four a.m. he sits down at his computer and logs in to his site at Global Ministries International and checks his messages. Because inquiries come into GMI's website from all over the world, time makes no difference. Someone is always up and writing. Someone such as the person who sent this message from Ghana: "I happen to be Muslim but thanks be to God I have accepted Christ as my Saviour. Help me be more powerful in the Lord; spiritually strong in my new Christian life."

Whoever you are—missionary, office worker, bread truck driver, or whatever—you never need to stop living in a way that will leave this world a better place than you found it. You never need to stop working for the sake of eternity.

A Legacy in Progress

Statistics indicate that many baby boomers will spend twenty or thirty years in their "retirement" mode. Imagine—up to one-third of your life in a new second-half adventure season with no end of exciting possibilities.

Twenty to thirty years is a good long time to draft out a worthy legacy. We're not talking finances here, of course. Legacy has nothing to do with money. It has everything to do with handing along something of eternal worth.

Jesus was talking legacy when He told those around Him to go into all the world and make disciples of the nations (Matthew 28:19). He was talking legacy when He sat on the mountainside and spoke the Beatitudes (Matthew 5:1–12). He was talking legacy when He said, "Do not store up for yourselves treasures on earth, where moth and rust destroy, and where thieves break in and steal. . . . For where your treasure is, there your heart will be also" (Matthew 6:19, 21). He was talking legacy when He said, "Come, you who are blessed by my Father; take your inheritance, the kingdom prepared for you since the creation of the world. For I was hungry and you gave me something to eat, I was thirsty and you gave me something to drink, I was a stranger and you invited me in, I needed clothes and you clothed me, I was sick and you looked after me, I was in prison and you came to visit me. . . . Whatever you did for one of the least of these brothers of mine, you did for me" (Matthew 25:34–36, 40).

It Takes the Whole Family

A full 97 percent of the people who inhabit the world's least evangelized countries live within the aptly named 10/40 window (10 degrees to 40 degrees north of the equator), a band that encompasses Saharan and North Africa, almost all of Asia, and much of Southeast Asia. Roughly two-thirds of the world's population lives within this window. Besides being the least evangelized people in the world, they are also the most impoverished and the ones who suffer the poorest quality of life.

Most of the countries in the 10/40 window either severely restrict or have completely closed their doors to foreign missionaries. So if the door is shut, how will people in those countries hear about Jesus? Through their own people. God has raised up indigenous missionaries from within the Christian movements started by early mission pioneers, and they are actively winning their own nations to Christ. Dr. B. E. Vijayam, the renowned scientist and dedicated Indian Christian mentioned earlier, is an excellent example. Through his umbrella group, TENT Ministries, much of India benefits from humanitarian efforts that bring help and hope to the poorest of the poor. His PROGRESS microenterprise programs have been so successful that the Indian government now supports them despite their Christian foundation. But also under the TENT umbrella is a major endeavor to train up pastors and evangelists and send them out to reach India's more than four thousand unreached people groups. The program has been highly effective under its Indian leadership. They send people who already speak the language and understand the needs of the people into their own areas. They understand the Indian culture. They don't need visas or airfare, and they live economically on the same level as their neighbors. This is how the gospel is spreading through India and China and many other areas of the world.

Still, the indigenous church cannot do the job alone. Reaching all people and all nations requires the united efforts of all the various parts of the worldwide body of Christ. It takes people such as the fifty-year-old California woman who went to Cambodia for five months to teach conversational English to Christian leaders. All she did was make herself available to talk to them.

It takes the Global Media Outreach volunteer who sat at her computer in New York and typed out an answer to S. in Malaysia who had implored: "I am the only one in my family who accepted Jesus as my Saviour. I don't have any support to become a Christian. Please guide me."

It takes "tentmakers" willing to go to severely restricted countries and live and work and take the time to develop trusting relationships with neighbors.

It takes Grace who is using her writing abilities to mentor a budding writer-pastor in India online.

It takes Helen and David who work together in their home so that cast-off people will know they are precious to the Good Shepherd.

And it takes church teams such as those sent from Northwood Church in Texas and from Tree of Life Church in California.

It is not the way it's done, you see, nor is it the person who is doing it that makes the difference. To reach the world for eternity is a job of endless variety to be carried out by the united efforts of the entire family of God. This is getting easier all the time in the increasingly global world in which we live. We can instantly communicate anywhere by Internet, which is what makes Global Media Outreach such an effective ministry. In 2008, 3 million people from all around the world clicked on to their site and 637,000 of them sent e-mails. Eighty percent were from outside the United States, many from closed countries, such as this one from Saudi Arabia: "I accept God as my personal savior; but I'm a sinner. I know I've done things which are prohibited by the rules of God like telling a lie and making trouble to anyone. I want to change and I want to correct the mistakes I've started. What should I do? Could you please help me?" Within the hour, that Saudi Arabian had an answer on his or her computer screen. Imagine a second-life adventure that includes responding to such a heart cry! No need to go to Saudi Arabia. Just go to your computer.

Eternity in Their Hearts

All their adult lives, Penny's and Allen's hearts were tender toward missions. But it was when they saw retirement coming that they decided to step forward and make their lives count for eternity. Allen loves golf, but he had no intention of spending three or four days a week on the golf course. He wanted to invest his life in God's kingdom.

Penny owned her own medical transcription business, which she ran out of her house, and Allen was a high school vice principal. Allen had Bible studies with other staff people, and he kept many Bibles in his office—in fact, they filled his entire top shelf. A conversation starter, he figured. A way to let anyone interested know he was always ready to talk about religion. Still, he was limited in how openly he could share his faith.

It was in 1998 at a church missions conference that the Lord spoke to both Penny's and Allen's hearts, and they began to pray about what God wanted them to do in their second half. As they prayed and discussed their options and talked with others at church, a strategy emerged.

"We are both Jewish," Penny said. "Our plan was to go to Israel and get citizenship, then to move there to live. As new immigrants, we would immediately be sent to language school to learn modern Hebrew. Then, after two years of language and cultural studies, we planned to work as evangelists in Israel."

At that time, Israel welcomed Jewish people from around the world so long as they were not believers in Jesus. A Mormon Jew, a Jewish Baha'i, a secular Jew—all could get citizenship so long as they met the one requirement of the "Law of Return" that requires that they have one Jewish grandparent and the documentation to prove it. (During the Holocaust anyone with one Jewish grandparent could be sent to a death camp.) But Christians were not included in this welcome. (This was changed in a 2008 ruling of the Supreme Court of Israel, which stated that "being a Messianic Jew does not prevent one from receiving citizenship in Israel under the Law of Return or the Law of Citizenship.") Since Penny and Allen had no intention of being untruthful, the application interview concerned them.

In 1999, Penny and Allen flew to Israel to apply for citizenship. They were told to come back in a month. But when they returned, the worker in the Ministry of the Interior kept them waiting and waiting as she made one phone call after another. Finally, after two hours, she said, "Our head office in Jerusalem is shut down because the Orthodox Jews are protesting a Supreme Court decision and everyone in the Ministry is Orthodox. We can't reach anyone." So with no questions asked, their application was approved. Penny and Allen were Israeli citizens. They flew home and sold their house and car, never planning to return to the United States of America.

Well-laid plans and a sound strategy—a good starting point. But Allen and Penny were to experience the truth of Proverbs 16:9: "In his heart, a man plans his course, but the Lord determines his steps." Allen simply could not learn to speak Hebrew comfortably. He studied and he practiced and he worked with tutors, but he just couldn't do it. Other immigrants settled quite comfortably into enclaves of English speakers where they attended English-speaking churches, but Allen and Penny didn't want to do that. They had gone to Israel to live with the people and develop relationships so they could tell them about Messiah. They couldn't do that without the language. After two years, Allen said, "I really believe the Lord wants us to go home."

Back in the States, they poured their hearts out to God. "What now?" they prayed. "What is Your will, O Lord?" For ten months they prayed, and for ten months all they heard was silence.

And then, after the couple had waited on the Lord for close to a year, Jews for Jesus approached them and asked if they would be interested in training as volunteers. The Jewish population in their area wasn't big enough to warrant a full-time missionary. The opportunity fit them perfectly. "It's wonderful," Penny says. "From May to September, when people are outside, we and our volunteers go everywhere we can and hand out tracts—around forty thousand during the summer season. In the winter, when it's cold and wet, we reach out to those we already know. We welcome people into our home, and we train volunteers. Last year forty-nine people came to the Lord—seven of them Jewish."

Allen does what he loves and what he is gifted to do—evangelize. And Penny, in obedience to Messiah, works alongside him. They train volunteers, and they follow up on inquiries that come in to the website.

"If a person is willing, we have a Bible study together," said Penny. "Often, before we finish the study, the person comes to the Lord because they can see so clearly that Jesus is God's answer to our sin. Our whole goal in Jews for Jesus is to make the messiahship of Jesus unavoidable to the Jewish people."

Penny and Allen have seen exciting things happen, both among the Jewish community and with Gentiles. Not everyone is pleased with their work, however. "Some people are very angry," Penny said. "But for most of my life, I never suffered any kind of persecution. If an angry person yells at me now and then, my suffering is minimal compared to what is happening to so many people."

With prayer and counsel and every right motive, Penny and Allen made their plans. They were willing to give up everything and move to the other side of the world to follow Christ. Their plans did not work out. But now, because of the validity they gained as Israeli citizens, because Penny can speak fluent Hebrew and Allen can read and understand it, they have a unique fit in their local Jewish community.

The Lord determined their steps.

Author and speaker Brennan Manning said, "The greatest single cause of atheism in the world today is Christians, who acknowledge Jesus with their lips and walk out the door and get on with their lifestyle. That is what an unbelieving world simply finds unbelievable."

Which is exactly why Penny and Allen, and Gary and Pat, and so many others see their second half of life as so vital. They are working today for eternity.

A relatively new Gentile believer we shall call Jennifer found the Jews for Jesus website and wrote: "I've just come to the Lord and I have this Jewish friend. What do I do?"

As soon as Penny got the contact information, she called Jennifer and made arrangements to get her a packet of resources to help her know how to talk with her friend. When Jennifer's friend found out, he was livid. But Jennifer continued to meet with Penny and pray with her. A year and a half later, Penny invited Jennifer and her friend to join a group at Penny and Allen's home for Passover dinner. They came. Since then, Jennifer and her friend have come to several other dinners at Penny and Allen's house, most recently for Sukkot, the Feast of Tabernacles. Jennifer and Penny still meet together regularly to pray for the young man. Penny is never too busy for that.

Your second-half adventure may be great fun. It may be breathtakingly exciting. It may be the most memorable venture of your life. Or it may not be any of these. Whichever, one thing is certain: If you choose to use your second half for God, it will affect eternity. As C. S. Lewis wrote, "All that is not eternal is eternally out of date."[10]

"He is no fool who gives what he cannot keep to gain that which he cannot lose." At the age of twenty-two, Jim Elliot wrote this now-famous sentence in his notebook. Six years later, he was martyred in the jungles of Ecuador along with Nate Saint and three other men. It was their story that inspired Gary Sheppard to go into missions.

Chapter 9

From Success to Significance

What do growing up in a Mafia family, pastoring an evangelical church, and being financially savvy have in common? They are all pieces of Charlie's life.

Charlie grew up in an East Coast neighborhood, tough and used to being in control. From childhood he understood two things: power and money. Early on, he learned how to get what he wanted, even if it meant intimidating others and striking fear into them.

He founded his own accounting and financial planning business, and because so many people were seeking sound financial advice, it proved quite profitable. Charlie was a success. True, his third marriage was about to end, but he would see that it ended on his terms. He was tough, he had money, and he had power. But then something totally unexpected happened. Out of desperation, Charlie's wife attended a Bible study, and there she came to know Jesus Christ. Charlie ridiculed and mocked her, but try as he might, he could not deny the change in her. Grudgingly he agreed to attend church with her one Easter Sunday, and—miracle of miracles—at the age of forty-four, Charlie, too, became a Christian.

Charlie began attending church regularly, and to his amazement, he found that he really liked it. But after a while he saw something that astonished him—Christian people had the same money problems as everyone else. Not only was this robbing them of peace, but it was destroying families. Their church of five hundred members had Bible studies and small groups for just about everything, but nothing was available to help people handle their finances in keeping with biblical principles. As it became known that Charlie was a certified public accountant, more and more people tapped him for advice. It was a ready-made ministry.

Because Charlie knew from firsthand experience that only God's Word brings lasting change, he began an intensive search for an appropriate Bible-based financial study. He and his wife started leading classes in their church. Immediately, it affected lives. "Most people are amazed to discover how much the Scriptures actually say about money," Charlie says. "There is more in the Bible about money than any other single subject."

Charlie did more than teach; he lived what he taught. Within two years, he and his wife, Maxine, were completely debt-free. When he heard about Crown Financial Ministries—an interdenominational ministry dedicated to equipping people to learn, apply, and teach biblical financial principles—he immediately volunteered to work with them. He presented seminars, counseled individuals, and trained others who wanted to do similar volunteer work.

"God made it clear to me that this was what I should be doing," Charlie said. "But I still had a great business and I hated to leave it. Even though it was extremely profitable, I didn't think I could sell it, because there was nothing tangible for anyone to buy. But then someone came along and offered me an amazingly good sum, just for its good name. That was a clear sign from God."

After he sold his business, Charlie continued working with Crown Financial Ministries, and in the evenings he attended seminary classes, which led to his ordination. He served as a senior pastor for several years. Because he could see the need for sound financial stewardship from both sides, more and more of his work with Crown was geared toward pastors. God had prepared him perfectly.

Passion, eagerness to explore the cutting edge, a determination to give back—these are well-known baby boomer traits. They are also traits that can well serve the kingdom of God.

"We Christians should model the way in being good stewards," Charlie insists. "Imagine what a witness we would be in hard financial times if we were living without debt!"

Significant Witnesses

In India, pastors tell of "prosperity" preachers who come from America and preach that Jesus promised His followers an "abundant life," which they define as wealth, health, and earthly comfort. They end their sermons with, "Praise God! Great is His faithfulness to us!"

But when the Indian Christians look around them, what they see is poverty, sickness, suffering, and persecution.

In his book *Don't Waste Your Life*, John Piper says: "The world is not impressed when Christians get rich and say thanks to God. They are impressed when God is so satisfying that we give our riches away for Christ's sake and count it gain."[11]

According to the World Bank, three billion people—almost half the world's population—struggle to survive on the equivalent of less than two dollars a day. They cannot get credit from a traditional bank, so they simply have no way to get ahead. The result is mass hunger, disease, and despair.

For some time now, organizations have been helping the poor with micro-loans. But now, individuals are getting in on providing help. A 2007 *Time* magazine article tells of retirees who are personally funding new businesses and nonprofits with their own savings—and are doing it successfully. The article starts with: "Money experts warn that it's a bad idea. But a steady flow of people past the age of 50 are funding new businesses and nonprofits with their retirement savings anyway—and having enough success (or fun) to brag about it." After giving examples as well as guidelines, the article ends with this sentence: "So be careful. But remember there are other risks in play too, like the risk of losing your sense of purpose and missing the chance to do something that excites you."[12]

At the age of fifty, Bill Gates, founder of Microsoft and the richest man in the world at the time, resigned his post as chairman of the board to focus his efforts and attention on the Bill and Melinda Gates Foundation. Worth $29.1 billion in 2008 and the world's largest foundation, its mission is to bring vaccines to poor children in Africa and India. Then in the summer of 2008, Warren Buffet announced that the philanthropies named in his will would not have to wait until his death to benefit from his multibillion-dollar fortune. His foundation would begin to distribute it immediately, and most of it would feed directly into the Gates Foundation.

Though few in the world could even come close to what those two are doing, a plethora of celebrities have been stepping forward to be counted as philanthropists, giving to everything from cancer centers in the United States to programs to benefit children around the world. Rolling up one's sleeves and doing good for others has become downright trendy.

In their twenties, baby boomers began their quest to find meaning in life. Now, after three decades of accumulating stuff, they are looking back to where they started. No longer is the boomer generation trying to change the world through upheaval and mass reform. Most are now striving to change one small part of the world—or maybe just to change themselves. They want their time on this earth to leave a positive mark.

Whether it's millions of dollars or a hundred dollars, whether it is full-time work or volunteer hours, generally people give because their altruism brings them some sort of significance. For the Christian, there is a biblical motivation. The Bible instructs us to do good, to champion the cause of the poor, and to make our lives matter.

We are not called to be millionaires, but we are all called to be responsible stewards of what God has entrusted to us, whether it be a great abundance or only a little. Whether they have a lot or a little, all those who use their gifts wisely will be rewarded with the same words from the Master: "Well done, good and faithful servant!" (Matthew 25:21). Yes, this refers to how we use our money. But it also means our other gifts—abilities, opportunities, and the days and hours we are given on earth.

"I had plenty of money," Charlie said of the first half of his life. "My money was my success. But God changed that. Now my significance comes from who I am in Christ, and through my opportunities to serve." Then he added, "I may be in my second half, but I feel like I'm still twenty!"

Your Microbiography

For years I taught writing classes to older people living in senior residences. They were in their late seventies, eighties, and nineties. During the course, I always gave them this assignment: *Write the significance of your life in 100 words or less.* It was amazing to me to see what people considered worthy of their one hundred words. Most of the men described what they had done for a living, and many women used their words to talk about their children. When I handed these back with the comment, "Yes, but tell me about *you!*" people seemed genuinely stymied. One woman wrote exactly one hundred words describing her faults and shortcomings. But I remember a certain man by the name of William who began his microbiography this way: "I escaped life at the age of sixty when I retired from my job and went to work doing good. That was when I became me."

Significance isn't about success; it's about meaning. It's not what pads your checkbook; it's what gives value to your life.

Tom understands the search for significance. "It's not that I was dissatisfied with the business world," he said of his former career. "It's just that I wanted something more. I wanted to use my knowledge and blessings to give something back. The business code where I worked was: *Make a difference, not just a dollar.* Well, I wanted that to be the code of my life. I wanted to leave a mark."

Many boomers have worked long and hard to accumulate things. But when the time comes that they leave this earth, they will have to leave all that mound of things behind. Other people will benefit from that dream home in the suburbs and the vacation house in the mountains, the cars in the garage and the boat at the lake. Someone else will have to go through the piled-high attic and the locked safe and sort through all their gathered treasures.

Of course, you should enjoy yourself. Certainly, live life to the fullest. The important thing is to understand that all of that is fleeting. And if you are depending on the fun and stuff to satisfy you, take note: you will be sorely disappointed.

The Journey Continues

Nineteenth-century psychologist/philosopher William James once said, "The greatest use of life is to spend it on something that will outlast it." If he had been born a century later, he would have ushered in the era of the baby boomers. Had he been a Christian, he would have more fully understood the truth of his words.

In their determination to give back, mature baby boomers are realizing that significance truly is found beyond themselves and their own lives. If we live into our eighties or our nineties—even if we blow out a hundred birthday candles—our days are numbered. And no one can reclaim days from the past. It's the way we leave this earth that shows the truth of where our treasure is.

Now is the time to rethink goals and values with eternal significance in mind.

"Do your little bit of good where you are," said Archbishop Desmond Tutu of South Africa. "It's those little bits of good put together that overwhelm the world."

In the seventeenth chapter of Acts we read how Paul and Silas made their way down the Egnatian Way to Thessalonica, the capital of Macedonia, home to a colony of Jews. As was his custom, Paul went to the synagogue and explained the Scriptures. Some of the Jews followed, and so did a large number of Greeks, and a few important women as well. This did not please the Jewish leaders at all. So they went to the marketplace and rounded up a group of troublemakers who started a riot in the city. Because it was known that Jason was a follower of Christ, the crowd rushed to his house in search of Paul and Silas. When the mob didn't find the men, they grabbed Jason and a handful of other Christians, and hauled them before the city officials shouting, "Here they are, the people who have been turning the world upside down" (see Acts 17:1–6 NRSV).

Can you imagine a mob pointing to Christian baby boomers and making that same accusation? "These are the people who have been turning the world upside down!" Talk about significance!

It could happen. Baby boomers, the generation of transformers, have only just begun to show the power of their second half. Only God knows what they can do.

Chapter 10

Pass It On

Despite baby boomer strides, Americans remain a narrow-minded crowd. In the fall of 2008, *Outreach* magazine reported some rather surprising research findings. Consider:

The number of Americans, as a percent, who have never known:
- A Buddhist: 59%
- An undocumented immigrant: 54%
- A Muslim: 46%
- A homeless person: 45%
- An evangelical Christian: 40%
- A political liberal: 25%
- A political conservative: 24%
- A former inmate: 15%
- A wealthy person: 12%

I wonder what the results of such research would show in 2018? In 2028? In 2048? Drastically different numbers most likely, simply because America is changing. But also, I hope, because today's baby boomers are changing themselves and their country.

Let's be honest: Many in the generation coming up behind us are disgusted with the self-important attitudes so often attributed to boomers. When they look at us, they don't see global concern and true desire to leave a significant mark in the world. They see broken marriages, egocentric choices, self-serving lives. The last thing they want to do is follow our bruised model.

The psalmist David wrote, "Even when I am old and gray, do not forsake me, O God, till I declare your power to the next generation, your might to all who are to come" (Psalm 71:18). Goodness knows, David's egocentric choice broke up a marriage. He had Uriah killed so he could have the poor man's wife, for goodness sake! What David did was the epitome of self-serving, and yet he was called "a man after God's own heart." He ended his life declaring the Lord's power, not only to his own generation, but for millennia of generations that followed.

Have the baby boomers been a narcissistic generation? Perhaps. But they have also been an accepting generation, a generation willing to look around them and see things through a wider scope. The boomers have also been great parents. Because of them, the next generation is smart and educated, creative and versatile, less racist and more globally minded, a great mixture of hopefully optimistic and realistically perceptive.

We have raised a generation that not only cares about the world, but that actively embraces equality and cooperation as well, and in a way we only dreamed of doing.

These are wonderful attributes. Yet our children, and our children's children, need mature mentors who can work with them and for them without feeling disrespected or threatened. They need us to be Moseses in their Joshua generation.

One younger ministry worker told me, "This present young generation coming up thinks they can change the world. Other generations didn't think they had much control. Other generations didn't think they could do anything that really mattered."

How soon they forget! I couldn't help myself; I just had to stop her and conduct a bit of baby boomer education.

But the fact is, every generation has its own place to fill. It is true that the next generation is more globally aware than boomers were, and the generation behind them is even more so. Young people today are growing up global. That wasn't the case fifty years ago.

Still, boomers have done an amazing job of breaking through barriers and setting a marching pace through the wilderness. Now, though, we need to prepare to pass the staff along to the next generation. This means readying ourselves for the transition, and it also means doing what we can to equip those coming along behind us so that they can effectively lead on into the global age. Fortunately, we have some excellent skills for doing exactly that: teaching and modeling and inspiring toward a better world.

Every believer is a disciple, and any believer can make disciples. It is our charge to disciple those coming along behind us and to ready them for ministry. We can do this in six specific ways:

1. Making Ready by Paving the Way

"I wanted my kids to experience life as the majority of the world lives it," Tom said. "I wanted them to know that for most people, life is not an American dream." Certainly there were many adjustments to make when his family lived in Uganda for two years—such as going to bed at sundown because the electricity was off so often, and no television. But other adjustments were a pleasant surprise. Culturally, Uganda is basically a moral country. The culture shock didn't so much come with the family's move to Uganda but with their return to the United States. "After two years away, the kids were shocked at what they saw plastered on billboards and on television," Tom said. "But then, after nine months or so, no one even noticed anymore."

We have paved the way, but we can't stop there. That paved way must constantly be touched up and refinished. Sometimes it even has to be completely repaved. Here are a few ways that is being done:

One baby boomer who understands the importance of paving and refinishing helped to develop the Morningstar Institute housed in Southern Nazarene University's School of Business in Bethany, Oklahoma (morningstarinstitute.org). Morningstar's primary purpose is to combine academic training, research, and actual field experience in order to raise up Christian leaders for tomorrow in the areas of international development and poverty alleviation.

Finishers, too, is a leader in paving to tomorrow. Finishers.org was designed with baby boomers in mind. Funny thing, though—young people kept going to the site because they had no other workable options. Now that is changing. The site of MissionNext.org is specifically designed for next generation missions. Already Finishers is passing their experience along.

Mike is paving the way by pointing Christians to such secular opportunities as Devex.com. This site posts exciting job opportunities with USAID, the World Bank, and positions with health practices, AIDS practices, and many, many other organizations. It is a great resource for men and women who prefer to do kingdom work from within a secular organization. "It isn't an easy thing to accomplish," Mike warns, "but neither is it impossible. And there are many, many opportunities there that we should at least consider."

"I took my son to Honduras on a business/mission trip," Tom said. "He really wanted to go, and we had a good time, but the next year he didn't want to go back. He had his own things to do."

So how can an interested second-halfer help keep a younger person's sensitivity sharpened? Do anything you can, but don't push. Trust God to move in the lives of those who are coming after you just as He moved in your own life

2. Making Ready by Example

We have the experience. The way we use that experience may be the most enduring gift we can give the generations coming along after us. Specifically, you can:

- **Practice what you preach.** "I walk the talk," Charlie says. "When I give seminars, I have no book table. I sell nothing. All I do is bring a message. When we get our own house in order, we don't need to knock on doors to tell people we are different; they can look at us and see it for themselves."

- **Speak up.** It is always helpful to let your government officials know your opinions and concerns. But the beginning of the Obama administration "is probably the best opportunity we've had to be heard for a long time," Mike said. "We just had eight years of faith-friendly government, and those policies aren't about to change anytime soon. Plus, both the secretary of state and President Obama are pro-faith-based. Also, both the Republican and the Democratic parties are pro-faith-based. Only a small percentage are opposed." If Mike is correct, and both sides of the political spectrum are willing to listen with faith-friendly ears, this is definitely the time to speak out. But even if that is not the case, we would do well to change the example set by some baby boomers of writing the government off as no friend to Christians. Now is the time to speak up and set a positive challenge for working together—government, business, and God's people. It's not possible in all things, nor with all groups, but we can move forward without the knee-jerk "us against them" approach.

- **You can involve your children and grandchildren in mission work.** Today, more intergenerational family groups than ever are volunteering to work together on mission projects. Even if you cannot go yourself, you can be a strong force of influence and help. With equipment, funds, and prayers, Pat and Gary sent a part of themselves along with their teenage grandson on a mission trip to Quebec. Evidently the Lord is nudging the boy, because since that trip he made three other trips to work on mission projects, another time to Quebec and twice within the United States. Of course, the family involvement goes deeper than just one trip since missions is such an integral part of Pat and Gary's family. Their son and his wife, the grandson's parents, went to Côte d'Ivoire for a year. Another son is actively working toward early retirement so that he can go back to Africa where he was born. Your mission roots likely don't run as deeply as Pat and Gary's do, but you can still look for ways to involve the next generation in the kingdom work that means so much to you.

3. Making Ready as Teachers

The apostle Paul was clearly a strong believer in the principle of passing the staff of leadership along by means of training teachers who would in turn train more teachers. In 2 Timothy 2:2, he instructs his own student Timothy to entrust all that he had been taught to "reliable men who will also be qualified to teach others."

"I hope I never retire," said Tom of his job as chair of the business school at a large Christian university. Then he added, "But then, teaching is sort of like being retired. Academia has been picking up a lot of people of retirement age who want to make a difference. Students respond well to those older instructors because they respect their experience. Older instructors have firsthand illustrations that make their courses come alive."

Not that teaching is restricted to the classroom. Consider the value of mature, experienced Sunday school teachers and Bible study leaders. Or the contributions of Grace, who is teaching writing online to the young pastor in India. Or the fifty-year-old woman who spent five months in Cambodia helping students to learn English just by talking to them. In fact, think of the many men and women who teach English in so many different places all around the world.

4. Making Ready as Mentors

It's one thing to be a teacher, and another to act as a mentor. The Encarta dictionary defines a mentor as *an experienced adviser and supporter:* "Somebody, usually older and more experienced, who advises and guides a younger, less experienced person."

Yes, that's it exactly. We can ready the younger generation by advising and guiding them. This, too, is a scriptural principle. Titus 2:1–5, for instance, demonstrates how Paul instructs his student Titus, then Titus is told to teach the people. In addition, the older women are to mentor the younger women.

"Crown Financial Ministries has a mentoring program that passes along biblical principles," Charlie said. "In any group, some people might be as young as thirty and some as old as sixty. The younger ones watch the older ones and learn from them."

But you don't need to be part of an organized group to be a mentor. Mentoring is what gives value to the writing or telling of your own faith story. When you share your journey, you model investing in a second-half adventure to those who are not yet there. Through your own life, you show what it means to "trust in the Lord with all your heart and lean not on your own understanding." Your own experience will demonstrate the truth that when you "acknowledge him," then "he will make your paths straight" (Proverbs 3:5–6).

5. Making Ready through Encouragement

Many people can encourage and counsel a young person who is considering mission options. Anyone can pray with that person and point out appropriate Scriptures. But few can do it as effectively and with as much power as someone who has been there. When the counsel, Scripture, and prayers come from a person who has already considered those options personally and who is living out the results, then the encouragement takes on a whole different hue.

Linda, who is now teaching English in Ukraine, forwarded this note that she received from one of her students: "Thank you so much for your friendship. You teach me not only English—you also teach me to live right." She included the note in her regular correspondence with a young woman who is considering coming to join her. Those simple words, passed along by the person God was using to change a life, made up the younger woman's mind. She will be on her way in the spring.

Recently six of Pat and Gary's nine grandchildren were visiting them. As is their usual practice, Gary read a missionary story during family devotions. Their ten-year-old grandson, his brow wrinkled in serious contemplation, said with some frustration, "Grandpop, for a long time I've wanted to be a medical doctor. But I also think I'd like to be a missionary." When Gary explained that he could do both at the same time, the boy's face lit up with excitement. "Great!" he exclaimed. "That's what I'll do when I grow up! I'll be a missionary and a medical doctor!"

6. Making Ready through Challenge

Again and again, people I talk with stress the fact that the evangelical community needs to unite and work together as a body. Not all alike (a body is made up of many different parts, remember) but all united in one goal. "Muslims think all we care about is being crusaders," said Mike. "So much could be done if Christians could work alongside our government and private businesses. Christians are already committed to helping people, to offering relief and humanitarian work. Unlike business or government, they work without pay. We need the government to give us the freedom to answer questions about our faith without fear of reprisal. But we need to be willing to assure others that if we agree to certain guidelines, we will follow them."

Rick Warren of Saddleback Church has already thrown out this challenge—from his pulpit, in the pages of his books, and through his well-publicized P.E.A.C.E initiative. Now is the time to encourage the next generation to grab it up and change the adversarial way things are too often done.

One idea offered is the development of a state-of-the-art website that would match up the needs of people with the capabilities of

NGOs (nongovernmental organizations). For instance, if farmers in Cambodia need cows, they could directly contact an organization in the United States that has a program that provides cows. Faith-based organizations would be welcomed on this website. Of course, this is not a paradigm that would fit every organization. But it would be a way for some evangelical groups to work alongside the government and begin to eliminate the animosity between the two. Perhaps the next generation will see this possibility become a reality.

Many American churches already see the local church as a global church. Certainly Saddleback does. So does Northwood Church in Keller, Texas, which has people serving around the globe. Besides their major work in Mexico and Vietnam, Northwood people are making over houses in rundown neighborhoods in their own backyard, conducting counseling in Morocco, and digging water wells in Guatemala. Pastor Bob Roberts says, "For me, it's not about missions; it's about the kingdom of God. That's what can change society."

The Tree of Life Church in Fremont, California—a Chinese congregation—also sees the church as global. It is a congregation of 180 (not counting the children and youth) yet each year it sends out five or six mission teams. In 2009, their schedule included Thailand, China, Indonesia, and two trips to India. The previous year, teams went to Vietnam and Malaysia as well as to India, China, and Indonesia. I asked Agnes Hoang, the missions pastor, if everyone in the church was involved in the missions program. "A good portion are," she said. "They give in prayer or in money, or they go and see."

"Any church can make this type of commitment," says Bob Savage of Partners International. He should know, because he helps churches across the country do exactly that. For instance, a church in Colorado "adopted" a town in China so that their members could focus their efforts and make a long-term difference in that place. Each year they take cross-generational teams over to teach English. A church in Dallas, Texas, regularly sends teams to their area of focus in Indonesia. Just recently, in answer to the request of the Indonesian Christians, the Dallas church sent five professional counselors to train local pastors in counseling techniques. Another church in California just sent a research team to the Middle East to explore ministry opportunities in that area.

"People are looking to get involved with their skills and abilities," Bob Savage said. "Small churches can do this as well as large churches. It often means meeting a lot of families and drinking a lot of tea, and being friendly and speaking conversational English. We at Partners International are looking for people who want to partner with indigenous people over the long term."

Church teams are cross-generational, "from teens to eighty," says Bob Savage. "The young ones relate well and the older ones are greatly respected." And when the church commits to such a ministry, no one person needs to go and stay more than a couple of weeks—although many people end up going back every year.

Agnes Hoang says that at the Tree of Life Church, second-half adults are the first to volunteer to go on trips because they are the ones in the best position to pay for it. "The travel is expensive," she says. "But they are also valued for their life experience. They are able to see from a different perspective." Agnes told of a group that went to Indonesia who was praying with a group of local Christians. "The older woman in our group was especially keenly aware of people's needs," she said. "Her praying touched many hearts."

A Chinese proverb says, "Flowers leave some of their fragrance in the hand that bestows them."

That is certainly true of kingdom workers who grab hold of the baton passed to them by the faithful cloud of witnesses in Hebrews 12:1–2. Keeping our eyes on Jesus, we run the race specifically marked out for us. And as we come closer to our turn to pass the baton along, we prepare to join the cloud of inspiring examples so that we, too, can cheer on those still running.

"Our legacy is alive as long as our influence survives, for good or for bad," Charlie says. "And our legacy influences the next generation."

And the next and the next and the next . . .

Chapter 11

A Second Half
Well-Lived

I got an e-mail message from Rich, who has been struggling with the whole idea of retirement. Here is what he wrote:

> I talked to the Finishers office today after a call by those inviting
> me to teach in Delhi. Also talked to my wife about Delhi and she
> does not feel a call there, so I would not go for a semester with-
> out her. But what I thought was hopeless is turning out to be
> pretty interesting. Don't know where it may go, but I am desper-
> ate to try. What I need most of all is to finish well.
>
> —RICH

As I read Rich's note, I couldn't help but think of my neighbor Ed. Ed retired the day he turned sixty-two and he lived to be eighty-six. For almost a third of his life he slept until ten each morning, then spent the rest of the day playing solitaire and watching television. As time went on, his life became more and more ingrown, and Ed grew angrier, grouchier, and increasingly self-absorbed. Just before he died, he told his son, "If I had known I would live this long, I would have taken better care of myself."

What a difference from my friend Olga who went home to heaven last year at the age of ninety-six. When I visited her a week before she died, she showed me her list of goals for the next five years. The Bible would have said Olga died "at a good old age."

Abraham lived to be 175 years old, and the Bible says he died "at a good old age, an old man and full of years; and he was gathered to his people" (Genesis 25:7–8).

At Moses' death at the age of 120, he is referred to as "the servant of the Lord" and it was God Himself who buried him. "Since then, no prophet has risen in Israel like Moses, whom the Lord knew face to face" (Deuteronomy 34:5–6, 10).

Gideon "died at a good old age and was buried in the tomb of his father" (Judges 8:32).

David also "died at a good old age, having enjoyed long life, wealth and honor" (1 Chronicles 29:28). Of all the honors bestowed upon David, the greatest was that he was known forever after as a man after God's own heart (Acts 13:22).

Certainly, all of these men were blessed with long lives. But the number of years was not the important thing. The important thing was that they all lived well. Every one of them is listed in the Hebrews 11 hall of faith. Faith is a rock-bottom requirement for a life that finishes well, for everyday people as well as for the greatest of men and women.

Many boomers are not yet thinking about the finish line. That still seems years down the road. Tom said, "I don't know whether anything I do will live on after me or not. I wish it would. But give me another twenty years on that."

Still, the thing about finishing well is not to put too much stock in making up for lost time with a good final sprint across the finish line. A good race requires a consistent run.

In an oft-quoted survey, people ninety-five and older were asked how they would live their lives differently if they had the chance. The top three answers were:

#3— "I would reflect more."
#2— "I would risk more."
#1— "I would do more things that live on after I'm dead."[13]

We have a chance to do those things right now!

#3: Reflect More

There are many positive ways to reflect, but one of the best is to meditate on God's Word. And a good place to start is with the Psalms. You might want to consider these:

- *Psalm 18:* A celebration of God's faithfulness, God's righteousness, God's gentleness, God's majesty
- *Psalm 23:* A wonderful psalm of reflection when you seek God's will
- *Psalm 27:* A psalm of waiting on the Lord
- *Psalm 29:* Reflecting on praise to the Lord who brings peace in the storm
- *Psalm 37:* A psalm of godly wisdom
- *Psalm 61:* A prayer for restoration
- *Psalm 63:* Reflecting on the security of God's presence
- *Psalm 96:* A psalm that calls all nations to praise the Lord
- *Psalm 98:* Reflect by singing to the Lord a new song
- *Psalm 112:* Blessed reflections on fearing the Lord
- *Psalm 138:* A song of praise for God's saving help
- *Psalm 150:* A final hallelujah reflecting on the message of the Psalms

#2: Risk More

In Hebrews 11: 6 we read, "Without faith it is impossible to please God."

But what is faith? It is "being sure of what we hope for and certain of what we do not see" (Hebrews 11:1).

Which by definition means that stepping out by faith requires risk. Unless we risk so much that we actually have to depend on God, we are not practicing faith.

But there's more. Practicing faith means *doing* something. As James wrote: "What good is it, my brothers, if a man claims to have faith but has no deeds? Can such faith save him? Suppose a brother or sister is without clothes and daily food. If one of you says to him, 'Go, I wish you well; keep warm and well fed,' but does nothing about his physical needs, what good is it? In the same way, faith by itself, if it is not accompanied by action, is dead" (James 2:14–17).

Most of us expect to live to "a good old age," and most likely, the majority of us will. But of course, none of us can predict the future. So whatever we are going to do, we had better get going and do it now. Challenge yourself by taking lessons from those who knew Jesus best—His disciples.

- If Christ tells you to bring your own brother, as He told Andrew, go get him today.
- If Christ says to you, "Follow me," as He said to Philip, follow now!
- If you look at your life and despair because there doesn't seem to be much of value there, remember Matthew and know that God can redeem any situation.
- When you are tempted to call attention to your efforts, remember Jesus' rebuke of James the Less.
- Remember Thaddeus and know that to love Christ is to obey.
- Think of Simon, and let his life challenge you to never lose your passion to fight for right and justice.

- If Christ is urging you to speak of your faith to a friend, remember Bartholomew who owed his faith to a friend who introduced him to the Savior.
- Remember John who was willing to risk everything to follow Christ, even though "Eyes have not seen what is coming!"
- If you are a man or woman of importance, be challenged by James the Greater who, despite his exalted standing, had no desire to put himself in a position of prestige.
- Although faith takes risks, think of Judas and remember that taking a shortcut for your own personal advantage can be disastrous.
- If your faith falters at times, think of Thomas and read again his statement in John 11:15–17, then read his stirring confession of faith in John 20:88.
- Think of Peter and keep your eyes fixed firmly on Jesus.
- Remember Paul and finish well.

#1: Do More That Will Live on After You

A life well-lived is a life of faith. It is a life of boldness tempered by wisdom. It is a life that offers everything it has to God so that He can take it and multiply it for His glory. Such lives are needed in every age, but never more desperately than today.

Now is the time to make *evangelical Christians* synonymous with "caring people who do good things in Christ's name to make our suffering world a better place." Too long the popular opinion has been closer to seeing evangelicals as judgmental hypocrites who only want to jump into culture wars. "The public perception is that we are mean and negative," commented Jimmy Draper to the *Boston Globe*.[14] Too often our response to this perception has been to assume a defensive stance and to close ourselves off in our own Christian communities where we make a great show of our own evangelical rules, speak our own evangelical language, and immerse ourselves in our own evangelical media. Everyone else is locked out. It is *us* against *them*.

Now is the time to change that.

Let us throw down our defenses and allow the outside world to see us for who we really are. After the devastating 2004 Asian tsunami disaster, evangelical relief groups such as World Vision, World Relief, and Compassion International ably handled a huge influx of money, and because of their established relationships, they were equipped and ready to respond on location within hours. Following Hurricane Katrina, the Salvation Army, Southern Baptists, and an untold number of other Christian groups and churches showed up in force to offer help of every kind. Right now countless Christians are quietly feeding the hungry, building houses for the homeless, digging wells for the thirsty, bringing healing to the sick, and living out the gospel of Jesus Christ in this country and around the world.

A volunteer working online with Global Media Outreach logged on to find this message from China: *"I'm very happy when I found this website. I believe this will help me with my daily walk with Jesus. Since I am in a non-Christian country, please send me information to help me grow as a Christian."* Because that volunteer lives in this free country with unlimited access to every kind of resource, he was able to answer immediately and provide the help and encouragement his Chinese brother needed.

Baby boomers, through their second-half adventures, can contribute a whole new understanding of what it means to be a follower of Christ. They can do this by refusing to sit comfortably on the sidelines and tune out the rest of the world. They can do it by following in the footsteps of Jesus, who healed and cured multitudes.

Who met individuals where they were. "Everyone who drinks this water will be thirsty again, but whoever drinks the water I give him will never thirst. Indeed, the water I give him will become in him a spring of water welling up to eternal life" (John 4:13–14).

Who, in natural conversation, talked naturally of spiritual things. "God is a spirit, and his worshipers must worship in spirit and in truth" (John 4:24).

Who listened to questions and gave respectful answers. Woman:

"I know that Messiah (called Christ) is coming . . . " Jesus: "I who speak to you am he" (John 4:25–26).

Who understood His listeners before He preached to them. "Then, leaving her water jar, the woman went back to the town and said to the people, 'Come, see a man who told me everything I ever did. Could this be the Christ?'" (John 4:28–29).

No, I am not at all suggesting we subscribe to the idea that Jesus was merely a great moral teacher and that if we take His advice, we can establish a better social order on earth. (Although, He was a great moral teacher, and we certainly could.) I realize that the humanitarian message is in no way the full message Jesus came to earth to bring. And in no way am I suggesting that we abandon the message of salvation through faith in Christ. It's just that when we take time to build caring relationships, we make ourselves more credible witnesses of the truths that might otherwise be rejected out of hand. When we speak with gentleness and respect, the sharp edges fall from our words and make them less likely to grate on the ears of those who have been taught from babyhood to turn their backs on us. It's not just when we preach or quote Scripture that we mirror Christ. In everything we do, we show the One to whom we belong.

Always, there will be critics, but let us not be the critical ones. Always there will be the intolerant and the judgmental, but let it not be us. Always there will be objections, but let us not be the ones who are objectionable.

Now is the time for you to light your candle and hold it high. Now is the time for Christ's disciples around the globe to unite and together to light the world.

Finishing Well

Pastor Bob Roberts of Northwood Church takes Jesus' words in Matthew 25:31–45 seriously. God will indeed call us to account for our time on earth—for what we did for the hungry and the thirsty and the imprisoned. "It means the goal of the church is not just to get converts," he said. "It is to make disciples. Converts grow churches, but disciples change the world."

It is within the makeup of the baby boomer generation to need to make a difference. They long to have lives that count and to leave the world a better place. I just opened up the AARP magazine and saw an article titled *Ten Who Inspire: These go-getters are putting their passion into action to make the world a better place.*[15] The ten profiles include celebrities, businesspeople, and professionals, as well as people attracted to specific causes because of their own circumstances. Such accounts are everywhere, and they truly are inspiring. Although their stories are often missed, in every humanitarian endeavor, people of faith stand shoulder-to-shoulder alongside the most inspirational people on these lists. But there is a difference: people of faith have an added incentive. We know that the time will come when we will stand before God and give an account of what we did with what we were given.

When Charlie was asked to speak at Crown Ministries' Founders meeting, he chose the topic of leaving a legacy. He told the story of David Livingstone, the British missionary who opened up Africa to the gospel and spent much of his life there. Stricken with malaria and dysentery and near death, Livingstone insisted on being propped up on his knees so that he could continue in prayer just as he always did. That is how he died—on his knees, praying for the continent he loved and had given so much of his life to evangelize.

His mourning African friends knew he must be buried in England among his own people. But first, according to Livingstone's wishes, his heart was removed and buried under a mvula tree.

From all areas of Africa, tribal leaders gathered to honor the great man of God. They ceremonially wrapped his body and hand-carried it out of the jungle, through hostile tribes and friendly, to the coast where a ship waited.

David Livingstone was buried in Westminster Abbey in London amid great honor and ceremony. But his heart remained in Africa.

"Where is your heart going to be buried?" Charlie asked his audience. "On the golf course? Golf is fine, a good way to relax. In your needlework? It's a creative endeavor, to be sure. By the television? Lots of interesting programs on. On a cruise ship? Travel is wonderful. Nothing wrong with any of those things. But where will your heart be buried?"

When I stand before the throne of God on judgment day, I do not want to hear the glorious Savior demand: "That's *it*?! With all the blessings I poured out on you, with all the multitude of opportunities I heaped in your path, with all the endless resources I sent your way— even then, this is *all* you accomplished?!"

How about you?

Finishing well means one day hearing,

Well done, my good and faithful servant. . . . Come, you are blessed by my Father; take your inheritance, the kingdom prepared for you since the creation of the world.

—MATTHEW 25:21, 34

Notes

1. C. S. Lewis, *The Screwtape Letters*, Letter XXVIII (New York: Macmillan, 1982).

2. June, 2004, report from the Harvard University of Public Health—MetLife Foundation on Retirement and Civic Engagement; the report can be found at www.reinventingaging.org.

3. C. S. Lewis, *The Allegory of Love* (London: Oxford University Press, 1938).

4. This study was commissioned in November 2007 by Experience Wave, a Washington, D.C.–based campaign that aims to help older adults stay engaged in work and civic life.

5. This quote is found at www.quotedb.com and many other sources.

6. *The New Retirement Study*, conducted by Merrill Lynch, 2007.

7. March 2008 report from AARP, conducted in 2006 by research firm Focalyst.

8. Shirley Bragg, "Baby Boomers Expect to Beat the Odds with More Active, Longer Lives, "citing Rehabilitation Institute of Chicago survey. Online at beauty.about.com/cs/aginggracefull1/a/babyboomersage.htm

9. C. S. Lewis, *An Experiment in Criticism* (Cambridge: Cambridge University Press, 1961).

10. C. S. Lewis, *The Four Loves* (New York: Harcourt Brace Jovanovich, 1960), chapter 16.

11. John Piper, *Don't Waste Your Life* (Wheaton, Ill.: Crossway Books, 2003).

12. Dan Kadlec, "Turning Savings into a Start-Up," *Time*, Aug 2, 2007, 54.

13. Dale Carnegie & Associates, *The Leader in You* (New York: Simon & Schuster, 1993), quoted by Tony Campolo in his sermon "If I Had to Live It Over Again."

14. "Save the E-Word," Christianity Today, October 2006. Online at: christianityto-day.com/39051.

15. *AARP Magazine*, Jan/Feb 2009, 37–43. Online at: aarpmagazine.org/people/in-spire_awards_2009_close.html.

Appendix

Finishers Project works with approximately one hundred mission organizations. Many other groups are also working to accomplish the same kingdom ends and also provide opportunities for those who desire to make an investment in eternity.

The organizations listed here are the ones mentioned in this book.

Crossworld
Business as Missions (BAM)
www.crossworld.org
E-mail: get.involved@crossworld.com

Crossworld has nearly four hundred missionaries on eighty teams in twenty-five ministries around the world. It serves the worldwide church by mobilizing teams to make disciples and train leaders. BAM is a program offered within the Crossworld organization where real business is integrated with real missions. It is defined by legitimate economic activity conducted through a workplace professional who, by virtue of his or her position, is able to share the love of Christ and His message of salvation.

Crown Financial Ministries

www.crown.org

This interdenominational ministry is dedicated to equipping people around the world to learn, apply, and teach biblical financial principles. Located in the United States, Canada, Latin America, South America, and Africa—and expanding into Europe, India, Asia, and Australia—Crown has taught or equipped more than 50 million people in over eighty nations. The organization relies on approximately 250 employees and over 10,000 volunteers worldwide.

Finishers Project

http://finishers.org

The goal of the Finishers Project is to challenge North American adults, especially those at midlife, to make an informed decision about opportunities in local and global ministries. Finishers accomplishes this by providing people with individualized information, coaching, and ministry matches. The selected pathways come through partner agencies and churches.

Global Media Outreach (GMO)

www.globalmediaoutreach.com
If you want to join: www.GMOJoinUs.com

Global Media Outreach uses cutting-edge technologies to reach the world for Christ. From the 5 million daily Internet searches for spiritual help, thousands come to GMO websites where they are answered by one of the 1,800 plus volunteers (Online missionaries) from around the world.

Gospel for Asia

www.winasia.org

Gospel for Asia trains and sends indigenous missionaries to share the good news of Jesus Christ to those who have never heard.

Grace International Ministries (GIM)

Phone: 209-480-1107

www.grace-international-ministries.org

GIM sends English as a Second Language (ESL) teachers to Japan. The classes are an outreach program for the Japanese Christian churches. The emphasis of GIM is relational, global evangelism offered through the ESL classes, under the guidance and oversight of the local Japanese church.

Habitat for Humanity (HFHI)

www.habitat.org

A nonprofit, ecumenical Christian housing ministry, HFHI seeks to eliminate poverty housing and homelessness from the world and to make decent shelter a matter of conscience and action. Habitat has built more than 300,000 houses around the world, providing more than 1.5 million people in more than 3,000 communities with safe, decent, affordable shelter.

International School Project (ISP)

www.isptrips.org

ISP offers year-round opportunities that meet a wide variety of interests and needs. They say: "Whether you're drawn to a small discipleship team in Ukraine, a groundbreaking large conference in Mongolia, or just about anything in between, we have a trip for you!" The organization's website lists its most current schedule of upcoming trips and needs.

Jews for Jesus

www.jewsforjesus.org

This organization exists "to make the messiahship of Jesus an unavoidable issue to our Jewish people worldwide."

Leadership Development International (LDI)

www.ldichina.com

The goal of LDI is to help people succeed, both personally and professionally. They work in the areas of education and business training programs that combine innovative learning techniques with the principles of character and truth, emphasizing leadership. This organization especially needs people with years of business experience to serve as business consultants in China.

Living Water Quilts

www.LivingWaterQuilts.org

This project is about sharing the great news of Jesus through small group quilting sessions. Each element in the biblical account of the Woman at the Well as told in John 4 is represented by a shape within a quilt block. As the block is pieced, the Woman at the Well's life is also pieced together. Attendees take home a completed quilt block, the knowledge of Jesus, and sometimes an eternity-altering decision.

Mission Aviation Fellowship (MAF)

www.maf.org

Through aviation, communications, and various technologies, MAF makes it possible for individuals, communities, and nations to be transformed by the gospel of Jesus Christ. They use retired airline pilots to assist in training.

Operation Mobilisation (OM)

www.om.org

Working in every continent and on every ocean (via two oceangoing ships), Operation Mobilisation seeks to demonstrate and proclaim the love of God. In every location, OM teams adapt to the local culture and situation in order to find the best ways to share Jesus.

These include literature, creative arts, friendship, Bible studies, video and cassette tapes, correspondence courses, relief and development work, and much, much more.

Partners International
www.partnersintl.org

A global ministry, Partners International works to create and grow communities of Christian witness in partnership with God's people in the least Christian regions of the world. This organization pioneered the approach of partnering with indigenous Christian ministries. While its major ministries are church planting, leadership training, holistic witness, women and children, and ministry development, they also provide educational consulting services to partner ministries.

Reach Across
www.reachacross.net

Reach Across shares the gospel with Muslims and seeks to serve them in practical ways. They offer both short-term and long-term service opportunities and encourage approaches that integrate practical service with spiritual ministry.

SIM USA
www.sim.org

SIM is a community of God's people who delight to worship Him and are passionate about the gospel, seeking to fulfill the mission of Jesus Christ in the world by planting, strengthening, and partnering with churches around the world.

Teach Overseas
www.TeachOverseas.org

This unique ministry offers "the wisdom of experience with a cutting-edge sensibility." Each year, they train and send hundreds of Christians to teach English, business, and other subjects in China, the Czech Republic, Hungary, Kazakhstan, Kyrgyzstan, North Africa, Russia, Slovakia, and Vietnam. To date, over 100,000 students around the world have benefited. An openly Christian organization, Teach Overseas has developed an excellent reputation with national governments and local school administrations.

World Concern
www.worldconcern.org

Inspired and motivated by Jesus who taught us to care for the poor, the forgotten, the despised, and the marginalized, World Concern seeks to relieve human suffering and to bring hope to the people they serve. Its activities include caring for AIDS orphans, rebuilding homes after disasters, fighting child trafficking, providing business loans to poor women, teaching sustainable agriculture, preventing HIV/AIDS, and digging water wells.

World Vision
www.Worldvision.org

World Vision is a Christian humanitarian organization dedicated to working with children, families, and their communities worldwide to reach their full potential by tackling the causes of poverty and injustice. Motivated by faith in Jesus Christ, they serve alongside the poor and oppressed as a demonstration of God's unconditional love for all people. At present, they serve close to 100 million people in nearly 100 countries around the world, reflecting Christ in each community.

Wycliffe Bible Translators
www.wycliffe.org

Wycliffe's vision is to see the Bible accessible to all people in the language they understand best. To accomplish this, Wycliffe also focuses on literacy development, community development, and church partnerships.

With Deep Appreciation . . .

I cannot say enough thank-yous to the wonderful second-half adventurers who opened their hearts and lives to share their stories with me. Without all of you, this book could not have been written.

To everyone involved in the Finishers Project, thank you for the kingdom impact you are making all around the world. My special appreciation goes to Don Parrott, CEO/ President, and Nelson Malwitz, Founder. They saw my vision for this book, and from day one, they were behind me. I extend to them my deepest appreciation for helping it to become a reality.

Thank you to everyone from mission organizations who carved time out of their busy days to talk with me, to collect information, to answer all my questions, and to help me in so many other ways. You were a gift from God!

I also thank Moody editor Betsey Newenhuyse who saw the value of this book from its conception and championed it all the way through to completion.

Thank you, too, to my husband, Dan Kline, my chief encourager, main editor and critic, and my best friend.

THE JOYS OF SUCCESSFUL AGING

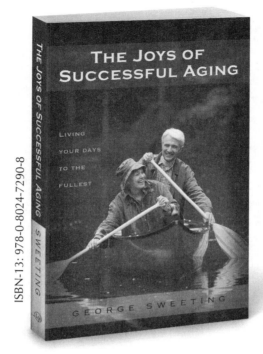

The last years of life can be joyful and fulfilling; though for some, aging is a challenge. Joy and aging are seldom linked together. However, Dr. Sweeting has discovered many unexpected joys in his senior years and shares them in this insightful and easy-to-read book for the Builder Generation.

1-800-678-8812 • MOODYPUBLISHERS.COM

THE MISSIONARY CALL

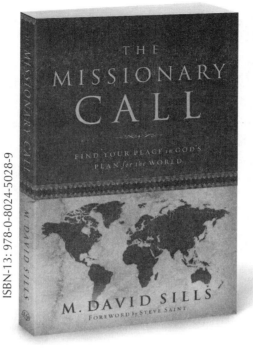

ISBN-13: 978-0-8024-5028-9

Christians of all ages recognize the heartbeat of God to take the gospel to the nations and wrestle with the implications of the Great Commission in their own lives. *The Missionary Call* explores the biblical, historical, and practical aspects of discerning and fulfilling God's call to serve as a missionary. Pointing the reader to Scripture, lessons from missionary heroes, and his own practical and academic experience, Dr. Sills guides the reader to discern the personal applications of the missionary call.

1-800-678-8812 • MOODYPUBLISHERS.COM

THE SHORTEST BOOK EVER ON SAVING FOR RETIREMENT

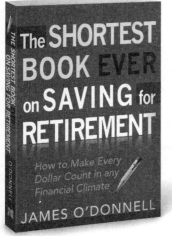

This book gives the facts–just the facts–on saving and investing for retirement in words everyone can understand. Our nation is facing a financial crisis of monumental proportions, and we need to invest carefully.

A former Wall Street pro, James O'Donnell uses simple, concise terms in a readable style to address the most crucial issues that affect your future financial health–whether you know it now or not!

SPLITTING HEIRS

You can't take it with you. But the wealth you leave behind could be the best thing that ever happened to your loved ones–or the worst. By approaching these important topics with clarity, conviction, and a little bit of humor, financial advisor Ron Blue explains why it is important to make these decisions now–instead of forcing your heirs to do it later. Even if your nest egg is small, it can have a huge impact on the next generation. With practical tips, tools, charts, and worksheets this book will foster a real appreciation for the precious resources that God has entrusted to your care.

W9-BSH-738

Praise for the novels of
New York Times and *USA TODAY* **bestselling author**

KAREN HARPER

"A strong plot, a pair of well-written characters
and a genuinely spooky atmosphere add up to
yet another sterling effort from Harper.
Fast-paced and absorbing, this one will keep readers
turning pages far into the night."
—*RT Book Reviews* on *Deep Down*

"The story is rich...and the tension steadily
escalates to a pulse-pounding climax."
—*Publishers Weekly* on *The Hiding Place*

"Strongly plotted and well written, featuring a host of
interesting characters, Harper's latest is a winner."
—*RT Book Reviews* on *Below the Surface*

"Harper keeps tension high as the insane villain
cleverly evades efforts to capture him. And Harper
really shines in the final act, providing readers
with a satisfying and exciting denouement."
—*Publishers Weekly* on *Inferno*

"Harper spins an engaging, nerve-racking yarn,
alternating her emphasis between
several equally interesting plot strands.
More important, her red herrings do the job—
there's just no guessing who the guilty party might be."
—*RT Book Reviews* on *Hurricane*

"Well-researched and rich in detail...
With its tantalizing buildup and well-developed
characters, this offering is certain to
earn Harper high marks."
—*Publishers Weekly* on *Dark Angel*,
winner of the 2005 Mary Higgins Clark Award

KAREN HARPER

FALL
FROM
PRIDE

MIRA®

Recycling programs for this product may not exist in your area.

ISBN-13: 978-0-7783-1340-3

FALL FROM PRIDE

Copyright © 2011 by Karen Harper

Cover photo credits: (barn interior) Erin Mountain Davison/Flickr/Getty Images, (barn) Bill Coleman, Inc. © All Rights Reserved. www.amishphoto.com

For questions and comments about the quality of this book please contact us at Customer_eCare@Harlequin.ca.

www.MIRABooks.com

Printed in U.S.A.

For my family and friends who love those relaxing, lovely trips to Ohio Amish country.

As ever, for Don.

1

"Sarah, you won't believe who just drove in. Passing by, that's what he said. It's Jacob! In a fancy car, too. He's right outside the barn."

At her younger brother's words, Sarah Kauffman's insides lurched. She had once cared for Jacob, but since he'd been shunned, it was *verboten* for him to be here. No way she wanted to see her former come-calling friend, but someone had to get him away from Gabe and his buddy group. Her family had invited the young people for a barn dance tonight.

"If the kids won't tell him to leave, I will," Sarah said as she circled the long plank table laden with food. "He's a bad influence, and you *youngie liet* don't need that in your running-around days!"

She hurried outside and down the sloped approach to the barn, her eyes scanning the clusters of boys huddled by their courting buggies or the two cars someone had driven in, and beyond all that, with its headlights still glowing golden, Jacob's red car stood out like a beacon.

No, she thought, the glow was not where headlights should be, but higher, farther off, behind the car and buggies so that they stood out in stark silhouette.

She moved to the side and squinted across the dark distance. The glow was growing, wavering. It was coming not from something on her family's property but from across the newly planted fields that stretched to those of Bishop Esh.

Ignoring Jacob's calling her name, she pointed, stiff-armed, at the distant blaze of color, but Jacob must have thought she was gesturing for him to leave.

"Hey, just came to say hi to all my ol' friends, 'speci'ly you, an' I'm not leavin' till we talk," he slurred, but she hardly heeded him.

What was that strange light? The moon rising low on the horizon? Someone burning trash? No. No! The Esh barn, where she had begun enlarging the quilt square she'd painted there two months before...the Esh barn was on fire!

"Fire!" she screamed. "Fire, over there—the Esh barn! Does anyone have a phone? Call the fire department!"

Sarah lifted her skirts and ran through the scattered boys, past a smooching couple who jumped to their feet. She almost tripped over some beer cans on the grass. Smooching and drinking—now she knew why their guests hadn't spotted the fire.

She raced past their *grossdaadi haus* where her younger sister, Martha, was tending to their eighty-year-old *grossmamm* tonight, past the family garden and into the field.

Laboring through the rich, damp soil, she sank ankle-deep with each lunging step, once falling to her hands and knees, but this was the fastest way to get there, even compared to a buggy or Jacob's car. *Schnell! Schnell,* hurry, hurry, she urged herself. Human lives, the horses, the stored hay and straw, the old barn itself…and her bold painting of an Amish quilt square. She jumped up from her knees and clambered on, hearing voices behind her of others coming, too.

Out of breath, a stitch in her side, she ran on, to warn the Eshes—Bishop Joseph and his wife, Mattie, almost her second parents because she and their girl Hannah had been so close…. Were they home tonight? Already gone to bed? Their house looked dark, but the glow of kerosene lanterns didn't show sometimes. Didn't they know their livelihood, their future, was on fire? The flames seemed high in the barn, reaching downward as well as up. Maybe the firemen could use her painting ladders to spray water.

It seemed an eternity until she reached their yard, screaming, "Fire! Fire!" She prayed no one would be trapped in the barn, that they could get the work team and buggy horses out if they were in for the night. She knew that barn as well as her own. It was where she, Hannah and Ella had played as children, tended animals, the barn where the bishop had been brave enough after much discussion to let her paint her very first quilt square and then let her enlarge it when he saw how well the others were received.

Exhausted but energized, Sarah stumbled into the Esh backyard, her dress and hands smeared, clods of soil clinging to her shoes. The belching heat slapped her face. What had been a glow in the hayloft was now a red-and-orange monster inside the barn trying to get out, licking at the windows, curling its claws around the eaves. Shouting, she beat her fists on the back door of the dark house, but no one came.

Turning back toward the barn, she saw that Jacob, Gabe and several other boys had followed her across the fields. Using someone's jacket to avoid burning their hands, they lifted the bar on the barn door and pulled it open. That only fed the flames, which made a big whooshing sound and drove everyone back. The beast's breath came hotter, orange fires from hell. She could see its fiery fingers reaching for the pattern of the six-foot-square Robbing Peter to Pay Paul quilt square she'd been enlarging from her wooden ladders and scaffolding earlier today. She'd left them leaning against the barn. Maybe they'd been burned up by now.

Her agony was not only to see the barn burn but her quilt square, too. How proud she had been of her work, the beauty of the striking design. Bishop Esh had chosen that repetitive, traditional pattern because he said it would remind folks that Paul and Peter were equal apostles—a Bible lesson, even on a barn.

Sarah watched in awestruck horror as the flaming beast devoured her neat white and gold circles within the bright blue squares. The paint crackled and blistered. Was it her imagination that the colors ran like blood? Was this a sign that she should not have asked to place it on the bishop's barn—shouldn't have been so worldly in her pride over it? She'd even felt a bit important when the local newspaper had put this painting and her picture—not of her face, of course—on the front page. But for so long she'd felt different from her Amish sisters and friends.... She stopped herself, knowing her line of thinking was a danger and a sin.

"Their plow team's in the south field!" someone yelled. At least that was a blessing. The six big, blond Percherons that pulled the farm equipment were safe.

"The Eshes must not be home!" Sarah shouted, ignoring Jacob, speaking to her brother and the other boys.

"I called the fire department on my cell," Jacob yelled, coming closer. "They'll be here ASAP."

She wasn't sure what "a sap" meant, but she asked him, "So there are no buggy horses inside, either?"

"Naw or we'd hear them, even over the roar, that's sure!" he shouted as he came closer. She hadn't seen him for months and she couldn't see him well now, only his bulky, black silhouette etched by leaping lights. The fire made a deafening roar. Inside, something heavy fell and little golden lines ran madly between the old, weathered boards. Barn swallows from under the eaves circled madly around the increasing clouds of ash-and-cinder-laden smoke.

It seemed an eternity before the fire engine pumper truck screeched in from the closest town of Homestead with six volunteer firemen, three of them Amish. When Sheriff Freeman's car pulled in with the siren sounding, several other firefighters spilled out to help. They pumped what water they had in the truck through two hoses, then, when that was quickly gone, rigged a hose to draw water from the pond. It was too late to save the barn, so they watered down the roof of the house and outbuildings to keep flying debris from burning them, too.

As word spread or they saw the seething sky, other Home Valley Amish arrived in buggies, some *Englische* neighbors in their cars. Even before the Eshes raced up the lane in their buggy, back from visiting Mattie Esh's sister on the other side of the valley, even before the local newspaper editor, Peter Clawson, started taking pictures, the big, old barn with Sarah's bright painting on it had burned into oblivion.

Nathan MacKenzie took the call on his cell phone. His digital clock read 3:24 a.m. Something terrible must have happened, and he hoped it wasn't bad news about his foster mother. His heartbeat kicked up. It was his boss, Mark Lincoln, the state fire marshal of Ohio.

"Nate, I need you to check out a big fire in Amish country, pronto. I want you there shortly after dawn."

"Amish country?" he said, raking his fingers through his short hair. "Northeast but south of Cleveland, right? That's Stan Comstock's district."

"Our northeast supervisor's in Hawaii for his daughter's wedding and won't be back for about ten days. It's a barn fire, Nate. Went to the ground—no one inside but for them a huge loss. Two volunteer firefighters were slightly injured when a beam fell. They should have been outside at that point, and I'm not sure how much correct protocol was followed. I just got calls from both the county sheriff and the local newspaper editor. I'll input what I know to you online including GPS specs for getting there. It's in a rural area called the Home Valley outside Homestead, Ohio, in Eden County. Real pretty rolling-hill country."

"And it was arson?"

"We won't know until you take VERA up there and get a good look. But the thing is, the newspaper guy says the Amish in Pennsylvania had a rash of hate-crime barn arsons a couple of years ago, and we can't take a chance with this. You'll have to handle things with kid gloves, not go in like gangbusters, even with VERA, you hear?"

"Of course," Nate said, fumbling in the dark for his jeans. VERA was one of the two expensive, state-of-the-art technology-laden vehicles that served the state Fire and Explosion Investigation Bureau, usually called the Arson Bureau. And VERA was Nate's idea of the perfect date to investigate arson on the road.

"You know much about the Amish?" Mark asked.

"Good food, handmade furniture, quilts, buggies, black clothing, no electricity, old traditions. How's that?"

"When you get a chance, research their belief system or find someone Amish you can trust there to translate their ways for you. Whatever you turn up, they're going to tell you this was God's will. They'll rebuild and forgive the arsonist—if that's what it was."

After Mark hung up, Nate muttered, "They may forgive, but I won't."

2

Sarah glanced out the window of the Esh farmhouse again. The beast that had devoured the barn left only a pile of blackened bones. The emergency vehicle carrying the two injured firefighters—Levi Miller, Amish, and Mike Getz, *Englische*—to the regional hospital had pulled away. Both had been struck by debris when a flaming beam fell and temporarily trapped them before they were rescued. Word was that, despite broken bones, both were expected to recover just fine.

Jacob had been asked to go, but other than that, no one had left. It was as if the circle of Home Valley neighbors were mourning a mutual, fallen friend. Since the Amish held worship services in their homes or barns every other week, and it was an off Sunday, many had buggied in. Others had arrived, including Ray-Lynn Logan. The owner of the Dutch Farm Table Restaurant in Homestead had parked next to the sheriff's car and was handing out doughnuts and coffee. Ray-Lynn was Sarah's friend and an outspoken admirer of her painting skills.

Sarah was exhausted and filthy, but to please her devastated hosts, she sat at the Eshes' kitchen table to eat. Mattie Esh and her two oldest daughters, Ida and Ruth, both married and living nearby, were turning out scrambled eggs and bacon to be washed down by hot chocolate. Sarah had been thanked repeatedly for spotting the flames and for rushing here to warn the family. But she still felt as if someone had died, not only the old barn, but the painted square that had meant so much to her.

"Still can't figure a cause," Bishop Esh muttered to his wife. "No kerosene lantern out there, no green hay to smolder in the bays or loft, no lightning storm, and at night."

"God's will," Mattie told him, tears in her eyes. "We may not understand His ways but must learn to accept."

"So who's the preacher now?" her husband said, his voice tired but kind. "We'll rebuild, Lord willing."

Sarah offered to help clear the table, but they wouldn't hear of it, so she went outside again. She wanted to head home to wash up and relieve Martha from taking care of their grandmother, but she just couldn't leave yet. If—when—the Eshes rebuilt, would they want another painted square? It had gone a long way that the bishop had let her put one on his barn, even though it was fairly small at first. What was worrying her most was that some of Gabe's friends at the *danze* last night had been smoking around her family's barn. It was a fair distance across the field, so surely none of them had sneaked over here to get more privacy for their doings, then carelessly thrown a butt or match down. The Amish never locked their barns, even if, in these modern times, some had begun to lock their homes.

From the back of her van's tailgate, Ray-Lynn, still handing out coffee in paper cups, motioned Sarah over. The Kauffman women, Sarah's *mamm* and married sister, Lizzie, made the half-moon pies for Ray-Lynn's restaurant, and Sarah delivered them fresh daily in her buggy. Like most everyone else around, she loved to talk to Ray-Lynn. Even in the grief of this morning, she was like a spark of sunlight.

The shapely redhead was about to turn fifty, a widow whose dream had always been to have her own good home-cookin' restaurant in Cleveland—that is, before she'd fallen in love with Amish country. Her husband had suffered a drop-dead heart attack six years ago, just before they were to buy the restaurant, once owned by an Amish family who couldn't keep up with the state's increasingly strict health inspection codes.

But newspaper owner and editor, Peter Clawson, had gone in as Ray-Lynn's partner, and she had made a real go of it, expanding to three rooms and a big menu. The Dutch Farm Table was the most popular place to eat and meet in town for both the local English and Amish, and, of course, tourists. They used to come by the busload, though they'd been in shorter supply lately in the far-reaching American recession.

"Good for you to spot that fire, Sarah," Ray-Lynn said, and gave her a one-armed hug. "Gonna get your name in the paper again."

"It didn't save the barn. Maybe you can tell Mr. Clawson not to overdo it, especially so soon after that article about my barn quilt squares."

"It may be a biweekly paper, but he's putting out a

special edition over this. I'll bet we get folks here to gawk at the burned barn, let alone your other paintings. And if the Cleveland or Columbus papers pick this up, especially if it turns out to be foul play—"

"Foul play? Did you hear that someone set the fire?"

"The sheriff just wants all the bases covered, so he called the state fire marshal's office," she said with a roll of her snappy brown eyes. "But barn burning's not the way we'd like to get buyers and spenders 'round here, is it? Personally, this painting," she went on, pointing at the patch of empty sky where Sarah's quilt square used to be, "was my favorite so far. Hi, ya'll," she called to someone behind Sarah as she gestured them over. "Coffee here, doughnuts all gone."

Though Ray-Lynn had lived in Cleveland with her husband for years, it was no secret she'd been born and bred in the deep South, so she drew her words out a lot more than most moderns did. She even had a sign in the restaurant over the front door that Sarah had painted. It read Southern Hospitality and Amish Cooking—Ya'll Come Back, *Danki.* And she was always trying to talk Sarah into painting a huge mural of Amish life on the side wall.

Secretly, Sarah yearned to paint not static quilt patterns but the beauty of quilts flapping on a clothesline, huge horses pulling plows in spring fields, rows of black buggies at church, one-room schoolhouses with the *kinder* playing red rover or eckball out back, weddings and barn raisings....

But all that was *verboten.* No matter what Ray-Lynn urged, Sarah knew an Amish painter could never be an Amish artist.

* * *

The moment he turned off the highway onto the narrow, two-lane road at the sign Homestead: 4 Miles, Nate MacKenzie felt as if he'd entered a beautiful but alien world. Another road sign bore the silhouette of an Amish buggy, so he cut his speed way down. Farmers plowing or planting in the fields used four-horse hitches and all wore black pants, blue shirts and broad-brimmed straw hats. Here and there, little boys dressed the same way as their elders, and girls in long dresses and white aprons fed goats or played some kind of beanbag game barefoot. Clothes flapped on lines and no electrical or phone wires existed around the neatly kept houses, which all boasted large vegetable gardens. Though the roads were nearly empty, he passed one black buggy and saw many others sitting beside barn doors or in backyards. The fields, even the woodlots in this broad valley, seemed well tended, almost as if he had driven his big vehicle into a painting of the past.

He noted a beautiful painted square, of what he wasn't quite sure, on one old barn. Despite his need to get to his destination—"Two miles on Orchard Road, then turn left onto Fish Creek Road," his sweet-voiced GPS recited—he slowed and craned his neck to look at the painting. The design was amazingly modern, yet he figured it was something old-fashioned. Not a hex sign, for sure. A quilt? Maybe they sold quilts at that old farmhouse.

He turned his eyes back to the road and tried to shake off his exhaustion. He'd felt burned out from too much work lately, but he'd managed about five hours' sleep before Mark called, enough to keep him going. He thrived on adrenaline, one reason he loved this job, though this case could be a bit of a challenge with the unusual culture and all.

At age thirty, Nate MacKenzie was the youngest of the state's twenty-one arson investigators. Though he'd told no one but his foster mother, his goal was to work his way up to become a district supervisor and then chief. He had both law enforcement and fire training. He saw himself as a detective who dealt with the remnants of a crime, the clues hidden in the rubble and ruins. After the tragedy that had happened to his family, his career was his calling, his only real passion.

He passed a one-room schoolhouse with a set of swings and a dirt baseball diamond. Man, it reminded him of something from the old show *Little House on the Prairie*. But surely a group of old-fashioned Amish couldn't be too hard to handle, especially with his experience and the state-of-the-art technology at his fingertips. He would make a quick study of the Plain People by picking VERA's online brain so he'd know how to deal with them and in case he needed their help.

Sarah was about to head home when she saw something big and black coming down the road, then turning into the lane. It looked like a bulky, square, worldly emergency vehicle but it was bigger than that—why, it could almost swallow four buggies in one gulp. She hoped it wasn't some kind of hearse and one of the injured firefighters had suddenly died and was being brought back for burial.

She and the rest of the Plain People stood their ground and stared at it. Even Ray-Lynn quit talking. It had a truck cab and real fancy writing on the side, but, as it pulled in and stopped, the large lettering didn't

really make sense except for the first word: OHIO.
OHIO FEIB SFM VERA it read in big print with some
smaller script under that.

Bishop Esh, her own father, Ben, and Eben Lantz—
the three farmers whose lands adjoined—walked over
to greet the man who emerged from the truck cab. Even
without his big vehicle, he stood out as an *ausländer*.
Bareheaded, he was a good foot taller than the bearded
Amish men, even with their straw hats. He was clean-
shaven like unwed Amish men. His short, almost ebony
hair looked strange amid the blond and brown heads
she was used to. His body seemed all angles and planes,
maybe because he didn't look as well-fed as the Amish
men. He wore belted jeans and a white shirt under a
brown leather jacket, a kind hardly seen in these parts.

She wished she could hear what they were saying.
The men shook hands and walked together toward the
broken, still-smoking pile of beams and rubble. Sarah
sidled a bit closer while some of the boys went over to
peek at the vehicle.

She saw the visitor was not only speaking with the
men but was talking into a little wire that hooked over
one ear and curved around his face and stopped at the
side of his mouth. It was either a small kind of recorder
or a microphone like some workers wore at the McDonald's in Homestead when you gave an order and they
passed it on to the kitchen. The stranger seemed to be
repeating some things the men told him. Bishop Esh
was pointing and gesturing, then he swung around and
scanned the crowd and motioned—to her.

Feeling exposed, maybe because she was bonnetless,
since it was still back in her own barn, wearing only
her prayer *kapp* on her head and suddenly aware of her

soil-and-ash-smeared appearance, Sarah went over to join the men.

"Sarah Kauffman is the one who spotted the flames from her own barn, over yonder," Bishop Esh was saying as he pointed across the fields, and the man turned his head away to look toward their barn. Her father nodded to her. He'd said earlier he was glad she had done the right thing to run across the fields because it took him twice as long to hitch up the buggy and come over to help.

Their visitor spoke something into his curved wire, then turned back to look at Sarah. Their gazes slammed into each other, right between the two men who held the most sway over her life, and yet it was like they weren't there at all.

"I'm Nate MacKenzie, Mrs....Miss..." he floundered.

"Just plain Sarah is okay," she said, crossing her arms over her waist, as neither of them broke their steady gaze. She bit her lower lip. She hadn't meant to make that sound like a joke about the Amish being called the Plain People, but no one seemed to notice.

"I'm from the state fire marshal's office in Columbus, here to determine the cause of the blaze," their visitor told her.

The cause of the blaze. His words rotated through her head. Funny but she was starting to feel warm, as if the seething fire was still sending out flames. She was usually real easy with strangers, enjoyed talking to moderns with their outside experiences, so why should this man be different? Well, maybe it was just that big version of a worldly buggy he drove and his different looks.

Nate—that was probably really Nathan, a good Old Testament name—had strong features, a little cleft in the middle of his chin, which, along with his sharp-slanted cheeks, was peppered with beard stubble, like he'd been up all night and in a hurry, which he probably was. His lips were taut, his nose broad with a little bump, like maybe he broke it once. A thin white scar on his forehead slanted into his left eyebrow, but it was his eyes that entranced her. He had deep blue eyes when she thought dark-haired people mostly had brown ones. What a color that lake-blue would be for a painted quilt square—probably for the pattern of Ocean Waves, because that design, like her other favorites, seemed to shift, to move and beckon....

"The state fire marshal's office received calls from the sheriff and the newspaper editor about this blaze," Nate said directly to her. "I understand you ran across the fields. I'd like to interview everyone who saw the early stages of the fire. Actually, if it's okay, I'd like to have you show me the exact spot at your place where you first saw the blaze so you can describe size, color and positioning to me. A time frame of its spread pattern will really help."

Ordinarily, Sarah would have waited for the bishop or her father to approve, but she said, "I'd be glad to help. I was just going to go back over, and I can meet you there, or you can come calling—I mean, visit us when it suits."

Her father cleared his throat and said, "Sarah had a big loss here, too, Mr. MacKenzie. She's been painting large quilt patterns on barns to help draw visitors to our area, and this was her first one. Enlarging it lately, just yesterday, too."

"Please, call me Nate. I saw one of those on the way in. Very striking. Did you lose paint or paint thinner in the barn last night?"

"Yes, but the cans were all closed up tight," she told him, her voice steady now. "I tap them back in their grooves when I'm done. Besides, I use exterior latex paint, water soluble, not oil base that needs turpentine or something like that. I left my scaffolding and two ladders just outside the barn, leaning against it. That's the bigger loss, moneywise."

Nate, still watching her, nodded. The sunshine shot more directly into his eyes. She saw he had sunglasses in his coat pocket, but he made no move to put them on, maybe trying to blend in with her people just a bit. He no doubt felt like the outsider he was. Though she was Amish born and bred, sometimes even she felt like that, unwed at the lofty age of twenty-four, a painter, not a sewer of quilts like other women.

"Like I said, Mr. MacKenzie," Bishop Esh put in, "no lanterns inside the barn and only seasoned hay, not the green stuff that can catch itself on fire."

"No open accelerants from paint supplies, no spontaneous combustion from methane-emitting hay," Nate said into his mouth wire. "Would it be okay if I take Sarah over to your farm in my vehicle?" he asked her father.

"Sure, and I'll ride along," *Daad* told him. "My son, Gabe, can bring our buggy back over."

Sarah knew better than to feel prideful or important, but her people parted for the three of them like Moses at the Red Sea as they walked toward the big, black truck. "We call her VERA for Vehicle for Emergency

Response and Arson," Nate explained, patting the shiny hood as Sarah might her buggy horse, Sally.

"Arson," Sarah repeated. "Then you do think someone set the barn on fire?"

"Yet to be determined. Arson's the easiest crime to commit but often the hardest to prove. I know this barn—all your barns—are important to your way of life. If we can eliminate accident and act of nature, arson's what's left, and then I'll investigate that."

Nate wasn't sure if the Amish woman and her father were awed or frightened by VERA, but they climbed in the big front seat with him, Sarah between the two men. He was surprised they didn't fumble with their seat belts but clicked them quickly in place. She wore no wedding ring, but then he hadn't seen one piece of jewelry on any of these people.

Amazing that, with her honey-colored hair parted in the middle and pulled straight back under her messed-up small cap and with her old-fashioned dirty apron and dress—a peach-colored one, not black—with not a bit of makeup on her face, Sarah Kauffman was a real looker. She was a natural beauty with auburn, perfectly arched eyebrows over heavily lashed amber eyes that seemed to have little flecks of gold swimming in them. Surprisingly, mixed with the scent of smoke, she smelled faintly of lavender. Her full mouth pouted as she looked wide-eyed at the dashboard computer screen.

"Why, it has a map of our area on it," she said.

"It's called a global positioner, and it talks to me in a nice female voice if I want it to," Nate said as he backed up, careful that none of the crowd, especially the gawking boys, were behind him.

"Oh, now it's changed to a kind of TV screen that shows what's in the rear when you back up," she said. Her voice was mellow without a trace of the accent that the older men seemed to have.

"Sarah, Mr. MacKenzie knows what's in his truck," her father said.

"Oh, right."

"So could you tell me what you were doing when you first saw the fire?" Nate asked as he drove them out of the dirt lane to the road.

"My family was hosting a barn dance for my brother's buddy group," she explained. "Gabe is seventeen and during the mid to late teenage years, our young people are given a time of freedom called *rumspringa,* kind of a running-around time before they decide—or not—to join the church. I went outside to ask someone to leave and looked up above his car and—"

"His car?" Nate said.

"Right. Jacob Yoder's. He shouldn't have been there, and he was drunk, I think, and making noise, and I was going to ask him to leave."

Her father put in, "Jacob Yoder has been shunned for breaking the *ordnung,* Mr. MacKenzie. Lied to the bishop and aided an illegal theft ring of stolen cars, and was unrepentant."

"So he and Bishop Esh have a history—not a good one?" Nate wanted to ask more about shunning and breaking the *ordnung,* but he let it go for now. Mark was right about this being a foreign world, one he was going to have to navigate his way through. Find an interpreter of their ways, their culture, Mark had advised. He supposed he should rely on the bishop whose barn had burned, but sitting next to this interested, inter-

esting young woman, he had a better idea. He needed
a translator all right, because, despite all of VERA's
space-age charms, he felt like a Star Trekker who was
about to go where no man had ever gone before.

When her *daad* said he'd be out later and went into
their house, Sarah was surprised. It was unusual for
her father to leave her alone with an outsider, a man at
least, so *Daad* must trust this man. Instead of taking
time to change clothes, she decided to get his investigation going right away. She led him toward their barn
since he had asked her to show him where she had been
when she first noticed the blaze.

"By the way," she told him, "our barn is almost a
replica of the Esh barn, if you want to see how it looked
before the fire. Except it's usually neat as a pin, and we
all ran out and left it like this last night." She gestured
inside where a table with food sat and bales of straw
surrounded a now-empty circle.

"Yeah, it would help immensely if I could study its
structure," he said, lifting his eyebrows and looking
intrigued by something. He had left his mouth wire in
his truck. She wondered if he wanted to make her feel
more at ease with him, which probably wasn't going to
happen, because he just plain disturbed her somehow.

"Feel free to look around," she said, noting he at
last pulled his gaze away from her to glance high and
low inside their barn. "So," she went on, "I was helping *Mamm*—my mother—serve food behind that long
table there, and I came across this threshing floor—"

"Still used for threshing at harvest time?"

"Sometimes, but we haul modern gasoline threshers
now, pulled behind the horses, of course."

"But animal horsepower pulls them, so they're not actually fueled by gasoline? That means the hay baler Bishop Esh says he lost in the fire would not have had gasoline in it even off-season?"

"Right—modern equipment but real horsepower."

"In your field and the Eshes', I saw them—beautiful horses, big as the Budweiser team. But go ahead. You walked to what spot before you saw the fire. And what did it look like then?"

"I honestly don't know what time it was, if you need to know that—"

"I have the exact moment the call came in, so that will help."

"Anyway, I shouted for someone to call the fire department. Later, Jacob told me he'd called it in on his cell phone."

"Right. I have that info from the sheriff."

"When the buzzers alert the volunteers, it takes a while to get to the firehouse and then here," she said as she led him out of the barn.

"I've got all that and will be checking everyone out."

"Oh, sure, to get their descriptions of the fire, too. So I would say I was right here when I saw the golden glow in the distance, which was growing fast and turning orange. And it seemed to start high, then burn downward."

"Really? That could be a key clue." He was taking notes with just a regular ballpoint pen on paper now, nodding, looking across the fields where she pointed.

"I thought at first the fire might be the headlights of Jacob's fancy car," she added.

"If he was exiled, why—"

"Shunned."

"Okay, shunned. Then why was he here?"

"It really doesn't have anything to do with the fire," she assured him, hesitant to get into all that about Jacob's past, especially how it meshed with hers.

"You need to let me decide that, Sarah," he said, turning to her. "Just in case the cause of the fire is incendiary and criminal, I have the right to investigate anyone who could have caused it, even make an arrest."

"You're a policeman, too?" she blurted. Although her people rendered to Caesar what was Caesar's and got on just fine with Sheriff Freeman, the Amish way was to steer clear of government authorities like the ones who had persecuted—burned to death by the hundreds— her people in Europe centuries ago. Her *grossmamm,* Miriam, was always reading to her from the Plain People's heirloom book, the *Martyrs Mirror*—talk about horrible burnings!

"I'm a law officer under certain conditions," he said. "So what's with this Jacob Yoder I've heard mentioned more than once? He was shunned by Bishop Esh?"

"By all of the church, really. I—it will take some explaining."

"Then we'll do it in a later interview. Go ahead and take me across the field the way you ran last night and tell me how the fire appeared to change as you got closer, how the flames spread."

Happy to have a topic besides Jacob Yoder, she nodded, looking up into his intense gaze again before walking toward the fringe of the plowed field. In his work clothes, *Daad* came out of the house, and she told him where they were going. He nodded and headed for the barn past the *grossdaadi haus* where Sarah stayed at night with her grandmother and where poor Martha had been stuck during all the excitement.

"Wait a sec," Nate said so loudly she jumped. "Your barn doesn't have lightning rods. The Esh barn didn't, either?"

"Lightning rods show dependence on man, not God. If the Lord wants to protect a barn, He will."

"Then, ultimately, if the fire was arson, God's to blame?" Nate challenged, frowning.

"Not to blame," she insisted, but she'd never thought of it that way. She supposed there were other sides to some of the things she'd been taught since birth. "We live in an evil world," she went on, her voice more strident. "The Lord might allow it for a lesson, for our better good, to teach humility or bring our people closer—all positive things, gifts from above. We will work together to rebuild, to raise money for that if we must."

"So I heard. On the other hand, at least you don't have electrical wires coming in that could have caused a spark. I didn't mean to criticize your beliefs, Sarah. I'm just used to lightning rods on barns. Those or smoke alarms or fire extinguishers can save lives and buildings. And maybe God gave the inventors the ideas for those things through inspiration, like positive, useful gifts from above."

She had to admit that, in his own way, he was right. She must remember, she told herself, that this man was here to help them but that he was not one of them. She had to keep her fences up, however much she wanted to work with him to help the Eshes.

So, with Nate MacKenzie at her side, she plunged
into the field following the trail of her frenzied footsteps, back toward the burned barn.

3

Sarah heard the purr of a big motor even before she peeked outside the barn where she was cleaning up the *danze* debris. As if her thoughts had summoned him, Nate MacKenzie had returned in the masculine-looking vehicle that had a woman's name. After Sarah had walked him across the field and back, he'd driven VERA over to the Eshes' again to do some preliminary work, but now, midafternoon, here he was.

"Hi, again," he called to her as he headed for their back porch but then did a U-turn toward her.

He came over, carrying something in a sealed plastic bag, wearing his sunglasses this time. They wrapped around his eyes like dark brown twin mirrors in which she could see herself getting larger as he came closer. At least she'd washed up and changed clothes but, not planning to go out in company, she still didn't wear a proper bonnet over her clean prayer *kapp*.

"I did an initial walk around the ruins," Nate said, stopping at the bottom of the banked entrance to the barn. "Everything's still too hot to sift through and may be for a couple of days."

"Sift through? All the ruins?" she asked. That meant he'd be staying for a while.

"I may not have to, actually, to get proof of arson, though I'll need details for my report that point to how and who. The why may be harder to come by, but I found something key to my investigation. A rubber band around a bunch of about twenty matches," he said, lifting the plastic bag so she could see what was in it. "I found them on the ground about thirty feet from the back of the barn—not in this bag, of course. Bishop Esh says no one smokes in his family, nor does he keep matches around like this to light their kerosene lanterns."

"Oh, no!" she blurted. "But why would kids who might be smoking on the sly put a bunch of matches together with a rubber band?"

"So some of the kids in the neighborhood last night were smoking, kids who were here at your barn dance?"

"During *rumspringa,* it's fairly common. When the fire happened, I thought of it and worried a bit. But those matches are unburned, so you mean they might have dropped that bunch, but threw another pack like that into the barn?"

"Sarah, I'm not jumping to the conclusions you seem to be. It's just that this is part of an old arson trick amateurs use. They get some kind of long trailer—a wick—light the end of it, maybe far away from the object to be burned, and have it ignite some kind of combustibles."

"But you found no wick?"

"No. If one led into the barn, it would have been consumed in the inferno. Besides, you said the fire seemed fiercer high up, so that means someone had a very long wick if they were on the first floor. Of course, kids could have gone up into the loft."

"We can ask them."

"I will."

"Or a long wick means the person could even stay outside the barn to light the fire."

"That's another possibility," he told her with a nod. "A trailer, if it's long enough—sometimes soaked with an accelerant—can give the perpetrator up to fifteen minutes to vacate the property before the fire ignites. So it could have been kids, but before I look around your barn to get an idea of what I'll be searching for in the remnants, let's have that little chat about why Jacob Yoder was hanging around if he'd been shunned."

Deciding not to take notes or record Sarah as she talked, Nate listened carefully as they sat together just inside the barn door on bales of straw. His cell phone even rang once, but he glanced at it—a coworker in Columbus—then put it away without answering.

Sarah explained how she had broken her betrothal to Jacob even before he was shunned for helping hide stolen cars. She said that Sheriff Freeman could have brought aiding and abetting charges that would have sent Jacob to prison for a while, but he didn't because he thought the Amish could make him shape up better by shock treatment—that is, ostracizing him from the church, his family and friends.

"He could have blamed the bishop and wanted revenge against him," Nate said after she stopped talking. He hadn't interrupted. He found her fascinating, the way she managed to keep control while emotions obviously rampaged through her. Her full, lower lip had quivered, but her voice never wavered. Her naive beauty was riveting, and he tried not to let that distract him from what she said. "Or, he could have picked that barn because of your wall painting there," he added, "or because it would hurt the Eshes *and* you. Can you give me more details about shunning?" he asked.

"If he hadn't been a member of the church, he wouldn't have been shunned. But, once you're a member and you break the set of rules—the *ordnung*—that's that. But I don't see how he can be vindictive. Not only did he bring it on himself, but he was not sent to prison when he could have been. Besides, the church will take him back with open arms if he atones and returns to our ways."

"Since he was hanging around at your barn dance, does he think you'd take him back with open arms? Sorry, that's too intrusive."

"It's okay. To tell the truth, though I once cared for Jacob, it was a relief for me when we got unmatched—before he helped those car thieves. I knew he was keeping something from me and he was flying too high and too fast in worldly ways and questionable company. Now, if you want to look around our barn or ask more questions, go right ahead while I finish cleaning up."

He supposed he'd overstepped, pushing her about Jacob, but whatever cages he had to rattle, he would. As polite as she remained, her demeanor had shifted a bit from helpful to huffy. She started toward the long table, but he walked with her. "Can you tell me a little more about your quilt square paintings?" he asked.

"Painting is...dear to me," she began, her voice almost faltering. She stopped and turned to face him.

"I've done decorations on birdhouses and gazebos in my father's wintertime carpentry shop for years, but I thought I could do more than scrollwork and leaves and birds—if it was allowed."

"Allowed by your father and by Bishop Esh, I take it—and the church *ordnung*. As I said, the painting I saw was beautiful."

"Best say it was purposeful. Just like the rest of the people in the country, shaky financial times have hit Amish businesses hard. Busloads of visitors used to come to eat in our restaurants and buy homemade goods like furniture and quilts, but not so many lately. So I thought, and convinced our church leaders, that it would be good to have something new to draw them in—a quilt trail, so to speak, where they could go from barn to barn, maybe buy things, even garden products or eggs if the more expensive items were too deep for their pockets. Besides farming, I guess we've learned to lean on the tourist trade a lot."

"Maybe someone attracted to the decorated barns has a hidden agenda. Has anyone ever said something to you about not liking your paintings?"

"Not visitors. In general, our people don't believe in doing things just for pretty, as we say. Things can't only be pleasing as a decoration. Quilts, scented lavender sachets or candles, furniture—all has to be useful, purposeful for the common good."

"And some of your people thought the quilt squares were just for pretty?"

She sighed. "Despite the bishop's and the church elders' permission, a few of the brothers and sisters, yes. Some think I'm being too different painting squares instead of quilting them. The local newspaper did an

article and made me sound prideful when I try hard not
to be!"

Emotion swelled her voice and flushed her cheeks
with color. He wanted to comfort her. Was he nuts? He
had to stay objective here, but he decided his best bet
was to change the subject because, before she turned
away, she almost looked as if she'd cry.

"I hope you don't mind," he said, "but Bishop Esh
said I can park VERA and live on the woodlot at the
juncture of the three farms while I'm here. He told me
the best approach to it is from the lane that runs off your
driveway and cuts behind this barn."

"Sure, that's fine," she said, heading again toward
the long plank tabletop set on sawhorses. "I can point
it out to you." She started to wipe the oilcloth-covered
table with a vengeance.

"I've got food in VERA and I've been invited to eat
with the Eshes when I'm over there working, but I don't
want to impose on them more than tonight. I'm told the
Dutch Farm Table Restaurant is good."

"The best, if you don't want McDonald's or
Wendy's—a big battle between those two with all kinds
of specials. If you don't mind day-old half-moon pies,
I've got some here you can take with you. My mother
and sister make them for the Dutch Farm Table. Here,
help yourself," she said, opening a cake-size box and
extending it to him.

"One more thing," he said. He took a bite of one of
the crimped-edge, glazed pastry half circles, this one
filled with apple and cinnamon. Delicious. He talked
with his mouth a bit full. "Mmm, this is fabulous," he
said. "I just want you to know that I need to be suspicious of everyone, every possibility. Not just of kids

smoking, not just of Jacob, who may have a double motive, but even of the firefighters themselves. If a closer survey of the evidence in the ruins points to arson by a burn pattern or residue of accelerants, I'll be looking at everyone, even them."

"At the firemen? That doesn't make sense, Amish or English."

"It's the so-called dirty little secret of firefighters. A few of them want to fight fires because fires mesmerize them, make them feel powerful, release pent-up feelings. They revel in being the first one into a fire, the hero, or, if they're injured, even the victim who gets the glory or sympathy."

"So that means you'll even talk to the two who were hurt and not just to see how they describe the blaze? They were the first ones in."

"Exactly." He held the half-eaten, small pie up to his mouth and stared at her again. He was surprised she didn't protest that, if an arsonist burned the barn, he—or she, though a female was unlikely—could be Amish, even one in good standing, especially if they thought both the bishop and the artist had overstepped with "just for pretty" painted quilt squares. He hadn't mentioned that directly, but he couldn't afford to ignore any possibilities.

"The Eshes can prove where they were before the fire, and our people don't believe in insurance, so no one would burn his own barn for that," she said, anticipating his next line of questioning.

"The Eshes have an alibi, but in the modern world, as you call it, sometimes people do burn their own property to get the money for it."

He almost choked on the bite of half-moon pie he

took to cover up the catch in his voice. What he'd just said hit too close to home—his own lost home and family. All he needed was that old nightmare he had buried deep to resurrect itself. But what scared him even more was his gut feeling that it would be so easy for someone to burn another isolated, unprotected barn. He had to act fast to stop that from happening.

"Are they burning our people again?" Sarah's grandmother, Miriam Kauffman, asked her the night after the barn fire.

Her voice shaking, her expression distraught, the old woman stood in the doorway to the bathroom with her toothbrush in hand and her white hair in a long braid, ready for bed. Sarah told Martha, who had stayed last night in the small *grossdaadi haus,* that she'd take over. But Martha had wanted to hear every last detail about the fire and the fire marshal's arson investigator, so she was waiting in the living room. *Grossmamm* and Martha had watched the fire from the kitchen windows, until Martha had convinced her charge to go to bed, but talk of the fire was what had probably set *Grossmamm* off right now. That, and the fact she insisted on reading a few pages from the *Martyrs Mirror* every night before she slept.

"No, *Grossmamm,* it's all right," Sarah assured her. "No one is burning our people."

"*Ya,* the authorities are coming again for us!" she insisted. "They tried to burn the Eshes out, and they'll be here next! Soldiers like that man you were talking to outside today are going to slaughter us again."

"That man is here to help us," Sarah promised, putting her hands on the old woman's shoulders. "We are safe here on the farm, in America."

Sarah had considered taking the *Martyrs Mirror* away from her grandmother more than once. But that precious book had come down through her family, an heirloom. Poor *Grossmamm,* afflicted with Alzheimer's, sometimes thought the Amish were still under siege as they'd been in Europe, hundreds of years ago.

Sarah kept talking, slowly, calmly. "That man was sent by the state government in Columbus to find out about our neighbor's barn, why it burned. No Amish were burned or will be."

"I was afraid you would be lost in the fire."

"Me? No, I'm just fine. All I lost were some paint cans, my scaffolding and two ladders."

"They killed our people on tall scaffolds as a warning so all could see. They tied women to ladders, then tipped them into the fires just because they disagreed with the state religion."

"That's all in the past. No one is going to burn. Even the horses were safe from that fire. Now brush your teeth, and I'm going to read to you from the *Budget,* all kinds of news about our people visiting and how well things are going."

"Except for Amish martyrs being burned," Miriam Kauffman mumbled as she thrust her toothbrush in her mouth and bent over the bathroom basin where she'd left the water running.

Sarah sighed. She knew she resembled her grandmother in her height and coloring, so she sure hoped she wouldn't inherit the mental hauntings that plagued her. She'd been better lately, but seeing that barn fire across the fields had obviously set her off again.

The *Martyrs Mirror,* with its lifelike etchings, was in almost every Amish home, along with the Holy Bible, of course, and the *Ausbund,* which contained the words to the traditional Amish hymns sung in the regular church meetings every other Sunday. As for the *Budget,* that newspaper was the Amish community glue that held the Plain People together wherever they lived. Births, deaths, marriages, horse sales, new addresses or endeavors and chatty tidbits were listed on page after page. Yes, she was going to spirit away the *Martyrs Mirror* and substitute it with the *Budget* right now.

Later, Sarah was glad she did. Not only did the chatty items in the *Budget* calm the old woman, but Sarah noted one about the Eshes that explained why they might have been out last night. Mattie Esh's niece had just given birth to triplets, and they probably went to see them.

As usual, *Grossmamm* fell asleep quickly, and Sarah took the kerosene lantern with her down the hall and into the living area. Most Amish farms had a *grossdaadi haus* for the older generation. When the grandparents who had worked the farm and raised their children were ready to retire, they voluntarily turned over the big house to the eldest married son, or the one who wanted most to keep the farm going, and moved to the smaller place on the property. No rest home, retirement village or shuffling off the older generation among the Amish. They cared for their aging parents or grandparents on-site and included them in as much of life as they cared to be a part of. After their *grossdaadi,* Gideon Kauffman, had died five years ago, his widow had started to slip into another world. Alzheimer's, sure, and she'd had a doctor's care, but they were still going to keep her here and look after her themselves.

Sarah found Martha sound asleep, sprawled on the sofa, breathing heavily. She covered her up with a quilt. That sofa made into a double bed, so where was she going to sleep? They both had their own rooms in the big house, but it was Sarah's turn to stay here tonight. Should she wake Martha and send her away so she could have the hideaway bed?

She sat down in her grandfather's big rocking chair very carefully, because she knew it squeaked. Her eyes were so heavy. She hadn't slept last night...was dead on her feet today, except when Nate MacKenzie was around twice because he seemed to give her energy.

When her lids drooped, she saw fire, saw Nate's intense gaze. She wondered how he was doing living in VERA down by the pond on the woodlot.... And what if the woods, all those trees around the pond, caught fire and the blaze burned him, burned her, too, crackling...popping...

She jolted alert. Her heartbeat pounded. That sound! Gravel against glass, against the window? That was the signal she and her friend Hannah Esh had always used during their *rumspringa* years to get each other up at night when they wanted to sneak out. Not to meet boys like some did, but to go for a night swim in the pond in the summer or just stuff themselves with candy or listen to a transistor radio until dawn while Sarah sketched pictures and Hannah sang along with every Top Ten hit. They knew better than to get their friend Ella from the Lantz farm for such goings-on. No way Ella, as much fun as she could be, would take a risk sneaking out like that.

Again, she heard the sound of gravel against the window. As she stood and looked, the glass was like a big black mirror since they hadn't pulled the curtains closed. Sarah turned down the kerosene lamp and peered out, seeing at first only her own reflection. The *Martyrs Mirror,* she thought...now why had they put the word *mirror* in the title? She'd never thought about that. Were the Amish all martyrs to something or other? Did it mean to look deeply into your own life, to see yourself as you really were or to decide what you were willing to die for?

And then Hannah's face appeared, not the old Amish Hannah but the new one her parents were so riled about. Hannah and her friends in Cleveland had gone goth. Whereas Hannah was a natural blonde with eyebrows and lashes so pale they hardly showed, she now had red, spiky hair and eyeliner dark as sin. Sarah was used to seeing her friend in the soft pastel dresses unwed women wore, not in black, partly ripped and fringed tight pants and wearing silver chains and pins and piercings. Even now, Hannah looked like some kind of worldly Halloween freak. And she was gesturing for Sarah to come outside.

Sarah held up one finger and, her hands shaking, scribbled a note for Martha. "I had to leave for a little bit. Stay with G., please—S."

She grabbed the windbreaker she wished she'd worn last night and tiptoed out. Hannah here! She wasn't shunned so she could come back anytime, but she didn't. After she'd had the argument with her father almost three years ago, she'd left for Cleveland. Their daughter's loss was the cross the bishop and his wife bore, and Sarah's and Ella's loss, too. When Hannah's plan to record and sell her own songs didn't work out, her friends and family prayed she would come home. Instead, her worldly boyfriend got her a job in a recording studio mixing something or other, answering the phone and greeting people at the front desk, looking just like this.

Sarah and Hannah hugged hard. Hannah smelled of an exotic scent Sarah could not name. Something smoky. She'd had incense burning in her little apartment the one time Sarah and Ella had visited her in Cleveland. Or had she been over to her family's burned barn?

"Jacob phoned me," Hannah told Sarah as they stepped awkwardly apart. "I couldn't believe the barn was gone. It's supposed to be in the Cleveland paper tomorrow, but I had to see it first, before all the gawkers in the world come flocking in."

"You didn't have to come at night. Everyone would have been glad to see you."

"Give me a break. About like they'd be glad to have Satan himself drop by. But I knew I could come to you, that you'd go with me. I just can't go see it alone, any more than I could face my father. I parked back down the road by the graveyard and walked here. He—Jacob—said you were the one who spotted the fire and he called it in, but that you weren't back together yet."

"Yet? Never. He crashed our party for Gabe's friends. That's why he was here."

"Jacob also said there's a superhero here to save the day, solve the crime—if it's a crime."

"Word travels fast, because Jacob was asked to leave before the state arson investigator showed up."

"Will you go with me, Sarah? I can't go to Ella. I

don't need her telling me I've got to mend my ways and come back. She never did quite get the 'judge not lest ye be judged' bit, did she?"

"I guess accepting that comes with suffering, and she's been all wrapped up in traveling the road of her perfect Amish life."

Sarah instantly regretted she'd said that with such a sharp tone. But sometimes she resented Ella's sticking to the straight and narrow, when she herself would like to go her own way at times. How she yearned to paint entire landscapes instead of the geometric quilt squares that called for no more creative decision than what color of hardware store paint to use.

"In other words," Hannah said with a bitter laugh, "she still hasn't found out 'it's not all cakes and pies.'"

"I've been thinking lately that it's not all *quilts* and pies."

"You never did like to stitch quilts. And you think I'm a freak? But your painting—that's you. Jacob told me about the quilt square you did on our—my family's—barn."

"A real font of information, isn't he?" Sarah said, surprised again her voice was so sharp. Maybe Hannah's rebellious nature was rubbing off on her. And was Nate right to be suspicious of Jacob? Nate had said that some firefighters loved the attention from a blaze, but did Jacob, too? Nate had also said that some arsonists returned to the scene of their crime, not only to watch the fire, but even later to relive the excitement. Maybe that's why Jacob stopped at the very next farm. Or did he think his phoning in the fire would build bridges back to his people—and her?

The two young women started down the Oakridge

Road that linked their farms. Sarah was glad Hannah didn't insist on a run through the fields, like she'd done last night. They didn't worry that there would be buggies or cars on the rural road now, because traffic was rare even in the daytime, unless a buggy clip-clopped past or tourists pleasure-driving some back byways happened by.

As they sneaked around Hannah's childhood home, not going up the lane but skirting along the fence, Hannah cursed. "Damn! There's a hole in the sky where it should be! Nothing but blackness and stars! It's so—I can't believe it, all of that destroyed to almost nothing!"

Her family's team of horses plodded over to the fence as if to commiserate about the loss of their stalls, feed troughs and harnessing gear, the wagons and equipment they used to pull. Hannah put her hand out to one's muzzle, and he snuffled against her palm as if he were crying.

"At least you guys still know me," Hannah whispered.

"Why don't you write your family a note!" Sarah suggested. "They'd love to hear from you, know that you cared enough to come see it."

"It won't help them to know I was here and saw this," she insisted. Even in the darkness, with only the wan quarter moon rising, Sarah could see her friend's tears track down her cheeks. "The heart of the farm, so many good times here... I'm so sorry, so sorry about what I've done," Hannah cried, and began to sob so hard that some of her mascara ran down her face in dirty lines and smeared against Sarah's cheek as she hugged her again.

"Good evening, ladies." The deep male voice came

from behind them. "Sarah, I thought you were going to stay all night with your grandmother, and what is this person confessing she's sorry she's done?"

4

"What are you doing here in the dark?" Sarah demanded.

The other girl glared at Nate and tugged her arm free. He was so shocked by her appearance that he let her go. He read in her defiant stare that she wouldn't run, but he kept a light hold of Sarah's arm. It was the first time he'd touched her. She radiated warmth from what must have been a walk down the road from her farm.

"I'm going to ask the questions, Sarah," he said more harshly than he'd intended. "I'm Nate MacKenzie, state arson investigator," he told the other young woman, riveting his gaze on her. "I want to know who *you* are and what *you* are doing here in the dark."

Since he'd been in a sleeping bag near the back of the barn, Nate knew they hadn't come across the fields. He'd seen the Eshes turn off their house lamps over an hour ago, so he'd been startled to hear women's voices. Earlier, the bishop had sat outside with him for a while, over milk and cookies, no less. Nate had explained to him that he had obtained a search warrant to examine the ruins of the barn, but the bishop had said he had his permission and didn't need anything from the government to say so.

Bishop Joseph Esh had also reminisced about the barn, which his father had bequeathed him. Amish barns were almost a part of the family, he'd learned, the cornerstone of their way of life, necessary not only for running their fifty-or-so-acre farms but for keeping the generations working and worshipping together.

"This is Hannah Esh, from Cleveland," Sarah said when the stranger continued to glare at him in silence. "She's the Eshes' third-oldest daughter, but she hasn't lived here for three years because she's away building her career."

"It's okay, Sarah," Hannah said. "I can talk for myself. He just surprised me. I thought, at first, it might be my... Never mind. Mr. MacKenzie, a friend phoned to tell me my family's barn burned to the ground, and I wanted to see it without bothering them. I'm a big disappointment to them and am living in so-called worldly exile."

Hannah Esh, Nate noted, had a bitter tinge to her voice and a defiant expression on what could be—with that harsh makeup, he wasn't sure—a pretty face.

"She's not being shunned like Jacob. She left home before joining the church—perfectly permissible," Sarah said.

"Then she's able to be welcomed back with what you called open arms," Nate said.

"I'd appreciate it if you don't tell my parents I was here," Hannah said. "And I certainly don't want to see them tonight."

She stared straight at him when she talked. Like Sarah, a strong woman—or were all Amish women?

"I would think they would be happy to know you cared," he said.

"But only to visit to see a—a dead barn? I don't think so."

"Hannah, I need to know where you were last night, when the barn burned."

"Why?" she countered instantly, and this time her steady gaze did dart away from him, back toward where the barn had been. He heard Sarah suck in a breath, so she no doubt recalled what he'd said about arsonists possibly returning to the scene of the crime. And Sarah's quick mind would get it that Hannah, just as Jacob, had a motive to hurt the Eshes for rejecting her.

"All right," she said, cutting off Sarah, who seemed ready to leap to her friend's defense. Hannah folded her arms over her breasts. "I was in the recording studio, making a demo and mixing my own audio background."

"You're a singer?"

"I am, and trying to be a professional one."

"She has a great voice," Sarah added.

"So you're saying you were alone last night," Nate said, looking only at Hannah. "Who called you to let you know the barn burned?"

"No one you've met. Jacob Yoder."

"But someone I'm going to meet real soon. I need all your contact information, Hannah, including the name and address of the owner of the studio where you work—just in case there are more questions."

"And I'll just bet there will be," she said, her voice slightly shaky now. Ordinarily, he felt he could really read suspects, but with the barrier of her appearance, he couldn't. It was tough enough to try to read the Amish, but an Amish woman who had rebelled? Maybe he could get more out of Sarah about Hannah later. She was becoming his touchstone here—his translator, as his boss had put it.

"I'd like to be able to drive you ladies back to Sarah's but I jogged over from where I left my vehicle in the woodlot behind the Kauffman farm. So I'm going to walk you back."

"Not necessary," Hannah said. "No one's out in Amish country in the dark."

"Someone was out last night," Nate said, handing her a small pad and a pen to write down her contact information. "Someone, I'll bet, who had a big beef against either your father or Sarah, or both."

Sarah loved her job taking *Mamm*'s and Lizzie's half-moon pies to Ray-Lynn at the Dutch Farm Table Restaurant six mornings a week. Honoring the Amish tradition of no Sunday sales, the place had been closed yesterday. Sarah had to get up before dawn, but she didn't mind. *Grossmamm* was always still asleep and either Martha, if she wasn't in school, or *Mamm* if she was, came over to stay.

Some amazing sunrises greeted Sarah as she went out to the barn to hitch Sally to her buggy, but, she had to admit, never one as stunning as the orange, fuchsia and apricot blaze in the sky today. Cirrus clouds and feathery floaters made the heavens look like a kaleidoscope quilt—one with Nate MacKenzie standing near the barn, silhouetted by it all. *Ya,* if he'd only been wearing an Amish jacket and straw hat, what a painting that would make. As good as his word, he'd walked her to the *grossdaadi haus* last night and Hannah to her car down the road at the Amish cemetery. He seemed to turn up everywhere.

Somehow she managed to find her voice. "So you're an early riser as well as a night owl," she said as she carried her big flat basket with four boxes of half-moon pies into the barn. *Daad* and Gabe were already out in the fields with some of the work team, and the barn door stood open.

"I do what I must to solve a crime."

"You're sure it is?"

"I'll start going through the debris today, and then— if it is—I'll be interviewing others. Hannah just more or less knocked on my door before I was ready for her."

"She's had a hard time."

"So have her parents."

"Did they mention her to you?"

"Not a word, not even when I had a heart-to-heart talk with her father."

She nodded, put the basket down on a hay bale and pulled her buggy out of the back corner from among the lineup of the big carriage, sleigh and smaller carts. She saw *Daad* and Gabe had already taken the work wagon out. Trying to stay calm near Nate when she didn't know what was coming next, she went out to fetch her buggy horse, Sally, in the side field. Although the horses were often out in this mild weather where they could graze, she still took the mare's feed bag with her so Sally would get her grain and vitamins. She saw three of the family's work team of big Percherons were still grazing in the field. She whistled and her smart former harness racer came right over to the gate.

Again, she was grateful that the Eshes' horses had

not been in the barn when it caught fire. Could the arsonist, if there was one like Nate evidently thought, be Amish and know how important the horses were? No, not if he'd burn a precious barn.

She fastened Sally's feed bag on, brought her through the gate, past Nate, and backed her up to the double-seat buggy. Most Amish women, unless they were unwed, didn't have their own vehicle. Despite the fact it marked her as an unwed *maidal,* she loved her freedom and kept the horse well-tended and the black fiberglass buggy clean and shined. Although Nate was usually full of talk and questions, he came closer and leaned against a stall rail just watching.

"I have to have these half-moon pies at the Dutch Farm Table before they open at seven," she explained. "It's a real challenge in the winter, but I like the time alone to observe everything just waking up, any season of the year."

"I guess the speed of a buggy gives you time for that. I keep learning about things I thought I had answers to."

She wasn't sure if he meant about his investigation or the way they lived here, but she just nodded as she put the crupper under Sally's tail and the breast strap between her forelegs, then took the feed bag off so she could get the bridle on.

"When your father and brother opened up the barn this morning," Nate said, "I really looked around in here to get an idea of the preburn layout of the Esh barn. Then I searched German bank barns on VERA's laptop."

"Searched?"

"Oh, yeah, sorry. On my computer. I studied up—a

crash course on barns with three levels like yours and the Eshes'. I couldn't believe how your barn exteriors are misleading. I mean, there's so much more space inside than what I expected. It's like, don't judge a book by its cover, I guess, like with people, too. Sarah, I don't want you to get the idea I'm prejudging people, Hannah or Jacob or anyone else."

Over Sally's back, their gazes locked and held again, the way they too often did. She always felt a funny fluttering in her lower belly she'd never had with Jacob. This man made her blush, too, but at least her complexion usually hid that.

"I had to ask your friend those questions last night, get her info," he added in a rush.

"You're really barking up the wrong tree with her."

"You said that about Jacob, too."

"She loves her parents, but they wanted her back in the nest under their roof and rules, and it led to harsh words. She was crushed to see the barn was gone."

"Sarah, she's still bitter about all that. She's chosen to be about as far from Amish as she can get, despite the fact she's still dressed in black."

"She would never burn the barn!" she exploded at him, then put her hand up over her mouth as if she'd cursed. This man brought out all kinds of emotions in her she'd never known were there, or at least ones she'd never let out before. Why couldn't she just be like other Amish women, content with her lot in life? Why did she have to yearn for the forbidden—to paint pictures, that is?

"Okay, thanks for that testimony about Hannah," Nate said, his voice clipped. "You're starting to sound like an expert witness, but I guess I asked for that. See you later. I've got a long day over at the site of the burn."

As he strode away, she was upset she'd lost her temper. Patience and humility, not anger and pride, were what she needed. She went back to harnessing Sally but turned her head to watch Nate walk away. The man was too lanky, and she'd like to feed him up good. His head was down while he punched something into a little cell-phone type thing with both thumbs. He headed toward the back lane where he had VERA parked. She might have just kept staring, except Sally snorted and stamped her foot.

Just as she was heading out of the end of the lane onto the road, Sarah heard the purr of the big engine behind her. Nate in VERA, of course. Was this driven man, who needed some speed bumps in his life, as edgy as she? Was he annoyed to be slowed down by the buggy, impatient with their ways? May the Lord forgive her, but sometimes, Sarah had to admit, she was impatient with her people's ways. But right now she hoped Sally didn't leave any horse apples for his fancy vehicle to drive through. At least he knew better than to honk like some moderns.

As Sarah headed toward town under real horsepower, she craned her neck to watch VERA as Nate went the other way, toward the Esh farm.

Because a TV reporter with her cameraman and several tourists had been standing out in front, Ray-Lynn Logan had opened the Dutch Farm Table a half hour early. She was already there with a couple of her Amish waitresses, anyway, and her profits had been down lately. So she was glad to see Sarah Kauffman coming in the back door with the day's supply of half-moon pies, which sold much better than doughnuts. Full-size schnitz and shoofly pies and other Amish desserts like date-nut and carrot cake came in from area bakers.

"Not late, am I?" Sarah asked. She was out of breath and looked as rosy-cheeked as she did in bitter winter.

"Not our heroine of the day," Ray-Lynn told her, taking the basket from her hands and handing it to Leah Schwartz, who took it through the swinging doors into the kitchen. "You should see the special edition Peter put out. Got a real nice ad for the restaurant in it, too, but then he'd better, since he owns part of it. There's a copy on the counter. Oh, by the way, he'd like a more in-depth interview with you, and I'll bet the outside media coming in would, too. Two of those critters just left."

"No. It's a blessing I just happened to spot the fire first and I don't want to sound prideful. Someone else made the call."

"And he's got a lot to say—Jacob, that is," Ray-Lynn said, tapping her index finger on the middle paragraphs of the article under the large photo of the flaming barn behind the dark silhouettes of firefighters. "He kind of makes it sound like you were working together to call the fire in."

"Oh, rats," Sarah said, and leaned over the paper on the counter. "I did not tell him directly to make the call, but I figured he'd have a phone on him, even if half the other *rumspringa* kids did, too. I have refused more than once to see him, and we are not in cahoots of any kind."

In cahoots, that's a good one, Ray-Lynn thought,

pouring Sarah a cup of coffee, then reaching in her quilted apron pocket for money to take back to her mother and sister. The Amish had a fresh way of saying some things. Sarah Kauffman might not want to be in cahoots with Jacob Yoder, but she'd sure like to get Sarah to be in cahoots with her about doing some paintings Ray-Lynn could sell for her. The girl was extremely talented, and Ray-Lynn was willing to risk a lot to bring her Amish art to the world.

"I see there's a big interview here with Fireman Getz," Sarah said, obviously trying to shift the subject. "It says he has a broken arm but he doesn't regret going in first to try to put out the flames."

"More fool he, and that Levi Miller, too. Levi's cousin to my waitress Anna, you know, and she says both men got released from the regional hospital. Well, I bet I know why Mike Getz played the hero. He and his gal, Cindee what's-her-name—"

"Cindee Kramer. She works in the hardware store where I buy my paint."

"Right. Anyhow, they're not married but been living together—"

"I know. That takes extra nerve around here."

"They got into a real tiff in the restaurant last week, something about she didn't look up to him anymore, but I'll bet she does now. She had a real conniption at table eight in the back room. I was afraid he was going to start throwing things, but I'll bet he could run for mayor after those heroics," she said, pointing to the picture of him, smiling, no doubt, prefire, all decked out in his fireman gear. "What? You're frowning again."

"Nothing. I will just give the devil his due."

Ray-Lynn wasn't sure what that meant, coming from

an Amish girl, but she saw outside what she'd been looking for and muttered to herself, "Speak of the devil…"

The sheriff's shiny black cruiser with that bold light
bar had pulled up to parallel park in front. The restaurant door opened, and Sheriff Jack Freeman came in,
hanging his hat on a wooden peg, his sharp gaze scanning the room as if he'd find a robbery or kidnapping
in progress in this little burg.

"Morning, Ray-Lynn, Sarah," he said matter-of-
factly. He passed them with a nod and his version of
an official smile, then sat in his usual spot at the curve
of the counter facing the door with his back to the wall
so he could keep a good eye on things. Ray-Lynn used
to scurry to pour him coffee and take his order—even
when she knew what he'd order already—but she'd decided on another tactic now. No falling at his feet, just
take it easy, a bit hard to get.

While Sarah scowled over the newspaper, Ray-Lynn
sauntered down behind the counter and nonchalantly
poured Jack his coffee during their usual chitchat about
the weather. She was up for that much of their old routine, at least. She knew darn well he'd want sausage
gravy on buttermilk biscuits and two eggs over easy,
but she asked, "What will it be today, Sheriff? I'm sure
you've got a busy day ahead with the extra folks in
town, so I'll send someone right over to get your order."

She left him staring wide-eyed at her while she went
over to fill other people's cups at the tables.

Jack Freeman was a few years older than Ray-Lynn
but he was holding up better than most men his age.
No paunch, very few gray hairs, just enough to make
his auburn hair looked frosted at the temples. Unlike
the bearded Amish men, he was clean-cut, something

he'd never changed from his former marine days. He always looked slightly tanned, which set off his clear, brown eyes and white teeth. His black uniform was military clean and crisp-looking, pretty surprising since he'd been divorced for years and Homestead's one dry cleaner had gone out of business. It annoyed Ray-Lynn that she got kind of shivery around him. The man exuded authority and control, both of which she was itching to dismantle, at least in private, with her Southern gal feminine wiles. But he seemed to put up a big wall when she came on soft and sweet, so her new strategy was worth a try.

She ignored him but made a big fuss over seating four tourists from Columbus, chatting away to them, while Anna Miller took the sheriff's order. Good—she could tell he didn't like the lack of personal attention. It was another risk, but she'd decided some things were worth it.

She walked back to Sarah while Jack took out his own copy of the special edition of the *Home Valley News*. It was only about eight pages this time—a lot of ads, about half of them for businesses Peter had his finger in, even the Buggy Wheel Shop, which had only Amish customers who would go there to buy new buggies whether there was an ad or not.

"The rest of that fire article's not so bad, is it?" Ray-Lynn asked Sarah. "As I've told you a hundred times before, you're a fabulous artist and should be aiming higher than just quilt squares on barns. I know you're yearning to do more than copy patterns even if you do choose the colors."

"I wish he hadn't put my age in here," Sarah whispered, looking as if he'd written that she was a serial killer. "It sounds weird that a twenty-four-year-old woman still has her maiden name. 'Sarah Kauffman, age twenty-four, from the Kauffman farm next door.' Why do papers think they have to tell stuff like that, and who told him my age?"

"Listen to your friend Ray-Lynn, my girl. At twenty-four, you are still what the big, bad world would consider a young chick, believe me. Now, I know Amish women your age are usually wed by now, but it'll happen. Besides, not to sound like a broken record, but you've got other talents, and I'm real sorry to see that first pretty quilt square you did got burned up with the barn. You've got to branch out, so my offer is still open for you to paint an Amish scene on that long wall right there instead of that old-fashioned wallpaper. I'll never forget those beautiful drawings you showed me from your sketchbook."

"Thanks, Ray-Lynn. I haven't shown anyone but Hannah, Ella and you those drawings, so I guess we're keeping each other's secrets, right?"

"And secrets they will remain for now," Ray-Lynn said. The thing was, Sarah had eyes like a hawk. Maybe all artists did. Though Ray-Lynn had tried to hide it, her Amish friend had picked up on the fact that she was smitten with Jack Freeman. "You just keep that offer about the mural in mind now," she urged Sarah. "I'd pay you well for your time if we can just get permission from your powers-that-be around here."

"Can I take this copy of the paper to show the arson investigator?"

"Why, sure. But if you don't want to be interviewed, better steer clear of the Esh place. I think a camera crew and a few others went out there to talk to him—oops, more customers to be seated."

"I'm supposed to take some things to the Eshes, a chicken dinner when *Mamm* and Lizzie get it ready."

Though Ray-Lynn knew the Amish rarely showed affection in public, she gave Sarah's shoulders a quick squeeze. As she passed Jack, heading to seat more folks who'd come in the front door, she said, "I'll have Anna refresh that coffee while you're waiting for whatever you ordered, Sheriff."

5

It was arson. By noon, Nate knew for sure. He'd been interrupted more than once by curious Amish or others. Bishop Esh had said he trusted Nate's judgment so, with two of his sons, he was planting a cornfield to the south.

Nate had stonewalled the Cleveland reporter and her cameraman, though they still hung around by their van which read News Live at Five. He'd phoned the state fire marshal from the privacy of VERA. It was going to be an interesting case file. He hoped he wouldn't be recalled until the area supervisor returned from his daughter's wedding in Hawaii. He'd told Mark he had some leads already, though he hadn't told him he was convinced that there'd be another arson. He had nothing to back that up but his instincts, and Mark was a just-the-facts guy.

As he left VERA, Nate saw Sarah driving her buggy into the lane. His insides flip-flopped—probably, he told himself, because the reporter had asked him if he knew where Sarah was and he'd said no. He hadn't exactly lied. She could have been anywhere on the three

miles of road between here and the restaurant in Homestead.

"How's it going?" she asked as she reined in.

"Arson for sure," he told her. "I'm going to point
out the evidence to the bishop when he comes back for
lunch."

"We call it dinner," she said, "and I've got it right
here all packed up in my buggy. A lot more food than
you moderns are used to, I bet, but we've all been up
early working hard—you, too."

"If I ate like your people, I'd gain more than evidence
about an arson around here."

"You could afford to gain some weight," she said,
then blushed. "I mean, someone who jogs and walks
all over like you do, even though you drive your truck,
too."

"VERA's a gas hog, but I still call her my home
away from home. But I'm now as much of an expert on
banked, three-story barns as I am on VERA."

Twice he'd spent late hours online and learned that
banked barns were also called German barns—no surprise there. What was banked was the slanted, hard-
packed earth leading up to the broad double doors. The
only other entry was in the stone-constructed lower
level. Originally, that was where the barn animals had
stalls, though he'd observed that the local Amish kept
their horses in stalls and their buggies stored on the
second level called the threshing floor. A haymow or
loft was on the third level under a peaked roof with a
cupola on top to aerate the barn. Windows were small
and minimal but threw enough light inside, especially
if the double doors were open.

The most important thing he'd learned was that the

window or windows were all on the third level. So the arsonist had to have been up in the loft or on a ladder to get lit trailers to go through a window. Sarah's wooden ladders and scaffolding had been burned from outside the barn—but had they been used by the arsonist first?

"So how is VERA as a home?" she was asking.

"Cozy, maybe too cozy. I'll show you around, and then you'll see what I mean."

He didn't say so but he found the confines of the VERA's high-tech combination of lab/office/storage/ bathroom/bedroom a little claustrophobic, especially out here in the wide-open Home Valley surrounded by rolling hills. If the weather stayed mild and dry, he planned to keep sleeping out under the stars. It brought back the best memory he had of his dad when they used to camp out in Southern Ohio down by Old Man's Cave, before his whole childhood went up in flames.

"By the way," he said when their mutual staring in silence stretched out a bit too long, "you'd better stay in the house if you don't want to be interviewed. As you can see by their vehicle, the TV folks are still here." His BlackBerry tone sounded, and he looked down to see if it was his boss again. "I've got to take this," he told her. "It's my foster mother, and I always take her calls."

"Foster mother?"

"I'll explain sometime."

"I'll head straight in with the food and come out with the Eshes when you announce the arson," she said with a snap of her reins. "Unless someone tells the TV people who I am, they won't notice me separate from the others at all."

But even as he took the call, he couldn't help thinking

that Sarah somehow stood out. Even among the Plain People, she didn't seem plain at all.

Everyone ate before hearing Nate's verdict, maybe, Sarah thought, to fortify themselves for what was to come. Then, too, though no one said so, it was possible the bishop was hoping the media outside would leave them alone to hear about the autopsy of the barn fire in private. That's what it felt like, Bishop Esh had said, an autopsy of his dead barn, with the burial and then, hopefully, the resurrection yet to come.

At the Esh table the number of guests swelled, but then *Mamm* and Lizzie had sent over enough fried chicken, biscuits, gravy, applesauce, chowchow, dandelion salad, schnitz pie and rhubarb crunch to feed an entire work crew. Churchwomen were taking turns sending a noon meal to the bishop's family for a while. The Eshes had insisted that Sarah, Nate and Mike Getz, who showed up and had just done an interview with the Cleveland TV station, join them. Also, two church elders, Reuben Schrock and Eli Hostetler, who both had Sarah's squares painted on their barns, dropped by in time for dessert and coffee.

Sarah saw that Nate ate like a field hand, after they'd just had that talk about his gaining weight. And she also noted that Nate watched Mike Getz like a hawk.

"I know now it was a bad move," Mike, a big guy with a shaved head and goatee, admitted. "I shouldn't have rushed inside to try to pull some of the buggies out, but the barn looked like a goner and I wanted to save something."

He ate with his left hand since his right was in a cast. Sarah could see the clean, white plaster had writing on it already, including in pink ink, "Love Ya! Cindee" and a large heart. Mike's head seemed to sit directly on his broad, slanted shoulders—a man with no neck, and not, she thought, a lot of sense.

"But a broken bone's a small price to pay," he went on, his mouth partly full, "to help a neighbor."

Strictly speaking, Mike wasn't a neighbor of the Eshes but lived much closer to Elder Reuben Schrock and his family, over on Fish Creek Road.

"Have you rushed into other buildings on fire?" Nate asked. The entire Esh family, along with Sarah and Nate, had eaten first and it was mostly men at the table now, with Sarah and Esh daughter Naomi clearing dishes and serving more pie and coffee. Naomi was betrothed, and Sarah knew how badly she missed having her older sister Hannah here to help plan for the big event next autumn. Well, Sarah thought, maybe she and Ella could somehow convince Hannah to attend that day—if Sarah could talk Ella into building bridges with Hannah.

"I've always done what I could," Mike Getz was telling Nate. "I've been working with the volunteer department since I was twenty—for six years. Man, I think your job must be really fascinating, Mr. MacKenzie."

"It is," Nate said, "and I'd be happy to talk to you about it. I always like to meet dedicated firefighters."

Mike Getz just beamed. As she stood in the doorway to the kitchen, Sarah wondered if Mike had just gone to number one on Nate's list of suspects.

"We have something to announce," Reuben Schrock said, and cleared his throat. "Bishop Esh, we would like to hold a barn raising soon as possible with an auction of goods even sooner to raise some cash for the project and to build up the alms fund for the rebuilding and other needs."

"We are grateful," Bishop Esh said, his voice quiet, his face serious. Sarah could hear his wife, Mattie, standing beside her, sniff back a sob.

The other elder, Eli Hostetler, spoke. "Date for the raising to be determined, when we can clear the space and order the wood and all. But we'll be announcing the auction for next weekend at the schoolhouse, lest it rains."

Sarah knew her family and others would donate quilts and that outsiders would snap them up. For once, she almost wished she liked quilting bees, but she never had, standing out like a black sheep among the other skilled-at-stitching Amish sisters. At least some of *Daad*'s birdhouses would be for sale, a few things she had decorated. She wished she could contribute some painted quilt squares on wooden wall plaques, but her father had said he didn't think it was a good idea for her to be branching out too much.

When everyone rose from the table—still not hurried—and Nate passed Sarah, he whispered, "So is that alms fund like Amish insurance? Will you explain later?" He kept moving, not waiting for an answer.

They all gathered outside where Nate, standing knee-deep in the black bones of the barn, took over. The TV reporter, a blonde woman, scribbled notes while her cameraman held out a microphone on a long pole. The bishop had asked them not to film, and they'd agreed. It wasn't so much, Bishop Esh had explained to the reporter, that the Amish saw still or moving pictures as making graven images, which the Bible warned about, but that having one's picture taken or being featured in a magazine or newspaper story could make one prideful—that is, feel better than or separate from the community.

Sarah thought again of her interview with Peter Clawson, who had just come roaring in in his truck. *Had* she been prideful to speak to him and to be so pleased with the printed color pictures of her quilt squares adorning Amish barns? Community oneness was everything to her people, their essence, their very survival. So why couldn't she squash her desire to paint entire pictures of the Amish? Defiant independence to chase a personal dream fueled by a God-given talent had ruined Hannah's life so far.

Word really must have spread that the arson investigator was going to give his verdict. Most of the Lantz family from the third adjoining farm buggied in, including Sarah's friend Ella, her parents and four of her siblings. Sarah noted that Barbara, nearly sixteen, went over to stand by Gabe, but he shook his head at something she said and shifted a few steps away. Ella came over to stand by Sarah, linking arms with her as Nate's voice rang out in the hush. It was disturbed only by the spring breeze turning the windmill, birdsong and the occasional snorting of the buggy horses tied to the fence rails near where Hannah and Sarah had stood together just last night. She should be here, Sarah thought, and whispered that to Ella.

"*Ya,* Hannah should be home with her family and you and me, just like in the old days," Ella whispered as Nate's deep voice rang out.

"Arson is often proved by investigators finding a path of foreign accelerants that ignited, then spread, the flames. Accelerants can include grease, kerosene, gaso-

line and paint thinner, but I've been able to eliminate
the accidental spillage of those or even the presence of
those. Besides finding a bunch of matches—unlit—outside of the barn, I found evidence of accelerants within,
so let me explain and point that out."

His cell phone tone sounded. Sarah noted he ignored
it.

"The front door frame," he said, pointing to a big,
tumbled beam with a blackened metal handle on it,
"shows what we call alligatoring—shiny blisters." Several people leaned closer. The Cleveland reporter and
Peter Clawson scratched away on their notepads.

"This indicates a rapid rise in temperature of the
blaze, so nothing really smoldered. Evidence here," he
said, continually moving through the debris and pointing things out, "indicates it spread unusually fast, which
eyewitnesses corroborated. These beams were from the
roof—third or loft floor. Also, the fire seems to have
started in more than one place, one at the back of the
barn near a window, another near the east side window.
Multiple V-pattern burns are also major clues pointing
to arson.

"But how did someone reach those high windows
to get the fire going in the loft where hay was stored?
I'm surmising that the arsonist used one or both of the
ladders that were on the ground outside the barn, which
were then destroyed in the fire. In that respect, the arsonist either knew the ladders were available or stumbled into being able to use them. It meant he or she
could stay outside the barn rather than going in and
climbing the built-in ladders within to start the fire."

The arsonist had used her ladders! Why hadn't he
told her that—warned her he'd say that? At least no one

but Mattie Esh so much as glanced her way, but it made her sick that her equipment might have been a part of this—and that Nate had not confided that to her earlier when he told her it was arson.

"What might this accelerant be?" he went on. "I'm still running some tests in my mobile lab, but kerosene residue can be recovered from beneath floorboards, which it permeates. It can be found under the ash-and-water pastelike substance a hot, fast fire leaves behind. That was probably the case here, especially on the third floor or loft level, which was the ceiling of the threshing floor level. Bishop Esh reports that no kerosene was in the barn, not even an old lantern, and no gasoline in the farm equipment. No green hay to give off methane to cause spontaneous combustion, the latex, water-soluble paint cans were sealed." A few heads turned Sarah's way. "So my report, sad to say, in such a helpful, concerned community is criminal arson by a fairly primitive incendiary device lit from at least two points through small window access on the loft level."

"Any way to catch the firebug with what you got?" Mike Getz spoke up.

"Arsonists have a way of being caught in a trap of their own making," Nate said, staring at the big man. "The Esh fire is a crime and will be severely prosecuted by the state fire marshal's department in the state courts of Ohio. The penalty for such is long prison time. So spread the word that arson is never, never worth the risk."

Sarah noted that the portly, ruddy-faced Peter Clawson kept nodding fiercely, as he stood a few people in front of her. Sarah pulled Ella off to the side before he could turn around and ask her more questions. But she heard him tell the Cleveland reporter, "You can't say the guy isn't eminently quotable. You got some great sound bites, and I got another great article for the *Home Valley News,* and you can quote me on that."

The next day an Amish work crew of young men—overseen by Nate—removed the remnants of the barn. They hefted the ruined debris out of the stone basement level where a lot had fallen and hauled it away in their work wagons with Nate keeping an eye on every piece for more clues. Then the Amish scraped and raked the place flat, down to the stone foundation on which the new barn would be erected.

It was hot and sweaty work, even just mostly doing the overseeing. Nate needed a swim in the pond near the woodlot—who needed a shower when the old swimming hole was there?—and some coffee to keep going. The test on the composition of the residue from under the old barn boards had proved to be kerosene, but that was in full supply around here and didn't necessarily point to an Amish arsonist.

He drove VERA back past the Kauffman place, wishing he'd see Sarah, but no one was out for once—just laundry flapping on the line, blacks and pastels, men's and women's, big and small, the daily life of an Amish family, all hung tight together.

He parked VERA and stripped to his underwear and waded into the pond. When he saw the water was deep enough, he dived. It felt fantastic, cool, refreshing. Like a kid he swam on his back, splashing. He should have brought some soap out. He floated, then treaded water in the center of the pond, listening to the sounds of the wind through the maples and oaks, birdsong. He stared up at the blue sky with cotton clouds for he didn't know how long.

Suddenly a voice called out, "You shouldn't swim alone, you know. It could be dangerous."

as at the bottom, he will expect Jessica to have been here first.

Jessica's mother asked one. You should tell them what you know, he told he employees.

6

"Dangerous how?" Nate asked. He spun around to see Sarah with a large package in her arms.

"This just came for you at the house—FedEx," she called to him. "Now that you've announced it was arson and you're going to find the arsonist and send him to jail, what if he tries to hurt you?"

Nate swam toward her side of the pond, his muscular arms lifting from the surface at each stroke. When he was close enough to talk easily he stopped and treaded water. "You startled me, though I was expecting that package. It's my fire protection hood. It wasn't packed in VERA when I left. And thanks for worrying about my safety, but arsonists are usually cowards about confrontation. The arsonist wants my attention, not to get rid of me, but I'll be on my guard."

You won't if you're splashing around like a kid and not paying attention to who's approaching, she thought, but she just nodded. As he remained fairly motionless about twenty feet away, she could see a lot of skin through the water. What if he was in there buck naked, because why would he have brought an *ausländer* swimsuit?

"So you fight fires, too?" she asked, hugging the package to her breasts. She'd come out here barefoot, a common practice among her people in the warm weather, especially on their own property. She fought the desire to sit down and dangle her feet in the pond. Though she'd done that a hundred times and her family shared ownership of this woodlot with the Eshes and the Lantzes, it suddenly felt like forbidden, foreign territory.

"I don't fight fires if I can help it, but I don't hesitate to go into a partially burned building or even one on fire if it will help me trap an arsonist. If you wouldn't mind turning around for a minute, I'm not exactly clothed in here, and I'll get out."

"Oh, sure. Right," she said, and sat down facing away with her back to the pond. Beneath the shade of her bonnet, her cheeks flamed. She stretched out her legs. Her toes barely peeked from under her moss-green skirt. "I'll bet it feels good in there," she said, hoping he didn't think she was fishing for an invitation to join him. His voice had faded a bit, and she heard the water rippling as he evidently swam away.

"Sure does. I've got a washbasin and head—sorry, toilet—in VERA but no shower."

"I'll bet *Daad* will let you use ours if you want. I was going to send Gabe out with this package, but he took his buggy over to see his friend, Barbara Lantz, two farms over."

"I take it your family's close to them, but no quilt square on their barn yet?"

"It was decided first the bishop, then two elders,

then the Millers wanted one. I've done those, but since then, no one else has come forward to ask for another. But your mentioning the Lantzes reminds me there's a second reason to be careful in this pond. There's a strange, cold current in it sometimes," she said, still talking toward the trees. "I think there's an underground spring that flows through it, especially after a rain. When we were teenagers and swimming here, Ella did a little jackknife dive and just kind of stayed under. Hannah and I about went off our beans—panicked, you know. We dived and found her and pulled her up but we could feel the colder current pulling us deep down, very scary. We had to almost pump the water out of her. She—well, she changed after that, got very rigid and strict with herself and others, always followed every rule."

"So Ella Lantz owes you two her life," he said, his voice coming closer until he stood in front of her. He'd pulled his jeans on over his wet legs and his black T-shirt stuck to the muscles of his chest and his flat belly. His short black hair looked even darker all wet. For a second she couldn't recall what he'd just asked.

"Oh, we don't think of it that way," she told him. "It was the Lord who saved her, and we were just His way of doing it. No thanks needed, and we didn't even let outsiders know, though someone blabbed, and it got into the *Home Valley News*."

Nate reached down to her, and she gave him his package before she realized that he had meant to give her a hand up. His skin was cool from the water, or else hers was hot. Both barefoot, they walked back around the pond where he had VERA parked beside two big oaks. The vehicle had a tall, thin tower projecting upward from the back, and from that sprouted a five-branched antenna.

"Peter Clawson's really got his ear to the ground around here, doesn't he?" Nate asked. "I need to interview him about any leads he may have."

"He keeps a lot of Amish employed in businesses he at least owns part of—the Dutch Farm Table, the Buggy Wheel Shop, a bunch of others. But his paper is his pride and joy."

"Can I show you around VERA?" he offered with a sweep of his hand toward his big, worldly buggy.

"I'd like that, but better not right now. I have to get back. Gabe wants to see it, too, so can we come out later? And, oh, *Mamm* says come to supper—evening meal, not half the amount we eat midday, in about two hours."

"Tell her thanks. I'd love to."

She wanted to throw caution to the sweet breeze that had begun to dry and ruffle his hair and go into the back of VERA with him—it was cozy there, he'd said—but she knew she shouldn't. She was already too attracted to him, like he had some kind of magnetic field and she was a compass needle.

"Before you go, then," he said as he walked her back a ways toward the farm, "will you explain the alms fund one of the elders mentioned? It sounds like private Amish insurance, but I thought that was forbidden."

Forbidden, *verboten,* danced through her mind as she darted another glance up into his intense, blue-sky gaze. Again, she had to unscramble her thoughts to grab for the right thing to say.

"Not forbidden if we keep it within the Amish community," she explained. "We do not pay into worldly insurance companies or the American government's Social Security or ever use such funds, because health is a gift from God and that would be gambling against that in a way. But we do collect a percentage of everyone's wages on a regular basis and use that to support those in the group who have big medical bills—or something like a house or barn burned. The church deacon collects and puts the money in a savings account until we need it. No big corporations profit. The family in need does pay a small part of their bills first, before our fund is used."

"Like a deductible," he said, nodding. "It's really a private, small group insurance. Very smart—amazing..." He looked at her closely and he drew out the last word so it almost sounded like Ray-Lynn's drawl. His gaze caressed her as he peered within the dim shelter of her black bonnet.

"I've got to get back," she said, quickening her steps. "See you for supper and then Gabe and I can take a look at VERA later, if it's okay."

She didn't want to seem like she was running away, but in a way she was. Standing so close to him, both of them in their bare feet, had made her think of Adam and Eve in the Garden, and look at all the trouble they'd got into!

If the bountiful Amish evening meal was what Sarah described as less food, Nate was as astonished by that as he was by his crazy attraction to her. It was probably just the fact she was so different from any woman he'd ever known, he tried to tell himself—bright but naive, stubborn yet humble, plain yet stunning, modest yet sexy without even trying. Man, he had to keep his mind on the food and the conversation, because her father, Ben Kauffman, had been drilling him about some things and here came another calmly couched but key question. At least he'd waited for this one until they were on the coffee and fabulous strawberry short-cake with home-churned vanilla ice cream. How Nate could put this dessert away after chowing down on sauerbraten, homemade bread, German potato salad and noodles with gravy, he wasn't sure, but maybe he was about to pay the price for this great meal.

"So far, Mr. MacKenzie," Ben Kauffman said, "have you found any proof, even hints, that the barn burn-ing might be someone upset by Sarah's painted quilt square?"

"No, sir, I haven't. But it's something I've considered and will stay aware of. I realize that such a work of art is to be useful—not just decoration."

"In that case," Ben Kauffman went on, "I will allow—ask—Sarah to paint a square for our barn. I ran it by Bishop Esh. I want to stand up for the earlier decision that she be allowed to paint her patterns on Home Valley barns to bring more visitors in. Amish businesses are slow. Orders for my gazebos, kids' play-houses, birdhouses and other items are down. And I want everyone to know that I believe her painting was not and should not be a target of arson."

Nate could see Sarah was surprised and elated. Her amber eyes filled with tears she blinked back. *"Danki, Daad,"* she said. Darn, Nate thought, if he wasn't ac-tually catching on to some of the German they used. Sadly, he hadn't been able to speak to her elderly grand-mother at all. She rarely spoke English anymore, and seemed pretty afraid of him, not to mention confused about things. She sat at the other end of the table, eating, but with her eyes on him as if he might leap at her. Sarah had introduced them, then whispered something to the old lady about him being here to help and that he could be trusted. Also at the table were Sarah's mother, Anna, Gabe and Martha.

It really impressed him how the Amish generations stuck together. When he'd lost his parents in the tragedy, how he'd wished he'd had a grandparent or even an aunt and uncle to take him in. At least his childless neighbors down the street, Jim and Mary Ellen Bosley, had been willing to give him a foster home. But living so close to where it all happened had been hard. In a way, that empty lot where what people called "the death house" had sat haunted him all through his youth—and yet today.

"I'll have to replace my ladders," Sarah said.

"While you paint here, you can use the barn one and only buy one," her father said. "And those planks for the long tables you can stand on."

"I have a ladder in my truck Sarah can use," Nate offered, "at least while I'm here. And a safer scaffolding than planks—if you don't mind the suggestion. I won't need them—unless there's another blaze to investigate, and I hope not."

"We pray not," Anna Kauffman said.

"If the man in black comes back, there will be more fires." The old lady spoke for the first time and in English. "I heard Sarah tell Martha the fire burned the barn like a beast devouring it. That's what it will be like again if that monster keeps sneaking around my house at night."

Nate could see Sarah was embarrassed by the outburst. "If you mean Nate here," Sarah said, leaning toward the woman and taking her hand, "he's only in the neighborhood for a while to help. And maybe you just dreamed the man in black."

"No, I saw him with his horrible, glowing eyes when I got up to go to the bathroom. *Ya,* I did!"

Sarah's parents just looked at each other as Sarah helped the old woman away from the table. She was obviously demented. On the other hand, if she had seen someone, Nate wondered who, because it hadn't been him.

Ray-Lynn knew Peter Clawson was a bit of a loner, but she couldn't argue his generosity to others. Whether it was large tips for her Amish waitresses or his funding of local businesses, the man was magnanimous to a fault. And, if she thought she managed to catch all the local gossip, she was a rank amateur compared to Peter, who seemed to know almost everything about everyone. Why, if it wouldn't be frowned on around here, he'd probably run something called the *Home Valley Enquirer.* She sometimes shuddered to think that he probably knew what kind of toilet paper she used at her house, though at least she'd stopped his just dropping in.

"I suppose you're really going to talk up the Saturday auction to benefit the barn raising," she said to him as she rang up his evening meal at the cash register.

"If not talk up, print up. You bet I will," he said. "And not only for a broader distribution of the paper. The regular Thursday edition will have a full-page spread on it. The layout is already done. Lots of folks far and wide will come in for Amish goods at an auction, especially the cooking and the quilts."

"I just heard about the auction and chicken barbecue from one of my girls," she admitted as she handed Peter his change and watched him take a peppermint and a toothpick from her counter. "But then you always have your ear to the ground when it comes to business."

"That's right, Ray-Lynn," he said with a wink as he smoothed his straight brown hair back from his forehead. "And, let's face it, you are one of my most important business affairs."

She could have kicked him, but it seemed no one else had heard. She didn't like the suggestive way he'd worded that, because she'd done a good job holding him at bay. A good business partner, yes, but not a partner for life—no way. He was single, but he didn't seem to look at women—that is, besides her.

Peter, at age forty-five, was balding and it obviously bothered him. Why his being overweight didn't, she wasn't sure, if he was so doggone concerned about his appearance. At least with his hair, he wasn't to the stage where he'd tried a comb-over, but he was always messing with it. "Even if it's monkey business, I'm on top of it, so don't get too close to our illustrious sheriff, you hear now," he added with a smug grin.

For one moment, Ray-Lynn was at a loss for words. Now how had he found out about that? Surely, Sarah hadn't talked, so it must have been her own falling all over Jack that Peter had seen. Well, ding-dang. He was kidding her, of course, yet there was a strange edge to his voice. Surely, as well as Peter had seemed to take it that she wouldn't date him, he wasn't jealous.

"Monkey business?" she countered, hands on hips.

"You'd better keep your mind and newspaper on the serious stuff around here, and there's plenty of that lately."

"I don't like to show off my extensive knowledge of newspaper trivia, my Southern belle, but monkey business was what brought down presidential candidate Gary Hart, not to mention John Edwards. I suppose you don't remember the details, but Gary Hart dared the press to follow him around, and they did…and found that married man—pillar of American morality—with a young mistress aboard a yacht called *Monkey Business.* Do you remember that?"

"No, Peter, actually, I don't. I must have been too busy serving up mint juleps and sitting on the veranda with Scarlett O'Hara that year."

"My point is, the newspaper people Hart dared to find out his business brought him down, just as the *National Enquirer* torpedoed John Edwards. Goodbye presidency, goodbye power. Ah, the power of the press. I'll see you tomorrow, Ray-Lynn," he concluded, speaking as usual almost in one breath as he went out and let the wooden door swing closed behind him.

Ray-Lynn wouldn't have minded a bit if it had swung closed faster and hit him in his big rear end.

There was still a good hour of daylight left when Gabe and Sarah accompanied Nate to see VERA and to check if his ladder would suit for the quilt square she planned to paint on her own family's barn. Though she would have preferred to have painted the entire, realistic scene of the farm, Sarah was thrilled to have another pattern to paint, one she was being allowed to select this time. And she was touched that her father believed in her work, especially when he'd been reluctant at first.

More than that, she was excited to see VERA's insides at last. Gabe was, too. He kept chattering about wanting to sit in the driver's seat, no doubt dreaming about driving the big truck, whatever was in the back of it. As for her own dreams...

"Gabe, I'd like to ask you a question about the night of the fire," Nate said as the three of them walked along the farm lane toward the woodlot. "On the level now, I take it some of the kids in their running-around years try smoking cigarettes."

"Some," Gabe said, nodding so hard his bangs bounced on his forehead under his straw hat. "A few even try pot. We're allowed. I know it's not good. Some kids have problems giving it up later, even tobacco cigs, I mean. You know, after they join the church, but, yeah, it's kind of common, like maybe having a coupla beers."

"So is there any chance someone could have sneaked across the field, maybe been around the Esh barn the night of your party but, because the party, at least inside the barn, was chaperoned by your mother and sister, wanted more privacy?"

To Sarah's dismay, Gabe cheeks went as bright as a polished Red Delicious apple. She bit her lower lip to keep from either trying to help him out or questioning him herself. She recalled how out of breath and red-cheeked he'd been when he'd rushed into the barn to tell her Jacob was outside. Could he have come from way across the field and not only been outside their barn?

"I don't think so," Gabe said. "A coupla guys were smoking regular cigs outside behind the buggies—not me—but I have a time or two."

"I'm not blaming anyone for smoking or accusing them of being an arsonist," Nate assured him with a pat on his shoulder. "As I said, a single dropped cigarette or match in the hay was not how the barn fire started, but if some kids were over there, maybe they saw some-thing—something they don't even know was important for my investigation. I'd love to talk to them. I need all the help I can get," he added as they approached VERA. "And I can keep things confidential. You know that word, Gabe—confidential?"

"*Ya,* Mr. MacKenzie. I can ask around and keep my ears open."

"Good man," Nate said, and this time hit his shoul-der lightly with a balled fist.

Sarah and Gabe watched as Nate took a small bit of metal and plastic out of his pocket—not quite a key—aimed it in VERA's direction, then pressed something. They heard a double click and VERA's lights blinked once as if in welcome—or warning.

"Like a magic lock," Gabe said as he climbed up into the high cab next to Nate while Sarah sat by the passenger's side window. "Way cool."

Sarah kept silent while Nate explained and demon-strated the various dashboard instruments. He showed them how the GPS worked and how the computer could perform other tasks. But Sarah sensed that it was just being in the big truck cab that impressed Gabe most. He kept touching the outer edge of the steering wheel and glancing out through the windshield. So her brother had a good imagination, too, just different from hers, that's all, she thought.

"Do you want to see the magic techno-cave in back now?" he asked the wide-eyed seventeen-year-old.

"Maybe later," Gabe said, his eyes aglow. Barbara Lantz, Sarah thought, might be jealous if she saw how her brother lusted—yes, a sin, but so human—after this big, polished, black truck cab.

"Then while I show your sister," Nate said, "why don't you slide over in the driver's seat?"

"Nate!" Sarah blurted.

"Don't worry," he said as he got down and closed the door on the rapt boy who now had his hands on the steering wheel. He came around to help Sarah down. "He can't start it, can't go anyplace."

He gestured toward the back of the vehicle, and she went with him. She'd been tempted to see VERA up close earlier today and now she would. After all, as entranced as Gabe was up front, he was here as a kind of chaperone. So what could happen while an *Englische ausländer,* however entrancing he was, introduced her to his sleek, brilliant, mechanical partner?

7

At first, Nate showed Sarah things inside VERA she'd expected to see, like firefighting gear and an ax and shovel he'd used to examine the ruins of the Esh barn. He explained a scene light and demonstrated the neat collapsible ladder he said he'd loan her. She figured that was all to break her in easy when he began to show her the array of amazing instruments and machines neatly stowed inside VERA. But she was even more amazed by her feelings being so close to him. Despite Gabe nearby and the back doors being wide open, she felt so alone with Nate as it went from dusk to dark outside.

Nate's tour of VERA's marvels with brief explanations of their uses blurred by: a thermal imager, a digital camera, a laser range finder. He showed her handheld, wireless phones. Several years before she'd heard Peter Clawson call them walkie-talkies when he used them with his reporter, before times got tough and he started doing everything at the paper himself, except for some volunteers. Nate showed her his laptop computer and his printer, copier, scanner and fax machine. He said he had a fingerprinting kit but didn't show it to her. VERA had what he called a camcorder and a fourteen-inch color TV with a built-in DVD that played flat silver disks and worked off a generator or the truck's batteries.

"The antenna system you've seen on the roof is invaluable in the rolling terrain around here," he went on. "The tower retracts into a rear compartment—here, see—and is raised and lowered by a single switch to go thirty-four feet into the air. Five antennae then pop out so I can get signals for communication."

Signals for communication—his words echoed in her head. She hoped he didn't know how his closeness was getting to her, as if his occasional light touch on her elbow or back, the scent of his hair or skin, was giving her body silent signals.

He was right about it being cozy in here. Besides a narrow counter for lab work on both sides of the truck, a skinny central table with newspapers open on it took up some space. She saw the *Budget,* the latest issue she'd been reading to her grandmother, and the special edition of the *Home Valley News* spread out with some things underlined or circled in red ink.

"Any clues in there?" she asked.

"Just trying to learn more about the area and the people. You've been very helpful with that."

"Good. We all want to help you find who did it. You told my father you didn't think the fire had anything to do with my paintings. I appreciate that."

"I think it's more likely someone's out for revenge against Bishop Esh. But I'm glad you'll be working at home for a while, because I don't want to imply you don't have to be careful painting your patterns. That's what I'm looking for, a pattern. I'm just hoping—praying, as your mother put it—that I can find something that makes sense and leads to the arsonist. I can tell how much those painted quilt squares mean to you."

"What I'd really like to paint are entire scenes of Amish life," she blurted, though she was usually so guarded about sharing that. "Ray-Lynn Logan at the restaurant, Hannah and Ella are the only ones I've told. To my people, it would be too personal, too prideful, even if I didn't sign my name on them. Ray-Lynn said I have a folk style, kind of primitive, but that it would suit my subject matter. She said it would be something like a woman called Grandma Moses used to paint. She told me that several months ago, but I remembered the name."

"So you'd risk being a rebel to paint like that?"

"No, I'm fine doing the barn art. That's a big step for all of us."

"Your work might be like Grandma Moses, huh?" he said, leaning over the keyboard of his laptop. He tapped something, and the screen came alive, a picture of a group of men, including him, together under the sign Fire and Explosive Investigations Bureau. Then he typed in the words *Grandma Moses* and *art,* then another screen lit up with a series of paintings. He enlarged them one at a time while she stared at them in awe.

"Oh, yes," she said, her voice shaky, "if those rural hills and farm scenes were Amish—*ya,* I could do that, only with my own touches, in my own way." They leaned toward the screen together, so close her bonnet bumped his cheek. "Well, good for Grandma Moses," Sarah said with a huge sigh, "and that nickname probably means she was elderly, too."

"She took up painting very late, it says here, leaving the art of embroidery to follow her heart toward a new kind of art."

To follow her heart… Sarah suddenly felt almost as close to the long-gone Grandma Moses as she did to her own *grossmamm* Miriam. The Amish didn't embroider—too fancy—but she'd long ago given up stitching quilts unless she absolutely had to, and she'd suffered socially for that. Still, she did not want to be elderly when she got the gumption to try entire paintings, not with the latex paint she used on the barns but in oil paint on stretched canvas like she'd seen for sale in the back corner of the hardware store in town.

Nate left a big painting on the screen, one called *The Old Oaken Bucket,* with horses in the field, barns and hills, women in long skirts, even an Amish-looking man in the lower left corner of it. As much as Sarah was impressed with VERA's insides, that picture perked things up, almost as if it were hung on the wall. It seemed like a gift Nate had given her.

She meant to move away, but they were suddenly wedged in close. Her breasts brushed his chest as she sidestepped.

"Okay," Nate said, as if he needed to agree to something or was warning himself. "You know, I don't mean to pry, but I smell lavender perfume or something really nice on you."

"Not perfume," she told him, blushing. "My friend Ella Lantz has a great lavender garden and makes soaps and sachets to sell. That's just my—her soap. If you have a special someone, you might want to buy some of her Lavender Plain products, a gift from Amish country to take home."

"Ah, no. I mean, there's no special someone at home."

She nodded. Their eyes locked again. She felt his intense stare clear down to the pit of her stomach.

Wiping his palms on his jeans, he moved away and peeked out through a small front window at Gabe as he had several times already, then back at her. "He's still entranced," he said, tilting his head a bit as if to peer inside her bonnet brim. She had the strongest urge to take it off, but she tried to concentrate on what Nate was saying now. He seemed as desperate to get back to business as she did, so he showed her his firefighting gear and explained how it went on, piece by piece.

"In those storage bins," he said, pointing, "are PPEs—personal protective equipment—for a chemical or biological incident, coveralls, gloves, overshoes and a filter mask, some overlap from the fire gear I showed you. I'm a first responder in case there's a terrorist attack. VERA's equipped for Homeland Security, too."

"Like 9/11 or a chemical attack, but I feel like there has been a terrorist attack on our Homestead area, too—only, thank the Lord, no one got seriously hurt."

As he reached past her to show her the tiny fridge and microwave, they were standing too close again. "I can heat up my supply of MREs—meals ready to eat—in here," he said. "But the food everyone's been so kind to share puts those to shame, so I won't even show you. I keep a cot in there, but prefer my sleeping bag outside."

"Staking out the Esh barn."

"I haven't seen any sign of activity since the other night. The arsonist usually returns quickly to the scene. Sarah, I'm going to interview Hannah tomorrow. I know—you think she's innocent, but I have to follow every lead. I was hoping Mike Getz would come to me for another fellow fireman chat, but I'm going to check him out, too. And Jacob. But I don't want you warning anyone, tipping them off I'm coming or that they're on my list."

For once, he wasn't looking into her eyes but at her lips. That made her aware she had thrust out her lower lip, pouting over his still suspecting Hannah. He lowered his head just a bit. She could feel his breath, warm and strong. She tried to relax her mouth, but she was tense all over. She had the definite feeling he was going to touch her—kiss her. She almost swayed into him.

"Oh, what's that?" she asked, like a coward, pointing at a pair of strange-looking binoculars hanging above his head.

He looked up, then turned around. "Night goggles so you can see in the dark," he said. "Things look kind of greenish and grainy, but these can come in handy. I'll show you sometime, but we have to get you and Gabe back with the ladder before it gets too dark."

"At least, when it looks dark, peering out from a lighted place, it's always brighter outside than you think," she said, feeling both relieved and regretful her private tour was over. "But you're right. We'd better get back. I'll see if I can pry Gabe out of the driver's seat." She beat a too-hasty retreat out the back of the truck, stepping down on the flat, back bumper.

But she jolted when a pulsing sound emanated from inside, like when Martha accidentally walked out of Wal-Mart with something she hadn't paid for.

"What? What's that?" she cried, but Nate was already snatching up his cell phone.

"Where? Yeah, I can find it. Sarah," he shouted,

jumping out of VERA and slamming the back doors, "get in the front seat and put Gabe in the middle. Sheriff Freeman says the Schrock barn's on fire, and I want you two to show me the fastest way there."

Nate lowered the antenna, swung VERA around and started down the lane, driving fast. He turned on his brights in the deepening dusk. Gabe was going to get his ride. "Sarah, how far to Schrock's?" he asked.

"Maybe four miles—other side of town. Turn right on Oak Ridge."

"Is he the church elder who was at the Eshes?"

"Yes, Reuben Schrock, the auburn-bearded man who announced the barn building and the auction."

"And he has one of your paintings on his barn?"

"Ya," she said as her voice caught. "Tumbling Blocks."

He bit off a curse. As they roared past the farmhouse, he saw Anna Kauffman walking toward the *grossdaadi haus.* She stopped to stare at them. He rolled down his window and shouted, "Barn fire at Reuben Schrock's! Sarah and Gabe will show me where."

In the rearview mirror, he saw her run back to the house. He turned right on the road, heading toward town, toward what he knew in his bones was going to be another arson. It was exactly what he'd sensed and feared—a serial arsonist working under cover of night in an isolated area. Another Amish barn owned by another church leader. Another of Sarah's painted patterns—oh, yeah, he knew he'd find a pattern now.

"Nate, be careful," Sarah said as he looked both ways, then went through the single Homestead stoplight—which was red. The place looked dark and dead, but for lights in Ray-Lynn's restaurant and the little newspaper office. And, he noted as he accelerated again, in the two fast-food restaurants and what must be security night-lights in the Citizens Bank. The self-serve gas station was open, one of the few in the state, he figured, where you didn't have to pay before you pumped. According to his research, the town claimed about four hundred residents, but that had to include some outlying areas.

"The fire truck's still in the firehouse," Sarah reported, "but two cars are there already. We're going to beat them to the fire."

"Where do we turn?" he asked as he accelerated.

"About a mile yet, left on Fish Creek Road, but I can't remember if there's a sign. Nate, Mike Getz is a neighbor of the Schrocks."

"Bingo," he muttered.

Gabe, wedged between him and Sarah, was wide-eyed and mute either with fear or excitement. When Nate had questioned him about kids being in the Esh barn, he'd had a gut feeling Gabe had seen something the night of that fire.

"There!" Sarah cried, pointing. "On the horizon at about eleven o'clock. It looks like the sun's setting there—see?"

"The barn's not fully engulfed yet, so someone spotted it early. And it's not burning top to bottom but low. So much for that pattern."

"It's also a different kind of barn, not like ours or the Eshes'. Only two floors, a real sharp slanted roof to shed the snow, second-floor haymow doors that look like they're open."

"That will fan the fire—suck it upward, too. Okay,

we beat the fire truck here," he shouted as he roared up the lane past the Schrocks' house and outbuildings. "No lights on in their place."

"Maybe they're not home, either. That's a pattern."

"Gabe, you go pound on the back and front doors of their house," Nate ordered. "Sarah's going to help me suit up."

"Suit up?" she cried. "You're not going into that inferno?"

"I'm not some amateur, volunteer firefighter!" Nate shouted, for the roar of the flames was enough to muffle their words. "Just to take a look. Gabe, go!"

The moment Nate got out, the boy slid over and sprinted toward the house. "Sarah!" Nate yelled. "I can do it myself, but you can help get me in there faster!"

He dragged his equipment out of the back of VERA and threw it on the ground. The Schrock barn was gray with black trim and a high-gabled roof, shingles over planks. He couldn't stay inside long because Sarah's ruined quilt pattern called Tumbling Blocks was probably going to be the fate of this proud structure. And then he saw her running toward him.

Sarah saw the fire truck, its red-and-white lights pulsing, but without the siren, streaking down the dark road toward them. She wanted to stall. No way she wanted Nate going into a flaming barn. Look what had happened to Mike Getz and Levi Miller. With a quick glance at her still-intact painted square, she realized her entire world might be falling apart. And then she rushed to the back of VERA to help him pull on the protective gear he'd showed her about a half hour ago.

She tried to remember how it all went. Nate had it

laid out on the ground, and was already into the thick
pants and suspenders. She helped him jam his feet into
his oversize, steel-toed boots. Then she held his bulky,
beige jacket so he could get into it. He yanked on the
fire protection hood that had arrived in the package
she'd delivered before supper. It encased his head and
neck but not his face. Her fingers weren't used to the
oxygen mask he pointed toward, so he ended up pulling it on and tightening the straps himself. She helped
him put on the heavy fire gloves and handed him his
hat. It looked scorched and smelled of smoke.

Meanwhile, all around her, volunteer firemen were
hauling lengths of hose out of their truck. Sarah knew
Nate wanted to beat them inside. She wondered if Mike
Getz was among them, but surely not with a broken arm.
Then she saw him off to the side with Cindee Kramer.
Their faces, lit by orange flames, seemed to glow with
excitement.

Nate nodded to her and headed toward the barn door.
The firemen were still dragging out two hoses, one
from their truck and one to draw water from the pond,
as Nate walked toward the flaming hell.

Talk about VERA being claustrophobic when he
slept inside, Nate thought as he lumbered into the burning barn. Until the oxygen started flowing through his
mask, he always felt a moment of drowning panic. If
he breathed in before the flow was good, his eardrums
seemed to suck right into his head, but he was fine now.
Somehow, it was always otherworldly. He couldn't hear
anything but his own breathing, couldn't talk, could
hardly see, plodding under seventy-five pounds of gear.

At least he had hopes no one was trapped inside. He'd

seen burned bodies, curled in a fetal position—black, unrecognizable, flesh and fat gone right down to the bone, smelling like charred meat on the grill. Thank God, it seemed no one was home at the farm again. The arsonist was clever and careful. But Nate couldn't afford to be careful right now. He had to look in the guts of this structure to see if he could pin anything down. Already, even with two internal points of combustion observable from outside, he saw it was a different M.O. But it had to be the same person setting these, didn't it? A copycat arsonist was rare, no doubt especially in a rural area where harmony apparently ruled.

He didn't mind that this blaze brought back his fire training—it was the other memories he tried to fight. That night when he was eight and the roaring inferno of their home engulfed him. His mother screaming his name, coughing, gasping, crawling on the floor through the pall of choking smoke to where he huddled near his bed. The last time he saw her, her nightgown was ablaze. And then his father rushing in—too late....

This barn—again, the horses were in the field—had a large central bay and two side bays, one with stalls, one with stored grain. The flames were so fierce, he figured he could almost hear some of the corn popping, when he actually couldn't hear a thing. Popcorn—that's what Sarah had said while she helped him get suited up. The Schrocks had harvested a huge crop of popcorn last year, sold most of it to the Orville Redenbacher's company.

Just about six feet inside the barn, he was dazzled by a burst of flames and sparks—a small explosion in amazing hues, violet, magenta, chartreuse. Was he hallucinating? Chemicals this time?

When the flare-up spread away from him, licking at the wooden beams that supported the inner bay and stall walls, he shuffled toward the source of the colors, prettier than the sunrise had been that morning as he watched Sarah hitch her horse to her buggy. It almost mesmerized him. And it must be something incendiary, because it was at the tip of one of the V-burn patterns the firemen were trying to douse.

A stream of water from a hose bounced before his eyes, throwing something against his boots. Grunting, he stooped to picked up a remnant. He had a hunch what it was and it wasn't kerosene this time.

Sarah and Gabe stood off to the side, beyond the reach of the heat belching from the blazing barn. Once again, observers gathered as they saw the flames or the word spread. Nate was still inside, but then several of the firemen were, too, so they must figure the structure was sound enough right now. The flames were consuming her bright pink, green and brown tumbling blocks on the stark-white background. She imagined she could hear it crackling in protest. The Schrocks had picked the design because it looked like it was moving both up and down, depending on your point of view. She watched the paint curl and blur, making blocks seem to tumble like the barn beams and roof would if they couldn't get the fire out soon.

Sarah tried to stem the tears that prickled her eyelids, but she couldn't keep from crying. Her vision blurred to make the barn fire seem like Armageddon with the entire world aflame. Her quilt squares, now the barns of two families who had trusted her to paint them there, were under attack. Who hated the Home Valley Amish?

Did someone blame her for something? Sure, there had been hate crimes against her people from time to time. Some *Englische* blamed the Plain People for being pacifists, for their slow buggies, for just being different. No way it was smooth sailing in this life she'd been born into and then had chosen.

She wiped tears from her cheeks with both hands. And then she saw something glint from the darkness beyond the barn.

She couldn't tell what—who—because it was as if she'd been looking into the sun, but she was suddenly sure someone was there watching, standing back a ways, not joining the others. Despite drifting smoke, had it been eyeglasses or sunglasses or binoculars that had reflected the flames? Surely not just a distortion from her own tears. A big meadow stretched into the darkness, so why would someone stand in the middle of it?

Sarah hurried back to VERA, climbed inside and took down Nate's night goggles. She got back out and moved into the shadow of the big vehicle. She fumbled to get them on, had to end up holding them over her eyes. But her view was so blurry, just a sea of eerie green flecked by shifting, speckled grays, kind of like swimming underwater.

Yet she glimpsed a figure, someone moving away, apparently from watching the barn burn. Man or woman? *Grossmamm*'s man in black? Should she race across the meadow in pursuit, at least to see up closer?

But at that moment Nate emerged from the inferno, stumbling, unsteady, and she ran toward him instead.

8

Sarah couldn't tell what Nate was cradling so carefully in his gloved hands. He walked around her and deposited something on VERA's wide, back metal bumper. Embers? The small mass, looking like a smashed piece of wood, was glowing as if it had a life of its own. It suddenly sparked pink and purple.

He pulled off his helmet and mask, sucking in air, out of breath.

"Stay back from that!" he told her.

"What is it?"

"Not positive yet. What are you doing with my goggles?"

"I saw someone in the back meadow but it was blurry. Someone hurrying away."

He pulled off one of his gloves and wiped his sweaty face with his free hand. "Amish?" he asked.

"I couldn't tell."

"Male or female?"

"Not sure. I noticed at first because of a glint from the fire, on glasses or binoculars, I think."

He shrugged out of his jacket and, still wearing his protective pants held up by suspenders, took the goggles from her and put them on. He walked away and peered into the distant darkness for several minutes, then returned and handed her the goggles.

"Is there a road or another farm back that way?" he asked.

"A road and a farm, but way over the hill. Levi Miller's place, the Amish man who had his ribs broken when he and Mike Getz went into the first fire. He's the church deacon who has one of my painted squares on his barn. Other than Bishop Esh's barn and those of the two church elders you've met, Levi Miller's is the only other one I painted—so far, now that I'm going to do one on our family barn."

He frowned. "I need to run a test on that material," he told her, nodding toward the remnant on his bumper. "I'm going to smother it so it doesn't burn further." She watched as he put the glove he'd removed over it, pressing it down.

"But won't that hurt it, if you need to find out what it is?"

"I'll be testing the ashy residue, the chemical contents. I'm betting on oil-treated sawdust from cedar with a copper-based coloring compound. In other words, what's left when you break open and ignite an artificial fireplace log."

"I've seen those!"

"In town?"

"It must have been in the hardware store. I'm going there tomorrow."

"Don't you be asking who bought some. I'll take care of that."

They both jumped as a white light nearly blinded them, but it wasn't from Nate's evidence. Peter Clawson had arrived and was taking pictures of the scene with a strobe. At least Sarah could tell, if he'd shot a picture their way, she had her back turned to the camera. He probably wanted ones of Nate and VERA.

"Can you stay here with this—not touch it, guard it—until I see how the guys are doing with the fire?" Nate asked, peering closer at his prize.

"*Ya*—yes, sure."

"Where's Gabe?"

"Over there with some friends," she said, pointing.

"I'll be right back."

She watched him talk to the two firemen who were holding the hose that was drawing water from the pond. It actually looked as if they could keep this barn from tumbling down, although her tumbling blocks pattern was a goner. Peter Clawson approached Nate, and they spoke for a minute. Sarah saw Ray-Lynn, who had just driven in, and was standing near the sheriff's cruiser. Ray-Lynn didn't see her standing beside Nate's truck or she would have come over. Nate made a beeline toward Gabe and his friends, bending toward them in earnest conversation. Next, he huddled in private with Sheriff Freeman, who had arrived while Nate was still in the barn and had been keeping the growing crowd back.

To her dismay, Peter Clawson came over to her, but at least he kept his camera at his side.

"Another of your pretty paintings gone, Sarah."

"The barn is what matters."

"Of course. It's starting to look as if someone's holding a grudge—a big one—against Amish church leaders, doesn't it?"

"I pray that's not the case."

"Right. God's will."

"Do you doubt that, Mr. Clawson?"

"The thing is, the devil's loose on the earth, evidently with God's tolerance or permission. So, I see you're helping Nate MacKenzie."

"Not exactly. He had dinner with my family, then Gabe and I came along to show him where the Schrock barn was when the call came in."

"So what's that stuff on the bumper of his truck?"

The man wasn't taking notes as he had when he interviewed her about her quilt squares, but she didn't want him quoting her and she didn't want to give anything away that Nate wanted kept quiet for now. Yet she totally shocked herself when she looked straight into the man's eyes and told a lie. "I've decided to keep a burned piece of each barn where I had a painting, just to remember how kind the families were to let me do it."

"A quaint idea," he said. He squinted at her, then rubbed his eyes, probably stinging from the pall of smoke. The breeze wasn't blowing this way, but the entire area—including her clothes and hair—hung heavy with the smell. He started to say something else, then, to her relief, thought better of it and hurried away, taking pictures again.

She stayed right where she was, guarding Nate's evidence as she saw him leave Sheriff Freeman to walk over to Mike Getz and Cindee Kramer. To Sarah's surprise, Nate slapped Mike on the back as if they were old pals. Right then her parents buggied in and got out with Bishop and Mattie Esh.

Nate spoke to the four of them, pointing her out to

her parents before he walked back to her and stared at his ashy evidence again.

"Peter Clawson asked what that was, but I told him it was mine," she blurted.

"I appreciate that or he'd be after me with more questions. I don't want those or my answers in his paper. And to keep that from being a lie, I'll give you a bit for a dirty souvenir. But guess who phoned this fire in?"

"Not Mike Getz?"

"I knew I should hire you as my assistant. We've got another arson here but between you, VERA and me, one way or the other, we're going to nail someone soon. We have to before this happens again."

The next morning, after delivering her half-moon pies, Sarah had breakfast in a booth at the restaurant, waiting for the hardware store to open at nine so she could buy paint. While she ate, Ray-Lynn came and went to greet or cash folks out, but she sat across the table from Sarah when she could.

"So you're going to go ahead and paint a quilt square on your barn?" Ray-Lynn asked as Sarah finished her blueberry pancakes and sausage patties. "After two of them just went up in flames with their barns?"

"Shh. I discussed that with my parents and Nate last night, and we decided yes."

"Easy for him to say—and it's Nate now, is it?" she added with a wink. "Well, if he's camped out back of your barn like you said, maybe he wants to set a trap for the arsonist—or for someone else."

"Now, Ray-Lynn, no teasing. It's not that way and it's impossible."

"I thought all things were possible with God. But, okay, okay. Still, aren't you scared for your own barn?"

"The point is, we mustn't give in to fear. 'Yea, though I walk through the valley of the shadow of death, I shall fear no evil.' Barns and quilts are part of our way of life, and we have to stand up for that. What's happening here is hardly the valley of death."

"Not yet, anyway. I'm not a good ole Southern Baptist for nothing, my girl, so I reckon I could quote a thing or two from the Good Book myself. But the thing that keeps coming to mind right now is something my daddy used to say. 'Are we still ahead of the hounds?' And I'm not sure we are. But never you mind my rambling. You're a strong woman, Sarah—talented, too. Even if this attack on your people has something to do with your paintings, my offer for you to do a big mural here still stands. So I'm standing with you all no matter what."

"I'm grateful, my friend. Oh, by the way, I saw you at the fire last night, too."

For a moment Ray-Lynn looked upset. "Oh—yeah, when I heard the sirens, I let the girls take care of the restaurant and drove over, following the light in the sky. I didn't see you there. I didn't stay long. I decided it was time for me to get back here, fire or not, so I could close up."

"Not to change the subject but guess who just came in?" Sarah whispered. "No, don't even turn around if you're putting up fences between you and him."

"Good thought to keep giving him the cold shoulder, but unfortunately, I need to run this place," Ray-Lynn said, and reached over to pat Sarah's hand. "Talk to you later."

Sarah had to admire how Ray-Lynn handled the sheriff. Nice but cool as a March breeze. Polite but that was all. Sarah bit back a little smile as she slid out of the booth and took her purse with her money in it to buy new paint. *Grossmamm* always used to say that you catch more flies with honey than with vinegar, but Ray-Lynn's vinegar seemed to be working wonders right now, because when she did what she called her sashay away from him, Sheriff Jack Freeman was all eyes.

Nate fidgeted and stared at his computer screen, waiting for the chemical assay analysis reading to come up. Yes! A copper-based color compound in the ash residue. He'd only heard of one case where the arsonist started a fire by breaking open an artificial log and igniting it to burn the house of his former, remarried wife, but the story had been picked up in the media and he'd just happened to catch it. Now where had that case been? Out in L.A., maybe—but how long ago?

He jumped up and stretched. Such a chemically treated log made for a fast, hot and colorful flame and would eventually burn away completely, leaving no evidence, so his risking going into the blaze was well worth it. This arson was a far cry from the wick-and-accelerant approach of the Esh barn fire, yet it surely must have been started by the same person. Two barn burners using double ignition points and choosing buildings with Sarah's paintings was too similar to be a coincidence. Both incendiary devices used materials that were readily available in Amish country or anywhere. As soon as he talked to Mike Getz and Jacob Yoder—who were neck-and-neck as his top suspects, with Hannah running a close second—he'd stop by the hardware store in Homestead and see if he could get someone there to recall who had bought artificial fireplace logs. The problem was that purchases of those could have been made last winter or even in the fall. He was pretty sure the few Amish homes he'd been in didn't have fireplaces, but then Jacob wasn't technically Amish anymore.

The moment the bell over the hardware store door rang and Sarah stepped inside, Cindee Kramer called to her from behind the checkout counter. "Hi, Sarah! Boy, oh, boy, wasn't that fire something last night? Mike was so upset he couldn't help put it out, but at least he spotted it and called it in."

"Much appreciated, too," Sarah said, and stopped to talk. "That quick call probably kept it from burning to the ground."

Sarah knew she was supposed to leave all the questions up to Nate when he came by later, but with that lead-in, she couldn't help but ask, "So what was Mike doing when he noticed it—I mean, was he outside or something?"

"He ran inside from where he was grilling burgers out back and called 9-1-1. Even one-armed, he's great at barbecuing, great one-handed at a lot of things, tell you the truth," she said with a little snicker. "I'm so proud of him lately, picture in the paper and all, helping with these fires. But our burgers burned to a crisp," she added with a tight grin. "Could have started our own fire, I guess, one way or t'other."

Cindee had naturally curly black hair, and lots of it, in a kind of big halo around her head. Her thin face got lost in it, but that was the only skinny part of her because she had a real full figure, chest and hips. She'd been helpful picking out paint in the past, and maybe she was being helpful today, too, and just didn't know it. After all, Nate had only told Sarah not to ask who bought artificial fireplace logs.

"So is your barbecue pit right where you can keep an eye on your broken-armed wonder, in case he needs help juggling all of that?" she asked Cindee.

"Not really. It's out behind the shed, 'cause I don't like the smoke drifting into the kitchen and that keeps sparks away from our big woodpile."

Their woodpile? Then, did that mean they didn't use artificial logs? On the other hand, Cindee hadn't had Mike in view while he was outside, so he could have slipped away to start a fire practically next door.

"Wow, the entire neighborhood smells of smoke," Cindee went on. "Now that you mention it, I did go out to help him use the electric fire starter, but he said he could handle that by himself and he did, too. So, you in for more paint? Since some of the Schrock barn's still standing, will you redo your block quilt piece when it gets fixed?"

"I'm going to do a quilt square on my own family's barn—Ocean Waves pattern. Do you remember I showed you that one?"

"Sure do. You said it was your favorite, 'cause you'd love to see the ocean. I remember it kind of seemed to shift and move."

Sarah could hear Mr. Baughman, who owned the store, talking to another customer down one of the aisles. She and Cindee walked toward the back of the store, where the paint samples always intrigued Sarah. Little paper squares laid out by color and hue, she wanted to arrange them into a painting right on the spot. Although it was not a big store, it seemed to have everything packed in, items for both English and Amish customers. They passed kerosene lanterns and kerosene, then an array of battery-powered kitchen gadgets, since electricity, unless provided by a generator, was *verboten*.

"Exterior latex, couple of contrasting blues and a white, right?" Cindee asked.

"Right, but I'll have to decide which blues. I really appreciate your help. I'll drop you off a couple of half-moon pies when I take some to the Schrocks. My mother and sisters are making and freezing huge batches of them for the auction at the schoolhouse on Saturday." And that, Sarah figured, would allow her to take a look at their barbecue area. Could the burned barn really be seen from there?

"Can you believe the Schrocks missed that whole thing?" Cindee asked. "Told us they were going to hire a van driver to take the whole family to see relatives near New Philadelphia, coming back later today, so I bet they don't even know, with no telephones and all. Poor people when they get driven in and see that."

So, Sarah thought, Mike Getz knew ahead of time that the Schrocks would not be home last night. She had to report all this to Nate when she saw him again.

When Mr. Baughman peeked around the corner and said a quick, "How you ladies doing?" Cindee high-tailed it back to the front checkout desk. Sarah had always liked Cindee. Anybody who liked and knew paint colors the way she did was fine with her. At least Cindee hadn't brought up the fact that artist's tubes of oil paints, canvas and easels were on sale again, because Sarah could hear them practically calling her name from the other side of the store.

That night Sarah lay on the hideaway bed in the living room of the *grossdaadi haus,* unable to sleep. So much was happening so fast. Nate had not come back as far as she knew, but she'd left him a note about what she'd learned from Cindee, stuck in his sleeping bag he'd left on the ground. A nice way to spend the night, she thought—that is, him sleeping under the starry sky. She assumed he'd done a lot of interviews today, maybe even driven to Cleveland to talk to Hannah and her employer to see if she had proof of where she'd been during the barn burnings—an alibi.

She sure hoped it wasn't someone Amish or even former Amish doing this, including Jacob. Enough outsiders thought the Amish were a little crazy, or quaint. Quaint—that's what Mr. Clawson had called something she'd said.

She and Martha had kept the news of the second arson from *Grossmamm.* She'd gone to sleep pretty well tonight and hadn't stirred—at least, Sarah hadn't heard her in the bathroom. Strange how the old woman was so afraid of Nate, but then it might be best if Sarah was, too, because he really intrigued her...really made her want to...

Sarah gasped. She heard gravel against the big window right over her head. Was Hannah here again? What if Nate was right to suspect Hannah, and she had come to look at the second barn she'd burned? Or had Nate questioned her today, and Hannah had come to tell her to keep away from him? Or it could be Nate himself, wanting to talk to her, even though she hadn't heard him drive in. Yes, she'd mentioned to him that Hannah had thrown gravel against the window the night after her family's barn burned.

She heard a handful of dirt or gravel again. Sarah sat up and pulled the bed quilt around her cotton nightgown like a shawl before she cracked the dark green curtains to look out. No one—she saw no one.

She tiptoed to *Grossmamm's* door and didn't hear her stirring, so at least Hannah—or Nate—had not wakened her. Sarah hurried across the small living room, turned the single lock on the front door and stepped out into the warm, windy night, walking to the edge of the small porch.

"Hannah!" she called. "Hannah?"

Silence. Nothing moving but tree limbs. The hoot of a barn owl sounded so lonely. The familiar squeak of the porch swing pushed only by the wind grated on her nerves, scraping along her spine to make the hair on the nape of her neck stand on end. The thick hair she let down at night moved back and forth across her shoulders like a ghostly caress.

Too late, Sarah realized she should not have stepped outside and no way was she going farther. Besides, last time Hannah had showed herself through the window, and Nate probably would have knocked. After all, *Grossmamm* had said she'd seen a man out here...unless it had been Nate looking around to be sure everything was quiet that night....

She felt fear nibble at her, but when had any of them been afraid to go back and forth between the farm buildings even at night?

Her eyes adjusted to the darkness, but she still saw no one. As she turned around to hurry back inside,

Sarah felt gravel under her bare feet on the porch. So it hadn't been her imagination. If it was Hannah or Nate, it wasn't one bit funny.

She gasped. A note was stuck to the front door with a basting pin. It must have been there when she came out.

She took it inside with her, locked the door behind her and lit the kerosene lamp. She read, in large, hand-written, black printing, words from the Bible: "For wickedness burns as the fire; through the wrath of the Lord of Hosts the land is burned up, and the people shall be as fuel for the fire."

9

Sarah wished she could just run to Nate with this note—this threat—but it was too late and too far to go alone.

After checking on *Grossmamm* to be sure she was all right, she paced the floor in the small living room, back and forth, skittish at her own shifting shadow, peeking outside now and then. She circled the note, not touching it as if it would burn her. At dawn, she'd run to the house to show the note to *Daad,* talk him into going with her to take it to Nate. For once in her life, she wished they had telephones here at the farm, or that she had one of Nate's handheld phones so she could call him.

But had this note been left by the arsonist himself, or was someone else horning in? Recalling how Nate had put the evidence of the bundle of matches in a plastic bag, she went to the small kitchen and got a gallon-size bag and sealed the note inside. Nate had a fingerprint kit in VERA. Maybe if he eliminated her prints from when she tore it off and brought it inside, he could find other prints. But then he couldn't go around making people give theirs, could he? Especially her people. They would mistrust him then—government intruding on personal privacy.

Each time she paced past the table, she glared at the message through the shiny plastic. Just regular, letter-size, white paper. Nothing special to identify that. Who wrote in such heavy, big print, or was that to show defiance or anger? And the fact it was a Bible quote—from someone Amish?

Was she to be the messenger of this threat to the church leaders or the entire Amish community? She did not want to cause panic or have the news media get hold of this. But how did the sender know she was in the smaller house and not with her family in the big one? Someone had been spying on her—or, again, it was someone Amish, someone they knew, who knew her family's ways, her ways. But someone Amish would have written in German, not English, wouldn't they?

Worst of all her agonizing was the implied warning that people would die, that the arsonist might burn more than barns. "And the people shall be as fuel for the fire." Did the barn burnings with her quilt squares mean that someone was angry with *her?*

Near three in the morning, she finally got hold of herself. She'd fight back—well, not really, because her people never did that—but she would not just let someone terrorize her or her community. She'd asked Cindee questions today. Now she had to learn more about this, not just let it destroy her confidence and faith.

Sarah tiptoed into her *grossmamm*'s room to borrow her Bible to look for the exact location of the verse. Out in the living room, as she bent close to the single lamp, her hands shook, rustling the well-worn pages. As if

she heard *Grossmamm*'s shrill voice again, Sarah kept
recalling the etchings of her people being burned alive
from the pages of the *Martyrs Mirror*. That one picture
of a young woman tied to a ladder and being tipped into
the flames flashed before her eyes. She was perspiring,
but a chill snaked up her spine.

Sarah knew to look in one of the prophets for this
quote. Finally, she found it early in the big book of
Isaiah in the Old Testament. She whispered it in the
sonorous German, Isaiah 9:19. What followed were
other predictions of a dreadful future for those who
worshipped idols—or had this quote been plucked out
strictly for its mention of fire?

Curled on the couch, she eventually fell into a fitful
sleep, slogging from dream to dream. A fiery beast was
trying to burn VERA, flames licking at the truck, devouring it while she huddled inside with Nate, holding
on to the ladder he said he would loan her. They were
both barefoot and had been swimming, but even water
from the pond was not enough to put out the inferno
that burned them, burned her....

She woke to find she was uncovered and shaking
with the predawn chill. After looking out from every
window, she ran to the big house to talk to her parents
and fetch Martha to sit with their *grossmamm,* so she
could take Nate what might be his best clue yet.

Nate was surprised to see Sarah and her father on
VERA's back doorstep even before he took a quick
swim in the pond or shaved. But then he'd been surprised to find her note in his sleeping bag last night with
all the helpful intel about Mike Getz. In a way, that had

saved his day, because it had been one frustration after the other.

He'd made the hour-long drive to Cleveland and managed a quick interview with Hannah's boss, Myron Jenkins. Jenkins couldn't provide Hannah with an alibi for either night of the barn burnings, but of course, that didn't necessarily imply guilt. No one was home at Hannah's apartment, where she lived with two other women, and the neighbor he'd talked to had no clue where Hannah's boyfriend lived so he hadn't been able to question him.

When Nate returned to Homestead, he'd also struck out trying to trace where Jacob Yoder was living, so he was going to visit his previous place of employment in town today to ask some questions or even interview Jacob's parents. He'd also made an appointment to talk to Peter Clawson since the newspaper man was aware of all that went on in the area. The owner of the hardware store and Mike Getz's girlfriend, who worked there, couldn't recall who might have purchased artificial logs and certainly no one had lately. They were boxed away in sets of four—which could mean the arsonist had two more to use—in the back storeroom until autumn.

But one look at Sarah's face, and nothing else mattered.

"What happened?" he asked before either she or her father said a word. He wanted to touch her, hold her, but he didn't so much as move at first. Her pretty face looked ravaged; at the very least she hadn't slept or was sick.

Sarah extended a bagged note to him, and he scanned it. "Where and when was this found?"

"Last night on the door of the *grossdaadi haus* where

I stay with my grandmother. Someone wanted me to find it right away and threw gravel against the window to get me outside. I thought it was Hannah and went out...."

His insides lurched and not just at her admitting the note could have been left by Hannah. This could mean Sarah's paintings—she herself—was the target of the arsonist. But it did mention "the people," not an individual.

"You've got to be more careful," he scolded, much too loudly. Even Ben Kauffman startled. "You could have been hurt!"

"Danger and fear—it's not how we think around here," she protested. "I wasn't hurt. It just made it hard to sleep. That's a biblical quote from the prophet Isaiah."

He fought to calm himself, to think and not just react. "And you thought to bag the note for me. Sarah, you're priceless. I assume you touched it."

"Yes, but I thought you could take my fingerprints. *Daad* says it's all right as long as you don't send them to the government, just use them to see if there are others on the page you can trace. If it would have been stuck to the door with a thumbtack, I would have brought that for the same reason, but it was put there by a basting pin—a long one, sometimes used for quilt making, really common around here."

Man, Nate thought, this girl is bright. Bright and shining in his eyes. But maybe the arsonist also knew she was bright and bold. Nate had thought her painting a quilt square on her own property would keep her safe, but would it? And that person her maybe-delusional grandmother had spotted—odds were now that the person was real and could be the arsonist. But he or

she was also clever, probably too clever to get caught
returning to where the note had been left.

"I'll also see if there are footprints or anything
dropped near where you found this," he told her.

He tried not to frown, but this biblical reference
backed up a possibility he didn't like, just as the kerosene and fake fireplace log—and now the basting pin—
did. Such as maybe he was going to end up arresting
someone Amish, not that others couldn't cite scripture
for their own purposes. He was starting to realize what
Sarah feared most was probably true. The arsonist was
not some random outsider or even a "modern," as they
put it, with a grudge against the Amish. It was someone
right here in this tightly-knit community, maybe even
one of their own people.

"Sorry," Sarah said, interrupting his agonizing. "But
I think I—Martha, too—have made a mess of the gravel
there, walking in and out, so you won't find footprints."

"That's all right. You've done really well. I pretty
much struck out yesterday asking if anyone recently
bought artificial fireplace logs at the hardware store,
so now, with this and the note you left me about Mike
Getz, we have something to go on. Let's just hope the
perp—perpetrator—made a mistake and has his, or her,
prints on this page."

Finally, her father spoke. He had looked pretty upset
through all this, though Nate gave him credit for letting
Sarah talk. He called Nate by his first name for the first
time. "Nate, there's no way we can just keep Sarah to
home, and that doesn't look like a refuge now, anyway.
She said you have little handheld phones—no wires
attached. I'll ask Bishop Esh, but since all this—" he
gestured toward the note in Nate's hand "—I would say

her idea you might let her borrow one when she goes into town and back could be a good idea."

"It would for sure. I'll show her how to use it, and she can call me if she sees anything strange. The only thing is, when I need to drive somewhere, I have to put my antenna down so a tree limb overhead doesn't damage it," he explained, gesturing up at it, "and that might play havoc with our signals. I was going to ask, anyway, Mr. Kauffman, would it be permissible for Sarah to take me to see the other two barns that have her paintings—in her buggy? I passed one on the road coming in, but I'd like her to tell me something about the patterns she's painted that may relate to a pattern with the arsons. Besides, I don't want to be seen driving VERA there, in case the arsonist thinks I'm daring him or her to strike again. Of course, you or Gabe or Martha could go along."

Nate realized he'd said too much, but he'd really wanted to explain himself so he didn't alienate Sarah's family or hurt her reputation.

"With plans for the big auction Saturday and buying the wood and hardware for rebuilding the Esh barn," Ben Kauffman said, "we're all pretty busy. But if you sit behind Sarah's seat in her buggy, so you're not real obvious, I say okay."

"Great. Would you like to come inside VERA, Mr. Kauffman, while I take Sarah's fingerprints? We won't be long."

"I'll just sit right here on the back, then walk her home. You two can make plans about seeing the other barns."

Nate rolled Sarah's prints as fast but as carefully as he could. Her fingers were delicate but strong. Talented

hands, he thought. They sat, of necessity, very close together. Her hair smelled of that seductive lavender scent
again. Was her friend Ella Lantz's making and selling lavender soap and sachets so different from Sarah's
being able to paint scenes of Amish life? All three of
the best friends—Hannah, Sarah and Ella—seemed to
have special talents that didn't fit the mold around here.

He'd thought this assignment would be a piece of
cake, but that old Amish saying was really hitting home
right now. Sarah sometimes said quilts instead of cakes,
but he was learning the hard way that dealing with the
Amish was not all cakes and pies.

When Nate found no prints but Sarah's on the paper
with the Bible quote, it only drove home again that the
enemy was careful and clever. Would Hannah, Jacob or
even Mike Getz have thought to keep the paper clean
of their prints? Maybe Getz watched the forensic tech
shows on TV. And both Hannah and Jacob were living
out in the world where they could think of that, too.

He glanced at his watch. He had time to go into town
for breakfast at the Dutch Farm Table, then to visit the
Buggy Wheel Shop where Jacob Yoder used to work.
That would give him plenty of time to get back here to
go with Sarah—and guard Sarah, truth be told—to the
other two barns with her painted patterns. If the owners
were home, he was tempted to tell them to stay home
after dark every night. He didn't want to panic them,
but an empty house seemed to be part of the arsonist's
pattern. So how, then, were "the people" going to be
"fuel for the fire"?

As he drove past the Kauffman barn, he saw Sarah
up on a ladder, chalking out the perimeter of the square

for her painting. He stopped and unloaded his ladder and metal scaffolding, then set it up for her, so she had more stability. Since the barn burnings were at night—cover of darkness and more spectacular for the arsonist, he figured—he'd just take these back each evening when she was done in case he needed them. It would give him more excuses to see her, and not, he admitted to himself, just because she was proving to be such a help to him.

"Thanks," she told him. "I'll really need those when I start painting. I think it might rain this afternoon, which may wash my chalk marks off, but I needed to do something on this today."

"The threat of rain won't stop us from going out this afternoon, will it?"

"This fiberglass buggy and even the Amish woman who drives it won't wash away in a little rain—or a swim in a pond, Nate MacKenzie," she told him, her voice teasing, almost flirty. His wanting to respond to that, but realizing he should keep this all business, made him almost tongue-tied as they looked into each other's eyes a moment too long.

"So what's this pattern?" he asked.

"It's my favorite, because I'd like to see the Atlantic and Pacific oceans someday. I've seen Lake Erie and just imagined it was the ocean. It's called Ocean Waves. A lot of triangles close up, but it looks like rolling waves with whitecaps from farther back."

"Like an impressionist painting."

"What's that?"

"Just what you said. Up close you can't see the images, only the pieces, but if you stand back a bit, the impression of the big picture becomes clear. I think most of the impressionists were French. I'll show you some on the laptop sometime."

"There's sure a lot I don't know about art and artists."

"That makes two of us."

"Maybe finding out who's behind the burnings will be like that," she said. "You know, we're so close to things—to people—we can't see the big picture. Nate, what if it's someone right under our noses?"

Nate finally got to meet Sarah's friend Ray-Lynn Logan, and was surprised to hear she had a soft Southern drawl. She gave him a good looking over, even a bit of a quiz about whether he'd left a girlfriend behind in Columbus—which he truthfully denied—so he had to wonder what Sarah had said about him. He also ran into Peter Clawson, who said he ate most of his meals there.

"Ray-Lynn tells me you own a piece of the Buggy Wheel Shop," Nate said to Peter as they walked out of the restaurant together. "So you're even into investments that sound as if they're Amish-owned."

"A couple. I like to put my money where my mouth is, so to speak. Some of these ma-and-pa businesses around here have taken a hit in the stale economy. It doesn't just affect the big boys on the Wall Streets and Fifth Avenues of the country, you know."

"So you're a local philanthropist."

"I never thought of it that way, more like a practicalicist—and I know that's not a word. For instance, I'm offering a five-thousand-dollar reward for information leading to an arrest of the arsonist, and I thought you should be the first to know. Besides the Saturday benefit auction information, the reward will headline today's edition of the newspaper. I have no doubt the media flocking in to cover this second barn burning will have to quote the lowly *Home Valley News* on that. Now let me take a guess, Nate," he went on before Nate could thank him for offering the reward. "You're looking for information on the Yoder boy at the Buggy Wheel—well, not a boy by Amish standards."

"Did you know him well? I assume he left the Buggy Wheel Shop when he was shunned."

"Right on that. For someone Amish, Jacob was really volatile. Low tolerance for criticism, and I'd say shunning—their so-called *meidung*—is the ultimate criticism from his people. The boy got way out of line messing with a car theft ring and who knows what else. Not sure what Sarah Kauffman saw in him—an independent spirit, maybe."

"Volatile," Nate repeated, not responding to the who-knows-what-else or the comment on Sarah. "You don't have a forwarding address for him, do you?"

"I doubt if even his parents do, but I'll give you their address, in case you want to chat with them, too. Of course, you can always ask Sarah Kauffman more about him."

Not biting on that, either—Nate was starting to think Peter was quite a manipulator, but then a lot of what he called media mavens were skilled at spin—he took the page Peter ripped off a small spiral notebook. In taut back-slanted script—the man was left-handed—he'd scribbled an address on County Line Road.

"Thanks," Nate said. "And I'll see you tomorrow morning just to chat about how you see this whole barn-burning situation. You're obviously a great pair of eyes and ears around here."

"That I am. Eyes, ears—and mouth," he said with a little laugh. Despite the lack of traffic on Main Street, the portly man looked both ways before he crossed toward his newspaper office. On the glass windows of the brick building was marked in big, bold print—black shadowed with gold—Home Valley News, Peter Clawson, Owner/Editor-in-Chief.

10

It was a real parade of interesting men today, Ray-Lynn thought as she had a cup of sweet tea when the crowd slowed around ten-thirty, before the lunch rush. Not that Peter was intriguing to her, but he was a mover and a shaker and, despite lower subscription numbers for his newspaper, he evidently still had money to burn with that reward for information he was putting up. At last she'd gotten a close-up gander at that good-looking-in-a-kind-of-rough-and-hungry-way Nate MacKenzie. And now, here came Jack.

"Morning, Sheriff," she greeted from the front booth where she'd been sitting by herself to catch her breath, now trying not to be breathless at the fact he was here, for once off his precious schedule. Why, you'd think the man was still a marine drill sergeant. "A second breakfast or just coffee?" she asked. "Your usual counter spot?"

"If you don't mind, I'll just sit with you—coffee only."

When she nodded, he slid in across from her. Fortunately, Leah Schwartz came over with the coffeepot so Ray-Lynn didn't have to get up to wait on him.

"Everything okay?" she asked, trying not to sound concerned. If nothing else, she'd love to get something out of him about the arson investigation he and Nate MacKenzie were working on. "I'm sure you're busy with the second arson and more news media in town."

"Yeah, well—thanks, Leah," he told the girl when she poured his coffee. She widened her eyes at Ray-Lynn and beat a quick retreat. "The thing is, it's a case, and one that means so much to the Amish, of course— and so to me. They're the backbone of this community and, like you, I admire them a lot, so I want to catch the firebug fast, before he does more damage."

Ray-Lynn sat still as stone, her mind racing. As many times as they'd chatted, he'd never opened up to her like this. Here he was admitting his deepest frustrations, trusting her with his problems. Should she let up on the purely professional facade she'd erected toward him lately—the fence, as Sarah had put it?

"I'm sure you and the arson investigator will solve this. You—are you thinking the arsonist might be Amish and that will upset the Amish?"

"Don't know. Could be. I know the crowds that are coming in are good for your restaurant and other businesses, but I'm having to spend too much time on PR and riding herd on traffic to focus on helping Mac-Kenzie."

Her jaw could have dropped into her tea. Jack Freeman admitting he was upset? That he was anything but in total control? And unburdening himself to her as if he wanted her opinion or support?

"Do you or Nate have any leads?" she dared to ask,

wanting to reach over to cover his clenched hands with hers. He hadn't taken one swallow of his coffee. "You know—thinking the arsons are hate crimes against the Amish or something like that. There was a rumor that even the FBI might be sent in. Surely, you and Nate MacKenzie can handle things without that complication."

"They won't be called in unless the arsonist causes fatalities. Interesting that he or she—it's usually young white males, from what I've been reading up on it— hasn't even caused the death of a farm animal."

"Oh, great, an arsonist with a heart, with a soft spot for the Amish whose livelihoods he's ruining."

"Yeah. Well, sorry I dumped all this on you. I know you've been extra busy in here lately. I could tell."

He looked up from the coffee cup he'd been studying as if he could read the future in it. She glanced down into her tea—no tea leaves to read.

"I'm really glad you stopped by when it wasn't so busy," she told him. "And that you told me how you feel. It will be just between us, and that's a promise. However many folks I talk to every day, I'm good at keeping confidences."

She watched him drain his coffee cup in a couple of quick swallows. When he went for his wallet, she shook her head and reached out to stay his hand.

"It's on me," she said, wishing her voice didn't catch so it sounded as if she was upset or hesitant. "You do so much for all of us, make us and me feel safe."

He cleared his throat. "I really appreciate it, Ray-Lynn, appreciate you," he said, his voice gruff as he slid out of the booth, retrieved his hat from the wall peg and went out the door. But he did give a quick look back.

* * *

Nate's frustrating lack of progress continued at the Buggy Wheel Shop. Despite learning a lot about how they actually customized the buggy interiors for Amish buyers, he hadn't learned much about Jacob Yoder. Maybe that was because he'd been shunned, maybe because he'd kept to himself and had worked hard despite getting in with the wrong bunch of "moderns" after work—he got that much out of Jacob's former coworkers.

Since that didn't take long, Nate decided to drive out to see if Jacob's parents could throw any light on things. He was so used to having Sarah tell him where to find something around here it took him a minute to remember to just use his GPS to find County Line Road. When he got there, he found a long, hilly road with lots of mailboxes bearing the same names—Miller, Garber and Yoder—but he had the exact address.

Despite that, he drove past the place at first. Unlike the Amish properties he'd seen nearer to town, the small, gray frame house looked run-down. No barn, no outbuildings, no *grossdaadi haus*. But then it had no electric or phone lines running into it, either, no lightning rods. A buggy was almost hidden out back by the small garage that could house a horse. He never should have assumed that all the Amish around here were prosperous farmers.

It reminded him not to stereotype anyone he met here or anywhere else—including the typical profile for an arsonist, one he knew so well. Young, white male, age seventeen to mid-twenties; poor relationship with his father; an overprotective mother; weak social skills;

employed in low-paying jobs; possibly above-average intelligence but only poor to fair academic performance.

He turned around in the next driveway and went back to the house, parking on the driveway in front. He saw a white-capped woman glance out through the green curtains, then disappear. A bearded Amish man came to the front door, even before he knocked. At least they were both home, a break he hadn't had lately.

He introduced himself and showed his credentials, but they seemed to know who he was. After all, VERA always announced him. The Yoders—he had a feeling they both looked older than they were—sat on their sagging maroon couch, facing him as he sat in a wooden armchair.

"I realize your son, Jacob, is not part of the community right now, but I was hoping you could give me an idea where to find him. As you know, he phoned in the first barn fire and was a witness to it, so I'd like to get his description of it."

"What you know about Jacob, I'm not sure," his father said. "But in a shunning, even the family doesn't have anything to do with him."

"I understand that. But he could be living with friends you might have known or maybe you've heard where he's employed right now."

Mr. Yoder shook his head. "He phoned the fire in from the Kauffman farm. He was at the Kauffman farm that night." His expression didn't vary from a stony frown.

"Yes, he had stopped there either because he saw a lot of people at the party or perhaps wanted to see Sarah Kauffman."

"He shouldn't bother her. She broke it off before he was shunned."

Jacob's mother spoke for the first time. "It might have been one of the things that made him angry—then he made mistakes, hanging out with the wrong sort. Made the sheriff get after him."

"I understand the sheriff went to bat for him, though, didn't file charges that could have meant prison time."

Mr. Yoder nodded. Mrs. Yoder began to cry silently, blinking back her tears but not wiping them away. "He was a good boy," she said. "Worked hard. He is—was— our only child, you see."

That really surprised Nate. He hadn't come across a small Amish family yet. So, the only child would have been especially treasured by the mother. Maybe his father had been strict with him and the boy had resented it, but he was reading into things here.

Feeling he had walked into another dead end in a maze, Nate excused himself and got up to leave. Mr. Yoder accompanied him out onto the front porch.

"Mr. Yoder, a fairly good source told me that Jacob was volatile. Did he have a temper?"

The man sighed and glanced out at VERA. He closed the door behind him and led Nate away from the house before he spoke. "When crossed, *ya*. His mother—God help us—she spoiled him some. I guess Sarah did, too, at first. I pray you can find him and get him help if he needs it, Mr. MacKenzie—help for his head. I been trying to decide to come see you or not."

Nate's heart rate jumped. "About what, Mr. Yoder? Do you know something that might help protect your fellow churchmen's barns?"

"Only that the boy used to like to burn the trash in

the big barrel out back. And lit our cellar door afire with matches once when he didn't get his way and—" he gave a big sniff and wiped his nose with his sleeve "—carried around with him in his buggy one of those fancy fireplace lighters you just hit a button on and a flame comes out. We been a'praying it's not him, Mr. MacKenzie."

"The red car he drives—do you know its license plate number?"

"No, but I bet you can find out."

"I will and hope to find Jacob, too. Thank you for your honesty, Mr. Yoder. I can tell you love your son."

"The prodigal," he said. "But if he comes home, can't say I'd kill the fatted calf for him. I also been a'praying I wouldn't want to kill him instead, putting his mother through all this."

What an admission from an Amish man, Nate thought. Finally, he had a solid lead and prime suspect.

Nate texted an ASAP request to his office in Columbus for Jacob Yoder's license plate number before he drove into the Kauffman driveway. Despite the graying sky that Sarah had mentioned might mean rain, she had finished chalking the outline for her quilt square and had drawn some diagonal lines through the space.

As efficient and prompt as ever, she had her horse hitched to the buggy, so he parked VERA behind the barn instead of driving way back in by the pond. He'd been agonizing over how much to ask her about Jacob. Both Peter Clawson and Mr. Yoder had suggested he should, so why had he been hesitating? Was it the fact that she must have once cared deeply for Jacob that bothered him? It was a battle to keep things professional around her.

"Here," he said, getting his thinking back on track. He produced a handheld two-way radio that looked more like a cell phone. "Let me show you how to use this, in case you need to call me. But as I said, if I'm on the road with VERA, I'll have to put the antenna down that receives, so it might not work then—unless there are none of these beautiful hills between us. At least this is a broad valley."

Hills between us...a broad valley... There was so much that stood between the two of them. He had to stop thinking of her in personal ways, he lectured himself again as he demonstrated how to use the two-way, then walked back to VERA and took a practice call from her. Needless to say, she caught on right away as she did with almost everything.

"I've got chicken sandwiches and some lemonade," she told him as he came around the barn to join her again. "They're in a basket on the backseat, so you can serve while I drive. That's one thing about a horse and buggy. You can safely eat and drive."

She sounded nervous and her cheeks were flushed. Maybe it wasn't a good idea for him to go out with her like this, but he needed her help—talk time alone—and her father had okayed it. "Sounds great. Which barn first?"

"I was going to start with the Hostetler barn farther out, but considering the darkening sky, I think we should go to Levi Miller's first. Besides, that's closer to where I saw someone in the dark with your night glasses in case we want to look in that meadow. Upteyup," she said to Sally.

They pulled away, then slowed as her sister Lizzie ran out with a small sack of fresh-baked half-moon pies for them. She and her mother were still baking as many as possible to sell at the benefit auction the day after tomorrow. Maybe Jacob Yoder would show up for that, he thought. Surely, it would be a mix of the Amish and the English. But if he could get his license plate number, he could ask Sheriff Freeman to keep an eye out for him in this entire area. Nate and the sheriff had plans to join forces but, of necessity, they'd both been checking separate leads on this case so far.

Nate was really impressed with the interior of Sarah's buggy, as customized as those he'd seen being made in the Buggy Wheel Shop. Hers had roll-down leather curtains, a polished splashboard where a dashboard would be in a car, a hand brake that would rub against the tires, battery-operated front lights and turn signals and an emerald-green, crushed-velvet front seat.

"So how do you like the eight-to-ten-miles-per-hour pace of the buggy compared to racing around in VERA?" Sarah asked between bites of her chicken sandwich. Nate sat behind her as her father had instructed, but he was leaning forward and, despite the rising breeze, she could feel his breath and smell that clean, pine scent he always had on him. Would it linger in her buggy after he was gone?

"It sure gives me time to take in the scenery. Beautiful."

He no doubt meant outside the buggy, but she felt herself blush, anyway. "So, any luck with finding out who wrote that note?" she asked.

"Do Amish kids learn to print and write cursive in school?"

"*Ya*—yes. Because of the Bible reference, you think it was written by one of my people?"

"Or former people."

"Not Hannah again!"

"Probably not. Can you tell me anything about Jacob's personality?"

"A good worker but ambitious for more and fast. Maybe," she admitted, "that's one thing that drew us together at first. But, like I said, he got in with some bad people."

"So I heard. I talked to his parents."

"Oh. Can you locate him?"

"Nope, though I'm hoping to trace him through his license plate if I can get it from the Bureau of Motor Vehicles in Columbus."

"I have a better idea. You can get it from Gabe."

"Gabe?"

"He has a real talent for remembering numbers, working with numbers. All the *youngie liet rumspringa* boys were in love with Jacob's red car—bet you know what I mean. Gabe will know."

"I should have known to ask you first, Sarah, my Amish translator."

"So you feel like a foreigner here?"

"Less and less, thanks to you."

"Even with our technology gap? My people do use technology when it suits them, when it allows us to keep the family together, which things like TVs would not."

"Keep the family together— A worthy goal."

"Do you have family, other than your foster mother?"

"No, so I envy you that, the big, close families. My

biological parents died in a fire—an arson—when I was eight."

"Oh, Nate! So that's why—"

"Yeah, I guess so. The thing is, my own father set it."

"No! I'm so sorry," she cried, turning to face him, so close her bonnet hit his cheek, their noses almost bumped, their lips nearly brushed. "I'm so very sorry," she repeated.

"Yeah, me, too, for my loss of them, my mother, at least. My dad was a murderer, actually, though he didn't intend to be. I'm sure he meant to save us. He died of smoke inhalation. A fireman pulled me out, but my mother was burned too badly and died at the hospital. So, even setting the fire, my father didn't know what the heck he was doing. He set it up all wrong, trapped himself and us inside, waited too long to get us out—an insurance scam that went wrong. I don't know, maybe I'm trying to make up for him as much as I'm trying to fight arsons for myself.

"A childless couple," he went on, "Jim and Mary Ellen Bosley—I call her M.E.—who lived down the street, took me in. They were very loving, but I was bitter, really a brat at times. They stuck with me, wanted to adopt me but I said no, and now I regret that."

His voice broke, but he continued. "Jim Bosley passed away a few years ago, and I still see M.E. often and call her when I can. I should see her more than I do, but she still lives on the street where I grew up, so I get her to come to me or to meet me at a restaurant or somewhere. Once I left I never wanted to go back because I still can't bear to see the vacant lot where it all happened.

"Sarah," he said, almost leaning his chin on her shoulder when she turned away to watch the road again as they neared a stop sign, "I had a doting mother and a distant, thoughtless father I resented—my real parents, I mean. That's often how an arsonist is made. Not me, obviously, but do you think that could be the case with Jacob's parents, him being an only child and all?"

"Could be," she whispered. "I'm regretful that was the way it was for you, and I'd say that was true of him."

The minute they turned onto curving Orchard Road, the traffic picked up. Despite the road's picturesque name, it led to the interstate. Though Sarah kept the buggy well over, partly on the berm, Nate got really nervous as cars came close, then roared past, usually with people craning their necks to see who was in the buggy. Most drivers were respectful; however, a few honked. One yelled, "Get a life! And a car!" At least Sarah and Sally seemed to be used to that. The slow pace, which he had begun to savor, now put him on edge. No wonder buggy-car crashes were another cross the Amish had to bear.

"There it is," Sarah told him, waiting for several cars to pass so they could turn left. "The Miller house and old barn."

Yeah, Nate thought, it was the barn with the quilt square he'd seen when he first drove into town, and he'd been so intrigued by it he hadn't noticed how run-down the place was.

"It would make a great moody painting with that cloudy gray sky behind it," Sarah was saying, "a study in soft, muted grays with only the bright quilt square standing out, but I'd like to put some people and horses in it, too."

Moody was putting it kindly, Nate thought. To him, Levi Miller's farm looked like a scene from an old Alfred Hitchcock movie, almost a replica of the Bates house from *Psycho*. An old Victorian peeling paint, an antique barn that hadn't been kept up, though that was highlighted by Sarah's bright square painted in glowing blue, green and gold. How unkempt the property was, even to an uncut lawn and scraggly bushes. This was the second lesson he'd had today that the Amish were not all prosperous or industrious—in this case, not even good farmers.

As if Sarah had read his mind—a dangerous precedent—she said, "He doesn't have much land, and he's not really suited for farming like some of the men. The square is painted on this barn not only because he's a church deacon, but because it's on this road, which is busier than most. Tourist buses come this way from I-77, and it's the first square they see in Home Valley and on a traditional barn, though it's seen better days. I've heard tell tourists don't even notice the house or condition of the barn when they see the square."

"I can attest to that," he said. It was the closest he had ever heard her come to praising her own work, though she was just stating a fact. "So what's the name of this one?" he asked. "It's a beauty."

"Crown of Thorns. You know, like the Lord's enemies put on His head before they crucified Him."

"Let's hope that's not a bad omen. I keep thinking how your Tumbling Blocks design was painted on a now tumbled-down barn. Do you think there's any connection between the patterns painted and what's happened, though I don't exactly get Robbing Peter to Pay Paul on the Esh barn."

"I've thought about that, but I just don't know. As I said, some of my people think my work is too showy. But burning barns for that reason? It's too far-fetched."

"You'd be surprised what is and isn't far-fetched when it comes to investigating a sick crime like arson. It looks like no one's home, and I was hoping to tell Levi Miller that he needs to at least stay home after dark. So far, *that* is part of the pattern, that the arsonist strikes when the place is deserted, but probably just so he won't be seen and stopped."

Sarah reined the horse in by the barn door, but when Nate gestured her on, she pulled around to the side so they would be hidden from the road. "If the Millers aren't here," he said, "let's look around, anyway, and I'll leave them a note."

They got out and walked around the barn, just as it began to rain. It was as if the gray sky, even the faded gray barn, were crying on them, he thought.

"Hey, what's that?" he asked, pointing at three, small, furry bodies on the ground—without heads. Tiny pools of crimson blood indicated the little animals had bled out. They seemed to be arranged in a trail, leading around the next corner of the barn.

"Dead voles, I think. Barn owls or hawks sometimes behead them," she said, her voice shaky as she backed up into him, and he put his hands on her shoulders to steady her.

Together, they peered around the corner at the back of the barn. Suddenly, Nate needed steadying, too. A few more small, headless vole bodies were strewn there.

And someone—sure as heck not a barn owl or a hawk—
had scrawled in red on the back of the barn the bold,
printed words Mack—Keep Away!

11

"Is that blood?" Sarah asked as they stared at the writing, which was already starting to smear in the rain. Despite getting wetter, they both bent close to study it. "That much blood couldn't come from those dead little animals," she added, her voice shaky.

Nate touched a letter and lifted his fingers to his nose to sniff at it. "It's not clotting and there's no copper smell. It's paint. Fairly fresh."

"It's probably latex, like I use, but I avoid red, the color—" her voice faded as she thought again of Jacob's red car "—of martyrs' blood."

They straightened, both glancing behind and around, but the rain had closed them in like a curtain. When they retraced their steps toward the front of the barn, Sarah couldn't see the Miller house or the woodlot nearby, where someone could easily hide. They both jumped when a bolt of lightning flashed and thunder cracked too close.

They hurried toward where they'd left the buggy. Sally neighed and tugged at the traces. The whites of her eyes showed as she tossed her head. Sarah felt that frenzied, too. Despite the cover of the rain, she had the feeling they were being watched, but she didn't want Nate to think she was a coward or didn't have faith in the Lord's protection. "Sally doesn't like lightning," was all she said.

"Neither do firefighters. First that Bible warning to you and your people. Now this one looks aimed at me. Mack must mean MacKenzie. The writer must know darn well I'm not going to keep away. But keep away from what? Let's get the buggy inside the barn."

"Right. The Millers won't mind. If the arsonist left that message, he—"

"Or she..."

"—seems to know your schedule. He must have figured you would check the two other barns that have paintings. I wonder if there's a similar message on the Hostetler barn in case you went there." A rolling rumble of thunder shuddered through her as she led Sally inside.

"Or did he or she follow us, pass us on the road and paint it just as we drove up? We couldn't see the back of the barn from the road. The bastard—pardon my French—"

"That's English. Strong English."

"I was going to say it looks like the arsonist has been watching me—or you."

Nate's voice was clipped, and he looked tense and angry. That made her feel even more afraid. He was supposed to be the strong one with the answers, to be in charge here.

Nate glanced around the dim barn and rubbed his palms on the front of his jeans. "Being stalked gives me the creeps," he admitted, "about as much as knowing he or she is out there waiting to ignite another barn. We wouldn't be inside this one if it wasn't pouring hard enough that it would be difficult to start a fire right now. But if the arsonist is following us, we may be able to set a trap later." He kept staring at her as if waiting for something.

Sarah was suddenly aware of how she looked. Though she'd shaken her skirts, they clung to her legs just the way his shirt did to him. The only thing that was dry was her hair and face under her *kapp* and bonnet. Sally stamped and snorted even as the rumbling thunder grew more muted, but the skies kept pouring rain. It drummed so hard on the barn roof that it sounded like hoofbeats on a wooden covered bridge. She had to say something to break the screaming silence between the two of them. Her pulse pounded harder than the rattle of the rain.

"Do you think my grandmother may have actually seen someone lurking outside our *grossdaadi haus?*" she asked as she brushed drops off her sleeves. "Not a monster with glowing eyes like she said, of course, but I've been thinking we'd better believe her about seeing someone since that Bible note appeared. Still, she does imagine things at times. Nate, the reason she acts afraid of you is that she's haunted by the persecution our ancestors faced in Europe, especially burnings for our faith. It—it kind of haunts me, too, sometimes, all of us. She thinks you're the government official coming to take us away, to burn us out, burn us. I thought I'd better tell you that."

"You've been tremendous through all this, helpful and honest."

"Good," was all she could manage, when she wanted to say something better and wiser. "Good."

He came close and put his hands on her wet shoulders. She put her hands around his wrists, not only to touch him but to prop herself up. She wanted him to hold her; she felt he knew that. Her lips tingled.

They had not closed the barn doors, so the wind whipped in, chilling their wet clothes. He let go of her and went over to slide the barn doors closed. At the grating sound—or at the idea of being sealed in here with Nate—she went all shivery with goose bumps.

Just before he slid the door shut, a whoosh and a swoop of air slapped them as a big-winged body swept past and out into the rain.

Sarah let out a shriek, and Nate ducked. "Oh," she said, "it's just a great horned owl flying out. She's probably the one that killed the voles, though she hardly lined them up that way. I'll bet she's feeding nestlings inside here."

"I'll leave the doors cracked for her, then. Speaking of which, my crackberry is vibrating."

"Your phone?" she asked, rubbing her hands up and down her arms. It was good to talk of something rational, something normal.

"Phone and more," he said, digging it out of his front jeans pocket. "Email, weather, global positioning, everything. I'll show you later. It's really called a Black-Berry, but it's so addictive that it gets the nickname crackberry—you know, from crack…cocaine."

She shook her head and shrugged as he answered the phone. It was a reminder to her that they came from two separate worlds. He had to talk loudly over the storm, so she knew it was his boss and something about Jacob's license plate. Could her former fiancé be doing all this? Yes, she was almost starting to think—to fear—he could. Surely, Jacob had seen Nate's name in the *Home Valley News,* and he might figure he was called Mack instead of Nate. Could that Keep Away on the sign mean for Nate to keep away from this area or to keep away from her?

"That phone kind of runs your life," she told him when he punched a button and put it away. "It makes a crack in daily living, is that it?"

"Not exactly—kind of. Sarah, the Bureau of Motor Vehicles for the state says that there's no Jacob Yoder who has a license plate registered in this county or any other in Ohio. He must be driving with stolen plates, maybe ones he got when he was running with that auto theft ring. I'll take your advice and talk to Gabe when we get back to see if he knows the plate number."

To their amazement, the huge owl flew back in with a small snake in its beak, tilting to get through the door. They watched her glide into the side bay, then heard bloodcurdling screams.

"That can't be the snake! What in the—" Nate muttered, seizing her arm and spinning them around as if he would protect her from something.

"That's the nestlings, the baby owls," she told him.

He nodded. "Sarah, don't ever feel you don't understand my world—my tools of the trade," he said, patting his pocket where he'd put his phone. "I'm a babe in the woods when it comes to things you know, so—"

And then they heard the knocking.

But from where? Nate thought. What was that? Sure as heck not the owls. Outside or inside the barn? It seemed to be coming from the other side of the back wall where there was no window except high in the loft. His imagination ran wild. Was someone leaning a ladder against the barn, then moving it along? The arsonist had started one fire high, using window access. On the other hand, it could be a trap to lure them outside. He'd mentioned setting a trap, but could their enemy be one step ahead of them on that, too? Then again, it could be that the wind had shifted and a branch was knocking there or, in this ramshackle old barn, something had come loose to bang in the wind. The place had a hundred chilly drafts and strange fits of air movement.

He put his mouth close to Sarah's bonnet and whispered, "Close the door the rest of the way, but don't bar it in case we need to get out fast. I'm going up into the loft to look out that window, down toward where we saw the message."

"But what's that sound?"

"I hope it's a tree limb in the wind, but I'm not betting on it. Go."

She did as he said while he quickly climbed the rickety ladder to the loft. It was dark up here; the rain pounded overhead, closer, louder. As he felt his way along under the big roof beams, his eyes adjusted to the dark. Wan light seeped through the patched roof that had sprouted numerous leaks. The old floorboards creaked under his weight and once he felt the entire floor of the loft shudder. Cobwebs laced themselves across his wet face and snagged in his eyelashes. Half expecting he'd be peering out through the paned window into the face of an arsonist on a ladder, he pressed his nose to the glass, dusty on this side but running with rivulets of water outside. He turned his cheek to it, trying to look down, around.

Suddenly, the knocking stopped. The horrible shrieks had just been owlets, natural sounds, so maybe his tree limb idea was right. He'd scramble down, take a shovel or rake with him for a weapon and go outside to be sure. He wished he had the pistol he kept in VERA, but he'd locked it up there and had shown it to no one in peaceful Amish country.

Man, you're getting spooked by this place, he scolded himself. Creepy house, old barn, bad storm and then that bloodred message smeared on the barn that carried the implied threat Or Else! Did it mean to keep away from this arson case, the Amish or Sarah? And, if the latter, didn't that point to Jacob Yoder again?

He turned to go back downstairs and bumped into someone. It was Sarah, thank God. With the pounding rain, he hadn't heard her come up here.

"Did you see anyth—" she got out before there was a creak, a crack—and the floorboards under them gave way.

Nate grunted and Sarah screamed. He grabbed a beam, grabbed her. Slammed together chins to shins, they dropped partway through the floor, then stuck, suspended at armpit level. Her right arm was splayed along the floor where the rotting boards had given way. Nothing was in reach for him but her.

"Hold on!" he told her. "Hold on to me! Pull your arm in, 'cause we're going down."

As they fell, her black bonnet and cap were ripped away. They dropped amid dust, dripping rain and loose, splintered boards to land in a pile of hay, a tangle of arms, legs, her wet skirts and hair gone wild.

* * *

"You okay?" Nate gasped, lifting his head from their landing.

"In one piece, at least," she said, pulling her thigh-high, mussed skirts and slip down over her bared, white thighs and black stockings. She knew her voice sounded shaky, and it wasn't from the fall or their worsening situation with an enemy. Oh, no, she knew the enemy she struggled with right now was her own *verboten* desire for this man.

"Thank God for this pile of straw," he said.

"Hay. It's really hay."

"Sarah—you're beautiful. We could have been maimed or killed, but you're still teaching me...."

His voice faded and he looked at her intently. "And you *are* beautiful, you know," he whispered. "In lots of ways."

Still watching every move she made, Nate lifted himself on one elbow; his other arm was trapped under her, but he didn't move it. He looked at her, down, up, then deep into her eyes, that stare that always made her feel she was falling off a high ladder. She blinked to get some of the dust out of her watering eyes, which made a double image of Nate, his gaze devouring her.

The hay felt both prickly and soft beneath her bottom, back and limbs. He was so close—it was almost like being in bed with him. Suddenly she was aware of her body in a new, thrilling way. She was beautiful, he had said.... She should jump up, find her bonnet, repin her hair, which was splayed out under her head and shoulders with strands in her mouth that Nate gently drew out in a soft caress across her cheek.

Something was going to happen between them that

should not, but she wanted to know and cherish each moment. She wet her lips, held her breath.

"My boss, your father and Bishop Esh would never approve of any sort of roll in the hay between us," Nate whispered, his face coming so close to hers that his breath almost burned her. "But I can't help this."

And then he tilted his face slightly to the side, lowered his head slowly, as if to give her time to turn away, and kissed her.

Smooching, her people called it. But this was entirely new, like nothing she'd had with Jacob. Spinning, swirling. Had the fall knocked her silly? She lifted her free hand to touch the side of Nate's face, the crisp, damp hair at his temples, his earlobe, the strong back of his neck as the kiss went on. She opened her lips for him and only moaned when his hand, trapped beneath her hip, moved, caressed the curve of her there, then slid slowly up her waist and rib cage, over her breasts to pause before coming up to cup her chin. His head had jerked a bit. He'd sniffed in a sharp breath. She'd bet he'd never known Amish women didn't wear bras—that is, not until now.

Every part of her seemed to come alive at his touch. And still the kiss went on, moving, deepening. He might be hovering on top, but she met him halfway until their entire bodies were pressed together as hard as their mouths. He rolled them over, her up and around until he was on top again. A roll in the hay, he had said. They breathed in unison, then she could hardly breathe at all, before he slowly—reluctantly, she could tell—came up for air.

"I should say I'm sorry, but I'm not," he whispered, his voice deep and raspy.

"*Ya,* me neither."

"I want to look around outside. We've got to go back."

"Right. This barn could have burned down around us and we would not have noticed."

He grinned, then chuckled. "I love an honest woman."

"Don't say that—love."

"You know what I mean. I just—what's that sound now?"

"A buggy."

"Going or coming? I've got to go look."

He brushed himself off as he got up, but she saw pieces of hay clung to his back. He hurried past Sally and the buggy to the door. She heard him slide it open a little.

"It must be the Millers are home and going right to their house," he reported as she struggled to pin up her hair. He came back and watched her do it. She wished she was taking it down for him, not just stuffing it up under her *kapp* and the bonnet he retrieved for her and dusted off. Oh, why did this have to happen, because she felt doubly endangered now, by the arsonist and by her own feelings for this *ausländer* who would all too soon, unless there were more fires, take his VERA and go home.

After brushing all the hay off each other, they went to explain to the Millers some of what had happened in the barn. While Sarah waited in the house, in the lessening rain, Nate and Levi, and the Millers' oldest boy, Noah, went out to examine the broken loft floor and the back of the barn. They found the threatening words washed off and a maple tree limb that looked like it could have hit the back wall. When they returned to the house, Nate said they had seen the diluted, crimson paint along the edge of the barn's foundation. But Sarah had something to tell him, too.

"Nate, Mrs. Miller says when they pulled up just before we joined them, they found a note from Sheriff Freeman pinned to their front door."

His eyebrows rose. "From the sheriff? Pinned how?"

"Not with a basting pin—a thumb tack."

"Could I see the note?"

Sarah watched him stare long and hard at it, just as she had. It was in bold print, but not necessarily a match for the note she'd found. It was on lined, yellow legal-pad paper, not white letter paper. Besides, Sheriff Freeman as a suspect? Too crazy. The note simply urged the Millers to be sure they stayed home after dark and kept a good eye on their barn.

"Which we would do, anyway," Levi assured them with a nod as he pointed at the written warning. "Got a good notion to sleep out there with my hunting rifle, broken ribs or not I got from fighting the Esh fire. But Noah's nineteen now, so he could take a turn guarding the place, too. The barn's broken down, but it's all we got now with no money to rebuild."

Sarah had once known Noah well, for he'd been a close buddy of Jacob's, but she hadn't seen him for months. She supposed Noah missed the shunned Jacob, because he'd really looked up to him.

"So," Nate said to Sarah as they took their leave and headed away in the buggy in what was now only light mist, "I keep getting surprised about the Amish. Levi might shoot at a person rather than turning the other cheek. Jacob's father said he'd struggled not to want to kill his son for what he'd done to his mother and…" he said, looking sideways at her with a little crimp on the side of his mouth.

"And I kissed you as good as you did me. See, Nathan MacKenzie, you're finding out the Home Valley Amish are not some kind of saints but human. That sign on the barn said you should stay away, but I'd be real sad if you did."

12

Early the next morning, Nate hunched over his computer screen in VERA, parked out by the pond. He was searching for other possible arsons started by artificial fireplace logs, but he was having a hard time keeping his mind on his work. Surprised to hear a car engine close by, he glanced out and saw the sheriff's car. As Nate walked to meet him, Jack Freeman parked at the edge of the pond, got out, slammed the door and sloshed through the puddles toward VERA.

Nate had turned down an invitation from Sarah to join her family for breakfast. It wasn't so much that he couldn't face the Kauffmans after his passionate encounter with Sarah but that he'd already planned to eat at the Dutch Farm Table. He hoped to find Peter Clawson there so he could speak with him casually before they had their appointment. He had some things to bounce off that quick brain of his.

"Sheriff, I could have come in if you'd phoned," Nate said, extending his hand. "I know you're busy."

"That I am," he said as they shook hands. It was a

firm shake, almost too hard. He still wore the plastic
rain cover over his wide-brimmed hat, though it had
stopped raining sometime overnight.

"Anything new, Sheriff?" Nate asked.

"How about you call me Jack, Nate? Naw, nothing really new. I just thought we should touch bases
again, 'cause I can't see much progress, especially with
that second arson making us look bad. Thanks for the
voice mail about that note left on the Kauffmans' *grossdaadi haus* door and the one on Levi Miller's barn. I'm
keeping an eye out for Jacob Yoder's car, license plate
number or not. A red sports car really sticks out around
here. I took a look in the woodlot where he and his buddies had hidden those hot cars, but no sign of him there.
We got to catch us a break somehow."

"At least we know the Amish aren't hiding him, not
even his parents."

"You probably heard I covered for that boy, but I
won't again. If he's the one behind this, I'll kick myself
for getting him off scot-free, however hard his own
people came down on him."

"I understand. When dealing with the Amish, it
seems right to handle some things—well, differently,"
Nate said, wishing he hadn't touched Sarah and yet glad
he did. It felt so good to have her holding on to him,
her arms around him when they fell, her strong but soft
body pressed against his. No question, he was falling
for Sarah.

"By the way," Jack was saying, "I also hit the
Hostetler house with a warning, but they were planning to do a night watch, anyway. So—Jacob still your
number one suspect? He's mine right now."

"My interview with his parents indicated he has not

only motive and opportunity, but the background for arson. I felt really bad for them. I'd suggest we don't both question them, if you're thinking of that. They're really agonized over this."

"See—you've learned to care about the Amish, too, and you've only been here a few days. So what's your next move?"

"I had a short chat with Peter Clawson at the Dutch Farm Table, but I'm going to pick his brain—definitely a close observer of things around here."

"Peter's not only an asset to the community but sometimes an ass, too. Nothing's privileged information with him, so don't trust him with any inside intel," Jack said, pointing an index finger for emphasis. "Just a word to the wise on that. See you later and keep in touch."

"Will do, Jack. Thanks!" Nate called after him as he got back in his cruiser and slowly drove out.

Keep in touch, Nate thought. He'd do that for sure because both Jack Freeman and, he hoped, Peter Clawson were great sources of information and support. He'd rather keep in touch with Sarah in more ways than one, but he knew he shouldn't.

As Nate looked off into the distance, he saw Gabe walking down the lane, carrying something in a sack. He realized he hadn't mentioned to Jack that Gabe might know Jacob's license plate number, or that he had a hunch the boy had kept something back from him about the night of the first fire. He could only hope that, like Jack had miscalculated when protecting Jacob, he himself hadn't screwed up by not grilling Gabe harder—yet.

* * *

After her usual Friday run to the restaurant to drop off half-moon pies, Sarah was on the road again. She was heading Sally back toward the Schrocks' house with potato salad and pulled pork sandwiches for them and, of course, some pies. She had given half a dozen little pies to Gabe to take to Nate so they could talk privately about Jacob's license plate. And, she'd grabbed a few extras to drop off to Mike Getz and Cindee Kramer. *Mamm* said she didn't mind since she'd made so many for the auction and the barbecue.

The little gift for Cindee was the perfect excuse to get a glimpse of their back area to see if the Schrock barn could be easily spotted from there. Sarah would be able to tell if Mike was home, since their garage was so full of junk that they always parked in their small front yard. And if his truck was there, she wasn't going near the place.

Truth be told, God forgive her if she was wrong, she was hoping the arsonist was Mike Getz, just so it wasn't Jacob or anyone Amish. She didn't like the way Nate kept insisting the barn burner could be a woman. It just couldn't be Hannah, and Sarah had to convince Nate of that.

Surely Cindee's comments about Mike being able to handle the electric grill starter one-handed and the fact he knew the Schrocks were away from home meant he could be the arsonist. If the Schrock barn could not be seen from the area where Mike claimed he saw it, she sure meant to tell Nate.

Sarah kept Sally going at a good pace, because she planned to get back home soon. Some other buggies were on the road, taking folks to work. Both Mike and

Cindee should be at work, so she felt quite safe. No one was going to scare her away from doing her tasks and helping Nate, too. The arsonist was a coward, one who only did his deeds in the dark.

She saw Cindee's old car and not Mike's truck, so she pulled into their driveway. Cindee must be going into work later. Rainwater sat deep in the ditches along both sides of Fish Creek Road, but their raised blacktop driveway was dry.

Taking out the sack of pastries, Sarah climbed down and hustled around back instead of going to the front door. Because of their garage, she couldn't see the black skeleton of the burned barn, but maybe she could farther on. But no—the moment she stepped into their backyard, she could see that either Mike had lied to Cindee, or he'd spotted the fire from another position. Or maybe he'd gone over on foot to start the fire and then came back to call it in. He had called 9-1-1 quite early, and that saved the structure from the complete destruction that had ruined the Esh barn. He was a hero again. But shouldn't Cindee have known he didn't tell her the straight story?

On the other hand, what beef could Mike Getz possibly have against the Eshes or the Amish in general? Hopefully, he wasn't one of those Amish bashers who resented that her people were different. He might be a bit of what they called a redneck. But maybe an arsonist who started and fought fires for the thrill of it didn't need to hold any grudges against those he harmed.

Sarah saw the grill was an old, yellow-glazed brick structure, not a pit and not a metal one like many of the moderns and Amish used, the kind the Plain People would haul to the schoolhouse for the charity barbecue and auction. But she didn't see any fire starters here. Of course, he could have taken them inside with all the rain.

"Lookin' for something?" came a loud male voice behind her.

Startled, she spun to face Mike Getz.

"Sarah said I should bring you out some moon pies and that you wanted to ask me something," Gabe told Nate.

"You want to sit down in the front seat of VERA to talk?" Nate asked.

"Oh, yeah, sure."

"Want one of these moon pies?"

"*Mamm* said not to eat till dinner, but there's six of them in there."

Nate let Gabe sit in the driver's seat again while he got in the passenger's side. From his belt, he unhooked the two-way radio he kept with him in case Sarah called for some reason. He was wishing she would, not that she'd be in danger in broad daylight on her own family's farm, but just to talk. He put it on the dashboard, then opened the sack and let Gabe take a pastry before he did.

"That's not a tape recorder," he assured the boy. "It a two-way radio, in case your sister calls me."

"*Ya,* okay. I knew that."

They talked with their mouths half-full, just two guys, hanging out. Nate was pleased with the relaxed feeling, not only so Gabe would open up to him but because he really liked the kid. Actually, he hadn't met a Home Valley Amish person he didn't like, but then he hadn't seen Jacob Yoder yet.

Gabe kept his free hand on the steering wheel. Nate had never interrogated a witness here before, especially not one in the driver's seat.

"Sarah mentioned that you were really good at math—at numbers," Nate said. "You happen to remember the license plate number of Jacob Yoder's red car?"

Gabe nodded. "RGE 1297."

Nate took his notebook from his pocket and scribbled it down.

"You gonna drive VERA around to look for him?" Gabe asked.

"You got any ideas where I could look if I took you along?"

"Only what I heard."

"Which is?"

"It's not nearby. Just that he has a couple of English friends. Up I-77, halfway to Cleveland. I haven't been there, but I heard the general area." He told Nate the route to cut off from the highway, even the intersection where Jacob might have a friend.

"You're a big help, Gabe. Also, I was hoping there was something else—anything would help—that you might recall from the night of the first fire when you were near the Esh barn. I could keep all of it or some of it privileged information," he said, pointedly putting his notebook away. "But I'd really appreciate your help."

"Like you said before—confidential?"

"Absolutely."

Gabe sighed and wiped the hand he'd been eating with on his pants before he touched the steering wheel with it. He gripped it so hard his fingers went white at the knuckles.

"Well," he said, "Barbara Lantz and I were in the Esh

barn that night, in the loft, but we didn't do anything wrong—not about the fire, I mean."

"I believe that. So can you help me out? Anything you saw or heard could give me a key clue."

The boy's cheeks had gone bright red again. "At first we weren't really paying attention—about what was going on outside."

Nate bit his lower lip and waited. He knew more was coming. It struck him that this boy was trying to express how he himself had felt when he was with Sarah in the Miller barn.

"But then I heard a car and thought it was funny—strange—so I looked out. And I saw someone get out, check the house first, then walk toward the barn. We heard the barn door open down below us and thought we were gonna get caught."

"It was Jacob Yoder."

"No. At first I couldn't tell who it was, in dark clothes and all. I peeked out through a crack in the haymow door. She was just standing, looking up at the barn, staring up at where—I guess—Sarah's painting must have been. Then she came inside."

"*She*. A woman? Gabe, I need to know who you saw. I won't let on who told me."

Gabe heaved another sigh that shook his shoulders. "When we saw who it was and that she'd know us, we got ourselves down the back ladder to the first floor and out that side door *schnell*—real quick. We ran across the field toward our barn and went in one at a time, so I don't know what happened after that, but I—I been wondering."

"Was it your sister's friend, Hannah Esh?"

He shook his head. "Mrs. Logan. You know, who runs the restaurant in town."

Mike must have just pulled up in front, Sarah thought as her insides lurched. She'd overstepped. She'd risked too much. She was so used to everything being safe around here. And she was so unused to having a phone in the buggy that she'd grabbed the pastry sack but had come back here without what she really needed. Not that she could have phoned Nate for help right in front of Mike Getz, anyway. She'd have to talk her way out of this without a call to Nate.

"I just wanted to see the place you were working about the time you spotted the barn fire," she said, forcing a small smile. "Cindee told me." She was amazed her voice sounded so calm, when he really scared her. He looked big and bulky with his bull neck and his fists clenched at his sides. "I told Mr. Clawson I don't want my picture in the paper for spotting the first fire, but I thought—if you had a good place for a photo somewhere around here—I'd tell him to just use yours for spotting the second one instead."

She knew she was saying too much, but she couldn't help herself. He had her blocked in by the garage, the big brick grill and a board fence. Yet if someone glanced back at the right angle from the road, they could be seen, so he wouldn't dare to hurt her, would he? And wasn't Cindee home?

"You know how my people are about photos and interviews," she rushed on, "but you gave those Cleveland TV reporters such good ones, I was hoping you wouldn't mind more. Only—I didn't want to just ask

Mr. Clawson before I looked around to see if there was
a spot for it."

"I think it'd be better over by the ruins of the barn,"
he said. He still frowned, but he shrugged his big,
rounded shoulders and finally unclenched his fists.
"Yeah, okay by me if Mr. Clawson says so."

"The other thing is," she said, extending her sack
of half-moon pies toward him, "I told Cindee when I
bought paint for another quilt square that I'd bring you
both some of these, so she was expecting me."

"Yeah, well, she had car trouble so we switched for
the day. She's at the hardware store."

"Then please give her these, and I'll be going to drop
things off to the Schrocks. They're expecting me."

He took the sack. "The fire marshal know about this
picture idea?" he asked, still blocking her way out.

"He does know you're a double hero now, so he will
probably be glad to also be interviewed for the story,
if that's what you mean. I guess you know, Mr. Mac-
Kenzie was really impressed with you," she added, and
dared to step closer to him, hoping he'd move back and
let her pass. She figured showing indecision or fear was
not the way to deal with this man, especially since she
now had another piece of proof he could be the arsonist, at least on the second fire.

Sarah could almost hear the wheels of his thoughts
grinding away in that big, bald head. Did he have
enough in his bean to be able to write that note with
the Bible quote? Surely, he and Cindee would not be
working together, even though she had easy access to
the artificial fireplace logs at the hardware store. But
if Mike Getz was not guilty, why didn't he just let her
leave?

He shuffled aside and she edged by, fighting to keep from fleeing. She didn't relish having to tell Nate that she'd taken too much of a chance here. In case Mike checked up on her, she'd now have to tell Peter Clawson, whom she tried to avoid, that he should get a picture of Mike. But, as he'd said, it should be near the ruins, because he couldn't have spotted the fire from this backyard.

"Let me make sure I've got this right," Nate said to Gabe. "Ray-Lynn Logan went to the Esh house and found no one home. Then she came over to the barn, looked up at Sarah's painted quilt square and then came into the barn. You two took off so you didn't see what happened after. You're sure?" he demanded, realizing too late that his buddy-buddy tone had evaporated. "You didn't tell Sarah any of that, did you?"

"I didn't tell anyone and told Barbara not to, 'cause we were up there together when the barn dance was at my place."

"Sure. Sure, I understand that."

"Sarah will tell you I didn't say a thing. You can ask her if you want, but she went to take some food *Mamm* made with some of those—" he pointed to the sack on the console between them "—to the Schrocks. I heard her tell *Mamm* she took some for Cindee Kramer, too."

"To the hardware store?" Nate asked, but he knew better. Cindee lived with Mike Getz, so he could only hope Mike wouldn't be home on a Friday morning. Sarah obviously meant to drop them off en route to the Schrocks. And he didn't like that idea at all.

"Gabe, we've got to switch seats. I've got to go somewhere."

"If you arrest Mrs. Logan, don't tell where you heard that, okay? She's a friend of Sarah's and pays *Mamm* and Lizzie good wages."

"I'm not going to arrest Mrs. Logan. Move!"

As they changed places—Gabe would be sad to see that Nate was going to put him out at his house—Nate swore under his breath and, from the front seat, reluctantly lowered the antenna that would allow him to make or receive calls on the two-way. He might be overreacting, but letting Sarah in on so much—using her, really—had endangered her. Why hadn't she told him she didn't intend to stay on her family's property after what they went through yesterday? With that threatening note pinned outside the place where she slept, didn't she realize the rules in cozy Amish country had all changed? As clever as she was, his Amish sidekick had clearly not gotten it through her pretty head to be careful.

Sarah was nearly to the Schrock house when she heard a loud motor kind of clearing its throat behind her. VERA? Nate had said he would be coming out here after the debris cooled down with a search warrant to sift through the ruins.

She glanced in her rearview mirror. Her insides cartwheeled and not because it was Nate. She saw Jacob's bright red car following her pretty close. He was probably expecting she'd pull over when she saw him, but she had no intention of doing that. If Jacob was following her now, had he been following her earlier? Nate had mentioned they might set a trap, but she hadn't wanted to set one this way. She'd call Nate on this two-way radio right now and tell him exactly where Jacob

Yoder was, assuming that was him behind the wheel. The sun still fairly low in the eastern sky glared off the car's front windshield and in her eyes.

Sarah figured she had about three minutes before she could turn into the Schrocks' driveway. Surely, they'd be home. She grabbed the two-way, and hit the quick-dial number Nate had set up for her. Could she keep Jacob here long enough for Nate to get here?

But unlike when they'd practiced, the radio didn't make a sound when she turned it on. Even when she put the number in again, nothing appeared on the tiny screen but the word *Searching.* Maybe Jacob had been searching for her, stalking her. But that note on the Miller barn had been addressed to Nate. This was even more of a nightmare if the arsonist was someone Amish—even former Amish.

The red car's horn sounded twice. She giddyaped Sally faster, while she struggled to punch in the number yet again. Jacob's car bumped the back of the buggy. Once, twice, then hard enough to shove it into Sally and send both horse and buggy crashing into the water-filled ditch.

13

As the buggy slammed into the water, Sarah went flying, her hands still on the reins. She went under with a huge splash and came up sputtering and angry. Sally thrashed the surface into waves, trying to get up but was trapped in the traces. Before Sarah could scramble to her feet, Jacob leaped in, too. He grabbed her arm so hard it hurt.

"This is your fault!" he shouted, thigh-deep in the roiling water. "All you had to do was stop."

"Let me go! You could have killed me and Sally!"

She glanced back into the half-submerged buggy for Nate's phone, but it was gone. Yanking free of Jacob's grasp, she sloshed toward her struggling horse. Thank the Lord, the mare hadn't broken a leg. Though the road wasn't busy, surely someone would come along soon. Then she remembered that Nate needed Jacob's license plate number, so she glanced up and tried to remember it in case Gabe wasn't sure.

Jacob moved behind her toward Sally. He helped Sarah free the horse from the buggy so she could stand. Sally floundered to her feet, making even more waves. "It wasn't my fault. It was an accident!" Jacob shouted.

"*Ya,* one you caused! You caused anything else you shouldn't have?"

"Something else I caused? What's that supposed to mean?" Jacob demanded, this time gripping her wrist so tightly her hand went numb. He shook her hard. "You don't think I had anything to do with the fires? I saw you with him! He's been turning you against me!"

"You've been following me, haven't you, maybe sneaking around at night?"

It wasn't like her to lose control, but since Jacob was guilty of this rash act, he could have left the note on the *grossdaadi haus* and burned the barns, too. She told herself she should talk quietly, not only to calm Sally but to keep him here until someone came along. She should find out where he was living so Nate could question him. But as if he'd read her mind, he said what she feared.

"We can't talk here. Get in the car," he ordered, pointing at it. "Sally and the buggy will be all right."

"No. I need to get the buggy towed out. Can you help with that?"

He lunged at her and pulled her so close she could smell garlic on his breath. He hauled her to the side of the ditch, then dragged her, clawing his way up like a wild animal. She saw he had red splotches on his hands but no visible cuts. Paint. Red paint from that threatening note to Nate.

"Jacob, you're hurting me. Let go!" She realized he'd left the car engine running; the driver's door stood open. "You want to talk, fine," she forced herself to say. "We'll talk right here."

Seizing her upper arms, he pulled her to him, nearly lifting her off her feet. Up this close, she really looked at him for the first time in months. His flushed face was unshaven, and gray half circles shadowed his wild eyes. A frown furrowed his brow. He lowered his voice, but he sounded so menacing. She smelled something else on his breath—alcohol?

"We're not staying here. I don't want that nosy *ausländer* MacKenzie or one of my former Amish brethren to come along." His already-bitter tone turned mocking. "'Oh, there's Jacob Yoder, under the curse of the *meidung*. We all know he's evil, must have started the fires.' That's what you're thinking, isn't it, Sarah? And you're the one who once said you loved me, trusted me! Now you're listening to him, trusting him."

He loosed her arms only to seize her wrist and again drag her toward the open car door. He pulled hard, but she twisted the reins she still held around her right wrist so she was anchored to Sally. Her attempt at another calm command of "Let me go," was drowned by his shout, flecked with spittle.

"I said, get in the car! I'm innocent, and you have to help me. I know who lit the fires, and I'll tell you if you go with me. We'll call the sheriff, explain things to him to get MacKenzie off my back. Sheriff Freeman helped me before, but you'll help me now, won't you, for all we once meant to each other?"

"Stop hurting me. Violence is not our way."

"Our way!" he exploded again. "There is no 'our' anymore! I've been banned, banished! You don't think that's a kind of violence? And you're hurting me, too. Now get in this car, or I'll—"

Giving up all attempts at calm, Sarah tried to buck

away from him and screamed once, again. Someone might hear her, help her, maybe the Schrocks or even Mike Getz.

Then, roaring down the road toward them, came VERA. The square shape of the dark vehicle was unmistakable.

When Jacob turned to look, he shouted at her, "Judas! Jezebel!" He shoved her away.

She staggered back to the edge of the ditch, rolled into it and hit the water again, bottom first this time, next to where Sally stood. Despite heavy, soaked skirts and a curtain of drenched hair in her face, Sarah dropped the reins, got to her feet and clambered up the bank again only to see Jacob's car speed away. Realizing Nate might stop for her and lose him, she waved her arms and pointed as Nate slowed.

"It's Jacob. Go! Go!" she shouted.

VERA roared away in pursuit.

Nate stepped on the gas pedal and gripped the steering wheel hard. He was livid with Sarah for going out without telling him, for getting in this situation, but she had flushed Jacob out of hiding. He hadn't wanted to use her as bait, but had she done that deliberately? And he was furious with himself for not making her promise to stay home. At least he had Jacob in sight, but the car had a head start, and it was faster than VERA. A car chase was definitely not in his job description.

The red car—some kind of sporty one—must be doing eighty down this two-lane road. What if either of them hit a car or, worse, a buggy? People were out on the roads. He'd lose the trust the Amish had offered him. Police vehicles, even an occasional fire truck rushing to emergencies, sometimes hit and killed innocent civilians. He'd be pulled off the case; a crash investigation would take precedence over stopping the arsons.

As the red car crested a hill ahead and disappeared, Nate cursed the beautiful terrain again. It screwed up long-distance vision, communications and safety. He should call the sheriff, but he'd left his phone in the back of VERA. As he reached the top of the hill and saw a farm wagon pulling out ahead between him and Jacob, who must have just missed it, he knew the chase was over. He slowed, turned around in a driveway and went back. He wanted to check to see that Sarah was all right, find out what she'd learned.

"You didn't catch him." Sarah stated the obvious when he got back to where she was waiting. People he didn't know—a man and woman in a buggy—were with her and they'd managed to get Sally out of the ditch.

"I'll get the sheriff after him," he assured her. "I've got his license plate, and Gabe gave me a lead on where he might be staying. VERA wasn't built for high speed."

She looked like a drowned cat for the second time in two days, but beautiful nonetheless. Even her hair was wet this time. He was glad the others were there or he would have lost his temper over her endangering herself. She was definitely coming off this case, because if she got hurt he would never forgive himself.

"I'll be fine," she told him as if she'd read his mind. "These are the Rabers, and they can help us get the buggy out."

He thanked the couple, then gently pulled Sarah off to the side. "After this," he told her, "I'm not leaving you alone off your property—maybe not even on it."

"I had the phone with me but it didn't work—that is, before it went for a swim here."

"That, at least, was not entirely your fault. Let's blame the hills, or the fact I put the antenna down after I talked to Gabe and he mentioned you were going to stop at Getz's. But I see it was Jacob I should have been worrying about."

She petted and sweet-talked the horse while he got a rope out of VERA and, with Mr. Raber's help, tied it to the buggy. Reuben Schrock came along the road and together they got the buggy righted and out of the ditch.

Though he could tell Sarah wanted to argue with him, Nate asked Mr. Schrock to take Sally and the buggy to his place and said they'd retrieve them later, because he had to take Sarah to the sheriff to report the incident.

"*Ya,* sure," the bearded church elder told him. Then he added, "You think Jacob Yoder burned the barns, Mr. MacKenzie?"

"We're going to find out and stop him if he did," Nate promised, then thanked everyone again and hustled Sarah, who was starting to shiver, into VERA. As he went into the back to get a blanket for her, he realized whatever had just happened between Sarah and Jacob meant he had to keep her off the case for her safety and his sanity.

Sarah wrapped herself in Nate's blanket. The water quickly soaked it, but he must have known the seat would get wet. Ditch water from her hair and smashed bonnet dripped down her back. Though it was quite mild outside, Nate closed the windows and turned on the heater, but he kept glaring at her as if this was her fault—and, of course, Jacob's desperation aside, it was. And he hadn't even heard that she'd misstepped with Mike Getz today.

"Your career as assistant arson investigator is over," Nate said, his expression tense and his voice harsh. "He could have drowned you back there. It's my fault, too. I should have told you not to leave your farm—not that that wouldn't keep someone from coming onto it."

"I will not be kept a prisoner on or off the farm, even if the arsonist is targeting the barns because of my painted quilt squares. But I don't think Jacob meant to kill me. He was trying to make me go with him."

"Oh, fine. Abduction. And then when he got you alone, what?"

He darted another hard look at her, then hunched over the steering wheel. Though he was chasing no one now, he was still driving too fast.

"I was so angry I wasn't thinking that he could have hurt or killed me," she admitted. "Actually, when he shoved me into the ditch water, I recalled the horrible time Ella almost drowned."

"Don't change the subject."

"But I need to tell you about something else. I may not have found out whether Jacob was guilty of arson, but it might not be him who's lighting fires. I found out Mike Getz couldn't see the Schrock barn from where Cindee said he did, unless she was confused. So someone lied, and why?"

"I knew it! I hope Getz wasn't there when you trespassed."

"Unfortunately, he was, but I covered for why I was there. I told him I was going to ask Peter Clawson to take a picture of him again, and he fell for it, not to mention I had a sack of half-moon pies for them."

Nate muttered something under his breath. "Sarah!" he said through gritted teeth, "you've been a big help to me, but you've got to keep clear of all this so you don't get hurt. You have not been trained or sworn by the fire marshal's office!"

"Sworn? Sworn *in,* you mean? No, only sworn *at* by Jacob and now you. Nate, I'm scared the barn burner's targeting not only my people but my paintings—me somehow. But I'm in a good position to find things out."

"No way. You let me do that. So did Jacob say anything about resenting your paintings on church leaders' barns?"

"No, but he wanted to talk more. He was very upset that I've been working with you."

Nate muttered under his breath again and she was just as glad she didn't hear. "Did he say anything that could tie him to the arsons?" he asked. "He no doubt blames you and your people for what he's done to himself."

"Well, if I'm not helping you anymore, I guess I shouldn't say, but *ya,* he called me a traitor and more. Still, his being desperate to talk to me and angry at me for helping you doesn't mean he's guilty of arson. He denied he had anything to do with the fires but said he knew who did. That's possible, isn't it?"

Nate kept flexing his fingers on the steering wheel, opening them, then gripping it hard. She wondered if he wished he had hold of her neck instead.

"Isn't there a saying," he demanded, "'With God, all things are possible'?"

"So Mr. Nathan MacKenzie can quote scripture, too. I wasn't sure you had a religious bone in your body."

"You think I'm some sort of heathen? My foster mother took me to church. I'm a believer."

"But not a believer in accepting help from anyone."

"Sarah, why are we arguing?"

"Because you know you need me—for helping solve the arsons, I mean—and you don't want to admit it."

"I just can't stand it that you could have been hurt."

"You were thinking of setting a trap for whoever wrote that note on the Millers' barn. That's what happened, only I was almost trapped instead of Jacob."

"I refuse to use you as bait. But did Jacob admit to that much—painting the note on the Miller barn?"

"He didn't have to. He has dried red paint on his hands. But I suppose, unless you do some kind of chemical test on it, he could say he was just painting over scratches on his red car and spilled a bit of it."

"I admire the way you think things through. But I'm expecting the sheriff to go right out to arrest Jacob for assaulting you at the least, and we can keep him locked up that way."

Sarah kept noticing the way fields and trees, farms and woodlots, raced past so much faster than in a buggy. But that's the way she felt her life was going now, kind of out of her control, and it scared her silly, as did what she had to tell Nate next. He had accepted the Plain People's form of insurance, even their lack of lightning rods and fire alarms, but would he understand her refusal to help him with this?

"Then," Nate went on, "he can be detained so I can question him. Also, I'll want a complete statement from you of everything Jacob said."

"You can arrest him for assault, but I won't accuse him or testify against him. We don't do that. The government courts are not for us. We settle things our own way, in the church, among ourselves."

"Sarah! You say you want to help but you won't testify to the fact he even roughed you up?" Then to her amazement he lowered his voice. "Okay, okay," he said. "We'll get him for speeding and an illegal license plate, then. Anything to hold him for a while, until he can at least be questioned. You don't want to accuse him of assault, I get that, but the barn burnings are an assault on your people. I'm going to nail whoever's guilty, and I'm betting on Jacob, though I now have another lead I haven't had time to check out."

"Another possible arsonist besides Mike Getz? What happened? You're not thinking it's Hannah again, are you? You said most arsonists are men."

"Let it go for now. It's nothing you need to be concerned with."

"Of course I do, and you can't stop me. Or were *you* planning to abduct me and lock me up somewhere?"

"To keep you safe—I'd do it. I'm thinking maybe you shouldn't even paint that new quilt square on your own barn."

"My new painting is agreed on. I'm honoring my father's faith in me by doing it. He knows the risk. The decorated barns draw more tourists in, and the people need that to survive and prosper right now. The Lord will help us through all of this, and you should rely on Him, too."

"But that doesn't mean we should put ourselves in harm's way. The world can be an evil place, Sarah, obviously even your sheltered Amish world."

Of course, stubborn outsider that he still was, Nate was right about that. She had never actually argued with a man, the give-and-take like this, and it was strangely exciting. But if Nate MacKenzie thought she was some shy, sweet Amish woman he could question, kiss and then command to keep quiet, he was dead wrong. She wasn't saying so right now, but she was in this arson investigation with both feet.

Nate brought VERA to a stop in front of the small sheriff's office on the only cross street of the main one through town. Sarah had heard the building had only one cell. She hoped Jacob Yoder would soon be in it and tell them who the arsonist was. At least, if it was him, it would stop the fires, the ones in the barns, though not the ones in her body and heart for this stubborn *Englische* man.

After the sheriff heard what they both reported and headed out to arrest Jacob, Nate took Sarah home to dry off and change clothes before he formally deposed her in her kitchen. Sarah wore her hair in a damp, thick braid down her back. After Mrs. Kauffman fed them both, she hovered in the background, putting pastries into boxes and sacks. The sacks started crinkling a whole lot louder while Sarah told him about Mike Getz confronting her. It just proved to Nate again that however much he needed Sarah, he had to keep her out of the loop of the investigation.

"So," Mrs. Kauffman said after he took Sarah's statement, "somehow that modern, two-way phone didn't work for her. Sarah shouldn't get too involved with all your things, Nate."

The woman's words rang in his ears: Sarah shouldn't

get too involved.... Was it obvious, especially to a watchful mother, that he and Sarah were getting too close to each other?

As if to emphasize her mentioning a modern phone, his cell buzzed.

"Good info on Yoder's location," Jack reported. "We're getting to be a good tag team. I'm bringing him in. You can have first crack at him, then he's mine."

"I appreciate that. The only eyewitness won't testify against him, and he probably knows that. But I've got some other ideas."

"Bet you do. See you there."

"He arrested Jacob?" Sarah asked.

"Yes, but we won't have to hold him for assaulting you, so don't worry about not testifying."

Still hovering, Mrs. Kauffman said, "The sheriff helped Jacob once, but even our shunning did not bring him back. He has been taken over by *hochmut,* puffing himself up, putting himself first."

"Like the old saying 'Pride goeth before a fall'?" Nate asked.

"*Ya.* Exactly," Mrs. Kauffman said with a firm nod. "In his heart, Jacob is no longer Amish. *Hochmut*—pride—is what some of our people thought had misled Sarah when she began to paint the big quilt squares, until Bishop Esh spoke up for her. Now we have decided she should paint one on our barn to stand up for her, too. But Jacob may be a lost soul."

"I feel bad for his parents," Nate told her. Even in the dim light that always seemed to characterize an Amish home, he could see where Sarah got her looks. Mrs. Kauffman's face seemed a faded, plumper portrait of Sarah's, and both women moved with a purposeful grace. "I don't have a wife or children to worry about," Nate went on, "but I can grasp how it is to agonize over someone you love who has gone astray, like the Yoders for their only son." He almost said something about his father, but he had things to do. Knowing Sarah, though, she knew what he meant.

"You take care of yourself, Nate," Mrs. Kauffman said. "Sarah will be right here with me or taking care of her *grossmamm*. She and Martha can both sleep in the *grossdaadi haus* tonight."

Looking into the woman's clear blue eyes, Nate nodded. "I value Sarah's help in this and yours, too," he told her. "Everyone here has been very kind. Thank you for your hospitality and support." He almost added, *And for keeping an eye on Sarah.*

Nate fought to keep from meeting Sarah's stare as he made a hasty exit. But as he pulled away from the Kauffman house, he noted the big, bold lines with which she'd sketched her quilt square. The rain had erased some of it, but he had no doubt she would draw it right back there again. And though he was going to try to steer clear of her for both their sakes, he felt her drawing him in again, closer and closer.

14

"I had nothing to do with the local barn burnings. That's all I have to say, Mr. Fire Marshal MacKenzie!"

"Why don't you just call me Mack?" Nate countered. "Make that *M-A-C-K* and paint it on the side of a barn and line up a bunch of beheaded little voles pointing to it. You're in serious trouble here, Jacob."

Jacob shrugged and shook his head to get his bangs out of his eyes—he still sported an Amish haircut—but refused to meet Nate's glare. At least Jacob didn't deny knowing what he meant. He must have been following Sarah around and figured out that she was helping him with the arson investigation. Had Jacob hoped that barn burnings targeting her paintings would force her to go to him for help, but Nate got in the way?

Jacob cleared his throat and said, "It's Sarah's paintings on the barns that got her in trouble, not me."

"Got her in trouble how?"

"Whoever's starting the fires must be angry with her for being prideful, no matter what the bishop says.

It's got to be someone Amish, but I'm not part of that anymore."

"Being prideful. *Hochmut,* you mean?" Nate asked, using what he'd learned from Sarah's mother. Jacob looked surprised. "It's sad," Nate went on, "but I don't think Sarah can be proud of her former fiancé, running with thieves and being shunned. Then he knocks her buggy off the road, threatens and roughs her up."

They sat facing each other across a small, bare table in the only cell in the Eden County sheriff's office. Nate tried to read the young man's body language as he stayed slumped in his chair, hands thrust in his jeans pockets, one foot tapping against the table leg so it vibrated in a regular beat.

The sheriff had wanted to book Jacob for stalking, aggravated assault and attempted kidnapping, but he knew those charges wouldn't stick without Sarah's cooperation. He'd been through that before with the Amish, he'd told Nate. But charges for speeding, for DUI—Jacob had failed a Breathalyzer test when he drove in with the sheriff waiting at his place—and for driving with an illegal license plate would hold him for a while. The sheriff had read him his Miranda rights, but Jacob had still been eager to talk to Nate. If Jacob had really harmed Sarah, Nate wasn't sure he could have kept control, but he was trying to set a certain tone here—tough but fair.

"I know I shouldn't have got caught up by that car theft ring," Jacob said, frowning at the table. "But they don't give a guy a chance."

"They?"

"The Amish, especially the church leaders. Sarah and her family, either."

"I have the understanding that they'll take a penitent back."

He looked up, then away again. "A penitent?"

"Someone who's truly sorry and wants to mend his or her ways."

"They should stick with the person, not throw him to the dogs in the first place."

"What dogs have they thrown you to?"

"I never would have been taken in by car thieves if I'd been treated right, even before I was shunned. Sarah broke off our engagement and everyone supported her, not me."

"So none of this is really your fault. It's hers, right? I can tell you're angry about it."

"Not really, but it just isn't fair."

"Let's go over your statement again, then. The night of the first fire in Bishop Esh's barn, even though you were not angry with the unfair Amish, you just happened to be in the area and decided to visit some of them, specifically Sarah's family."

"This is America, freedom of choice and all that!"

"I've got to agree with you there. Maybe because the Amish give their young people freedom of choice to become Amish or not, you wanted to hang out with Gabe Kauffman and his friends."

"Those *rumspringa* gatherings—you know, our... their...so-called running-around time—have outsiders dropping in. I just thought I could see some people I used to know. But when Sarah spotted the fire, I was able to call it in, then ran over there with the rest, that's all."

"So before you showed up at the Kauffmans' that night, you were doing what and where?"

"Just driving around. Thinking about how I missed some of my old friends, trying to decide to see my parents or not. The others might not talk to me or eat with me, but my mother would. To tell the truth, I knew some of the kids at that party might not shun me, and I guess I needed that. But what I don't need," he said, sitting up straight but still looking down, "is some worldly fire cop coming in here and conning Sarah into helping him, overstepping with her."

Nate decided to ignore that. Jacob hadn't gone for his challenge about "Call me Mack," and he wasn't going to react to the overstepping with Sarah accusation. Instead, he said, "So you decided to follow her until you could get her alone, even painted a message on at least one barn for me to stay away from her." Using the same calm conversational voice, he added, "Was the Miller barn third on your burn list, Jacob?"

He sucked in a sharp breath. "N-no, but I'll admit something. Yeah, I painted that message to you there, but I didn't burn any barns."

"I've done your case study and you fit the profile of an arsonist. Look, Jacob, this is going to go a lot easier on you and your poor parents, especially your mother—yes, I've met her—if you just confess, come clean and get this all over with. Your mother, Sarah and her family, let alone the entire 'unfair' Amish community, will think more of you if you tell the truth and ask for forgiveness than if you keep up your lies."

Jacob's hands came out of his pockets, fists clenched. He banged them once on the table. "I can't afford a lawyer, but I want one."

"Sure, we'll get you a lawyer in here for free," Nate said, leaning closer to him. Man, it was difficult to deal with someone who wouldn't look you in the eye. He had to be lying. "And I won't question you anymore without him or her being present. Only, to your former people, who don't trust lawyers much more than they like government officials—"

"You're government and seem to be doing just fine with Sarah!"

"Lawyering up, as we say, won't win you much support with the Plain People you've already let down and hurt. And in your head and heart, they are still your people, Jacob—you know they are," Nate said, rising and going to the door, even lifting his fist as if to knock for the sheriff or the deputy he'd called in from Wooster to spend the night here at the jail.

"Think about it carefully, Jacob," he said. "The arsonist has been clever and careful with the two fires. Frankly, I'm in awe of him and Sarah is, too. No one hurt, probably not even a barn owl, so the arsonist's prison time would not be as long as it would be if he kept telling lies or lit a fire where someone got more than just financially and emotionally hurt. I'll get that lawyer for you now."

"Wait! I—I'll plead to harassing and stalking Sarah, to painting that warning to you on the Millers' barn and Hostetlers' in case you went there, but I am not a barn burner. I told Sarah I knew who it was but I don't— honest!"

The man looked distraught, but he finally met Nate's stare when he'd seemed so shifty and scared before. Naw, Nate thought. He'd bet the farm—if he had one—that this was the arsonist, but that didn't mean he wouldn't keep looking. Mike Getz still needed to be

questioned, as did Hannah Esh and even his new possibility, Ray-Lynn Logan.

"You want that lawyer now?" Nate asked.

"Changed my mind. Don't need one, 'cause I didn't
burn those barns."

Late that afternoon, Sarah helped her mother place
stacks of boxed half-moon pies in the big family buggy,
then helped her father load the wagon with birdhouses
he was donating to be sold at the alms auction the next
day. She liked the flourishes and designs she'd done on
these so-called condo birdhouses for purple martins
with their multiple entry holes. She wondered if those
beautiful birds lived like the Amish with the generations together. Would one of these holes be a sort of
grossdaadi haus?

She wished she had her buggy here and, for her donation, a collection of paintings of Amish life on stretched
canvas, maybe framed, or even small quilt squares
painted on wooden plaques, but that would really set
everyone to talking about her painting pretty—her
hochmut. But was it so prideful to wish she had painted
birds or flowers, all parts of God's grandeur, on those
birdhouses instead of circles and swirls? And to yearn
to create on canvas or wood the scenes that paraded
through her head and heart that would portray the Plain
People in all their simple yet busy lives?

But she didn't have paintings or her buggy. At first
Nate had said he'd take her to pick it and Sally up at
Mr. Schrock's, but he'd later set it up with her mother,
while she was drying off and changing clothes, that
Daad and Gabe would go get Sally and the buggy after
they packed these things for the auction tomorrow.

Her stomach twisted tighter. What if Nate really meant it that he would work on this arson investigation without her now? She sighed and went to the barn to stare up at the spot where she would paint her new quilt square, Ocean Waves. She and Sally and the buggy had made waves in that water-filled ditch today. If Jacob was the arsonist, at least they had him confined now.

She walked to the *grossdaadi haus* where both she and Martha would spend the nights together because of safety in numbers. Pretty soon *Daad* might even say Gabe should sleep out here, too, with his hunting rifle. Or he might put Gabe in the barn the way Mr. Miller had said his son, Noah, was guarding their ramshackle one. Tonight, hopefully, there would be no more notes with terrifying Bible verses tacked to the door, no more gravel thrown against the window, though that would be worth it if Hannah would only come back, even just to talk the way she did the night after the first fire.

As Sarah went into the living room, she could hear Martha reading to *Grossmamm* from the *Budget* in the bedroom before her late-afternoon nap. They'd had a family conference and decided that the *Home Valley News* was all right to read to her, too, but not the extensive coverage dedicated to the fires, because that might set the old woman off again, just as the tales of burning Amish from the *Martyrs Mirror* had.

In his most recent editorial, Peter Clawson said the arsons could be hate crimes against the peaceful Amish and that the state fire marshal's office must find out who was guilty and root out the perpetrators. She'd heard the newspapers were selling like half-moon pies around here lately.

Sarah shook her head and shoved back her dirty hair.

She had to wash it tonight, get the ditch water out of it. A mirror. She wished she had a mirror out here, even the small one they had in the house. No need for mirrors among her people since beauty was all on the inside of a person, but with Nate around, she sometimes wondered how she really looked to him. She sighed again.

Suddenly overcome with exhaustion, she slumped on the couch, not even taking time to open the hideaway bed she or Martha would use tonight, while the other took a turn in a sleeping bag on the floor. Nate liked to sleep outside in a sleeping bag. She'd left him a note there about Mike Getz and had stroked the deep marine-blue of the soft flannel lining of his outdoor bed....

She forced herself to think about the hues of blue paint she would use for the triangles of her ocean waves. Tomorrow was the auction and then Sunday was a church day—the Hostetlers' turn to be hosts. But on Monday, after she took the pastries to Ray-Lynn in town, she would set up the ladders and scaffolding and begin to paint. She would use Nate's ladder and his scaffolding, not shaky, but firm. No fear of being tipped off...tipped off into the fires...falling from pride into the fires...

They pressed her against the wooden ladder on the ground, ripped off her bonnet and prayer kapp. The crowd was screaming for blood, those who insisted on plain ways, who would not bow to the rules of the government's church. The flames grew higher, hotter, close, so close....

"For wickedness burns as the fire!" someone shouted as she was tied to the ladder. "The people shall be as fuel for the fires of hell! Burn them! Burn them for the fires of hell!"

The screams of others being burned—her friends, her family, her people—shredded her courage. She wanted to beg for her life. She wanted to struggle, but it was not their way. Accept. Forgive. Forgive them, Father, for they know not what they do. Much better to drown in the pond or the dirty ditch, ducked to death like a witch than this terror.

More men with angry faces came closer, bent over her, lifted her high on the ladder, tied her hands and waist and feet. If she could only fly up to heaven, not have to face the fire! The heat seared her already, burned her with desire for an outsider, an Englische ausländer, a man she could never have. Her precious paintings flamed to pain and ashes as the fires lit her skirts, her skin and...

Sarah heard someone scream, someone close. Was it *Grossmamm* afraid again?

"Sarah. Sarah! Wake up!"

Martha was kneeling by the sofa, shaking her shoulder. "You had a bad dream. You screamed. *Grossmamm* nearly jumped out of her skin and asked if the beast was outside again."

"The beast? Oh, sorry. Get back to her."

"We're just all on edge. It's all right," Martha soothed with a squeeze of her shoulder before she hurried back into the bedroom.

But it wasn't all right, Sarah thought as she hugged herself hard, then staggered to her feet and went into the kitchen to wash her hair. She leaned over the sink, her hands on the counter, propping herself up. Nothing had been right since that first barn went up in a blaze, taking her painting and her Amish turn-the-other-cheek beliefs with it.

* * *

After Nate filled in the sheriff about Jacob's claims of innocence for the arsons, he went outside and, exhausted, just sat in VERA's driver's seat. It was late afternoon, the time, he'd heard, Ray-Lynn Logan went home for a break before the evening rush. He knew which house was hers just outside of this little one-cross-street town with its two rows of commercial establishments and then a scattering of houses. He intended to keep an eye on things at the auction tomorrow, and he was sure she'd be in the thick of things there, too, so he'd probably never get any private chat time with her then. Yeah, he'd phone her just before going to her door. He had to check out the lead Gabe had reluctantly given him. Even if she wasn't somehow tied to the arson, she might have seen something. But why hadn't she come forward?

Before he could start the engine, someone knocked on his window. He jolted in surprise, then saw it was Peter Clawson. He turned the key so he could run the window down.

"I'd like your statement about Jacob Yoder's arrest," Peter said without any ado. "I'll get one from the sheriff, but you're still 'the Man' on this arson case."

"I've been wanting to talk to you for a couple of days," Nate countered. "Walk around and climb in."

"I'd rather have you come to my office. I have something you'll want to see."

Nate got out and locked up, then followed Peter across the street. "Working hard?" Nate asked as Peter held the front door of the newspaper office open for him. It amazed Nate that this was a one-man shop except for distribution, but with a small paper in the digital age, it was obviously possible and profitable.

"Always. To use a cliché—which I hate to do—I like to strike while the iron is hot, and these arsons are making things hot here."

"So what is it you wanted me to see?"

"Before I show the sheriff or write it up for the next edition—this," Peter said, and pointed to a piece of white paper with large, block hand printing on his cluttered desk.

Nate saw he'd placed the paper in a stiff plastic envelope, so it shone in the overhead lights. Nate read, "A fire goes before him, and burns up his enemies round about."

The handwriting looked the same as on the note pinned to Sarah's door, but to be sure, he'd have to scan and send both to a handwriting expert the bureau consulted with in Columbus. But the expert didn't like photocopies or faxes because the pressure of the pen point on the paper could reveal things, too. He was quite sure this handwriting was different from what Jacob had done on the Miller barn, even though the materials were so different.

"I checked," Peter said, sitting in his high-backed leather desk chair which creaked under his big frame. "It's a quote from the Bible, Psalms 97, verse 3—the Revised King James Version to be exact."

Nate began to sweat. He'd opted to keep the Biblical quote from the Kauffman *grossdaadi haus* privileged information, to avoid causing panic and undue speculation and so he could use it to be sure he arrested the right person. Besides the Kauffmans and the sheriff, only his boss knew about it. But if this man discovered he was withholding information from the public, he could skew it to look bad. He'd already written an editorial suggesting Nate should get on the stick—to use a cliché. Peter's pompous manner rubbed him the wrong way.

"What are you implying about this note?" Nate asked. "That it's somehow tied to the arsons?"

"Put through the mail slot of the newspaper that's been crusading to have the arsons solved. Don't you think so?" Peter demanded, thumping the desk with his index finger. "Fire…burns up…enemies. I'd bet my Phi Beta Kappa key that this is from the arsonist. He or she wants more notoriety, wants to stir things up even more, to cause fear and panic if I print this, but I can't see not printing it. You think I should?"

"As you said, only if you want to stir things up more. I suppose it would sell more papers if that's your main goal."

"It isn't. Absolutely, the truth matters, but I care deeply about this community. I've got money and years of my life invested here, but I can't sit on something like this. However, if I had a strong interview about your questioning Jacob Yoder today—you did, didn't you?—I wouldn't have room to include the note, because I need to save big layout space for coverage and photos of the charity auction tomorrow."

Nate sat down in the wooden armchair at the side of the big desk. He was uptight, but he tried to look calm. He leaned back and put his arms on the wooden arms of the chair. "That almost sounds like a bribe. Or even a threat, Peter."

"Not at all. I'm willing to let you take that piece of evidence to see if you can get fingerprints off it, though

I admit I touched it before I knew what it was, so you'll have to eliminate mine. Do we have a deal?"

"You can print that both the sheriff and the state fire marshal's arson investigator questioned Jacob Yoder, but he is only being held for DUI, speeding and driving with an illegal license plate at this time."

"You don't think the firebug is Jacob Yoder?"

"Do you? I respect how you seem to have your finger on the pulse of this place."

"I'd say the odds are good for Yoder. Motive—in spades. Proximity, at least to the first burn, ditto. To the second burn, hard to prove. But then, Mike Getz, maybe. Hannah Esh, possibly."

"I'm impressed."

"The power of the press—and the brain behind it."

Talk about pride and *hochmut,* Nate thought as he looked up at the framed certificates and famous newspaper articles on the walls of the office. Then, taking the plastic envelope, holding the note with him, he stood and walked over to read several of them.

"A Pulitzer for powerful reporting is my inspiration, my goal in life. It's what keeps me going in this little place I have come to cherish. And I think we're either up against an arsonist who is Amish—or one who wants to appear Amish—or a religious nut who hates the Amish. By the way, did I leave out anyone on your lists of possible perps? You can tell me that much, at least."

Nate turned to face Peter. He'd risen from his padded chair and sat on the corner of his desk. Wouldn't Peter be shocked to know that his own partner in the restaurant had been on the scene of the first fire just before it ignited?

"See you at the auction tomorrow," Nate said. "If you notice anything fishy there, let me know. When I nail the arsonist, I'll be sure you have the complete story before the big boys in the heavy-hitter papers in Cleveland or Columbus get a thing."

At that, Peter's chubby face lit in a smile that made him look like a Christmas cherub.

Ray-Lynn was hoping that Jack might be calling when her phone rang during her break at home, so she took her time answering it. But it wasn't him.

"Ray-Lynn, it's Nate MacKenzie. I know this is your downtime from the restaurant, but I'd like to stop by for a few minutes and ask you a couple of questions. It's important."

She gripped the phone hard. "In person? Not on the phone?"

"No, ma'am. I'm only a few minutes away."

"Don't you 'ma'am' me, Nate, because it makes me feel older than I am and more old-fashioned than I'd like to be. All right. You just drop on by," she said, trying to sound cheerful.

She poured him iced sweet tea and fed him lemon sponge cake while they talked about the auction. He seemed interested in her *Gone with the Wind* collectibles—porcelain statues of Scarlett O'Hara, Miz Melanie and Rhett Butler, with a collection of china painted with scenes from the movie behind them: Tara before and after the war, Rhett carrying Scarlett up the stairs, the burning of Atlanta. She chatted on about it all, wondering if this investigator knew she had her net out to catch a cop—the head honcho around here. And then, the other shoe dropped.

"I'd like to ask you where you were the evening of the first fire, about 7:00 p.m. on Saturday, May 22," Nate said, looking up from her small painting of the Tarleton twins with Scarlett on Tara's portico from the opening scene of the movie.

Ray-Lynn's stomach flip-flopped. Could he know somehow? She hadn't seen anyone else there that evening. What if Jack found out that she hadn't told him? What if the Kauffmans, Sarah, got wind of what she had planned?

Slowly, she swirled the tea in her glass. "I suppose someone saw me on Bishop Esh's property," she said, trying to sound matter-of-fact. "I was fixing to ask him if I could get permission to have one of Sarah's quilt squares painted on the front of the restaurant, but he wasn't home, so I just admired her painting there on his barn. I could use the extra oomph of the publicity, you see, and I'm not afraid I'd be an arson target here in town near the sheriff's office. Don't you think the arsons are targeting Amish leaders rather than her lovely art?"

When he didn't comment but just studied her, she rushed on. "I've already asked Bishop Esh if Sarah could paint a mural inside the restaurant. I didn't get anywhere with that but thought I would try my luck with a quilt square."

"Sarah mentioned you encouraged her art, even thought she had a style like Grandma Moses."

"She's very talented. I have a friend who runs an art gallery in Columbus in the Short North area, specializing in naive art—that is, paintings by untrained but talented artists, often rural, often somewhat primitive in style. Since you're from there, you surely know how arty that area is. If you saw Sarah's sketchbook she's kept for years—drat, I forgot it's supposed to be a secret—but you'd be amazed."

"So you looked at her quilt square on the barn and left."

"Oh—I did open the barn doors and glance inside to see if someone was there, just in case. It seemed dark, but sometimes you can't tell when they just have a lantern. I swear, Amish eyes are more used to darkness than ours."

"And was someone there?"

She hoped her voice sounded steady. It wasn't working to just try to charm and chatter at this man. She was afraid that part of what she was going to admit would get her the wrong kind of attention from Jack as well as from Nate. And if her ultimate plan came out, she could lose everything she'd worked so hard for.

"It was pitch-dark inside, but, as far as I could see, no one was stirring, not even a mouse," she said, and forced a smile. "I hope to talk to the Amish powers-that-be about Sarah's art again, but with all the dreadful goings-on, I just haven't had time, not with packing things to donate for the auction tomorrow and all. I didn't want to bother you or the sheriff since I'd seen nothing amiss there before the barn burned. I must have just missed the arsonist, though, and that gives me the absolute willies."

His eyes bored into hers.

"I—I'm sorry," she went on. Was she even making sense anymore? "It's just I didn't want any bad PR for the restaurant. I realize I shouldn't have held back, but I didn't want Peter—or Jack Freeman—all upset with me. I was afraid Bishop Esh would resent my request to act as a sort of agent if they'd let Sarah paint—get her in trouble, too, as if she were in on it—but my timing was terrible to go there, and I just figured I should keep quiet."

"You should have come forward. Next time you hear or see anything that could help, don't just say you'll 'think about it tomorrow,' got that?"

"I do—and you've seen the movie."

"My foster mother loves it."

"And you love her, so you sat through it more than once."

"I repeat, next time you know anything about anything, let me know and no stalling. It looks bad."

"Yes, yes, I understand. Thanks for all you're doing for all of us, and keeping an eye on Sarah, too, a close eye."

She wasn't sure if he got the hint that she knew things about him, too, that hadn't been shouted from the rooftops, but he simply nodded and went out. She leaned against the door with shaking knees until he pulled away in the big black vehicle, then went over to clear the table. On her way to the kitchen with the plates, she saw that he must have turned her Scarlett doll to face the china plate of Atlanta burning. Now what in heaven's name was that supposed to mean?

15

As the Amish worked together to set up the auction early Saturday morning, Sarah hurried over to her friend Ella Lantz's Lavender Plain products table to buy several things before the crowd swelled. Already people were parking cars in the adjoining fields, and a sea of black buggies surrounded the scene. Blessedly, the weather was lovely, crisp and clear. The fact that this was the first day of their Memorial Day weekend gave moderns an extra Monday away from work and they might be more eager to shop. Sarah wondered if the arsonist would be here—if it wasn't Jacob.

"I'll take some more shampoo and some of the sachet," she told her longtime friend after a hurried chat. She helped Ella unpack and lay out some of her goods. "Hmm," Sarah said as she picked up a small quilted bag of the sweet-smelling sachet, "I see you've included a note here that this can keep moths away. If I was a moth, it would draw me right in."

"You probably can't tell, but I've mixed in some rue,"

Ella explained. "I just didn't want to be selling things that weren't purposeful."

"Oh, right," Sarah said. It was back to that again, she groused silently, but perhaps Ella hadn't intended it as a criticism of her barn paintings. No, she was just getting too sensitive about that, but what if the arsonist was targeting her work? As she hurried back toward the table with her father's birdhouses, which she had promised to mind for a while, she felt she was being watched. And then she saw she was.

Nate had arrived and was looking her way, though he just waved and didn't come over but kept pacing at the periphery of the activities. She saw him walk in, then out, of the schoolhouse like a security guard, which, of course, her people would never hire. Well, she told herself as she settled in with her box of coins and small bills for change, she and Nate weren't the only ones nervous today. Sheriff Freeman had been here from the beginning, talking to the Amish men who would guide the cars in, looking around everywhere as if he could spot some criminal in the crowd. Even the Amish, who trusted all things to the Lord, were on edge. This was an important day, one that should make them all joyous instead of jumpy.

Daad had left a disappointed Gabe behind in the house with a loaded hunting rifle, though he promised to relieve him just after noon. Mr. Miller, who was unloading sacks of rhubarb next to their buggy, had said he'd left his boy Noah in their barn with orders to repair the loft floor and keep an eye on the place, even though it was broad daylight. Mr. Hostetler, too, who had a painting on his barn, had someone watching it during the night since the arsonist had struck in the dark. It was sad and scary, Sarah thought as she made her first sale of a birdhouse, that her quilt squares were starting to serve as hex signs, not ones that kept disaster away but attracted it.

Nate had surveilled the entire area, amazed at the variety of things for sale, everything from baked goods to beautifully crafted oak, cherry and maple furniture pieces, which he'd expected, to farm machinery, which he hadn't. He walked the rows of plows, spotted an antique-looking McCormick-Deering tractor and two types of machines he didn't recognize. Reuben Schrock told him they were corn binders and manure spreaders. Yard tools, new and used, were propped along the east side of the schoolhouse, some with prices, the rest waiting for bids to be written on their tags. Buggies, four wagons and a sleigh vied for places with bales of hay—or was it straw?

Meanwhile, both men and women prepared booths or tables that would sell every kind of what the Amish called "eats," such as ice cream, popcorn balls and submarine sandwiches, not to mention preparations for lunch—no, Sarah had said they called it dinner. Five hundred pounds of chicken would soon be cooking on smoking grills that were being set up. He'd only had half-moon pies and coffee in VERA this morning, and his stomach rumbled.

The hand-lettered signs that boys were pounding in the ground promised dinner starting at 11:00 a.m. It would consist of chicken, noodles or mashed potatoes, green beans, dressing, gravy, coleslaw and dinner rolls with a piece of either rhubarb cream pie or oatmeal pecan pie, iced tea or pop included. Rather than a price being posted, the meal was available for "a kindly donation."

Random items for sale included Ben Kauffman's birdhouses and made-to-order gazebos, various handcraft goods and even Ella Lantz's lavender items, which wafted out a cloud of fragrance that reminded him of Sarah. Strangely, the scent made his mouth water more than the sight of the food. Cute little kids toddled freely around, most barefoot, dressed like miniatures of their parents, while kids of elementary school age clustered around the playground's volleyball net, swings and slide.

Nate had also checked out the interior of the schoolhouse. It was hard to believe that at the end of the first decade of the twenty-first century, the school was a one-room building with a cloakroom and a potbellied stove. Not a TV screen or laptop in sight. It made him feel even more that he'd stepped back into pioneer days. The schoolroom was hung with quilts on clotheslines along the four walls, stretched from blackboard to blackboard or just hung over dowels between stacks of cinder blocks.

He'd talked briefly to the sheriff as he made his rounds. Jack reported that Jacob had paced in his cell most of the night but had eaten a good breakfast. They were awaiting a visit from Jacob's parents this morning, so Mr. and Mrs. Yoder were probably the only people from the area not coming today.

Many Amish nodded to Nate, said his name in passing or gave him a smile. Strange how that warmed him, not only to be accepted but to feel somehow included. Since he didn't want to call attention to himself, he slipped out back behind the two school outhouses and the rented Porta-John facilities to make a second phone call on his cell. Earlier, he'd talked to his boss, Mark Lincoln, to give him an update of Jacob Yoder's arrest. He told Mark that Jack Freeman was getting a search warrant for Jacob's car and single rented room in West Salem, a small town where the sheriff had made the arrest.

Mark had asked him how sure he was that Yoder was the arsonist, and he'd told him truthfully, "On the evidence, about seventy percent. On my gut, about twenty percent."

Mark had urged him to pull out all the stops to solve the arsons, which were getting higher profile by the day, thanks to news agencies and online servers picking up some of Peter Clawson's headlines and photos. Amish Barn Arsons Could Be Religious Hate Crimes was sure to bring in more outsiders to this auction today as would Plain People Targeted by Barn Burner. Was there a Pulitzer Prize for Peter Clawson in the future? Maybe.

"M.E., it's me," Nate said when his foster mother answered her phone.

"Nathan, so good to hear from you. You're all right, aren't you? Did you catch that barn arsonist? There are lots of stories about it in the newspaper here. Are you taking time to eat all right? I still think you're too thin."

"Are you kidding? I'm gaining weight the way everyone feeds me here, and you should see the spread they have today."

She had a hundred questions of concern. He usually called her on Sundays. She was seventy-four, and her health had not been the best lately. After seeing how tenderly the Kauffmans looked after their matriarch, Nate felt guilty he didn't see her more.

"As for the arsonist," he told her, "I'm still working on it, but you know what they say about all work and no play. I'm at an Amish sale and auction, and I just saw your birthday gift—a handmade quilt, but I'm not sure what colors you'd like."

He knew he'd better not tell her how much the quilts were likely to go for. A factory-made quilt from Wal-Mart or Sears was more her style. He thought he'd like to buy one of those beautiful pieces for himself, too—well, he'd rather have a painting by Sarah, but he didn't dare ask—and he wanted to contribute to the rebuilding of the Esh and Schrock barns.

"Blues, greens and golds would be lovely," M.E. said. He'd never been able to call her "Mother," and she understood that. So Mrs. Bosley had become Mary Ellen and then M.E. over the years. "You know," she went on, "I'd like for you to take me up there someday to see the area, after your work there is done—I mean, if you would just take a few days off."

"I hope we can do that. Okay, blues, greens and golds. I'll keep that in mind."

"Nathan, what are we going to do when I can't get out as easily to meet you somewhere? I know you don't like coming here, but what will we do? Even with this knee replacement, I'm just not as spry as I was when Jim and I were chasing after you."

"I'll talk to you later about that. It will all work out."

"I'm not moving out of this house I love. I've told you that before and I mean it. My married life and rearing you, my dear boy, all happened here, and they'll have to carry me out feetfirst."

"I know. I—I gotta go, but I'll talk to you soon. I—I love you, M.E."

He returned his cell to its case on his belt and went back into the schoolhouse to see if there was a quilt with blues, greens and golds.

Sarah saw that Peter Clawson had a camera with a huge lens. It must be one of those cameras where the photographer could stand back a ways yet get close-up pictures. When her father came from where the men were barbecuing chicken for the big feed—picnic tables were being set up near the playground—and took over selling his birdhouses, she went a roundabout way to where Peter was taking long-distance shots from the side field.

"Sarah, how's the birdhouse biz?" he asked when he saw her coming.

"Doing fine. How's the newspaper biz?"

"Hate to say it, but the arsons and the Amish make fascinating reading both here and outside the Homestead area."

"I happened to be talking to Mike Getz and thought, since he spotted the second fire, you might want a picture of him from where he saw it."

"I already used one of him with the lead article on the first fire."

"Just a thought. It's terrible to sound as if we're numbering the fires, isn't it?"

"You mean, like we're waiting for the next one—third time's a charm? You see, Sarah," he went on, crossing his arms over the top of his big-lens camera, "that's the thing that's pulling people in to read about these crimes. The contrast between the charm of Amish

country—including your quilt paintings—and the ob-
scene outrage of burned barns. You have to admit that
your artwork might be helping some sicko decide which
buildings to burn. I'd bet on it. Though now that your
family's going to have one, too, you must not agree
you're tempting fate."

"You know the Amish don't believe in betting or in
fate, Mr. Clawson," she said, and went back into the
crowd to help set up the tables for dinner. But what he'd
said scared her more than ever.

Sarah saw that Ray-Lynn was helping set up, too,
opening folding chairs. Way before eleven, a line of
folks waiting to eat wound around the grills and serving
tables. Sarah ended up dishing out a choice of mashed
potatoes or noodles while, with clear plastic gloves on
her hands, Ray-Lynn added a dinner roll to each plate
as people passed down the line.

Mike Getz and Cindee Kramer passed through as
well as numerous other locals she knew, but lots she
didn't. Both Amish and *Englische* seemed to see the
women serving as part of a fast-food machine, because
time after time, they discussed things as if they weren't
there.

"Do you believe these fires around here?" one
woman asked another. "Wasn't there a Hallmark Hall
of Fame TV special with Patty Duke that had something
about Amish fires? You know, the actress that played
that deaf and dumb girl, Helen Keller?"

"They must think we're deaf and dumb, the way they
carry on," Ray-Lynn muttered as the women moved on
to the dessert table.

"Welcome to being Amish with outsiders discussing your ways in front of you as if you only understand German," Sarah whispered. "Potatoes or noodles," she asked the next person and dished out potatoes.

"It's just like in the restaurant," Ray-Lynn said. "You wouldn't believe the things I sometimes overhear. We live in an in-your-face world, Sarah, not to say people don't still have deep, dark secrets. So, does Nate think Jacob's behind everything?"

"I haven't spoken to Nate since he interviewed him. Potatoes or noodles?"

"Ever think you'd like to paint this busy scene?" Ray-Lynn asked. For once Sarah wished she'd just shut up and serve. It was too much to keep her mind on this work, listen to Ray-Lynn, skim the crowd for Nate and worry about someone possibly coming through the line who burned barns.

Wishing another server would step up to take her place, Sarah didn't even bother looking up anymore. "Potatoes or noodles?" she recited.

"Noodles, please, Sarah."

Her hand jerked, and her heartbeat kicked up. She almost put a heaping spoonful of noodles on Nate's coleslaw instead of next to it.

"How is your day going?" Sarah asked him as Ray-Lynn popped a roll on his plate.

"I hope to buy a quilt for my foster mother," he said. "Thanks. You, too, Ray-Lynn."

And he moved on. He ended up sitting with Bishop Esh, no less, but it made Sarah nervous that he could look straight at her, which he did. Whenever she could grab a glimpse between moving heads in the line, it seemed he was staring at her.

"He cares about you," Ray-Lynn said out of the side of her mouth.

"Not a possibility. He cares about solving the arsons. And speaking of caring, how is your I-don't-care campaign going with you-know-who?"

"Better, but he's married to his work, too."

On it went in a blur—plates, people, food and worries...and disappointment when Nate left the table where she could see him and disappeared into the crowd again.

Nate could not believe the bidding for the quilt he had his eye on was going so high. Five hundred and twenty-five bucks already with four people still holding up their hands off and on. At least it was going to a great cause. Reuben Schrock himself was the auctioneer, and he was good at it, his voice rolling along in rhythm like a stick stuck in the spokes of a wheel. It was ironic that some of the money earned here today would go to help the Amish rebuild Schrock's barn, after enough was taken out for the Esh barn.

Ray-Lynn was one of the bidders upping the ante on the quilt, so she was obviously finished with dishing out food. That meant Sarah might be free, too. He'd been tempted to seek her out, but he should save it for later. Why be seen talking to her here with hundreds of people around?

"Five hundred fifty!" Nate called out.

The quilt was amazing with its cream background and interlocking rings of blues, greens and golds. When it was introduced, he'd learned the pattern was called Wedding Ring.

He figured M.E. would like that name. She'd really

loved her husband and still missed him. To have a love like that...but to be able to include a foster son in her life. Nate seldom thought of having kids of his own, but he wanted that, didn't he? It's just that he'd never found the right woman, especially since he'd buried himself in his work....

"Six hundred from the lady over in the corner, Mrs. Logan from the restaurant. So do I hear six hundred fifty? An-a do I hear six hundred and fifty for this Wedding Ring quilt, a-going once, a-going twice..."

Nate looked over at Ray-Lynn. Was she hanging tough with this because he'd caught her holding back information? Her gaze caught his and she frowned as if to dare him to bid more.

"Six hundred and fifty for a beautiful quilt and a good cause!" Nate called out.

That seemed to bring the bidding to an end. The crowd buzzed. He heard his name once or twice and the hissing sounds of the whispered word *arsons*. He went toward the front to write a check and get his quilt, when he had a crazy idea. Maybe he could get Sarah to paint this same design and give M.E. both the painting and the quilt for her upcoming seventy-fifth birthday. Women liked decorations in their house to match and go together, didn't they? Besides, if he was going to keep Sarah safe from involvement in the arson case—and involvement with him would only hurt her—he needed some excuse to have a little time with her. Or was that really dangerous thinking?

After Nate stowed his plastic-wrapped quilt in the back of VERA, he stood and watched a game called eckball. Kids stood in corners of a laid-out square about half the size of a baseball diamond and tried to hit people milling around inside with something they called a mush ball. Evidently, anyone who got hit had to get out, until only the winner was left.

That's what he had to do, he told himself. Keep tossing lobs at possible perps until only the arsonist was left, and he had to do it before disaster struck again. At least he had a good handle now on who the candidates for the arsons were, unless it was someone from out in left field. If he could not discover who it was, he had to find ways to eliminate who it wasn't, but he couldn't lock up everyone until the arsons stopped. Sarah had helped him get to know people here, introduced him to the culture during the one week he'd been here, but he had his feet on the ground enough now that he didn't need her. At least, that's what he kept trying to tell himself.

He went back to the eating area; Sarah, her older sister, Lizzie, and Ray-Lynn were among the women wiping off the tables nearby now that the food line was closed. He hoped the "kindly donations" requested for the hearty and delicious food brought in a ton of money. He'd put in twenty bucks for his meal, amazed at the Amish attitude that people would give more money than if charged a specific price.

"I'd like to help clean up," Nate told Levi Miller, who seemed to be heading up the men's work.

The man nodded and handed him a wooden brush with metal bristles. "Pitch right in a'scraping, then dump water on it. Promised to go relieve my boy Noah, so he can come for a bit, but think I let him down. He's upset today 'cause Jacob Yoder was a buddy of his, and he heard he tried to hurt Sarah Kauffman and got locked up for the arsons."

News sure traveled fast on the Amish grapevine, Nate thought. "He was questioned about the arsons, but he's being held on lesser charges right now," he explained.

"I'll tell Noah. And take him a good if cold dinner and hope he got some of those repairs on the loft floor done."

"Since I fell through, I'd be happy to help pay for supplies."

"No need. Real glad you weren't hurt and aren't trying to sue us like some moderns would."

A modern, Nate told himself, feeling as if cold water had been thrown in his face. He might feel a certain camaraderie with these people, but he was a modern, an *ausländer,* or outsider as they liked to say. And suddenly that made him very sad.

Nate kept a good eye on the heaped pile of silvery, glowing embers discarded from the grills as he helped scrape stuck meat and sauce from them, then poured buckets of water on some if they had to be loaded back in buggies right away for the trip home. Some grill owners had chores to do, especially the dairy farmers who had to see to milking. Mike Getz, even one-handed, came over to pitch in, which impressed Nate until he saw why. Peter Clawson was starting to take photos of their efforts to put the grill fires out. Like the Amish men, Nate turned away from the camera and bent over his work. Mike maneuvered to get his face in the shot.

The next grill was really black and hot; the water Nate poured on it hissed and sent up smoke, gray and wispy against the clear blue, late-afternoon sky. The plume of smoke seemed not to stop but drifted and curled into distant clouds.

No, that was not this smoke he saw.

His stomach tightened. He grabbed Levi Miller's arm as he walked by with a box of food, no doubt for his son.

"Mr. Miller, see that smoke in the sky?" he said, pointing. "Could someone be burning trash? What could that be?"

The horrified look on the man's face said it all.

"My place!" he cried as others came to look and point, too. "Have the sheriff call in the volunteers! Someone find and tell my wife!" Levi thrust the box into Nate's hands and was off at a run toward the buggies.

"Wow, where there's smoke, there's fire," Nate heard Mike Getz say.

But not an arson, please, God, not an arson in broad daylight, Nate prayed as he ran toward VERA while others ran to find the sheriff. Not with Jacob in jail and the rest of his suspects—except for Hannah Esh—right under his nose.

"Mr. Miller!" Nate shouted. "Your buggy's too slow. Come with me!"

16

Sarah was watching Nate when he and the men spotted the distant smoke. When she saw Mr. Miller run for his buggy, she moved away from the schoolhouse so she could see the sky. Oh, no! If not at the Millers' place, near it. At least there was not much wind today to fan the flames. And a fire in daylight—not at night?

She got to Mrs. Miller just after Reuben Schrock told her about the smoke. "But, if that's our place, Noah's in the barn!" she cried, then pressed both hands over her mouth. She looked as if she'd collapse.

Sarah held her up by one elbow. "If we can't catch your husband, you can go with me," she told her as Mr. Schrock supported her other arm.

"Where is Levi?" the woman asked.

"Somewhere in the line of buggies and cars heading out," Sarah said, scanning the area. "I don't see him now, but I do see a way."

She let Mrs. Miller lean on Mr. Schrock and ran to the schoolhouse lane just as Nate pulled VERA out of the field still crowded with departing, slow-moving buggies and cars. Four cars and several buggies blocked him from being able to get out on the road. Suddenly, from VERA came a rhythmic, loud croak like the honk of a goose. As the buggies pulled off to the side to let Nate through and the cars tried to get out of the way, Sarah and Mr. Schrock hurried Mrs. Miller toward VERA.

Once they were close enough, Sarah saw that Mr. Miller sat in the cab with Nate. As they hustled Mrs. Miller closer, she seemed to drag her feet until she saw her husband in the big black truck.

"Mrs. Miller's going, too!" Sarah shouted to Nate through his open window.

"Make it fast and secure the door once you're in!"

Her heart pounded. She was going to this fire with Nate, too. The sheriff's car, which had been parked along the road, sped away with its lights pulsing and shrill siren sounding loudly enough to drown out VERA's lower one.

Peter Clawson appeared, out of breath, red-faced, still toting his big-lens camera. "What's that smoke from?" he shouted at Nate, then saw who sat next to him. "Millers? Can I go, too? You owe me big-time, MacKenzie, and turnabout's fair play!"

She didn't hear what Nate told him, but Peter ran around in back, too. It seemed an eternity to Sarah as she and Mr. Schrock got the trembling woman in the back of the vehicle and both climbed in with her. Peter managed to get in without help. While Mr. Schrock closed and latched the back doors, Sarah ran to the small front window to the cab and rapped her knuckles on it. "Go! Go!"

The traffic ahead must have cleared, because they

careered out onto the road. The four of them in back grabbed for handholds. Sarah sat Mrs. Miller down in the single chair at the narrow table. Sarah and Mr. Schrock sat on the floor, wedged in, while Peter put his equipment on the floor but stood looking around inside VERA.

Sarah was soon back on her feet, propping herself up between the table and the counter. No wonder things inside here were all bolted down or stowed away. The once-familiar roads outside the front windshield she could peek through between Nate's and Mr. Miller's heads went by in a blur.

It annoyed Sarah that Peter began to question Mrs. Miller, so she told him, "Have a heart."

With a little shrug, he said, "But I have a head, too, and you know this fire doesn't fit the pattern. The decorated barn does, of course, but not the timing."

When no one answered him, he went back to eyeing the carefully labeled drawers and shelves. No doubt, Sarah thought, there would soon be a newspaper article on Nate's vehicle. But what did Peter mean that Nate owed him big-time and turnabout was fair play? She didn't like the way he'd called the barn she'd painted "decorated."

At least in the rush of things, Nate hadn't had time to argue about her going along. He'd said he wanted her off the arson case, but here she was, of course with her own finagling. If it was the Miller barn, if it was arson, didn't that prove Jacob wasn't the arsonist?

"Can you see the smoke through that little window, Sarah?" Mrs. Miller asked. "It can't be our place, our barn. Not in broad daylight, not with Noah there."

"Noah?" Peter said. "You mean someone was supposed to be protecting the barn?"

Mr. Schrock spoke, his voice shaking, but he addressed Mrs. Miller, not Peter. "Levi said Noah was doing repairs in the loft. Was it so dark he'd take a lantern up there? Is there hay or straw around?"

"Hay and lots of it," Sarah said, before she realized she should have let Mrs. Miller answer. "We're on your road now," she reported. "I see the sheriff's car way ahead, but we're going to beat the firemen."

"Minus two of them," Mr. Schrock said. "Mike Getz is on leave and Levi's with us. We'll do what we can."

Sarah could see now that it was the Miller place—and the Miller barn. She wasn't sure whether to tell Mrs. Miller or let her see it for herself when she'd have her husband to comfort her. But better forewarned, she thought. She'd want to know to prepare herself for the worst, if it was her family's barn.

"We're almost to your house, Mrs. Miller. I see a lot of smoke but not many flames coming from the barn. Let's pray Noah is waiting outside the barn to help fight the fire, too."

Nate was furious. He had not been sure he had an arsonist locked up, but he had been sure he had definite suspects, knew a profile of the criminal and had figured out his M.O. But this—if it was arson, and the barn and painted quilt square said it was—blew all his work away. Once he checked out Hannah Esh's alibi for this blaze, if she had a solid one, he had nothing. Yoder was in jail and everyone else was at the auction, including Ray-Lynn Logan, his long-shot possibility.

He'd thought solving these Amish arsons would be a walk in a pretty park. What an idiot!

"I don't see Noah," Levi said as Nate turned into the yard and parked close to the house. Sheriff Freeman was there, his light bar blinking as red as the few flames that were visible. He was walking around the barn with his gun drawn.

Nate didn't hit the digital electronic siren again but laid on his horn to see if that would bring Noah from the house or barn. The sheriff probably didn't know there was a missing person here. Levi was out of the truck, running for the burning barn. Nate jumped out as Peter Clawson climbed down from the back, then Reuben Schrock and Sarah climbed out with Mrs. Miller between them. Nate knew he'd broken protocol. No civilians in the way during an active fire, certainly none packed in the back of VERA, but the Amish had changed him. He saw Mrs. Miller hurry toward the house while Reuben ran over to fill in the sheriff.

"Do you want your fire gear again?" Sarah shouted to Nate. "I can get it ready."

"Yes! Good!"

She turned back toward VERA. What would he do without her—ever—a voice in Nate's head shouted at him.

Both of the Millers were screaming, "Noah! Noah! Noah!" Mrs. Miller was yelling into the front door of the house, and Levi toward the barn. Nate could see he was heading to slide open the big front doors, which were, strangely, both closed. Sarah's Crown of Thorns painting in blue, green and gold—M.E.'s colors—seemed to writhe behind the pall of drifting smoke.

"Don't open those doors, or the air will fan the

flames!" the sheriff shouted at Levi before Nate could. "Right now, it looks contained at the back, high up, maybe still mostly smoldering."

"Wet wood and wet hay from leaks in the roof," Nate shouted. "I checked it out on Thursday. But when the flames eat down to the dry stuff, it will really go."

The fact the fire was high up, Nate thought, was like the first fire, and this barn was built somewhat like the Esh one, despite the fact it was much older and run-down. And, like at the Esh fire, a ladder lay on the ground, next to the barn that he hadn't seen there two days ago. He had to get geared up and go inside to see if Noah had been knocked out or was down from smoke inhalation. That could be as deadly as the flames.

"Is there a first floor door in back, like the Esh barn?" Nate asked Levi and the sheriff as he held the Amish man's arm to keep him from lunging at the doors. Once he and Sarah had seen that painted note and the torrents of rain began, they had not made a complete circuit of the structure, nor had he when he came out with Levi. He knew now he should have.

"*Ya,* a door, but it's got years of vines all over it, sealed shut. What if he fell and bumped over a lantern while he was working? Fell in the loft like you did? Noah! Nooo-aaaah! I should have stayed with him! Nooo-aaah!"

Sarah was dragging Nate's fire gear over to the edge of the yard just a few feet from them, laying it out in order just as he had learned to do in fire school. The woman was amazing.

Then, they heard someone scream.

They all froze, looking at one another, listening for the muted sounds over the increasing crackle of roof flames. "Those great horned owl nestlings?" Sarah asked, cocking her head. But then the scream became not an *eeeeeee* sound but *"Help meeeee!"*

The sheriff ran back to his vehicle for something. Levi lunged for the barn doors, and Nate let him as he dragged his heavy fire pants up, pulling the suspenders over his shoulders. On her knees before him, Sarah untied his running shoes and yanked them off and shoved his boots toward him, so he could jam his feet into them. She thrust Nate's heavy jacket at Reuben Schrock; he held it for him as he shrugged it on. As Nate moved under the weight of it toward the barn, Sarah held out his hood, then his oxygen mask, for him.

Levi had one door partially open. The heat blast from the barn smacked them, even thirty feet away. Smoke belched out, blinding them as Reuben grabbed Levi to keep him from running inside. Like a harbinger of doom, the barn owl flew out past them with a whoosh of its huge wings. Mrs. Miller lifted and clasped her apron to her face, not to stop the stench of smoldering wood and hay, but to wipe away tears so she could see.

Nate jolted as a deep, loud voice behind him said, "Noah Miller, are you inside the barn? Noah, this is the sheriff. Where are you?"

The sheriff had brought out his bullhorn.

"Help me!" Noah called weakly from within.

Nate adjusted his oxygen mask and turned on the flow. He heard only his own breath. His Amish superwoman handed his hat and gloves to him. As Reuben held Levi back from plunging into the heat and smoke, Nate took the big flashlight she held out to him and walked into the burning barn.

* * *

Sarah moved and talked as if something within her had taken over. She blinked back tears from fear as well as from the stinging smoke. How could Nate so much as see in there? He'd said sometimes firemen found victims by crawling on the floor or by stumbling over them. The place where they'd kissed and caressed had become an inferno, and if Noah was trapped in there…

She remembered how Noah used to follow Jacob around. He was younger, but somehow they'd hit it off at school—or had that been at Lizzie's wedding? Jacob had the answers for everything then, and Noah had been thrilled when Jacob gave him attention, got him a job sweeping up and greasing axels at the Buggy Wheel Shop. She was grieving to think that another Amish barn with one of her paintings was going up in flames, but a life was much more precious.

Then she remembered the window high up. Nate had tried to look out of it during the storm, hoping to see what was making the knocking sound or even get a glimpse of someone who'd left that note on the barn.

The sheriff had gone back to his car. Sarah left the Millers and Reuben Schrock as they waited and prayed for Noah and Nate. Around the side of the barn, she saw the flames, and the worst of the black smoke roaring through the broken roof seemed to be on the other side. It was probably too smoky inside to see much, but she could try looking in through that high window.

When she ran around the barn, she saw the sheriff had driven out on the road and had left his car there with the light bar blinking. He was jogging back toward the barn after setting up orange cones to stop traffic coming from the direction of the freeway, but he'd left open the way from town. Peter was standing back a ways, photographing the burning barn. The flames from the roof reflected in his huge lens as if his camera was on fire. Where were those firefighters? It seemed she'd been here hours, but it was probably mere minutes.

Because she didn't want to pull the Millers away from their vigil, nor have Mr. Schrock tell her she shouldn't try this, she picked up only the far end of the ladder and dragged it around the corner and under the window. She was good at setting up ladders against barns, at managing her skirts as she climbed the rungs. She beat down horrible memories of her nightmare of being burned, tied to a ladder. She had to try this without the others seeing her.

When she got up to the level of the window, she saw her idea was useless. Smoke boiled inside, bubbling to get out. But when Noah screamed again, he sounded so close, as if he was just on the other side of the glass. That meant Noah was in the loft! If she could break this window, could he crawl out here? Firemen on ladders made rescues from windows. Nate surely couldn't climb that flimsy ladder they'd used inside to get to the loft, not in that heavy gear of his.

"Help me!" she screamed. "Back here!"

Peter hurried around and began to take pictures of her up on the ladder. Sheriff Freeman ran around the corner of the barn right behind him and yelled, "What in the Sam Hill are you doing, girl! Get down from there!"

"I can hear Noah close to here! I think he's trapped in the loft. If you have something to break the window, maybe we can pull him out here!"

Mr. Miller came, too, and started to climb the ladder,

before the sheriff pulled him back. "Get down, Sarah, and I'll try to break the glass with this gun handle. Get down and let me up!"

Something inside the barn gave way and the few flames eating through the roof roared higher, slapping them all with heat and light. Sarah scrambled down and the sheriff climbed up, quickly shattering at least one windowpane with the butt of his gun while Mr. Miller and Sarah held the ladder and Peter's camera clicked madly away. Mrs. Miller watched in horror.

Sarah saw the sheriff duck as smoke roiled at him like a black fist. If anything happened to Jack Freeman, Ray-Lynn would probably kill her. But if anything happened to Nate, Sarah could almost see killing herself.

"Noah! Noah Miller, you hear me?" the sheriff shouted.

Despite the gush of smoke, he yelled directly in the window, then called down to them, "Says he's trapped, half hanging down from the loft! Scared to drop down. You go tell Nate! I think he was coming back out."

"He can't hear a thing with that oxygen mask on!" Sarah shouted. "Tell Noah he has to let go before the hay under him catches fire! Nate can help him if he'll just drop to the first floor!"

The sheriff relayed what she had said back to Noah. She knew Noah didn't have long before the hay in the ground level would be aflame and roast him to death, like chicken on those grills today, if smoke didn't kill him first. It seemed to be chokingly thick even out here as she ran around to see if Nate had come out yet. Maybe when someone was being burned, the best to hope for was smoke suffocation. Maybe those Amish martyrs years ago could breathe in the smoke and not have to suffer from the flames. She pictured herself and Nate, hanging, caught halfway. No fire then, only the one between them.

Yes, thank God, Nate was outside. But now she'd have to send him back in. Finally, she heard the wail of the distant fire truck sirens coming closer. Should she wait for them and not tell Nate? But Noah could be dead by then.

She got in Nate's face—his mask, that is—and tried to gesture to him about Noah. Noah in the loft, caught, just like us. Noah's father almost ran inside before his wife held to him hard. Again, she ignored Peter's camera almost in their faces.

Sarah thought Nate nodded. At least he lumbered back inside and, in what seemed an eternity, came out dragging Noah with his shoes and trousers tattered and mostly burned off. The skin from his torso looked blistered and his legs blackened and—and loose. Hefting him by his arms so only his feet dragged, Nate and the sheriff laid him gently on the grass, at least forty feet back from the barn. He screamed once as they set him down, twisted in agony, then lay still.

Sarah and Reuben Schrock had to hold the Millers back from touching him, even his head and upper torso, which didn't look so ravaged. Sheriff Freeman got on his phone; Sarah could hear him telling someone at his office to call for MedFlight and talking about the Cleveland Clinic. Noah started hacking up black spit and gasping for air.

Nate pulled his head gear off. "No—don't cover him, either!" he told Mrs. Miller as she took off her apron and knelt next to her son. "Don't touch him, or his skin will come off. It's bad enough I had to drag him, but the hay was going to go."

The barn suddenly roared as scarlet and orange flames battled with the billowing smoke. Nate knelt next to the burned boy and put the oxygen mask over his nose and mouth. "Breathe, Noah. Breathe, breathe," he recited as Noah started to suck in the air. Sarah knew his lungs could be damaged.

Sheriff Freeman finally told Peter to get away, and he did, turning his attention to the firemen fighting with the flames. Though the volunteers worked feverishly to douse them, those around Noah Miller hardly looked away as the boy fought for his life.

17

An endless half hour went by as Nate kept Noah breathing rich oxygen and the volunteer firemen fought the blaze. Nate could recall vivid details of the moments the Columbus firemen had pulled him from his burning house. One of them had put his oxygen mask over his mouth and nose that day until the emergency squad arrived. He tried to shut out those haunting memories, but concentrating on the here and now was terrible, too.

With whispered prayers, the Millers and Sarah knelt around them in a little circle, as if to protect Noah when that wasn't possible anymore. They could see he was suffering, gasping for breath, even with the flow of oxygen. He moaned but did not move. Nate knew that third-degree burns over fifty percent of the body would be fatal. Noah's legs were definitely third-degree with peeling flesh, but his torso seemed second degree with blisters. The smell, not only of smoke, but of burned flesh was stomach-churning.

Nate sent Sarah over to the sheriff, who was helping the firefighters, to suggest he put up more orange

cones to stop traffic both ways on the road. "Tell him
to signal the medical helicopter to land there, instead
of near the barn. We can't have the fire fanned by the
wash from the chopper's rotors coming too close."

A few minutes later, the helicopter landed out on the
road in a whirl of air and noise. When the two flight
nurses—one man, one woman—rushed toward them,
pushing their gurney up the dirt lane from the road,
Nate identified himself and helped them lift Noah onto
it. He followed along to the helicopter and watched as
they switched Noah to their oxygen supply and started
IVs. It helped to learn that one of them was a burn specialist. They said one person could accompany the patient. The Millers decided Noah's mother would go.

As frail as she looked, Nate admired how Mrs. Miller
had held up in the face of all this, even better than Levi.
He felt for them, felt he knew them, after all he had
been through with his own family. Sarah had said Mrs.
Miller had nearly collapsed at first, but he'd seen her
come through strong when Levi almost lost control. His
mother would have been like that—if she had lived.

"Nate, you okay?" the sheriff asked. "Soon as I get
this traffic moving again and not just gawking, I'm
going to get someone to drive Mr. Miller and Reuben
Schrock to the hospital in Cleveland."

Nate nodded. He should volunteer, because then he
could go directly to question Hannah Esh again, but
Levi and Reuben would need someone who could stay
with them for a while. Exhausted, he blinked back tears
he wiped away with his filthy hand, realizing for the
first time how his eyes watered and stung from the
smoke. That was it, wasn't it—just the smoke?

Sarah came up to him with a wet towel. He hadn't

seen her for a while, but he realized she must have been helping Mrs. Miller get some things together. As the chopper took off, turned tail and flew away to the north, Nate realized an Amish woman and her son were taking a forbidden airplane ride. When it was necessary, the Amish adapted. If he sided with Ray-Lynn to try to get Sarah a chance to paint, would she be willing?

"Thanks for all your help—again," Nate told Sarah as he wiped his face and hands with the towel.

"You've seen things like this before, Noah's injuries, I mean," she said, her words barely discernible over the noise of the departing chopper. "Do you think he'll make it?"

"I hope—pray—so, but I'm not sure." But he was sure he wanted to question the boy as soon as he could, right after he had a chat with Hannah Esh.

After the fire had burned itself to a tumble of black, charred barn bones, Sarah knew she should leave with some of the Amish who had finally arrived from the auction in buggies. But she left the Miller farm as she'd come, in the back of VERA with her mother with her and no one in the front seat with Nate. She was grateful to have someone Amish here instead of Peter Clawson.

As far as she knew, he was still asking questions and taking pictures back at the Millers'. She, like Nate, had noted that Mike Getz had arrived and was helping fight the fire, one-handed. Ray-Lynn had appeared, too, and was handing out coffee and doughnuts, just as she had the morning after the first fire.

"Isn't this VERA something?" *Mamm* said, looking around wide-eyed. In the deepening dusk, Nate had lit the interior for them, and the chrome and white walls shone. "Looks like a modern kitchen. Oh, I pray Noah will be healed. Did you hear anything those rescue people said?"

Sarah responded to that and *Mamm*'s other questions, but nothing seemed to stick in her brain except that three times someone had targeted barns with her paintings on them. It scared her to death that she'd overheard Nate tell the sheriff he was going to question Hannah again. She prayed silently that all this could somehow help bring Hannah home, but the right way, not charged with arson by the man Sarah wanted so to help.

Nate drove up their lane to drop them off at the house, but he turned VERA out toward the road, not the pond, before he got out. Sarah's stomach knotted tighter. Was he going back to the fire or after Hannah right now?

Martha ran from the *grossdaadi haus* and Gabe from the farmhouse to meet them, both full of questions until *Mamm* said that *Daad* would be back in the buggy soon and they would all talk then. Sarah knew Nate was going to drive away before she could talk to him, but his so-called crackberry sounded and he took the call. As he listened, he looked at Sarah. Everyone stopped talking. Sarah feared Nate might tell them that Noah Miller was dead.

"Okay, just a minute," he told whoever it was.

"Sarah," he said, "Hannah Esh wants to talk to me and insists I bring you along. Will you go with me?"

"*Ya,* but clear to Cleveland?"

"She's parked by the cemetery, just down the road. She says she's been in the area all day."

Sarah gasped and clapped her hand over her mouth. Hannah here all day when nearly everyone else was at the auction? Was she going to confess to the arsons and surrender to Nate so she wanted her old friend there to support her?

Just a week ago, Sarah would have asked for permission to go off with Nate in VERA, but she took her hand down from her mouth and squared her shoulders. "Sure, I'll help—hopefully help Hannah and you."

After Nate told Hannah to stay put and they'd be there soon, *Mamm* told Sarah, "See if you can bring her back here. Tell her we all want her to come home. She can stay here if she needs—you know, needs a place to live halfway home."

Sarah nodded and climbed up in the passenger seat of VERA while Nate got in and closed the driver's side door.

"As I said, I'm really grateful for all your help today, especially after I came down so hard on you before. I just don't want you to get hurt," Nate told her as he drove out of the lane and turned onto the road.

Her voice snagged with emotion. "I want to help." It was unspoken and that simple, but somehow she knew they were working together again. But what would she do without him when this was all over, one way or the other?

"When I was inside the Millers' barn that first time today," he said, "I could see the fire was set from inside, probably from spilled—or poured—kerosene or gasoline, far back in the corner near no windows or doors. That keeps up the pattern of a different incendiary method for each barn burning, but it's hard to believe our clever, careful, after-dark arsonist would set a fire in the lower part of the barn while Noah was using a hammer and saw in the loft. If I don't get a confession here from Hannah…"

"Then you will have no suspects left?"

"We'll see. By the way, Ray-Lynn tells me she's approached you about doing some paintings, not to be sold around here, but through an art dealer friend of hers in Columbus. She let slip you have a book of sketches she admires."

"*Ya*—yes to both things. But I can't take that step yet and she knows it."

"Yet? Then you've considered it?"

"Only in my wildest dreams, but I dream about a lot of things that will never be. Why did you bring that up now?"

"As different as these fires are, besides the common link of the barns belonging to church leaders, your paintings are what they all have in common."

"I know. Someone hates me, you think? Nate," she said, turning in her seat belt to face him, "you don't think that Ray-Lynn… I mean, I suppose if all my barn paintings were ruined or I couldn't do more of them, I'd be more ready to try paintings of Amish life. Or are you thinking the arsonist might want to draw big-time attention to my art instead of ruin it? But—"

"Okay, okay, we'll let that go for now, but I'm getting desperate enough to set some sort of trap at the Hostetler barn and stop your work on your own barn."

"No, I won't stop. I can vouch for Ray-Lynn just like I can for Hannah, if you think someone who cares about me is trying to draw outside attention to my work."

"Some people are not what they seem. I've learned that the hard way. Besides, you can't vouch for either of them. You weren't there, weren't with them."

"I know my friends! And that fire demon from hell is not going to scare us or stop us, not me, not the brethren and sisters. Let's set a double trap, one at the Hostetlers' place and one at ours. I know that's what my *daad* is starting to think now, Bishop Esh, too. There—up ahead, see?" she said, pointing through the windshield into the deepening dusk. "There's Hannah's car."

As they got out, Hannah appeared, hurrying down the hill from among the simple Amish gravestones. Sarah knew she used to visit her *grossmamm*'s grave a lot. They had been very close, just the way Sarah was— had been—to hers. In VERA's headlights, Sarah could see Hannah's hair was still spiky and red, her black leggings, skirt and top slashed and torn, but she'd toned down the dramatic makeup.

"Wow, that thing's quite a ride!" Hannah said, pointing at VERA. Her light tone surprised Sarah. She didn't sound like someone who was about to confess to arson.

Hannah hugged Sarah, emanating that same incense-smoky smell—not cigarettes—then extended her hand to Nate to shake it. Sarah had to remember to tell Nate that Hannah had smelled like that for over a year, so it was not barn smoke, but her insides twisted tighter. What if Hannah was to blame?

"I was hoping you two would do a big favor for me," Hannah told them. "I don't know who else to ask or trust here, or who would agree."

"Talk," Nate said as Sarah held her breath. She could tell how tense he was. His muscles seemed coiled, as if he'd leap at Hannah.

"I was trying to get up the nerve to come to the auction today," she admitted with a big sigh, "but I just ended up here, walking all over, waiting for you to be free, driving around some. I tried your cell number you gave me a couple of times late afternoon, Mr. Mac-Kenzie, but you weren't answering, and I didn't want to leave voice mail. I even drove past the auction twice, but when I came by a third time, everyone was peeling out. I have one hundred and thirty-five dollars saved up and I want to donate it—anonymously—to the fund to rebuild my family's barn. I thought if you took some of it and Sarah donated some, they'd never realize or question the source."

"That's why you were hanging around here all day?" Nate asked as Hannah dug a wad of bills out of her black leather purse. "Don't you know about the fire at Levi Miller's?"

"I—no. Not another fire!"

"Or that Jacob Yoder's in jail for questioning for the arsons?" he went on, his voice hard. "But unless he lit Miller's barn from behind bars, it has to be someone else."

For one moment, Sarah thought her friend would turn and run.

"I—I haven't been online or seen a paper, not even the *Home Valley News,*" she said, looking panicked. Her gaze darted from one to the other. "It's not me, if that's what you're thinking!" She thrust the roll of bills at Sarah. "I came for this and that's all. I told you before I did not burn my parents' barn. I came to donate to help rebuild it and I have nothing against the Schrocks or Millers. All I know about the Millers is that Noah used to be a friend of Jacob's—you knew that, Sarah. What? Why is Sarah crying?" she asked Nate instead of Sarah herself.

"Noah Miller was badly burned in the blaze today and may not make it," Nate told her.

Hannah gasped. This whole thing was a surprise to her, Sarah was sure of that. She couldn't be hiding all that guilt, even though Sarah had seen her hide things from her parents.

"And," Nate went on, "if there's a death from an arson, that can bring in the FBI and that will make everything around here ten times tougher—not easier, believe me—for the Amish and my investigation. Sarah, take your friend's money so we can donate it for the cause, but we're all going to step inside VERA right now for an in-depth interview about everything you did today, Hannah."

"I didn't do it—anything! And don't start thinking that was a bribe!" Hannah shouted as Sarah took the money in one hand and squeezed her friend's hand with the other.

"Look, Hannah," Nate said, stooping to get right in her face, "I just need answers. I'm not accusing you of anything yet."

Yet, Sarah thought. She could feel Hannah trembling, and it vibrated clear through her. Nate showed Hannah a badge he carried in his wallet and explained he had the right to question her either here or at the police station if she preferred to do it there.

Sarah was soon shaking, too. How had this happened that she was helping a government authority, and worse—one she was afraid she was coming to love?

After nearly an hour of what Sarah considered harsh questioning, the same things asked, over and roundabout, from every direction, Nate finally let Hannah

get in her car and leave. Her alibis—Nate's word—
could not be verified with anyone she'd been with.
But Hannah had spoken as passionately as ever, Sarah
thought, and she was certain she was telling the truth—
she just had to be.

They had tried to talk her into spending the night
with Sarah at the *grossdaadi haus,* but she wanted to go
home, though Sarah had noted when she said the word
home, her voice had wavered.

"You know where your home is, really, don't you?"
Sarah said to her in German as she hugged her hard.
"You come back, stay with us for a while in transition.
Mamm said so, like the Kauffman place can be your
halfway house to really going home. Besides, Seth—"

"Don't talk about him!" Hannah insisted, also in
German. "I just can't. Please, Sarah, if you don't have
to, don't tell my people Mr. MacKenzie thinks it might
be me, because it isn't!"

"I know. I'll work on him."

"I can see you already have," she said. She got in her
car and pulled away. Sarah watched the red taillights,
like two feral eyes, fade into darkness.

In VERA, going back to the Kauffman farm, Nate
said, "Sarah, I'm just trying to clear her, honestly. When
you two spoke German, did she say anything that would
help?"

"Not help you, nor me and her family because we
want her to come home. I trust her, Nate."

"And that goes a long way with me—really. I think
your instincts are good."

But a mess lately, she thought, because she wanted to
throw herself in his arms the moment he stopped VERA
near the *grossdaadi haus.* Leaving the motor running,

he hurried around to open the passenger's side door for her this time.

"I heard her say my name in German, but who's Seth?" he pursued. "You mentioned a Seth."

"You have good German ears, *ausländer*. He's the man she thought she'd marry. He—he married someone else."

"He or his wife don't belong to any of the families with the burned barns?"

"No! No. It's a long, sad story."

He walked her to the porch steps. She got the key out from under the pot of newly planted geraniums. Maybe it was because she was just remembering how much Hannah and Seth had once loved each other, but this reminded her of what a come-calling friend would do, walk a *maidal* to her door. And then, there would be a good-night smooch, of course, but she wasn't expecting that now, only wanting it badly.

"Sarah, would you trust me enough to let me see your sketchbook?"

"Sure. I'd be pleased. It's just inside, and I can get it back from you tomorrow."

"I'll need to spend time at the Miller barn, then I'm going to the Cleveland Clinic, hopefully to interview Noah, but I'll see you get it back safe and sound. I know the drawings are wonderful."

While he waited on the porch, she unlocked the door and slipped inside. Deeply touched by what he'd said—it was as if he'd embraced or caressed her with those words—she stood for a moment in the dark, her hands clasped between her breasts. Hannah and Ray-Lynn believed in her work. Now, perhaps Nate would, too.

Her eyes adjusted to the deeper darkness. Martha

was asleep, breathing loudly, on the hideaway bed in the living room. Tiptoeing around the bed, Sarah retrieved her sketchbook from the back of the end table drawer where she kept it under her Bible. As she took it out to Nate, she realized she hadn't looked at it for months, maybe since she'd showed it to Ray-Lynn, then refused to show it to that art dealer friend of hers from Columbus. Yet how much it meant to her, precious memories, a dream deferred, the outpourings not only of her hand but of her head and heart.

She gave the book to Nate and leaned back against VERA's warm hood next to him, so close their arms touched. The motor was still running, so she knew he didn't mean to stay long. They were not in the headlights, but enough light reflected that they could see.

"I'll take good care of this," he promised. "My face and hands are the only clean part of me. Time for a dip in the pond."

"You be careful, swimming alone at night."

"Come with me, then."

"I'd better not," she said, but she wanted to go really bad. She watched him open the book to the first sketch, then went to the next, then another. Why was he looking at them so fast? Oh, maybe because she'd not only sketched people but had dared to draw their faces, when that was forbidden. But she couldn't help herself, for that was part of her art. Truly, her love of this place included the faces of those she knew and loved, smiling faces, serious faces, worshipful faces—

"Sarah, I can tell you didn't do these flames, these fires—did you?" he asked.

"Fires? What fires?"

She leaned closer, squinting to see. With a gasp, she

grabbed the book from him and bent into the glare of
VERA's headlights, flipping through faster, faster, clear
to the back of it. On every drawing, in what looked like
dried blood, someone had scrawled leaping, streaking
flames burning buildings, barns and—and her people.

18

Sarah's knees buckled. As she started to slide down VERA's hood, Nate grabbed her and held her to him, her shoulder under his arm.

"No. No, I never... Who would do this?" she whispered, still fanning through the pages, then just pressing the sketchbook to her breasts as if to comfort all the people inside it.

"And why?" Nate demanded. "Do you think someone could have broken into the *grossdaadi haus,* looking for something else, then saw this? When did you see it last?"

"A couple of months ago. It was hidden. It hurts for me to look at these sometimes."

"Because you want to draw or paint more than that?"

She nodded jerkily.

"It looks like blood."

"I know. Quite a bit of it. I—now I'd have nothing to show an art dealer, anyway."

"Did Jacob ever see the sketches?"

"No."

"Martha or Gabe? Your parents?"

"As far as I know, only Hannah, Ella and Ray-Lynn, but…"

"What?"

"Well, you know my grandmother gets off her bean sometimes over how our people were persecuted and martyred in Europe, burned to death among other torments. It's the reason the Amish came to America. She fears we'll be burned out again and she keeps trying to warn us. What if she found this and did this?"

"I take it she's not working with knives in the kitchen anymore. Does she have any cuts on her?"

"Cuts and bruises. You've seen her, Nate. We try to keep sharp things away now, and she doesn't quilt anymore. But she still dresses herself and we close our bodices with straight pins."

He looked at her breasts, squinting as if to see the pins. She went on in a rush, "I guess a pinprick could make drops of blood to smear like this, but she must have done it time after time."

"Or we're back to someone else who found your art and wanted to warn or punish you because he or she knew it was *verboten*. The art itself and drawing in the faces—right?"

Sarah nodded. As distraught as she was, it touched her that Nate was not only recognizing German words but using them now. And that he'd come to know her people well enough already to realize images of Amish faces were as frowned upon as prideful drawings.

"So you can't ask her if she did this?" he asked.

"I could, but these pictures would upset her. Her copy of the *Martyrs Mirror* has some etchings of Amish being burned, and those haunt her."

"Who knows about that book?"

"All the Amish. It's second only to the Bible for us, and we have a hymnal of song lyrics passed down, too, the *Ausbund*."

"Your grandmother never goes out and around on her own, does she?"

"You don't mean does she wander the nearby fields to ignite barn fires!"

"I mean, if she found this book, wherever you had it stashed, what if she showed it to that person in black she thought she saw."

"I don't think she imagined that anymore, not since I saw someone through your night goggles in the field when the Schrock barn burned. But show it to a stranger while he defaced it—no."

Suddenly, she couldn't keep the sobs inside. Holding the ruined sketchbook to her breasts with one hand, she pressed the other over her eyes. As she sucked in air and her shoulders shook, Nate took the book from her and put it on the hood, then pulled her into his arms. She clung tight to him, crying, shaking both of them. Then, suddenly, he picked her up and sat down on the grass with her sprawled across his lap.

It was dark, though the gold streaks of VERA's headlights still stabbed into the night beyond. She shifted in his lap, turned to him and clung, lifting her face toward his. She meant to tuck her face under his chin, but suddenly his comforting turned crazy, his hands everywhere, his lips on hers, soft at first, then strong, demanding.

Thinking she would explode inside, she met him kiss for kiss, opening her lips to his. Nothing else mattered but his touch, his strength, his need battling with hers.

These runaway feelings—*ya,* she'd never known herself before this.

"Sarah, Sarah," was all he said, and then they kissed again, longer and deeper as her arms around his neck held him to her. They sprawled on the soft grass, already wet with dew. Everything bad seemed washed away, all her fears. She would not have cared if the entire world was lost right now, flamed into the fires she was feeling. Dizzy, dazed. Nate. She wanted Nate MacKenzie even more than she wanted to paint.

They jolted apart as they heard her *daad*'s voice, probably from the farmhouse porch, but too close.

"Sarah? Nate? *Mamm* wants to know did Hannah say she'd come back?"

Suddenly bereft of Nate's touch, Sarah stood, settling her skirts. How she found a steady voice she wasn't sure as she walked around the front of VERA where he could see her in the headlights and called to him, "She left. I think she's missing everything here, though."

"A lot can be learned from your old friends Hannah and Jacob," *Daad* called to her, not coming closer. She heard the porch swing. How long had he been sitting there? "They both wanted something away from our people outside the Home Valley and both are unhappy and in real trouble."

Was that a clever warning to her about Nate? About her painting? Did *Daad* think Hannah could be guilty of the arsons?

"I'd better get going," Nate said, keeping his voice low. "Can I take the sketchbook to look at it carefully, maybe run a test on the blood?"

"*Ya,* it's no good to me now—ruined."

"Anyone looking at it carefully could still tell a lot about the artist, the skill, the potential."

"You don't think someone would look at it and think the artist is a pure maniac?"

"Pyromaniac?"

"That's it."

"I think your raw talent shines through. This book would have to actually *be* burned before someone wouldn't see a unique artist at work here."

He walked around the truck cab and got in. Sarah stepped up on the *grossdaadi haus* porch, feeling the lack of him—physical, sure, but emotional, too—the moment he drove away. She could not bear to go speak to her father now, so she went into the *grossdaadi haus* and locked the door behind her.

She tiptoed into the bathroom, hearing her *grossmamm*'s gentle snoring in the next room. Could she have defaced the drawings? It must have been her. If not, since the sketchbook had been hidden, she'd have to start believing in a demon who left damning notes around, where she was sure to find them.

On the way out of the Home Valley the next morning, Nate saw the buggies of Amish families as they headed to church. Services were held in homes or barns every other Sunday, and the Hostetlers were hosts today. All those people—about thirty local families—would gather in the Hostetler barn with Sarah's painting on it with an arsonist loose, one he couldn't catch. He pictured Sarah's sketch of buggies parked around a barn for a church service and the bloody flames someone had smeared across it all.

He wondered if the arsonist would be at church. If so, it wasn't Jacob Yoder, though he was back in the mix of suspects again at least for the first two barn burnings. Could the third have been a copycat arson? At dawn this morning, Sheriff Freeman had served the search warrant to go through Jacob's rented room and car in West Salem, a small town about a half hour away. Nate had just met with the sheriff at his office.

"That third fire makes it look like Jacob's not guilty, but I've got to show you what I found on his bedroom wall," Jack had said, and pointed to a folder he shoved toward Nate across his desk.

Inside were at least ten newspaper articles about the first two fires—pieces of tape still attached—roughly ripped from the *Cleveland Plain Dealer* and the *Home Valley News*. One of them had printing in small block letters up the left margin: "Serves them right for treating me wrong" and another had "God's Justice!"

"I guess he's back on the list of possible perps for the first two arsons," Nate admitted. "First tier."

"You got a second tier?"

"Just people of interest. Not counting Hannah Esh, two other females on the fringe of things. Women involved in something like this are rare. But Cindee Kramer for one. I talked to her about an hour ago, got her out of bed while, luckily, her charming friend Getz was still asleep. She claims she was confused about where she told Sarah that Getz was standing when he saw the second fire. She has easy access to artificial fireplace logs. Maybe she's working with Getz or just covering for him. And I found out only recently that

Ray-Lynn Logan was at the Esh place just before the first fire ignited, even opened the barn doors."

The big man jerked back in his chair as if he'd been slugged. "Ray-Lynn there then! You gotta be kidding me!"

"One of the Amish kids told me so I talked to her. She said she saw nothing and didn't want to get involved. She was there to ask Bishop Esh if Sarah could paint a quilt square for the restaurant. Let's just say she's been encouraging Sarah to branch out with her painting."

"Ray-Lynn should have told me that and told me you talked to her."

Nate thought Jack looked as if he'd chew his desk apart. His ruddy complexion had gone bright red.

"Jack, you okay?"

"Yeah, sure. Just surprised about Ray-Lynn, though it proves nothing except she needs a good shaking up for withholding evidence. Anyhow," he went on, though Nate could tell he was still steaming, "about Jacob. I found nothing but those articles in his possessions to implicate him. Thing is, his parents want to get him out on bail. Don't know where they'd get the money, though. I can stall them until tomorrow, but, after that, I think he's sprung unless we got more than these articles. Anger at the Amish does not an arsonist make."

"The printing doesn't look like a real match for the two threatening notes, either."

"I gave Clawson a bad time for not bringing that note he got at the newspaper office straight to me, but then you're the one he really wants info from. Let's just pray there are no more fires and that you get information out

of poor Noah Miller. He might have seen something
before that barn blaze."

As he'd left the sheriff's office, despite being hungry,
Nate avoided Ray-Lynn's crowded restaurant. Jack had
said she usually kept it closed on Sundays in defer-
ence to Amish beliefs about no Sunday sales. But he'd
also admitted he knew that she'd been ticked off at the
Amish lately for forbidding Sarah's artistic talent to
blossom and that Ray-Lynn needed the money. Nate
wondered if she could also want money from helping
Sarah sell her art. And if Sarah's barn paintings were
destroyed...or got her more publicity...

Sarah was at the center of things again. Nate agonized as he passed more buggies. Sarah, his helper, his
distraction, his passion. He sighed, and tried to force
his mind back to business. She'd said that after the long
church service of preaching and singing, the Amish
shared a simple meal. He'd been invited to both and
would have liked to attend, but he'd called the Cleveland Clinic and—since he was an official on the arson
case—was told he would be allowed a few minutes to
speak with Noah Miller. His condition had stabilized
but was still serious.

Driving past the burned Miller barn, which he would
examine more closely when the ruins cooled, Nate left
Eden County and turned north on busy I-77. The pace
picked up. Lately, he'd gotten used to slower driving,
and he had to force himself to keep up to the speed
limit. He needed to push this investigation. Funny how
the Home Valley area seemed so sheltered by gentle
hills, yet a serpent had gotten into paradise.

Partway to Cleveland, he got a call from his boss. He

put him on speakerphone so he could drive with both hands.

"I got your message, Nate. Have you talked to the burn victim yet?"

"On my way right now. They stabilized him, some second-degree burns, some third."

"He dies, and we get the FBI in on this."

"The Feds will come in strong and that won't work in Amish country. I've been learning the hard way there are special dos and don'ts around here. At times I still walk on thin ice, even though the Amish have embraced me."

Nate wished he hadn't used the word *embraced*. That sounded strange. He knew Sarah was never far from his thoughts.

"By the way," Mark said, "Peter Clawson called me for a phone interview Friday."

"A real go-getter, that guy."

"He insists there's an estranged daughter of the family from the first fire you're not looking at, maybe because she's a neighbor and friend to Sarah Kauffman, the one you said is helping you."

Nate gripped the steering wheel harder. He'd mentioned Hannah to Mark, but what was with Peter Clawson horning in?

"I've interviewed Hannah Esh twice," Nate explained, "once just last night. Her alibis are vague but plausible. She's on the list and is getting cut no extra slack."

"Glad to hear it. Well, you know the big-fish-in-little-pond syndrome, and I suspect Peter Clawson has it in spades. I've read his paper online. After you interview the fire victim, let me know if you still think the third fire is atypical."

"Roger that."

"One more thing. Are you going to publicize those two threatening quotes from the Bible or still sit on them? Clawson's pressing to publish the one he got."

"For now, unless Clawson blows it, I'd like to keep them quiet. We don't need more upheaval around here. But if a third one shows up, I might change my mind."

"It's your call. You know what you're doing. Talk to you soon."

And he'd talk to Peter Clawson soon, Nate thought. He would get on his case if he kept meddling. How Ray-Lynn, whom he hadn't mentioned to Mark as a person of interest but maybe should have, put up with Clawson as a partner was beyond him. Of course, if she could act as agent for Sarah's art, maybe she'd earn enough to buy full control of the restaurant and get Clawson off her back, too.

Sarah was glad that church was in the Hostetler barn today instead of the house. Not only did it allow the nearly one hundred and fifty Amish in their district to sit in the same room—men and women on separate sides of the aisle on backless benches—but their presence seemed to bestow a blessing on the only barn left with one of her quilt squares. The painting was Sunshine and Shadows, with its contrasting pattern of yellow, white, gray and black. *Ya,* she thought, life was like that, too. Much joy but much sorrow.

She stood with everyone for the first hymn, led by the deep-voiced *vorsinger,* or song leader. As usual, it was Seth Lantz, Ella's brother, the man Hannah should have married. Sarah remembered how beautifully their voices had blended together. For sure, Seth's sin was part of the reason Hannah left home. Sarah's rejection of Jacob didn't help him, either, but what he got into wasn't her fault—was it?

The barn had been swept and scrubbed. She loved being in it, feeling its strength over and around them. Her eyes took in the rows of her people all dressed up for the service as the chantlike first hymn began. Like some of the others, it had been penned by imprisoned Amish martyrs in Europe awaiting their torture or deaths. No wonder *Grossmamm* had fears buried deep inside her, despite the fact that was generations ago and they were safe here in America.

But lately, not safe enough. Noah Miller might die and was horribly burned. Someone was waging war on their barns, someone still hated and persecuted the church leaders—perhaps her, too—for her prideful art. Tears in her eyes, she sang the traditional hymn in German.

We wander in the forests dark,
With dogs upon our track;
And like the captive, silent lamb
Men bring us, prisoners, back.
They point to us, amid the throng,
And with their taunts offend,
And long to let the fire or ax
On heretics descend.

After a hymn of praise, Bishop Esh began to preach, gesturing broadly, walking back and forth before the congregation. Forgiveness and turning the other cheek were his first topic. He shared passages from the Book of Psalms that promised protection even in the hardest of times, which, as far as Sarah knew, was right now, the worst since the old days of death and burnings.

"'I called on the Lord in my distress...I will not fear, for what can man do to me,'" Bishop Esh recited.

He was much heartened she knew, by the thousands of dollars raised at the auction that would go toward his new barn and some toward the Schrocks'. Now there would be huge medical bills for Noah. The local lumber mill had donated part of the timber for the new barn, and it had been announced this morning that the raising would be this coming Saturday. Nate had said he wanted to help. She hoped he had the arsons solved by then but she still wanted him to be around to be part of that. His completing his work here was something they all hoped for, yet something she dreaded.

As the congregation knelt in silent prayer with their elbows on their benches, Sarah prayed extra hard for her own weaknesses and sins. But she prayed, too, for the *Englische* man she would never have but would never forget.

Nate followed the Cleveland Clinic burn unit nurse down the hall into the sterile area of private rooms. The nurse had said they'd worked hard to stabilize Noah, to keep him from going into shock. This afternoon he would have a hyperbaric treatment in an oxygen chamber, the beginning of months of painful but necessary healing and rehab.

Like her, Nate wore scrubs and booties and had been warned not to touch Noah or anything in the room. "The third-degree burns on his legs are, in effect, an open wound," the nurse told him.

An open wound. The words stuck in his mind. Once you lost someone in a fire, there was always an open wound, even when your body healed, even when someone gave you a good home and the years passed. But you always longed for your own people and place.

"His mother's sitting with him, and I believe his father and two friends who came with him have gone to the cafeteria," the nurse said as they stopped at one of the closed doors. "If you'd like me to have her step out, I will."

"Yes, I'd appreciate that."

She put her hand to the door but didn't open it. "Did the young man start those Amish fires?" she asked. "I've been reading about those in the *Plain Dealer*."

"That's what I need to talk to him about."

The room seemed bare with just the raised bed, a bank of blinking monitors, the IV stands—Noah had two tubes snaking into his arms—and minimal furniture. Mrs. Miller rose from a chair and came over to them.

"I can't thank you enough for pulling him out of the barn, Mr. MacKenzie. I thanked Sarah Kauffman, too, for her quick thinking. And the sheriff. We might have lost Noah, sure could have."

"Has he said anything about the fire?"

"Just that he's sorry, very sorry. I'm sorry he didn't see whoever set it to help you out, but he must have been so busy in the loft when that person sneaked in, that's for sure."

Nate nodded, thinking how Hannah had kept repeating that she was sorry the night she came back to see her family's newly burned barn. He regretted that Mrs. Miller might not be so grateful to him when she learned why he was really here. After a brief talk with the nurse and another peek at her son, she left the room.

Nate approached the bed quietly. Noah's legs were uncovered and looked horrible. His torso, where he had more shallow burns, was covered with white gauze. He hated to wake him because the pain must be awful, despite the meds they were pumping in him, but it had to be done.

To Nate's surprise, Noah opened his eyes. They were bright blue, feverish above the breathing tube attached to his nostrils.

"Noah, you know who I am?"

"Ya."

"I need to hear what happened in the barn to start the fire. I know you'll tell me the truth. I don't think the arsonist was anywhere around. Did you accidentally spill that kerosene and ignite it somehow?"

His eyes widened in surprise. He grimaced slightly. Nate could see even that movement hurt him as a deep frown furrowed his brow. Tears tracked from the corner of each eye into his hairline.

"Ya," he whispered.

"I thought so from the burn pattern. Was it an accident or not?"

"I—it's an old barn. We need a new one."

"That's not what I asked. After the kerosene ignited, why did you go back into the loft?"

"I left *Daad*'s tools up there—forgot. Expensive."

"Exactly how did that lantern spill and ignite downstairs?"

"Needed more light up there. You remember, *ya?* Dark up there."

"Noah, I know you're in pain, but you know your people are, too, fearing the arsonist will strike again, so I have to find him."

"It's not me."

"I know it isn't. I asked your father last night where you were during the other two fires. So maybe it's still Jacob Yoder."

"He wouldn't. Can't say more. Sorry, that's all," he said, and closed his eyes.

"All right, then. I'll tell you a true story, since you won't tell me one. The reason I am so dedicated to my job is because my father deliberately lit our house on fire when I was a boy, much younger than you."

Noah opened his eyes and fixed them on Nate as he spoke. "He wanted insurance money for the house because he was going into debt—didn't have as much money as some of his friends and neighbors. I know the Amish don't have insurance, but they have donations and barn raisings."

More tears ran down Noah's cheeks.

"But my father made a mistake. He didn't know the flames would spread that fast. He used an accelerant that got out of hand. He was going to be a hero and get us out. But my mother was burned so badly in the fire she died, and my dad got trapped, too, and died. The fire got out of his control and trapped him. Is that what happened to you? You lit it so you'd get a new barn and so your friend Jacob wouldn't look guilty? You ran back up to the loft for the tools, but fell through the hole in the rotting floor and got trapped, right? I'm trying to help your family and your people, Noah. I need the truth. Is that what happened?"

Noah closed his eyes tightly; his lips moved. Nate could barely hear the response, one he wanted yet dreaded because it would make a bigger mess than he was already in with the Amish in this case.

"Ya," Noah said. "I did it."

19

After the chaos of the weekend, Sarah was glad to get back to her normal Monday morning schedule, even if it was the Memorial Day holiday for worldly folk. As she carried her basket of half-moon pies through the back door of the Dutch Farm Table, she saw the place was already full of *ausländers*. She peeked in all three rooms but didn't see Nate. He'd driven VERA past the *grossdaadi haus* toward the pond late last night and had left early. Though she longed to see him, she had her whole day planned. After having breakfast with Ray-Lynn, if her friend had time to sit down, she was going to begin to paint the pattern on her family's barn.

Sarah wanted to get a start on it before Bishop Esh and other church leaders called on *Daad* this afternoon to discuss whether setting a trap for the arsonist would be permissible. Despite her belief in forgiveness, she couldn't see why they would even hesitate. The arsonist was a dangerous criminal who needed to be caught and that was that.

"You didn't get any sleep, did you?" Ray-Lynn greeted

her, took the basket and handed her the money right away. She looked upset and rushed.

"Not much, but how about we tell each other we look and feel great?"

"Ah, the power of positive thinking, though even little lies are not very Amish. Here, sit at the far end of the counter, and I'll be back to chat if I have time. We're full of gawkers and media-types this morning, so hide under that bonnet if you don't want to be bothered. In other words, try not to look like your picture in the special edition Peter put out this morning. He must have been up all night, too. I'll be back in a sec," she promised, and darted away.

Her picture in the paper? That's all she needed after the comments and looks she got about the feature on her painted barn squares, Sarah thought as she climbed into one of the tall-legged, wooden chairs and slid a copy of the paper down the counter.

"Oh, no. Oh, no, oh, no!"

The story about the fire had bumped coverage of the community auction off the front page with the headline Amish Heroine Helps Save Man Trapped in Barn Fire. Arson #3?

She forced herself to read it slowly, whispering, her lips moving.

The antique Levi Miller barn on Valley View Road went up in flames at approximately 3:30 p.m., May 29, the third Amish barn in the Home Valley area to be ignited under mysterious circumstances. The Miller son, Noah, 19, was medevaced to the Cleveland Clinic with life-threatening burns after being trapped in the barn.

He was rescued by the heroic efforts of Sarah
Kauffman, 24, the Amish artist who painted the
quilt patterns on the Miller barn and two others
that have burned; Nathan MacKenzie, 30, State
Fire Marshal Arson Investigator; and Eden County
Sheriff Jack Freeman. MacKenzie has been investigating the Amish barn arsons for a week and is
"the best the state has to offer," according to State
Fire Marshal Mark Lincoln of Columbus.

Although the target of the fire fits the pattern
of the previous Amish barn arsons, some of the
circumstances do not, such as time of day and the
fact this barn had a person working inside, who
evidently did not see or did not stop the arsonist.
The old edifice was well-known in the area not
only as a historic building but as one of the first
barns to bear a painted quilt square.

Wide-eyed, Sarah studied the largest of the three
color photos. It was her all right, a full, clear profile of
her face because she'd shoved her bonnet back to see
better. She was up the ladder. A distraught Mr. Miller
and the angry sheriff were standing below her. Right
under that, two other photos were almost as large. The
one on the left was of Nate in his fire gear, emerging
from black smoke and flames, pulling Noah after him.
The one on the right was of her half-burned quilt square
on the barn with two streams of water from the pumper
truck crisscrossing in front of it.

"I'm not an Amish heroine," she told Ray-Lynn, who
bustled up and poured her a cup of coffee. "I'm just
trying to help."

"I know you feel that way, and this doesn't help with

the humility I know you all value. But you *are* a heroine. Listen, Sarah," she said, leaning close and putting one hand on her shoulder. "I don't want to see you scolded or persecuted by the people you love, but you have got to realize that your painted squares make you special. If you'd ever agree to draw and paint the Amish daily life scenes you've shown me, the sky's the limit."

"I just want us to catch and stop that arsonist. None of us need this kind of publicity," Sarah said with a nod and glance that encompassed the entire restaurant.

"I can't argue how good it is for business," Ray-Lynn admitted. "So, are you still fixing to help Nate?"

"He's got his feet pretty well on the ground now, but when I can."

"You should let him see your sketchbook. Maybe when he goes back to Columbus, he could show it to my friend for us."

"I can't think about all that now." She sighed and took a sip of the coffee. She almost told Ray-Lynn Nate had already seen the sketchbook and about her sketches being defaced with blood and flames, but something held her back from sharing that.

"Gotta go," Ray-Lynn said, "but I was just wondering if Nate has said anything about other suspects, if Jacob Yoder doesn't pan out."

"You'd better ask him," Sarah said. For once the pancakes with strawberries Leah Schwartz placed in front of her didn't look good at all. If she'd lost her appetite, things were getting to her really bad.

Sarah had a good start on her Ocean Waves painting when the church leaders—minus Levi Miller, who must still be at the hospital with Noah—arrived in separate buggies. Bishop Esh, elders Reuben Schrock and Eli Hostetler, and two deacons went into the house to meet with her father. To her surprise, Nate drove up in VERA, parked on the lane, then jogged back to her house and, with a wave, went inside, too.

Was he invited to let them know how Noah was doing or was he going to plead his case for staking out Hostetlers' and this barn? No doubt the Amish leaders weren't happy with the newspaper coverage. Sometimes, she had to admit, it would be nice to live in a community where the women could sit in a gathering of leaders making big decisions, but that just wasn't their way. The home and children were the woman's realm, and that didn't include painting pictures of people on barns or anywhere else.

Nate saw that the meeting was going to be around the Kauffmans' big kitchen table. That was fine with him, except the seat they'd left gave him a view of Sarah out back, up the ladder, which was distracting. Every time she leaned or stretched to paint, her raised hem flaunted the edge of a white slip and her shapely black-stockinged legs. It was incredible that a glimpse of stocking could be arousing in this day and age, but she always got to him that way.

He fought to keep his eyes on the eager, bearded faces as he told them Noah's condition had stabilized but that he faced a long, painful battle for full recovery.

"We'll need more money raisers, another auction and dinner," Bishop Esh said. "Let's hope the women can go back to quilting soon. We have some money in reserve to help the Millers with the hospital costs, but we have three barns to rebuild now, not two. Anything else about this third arson before we discuss plans for stopping the arsonist, Nate?"

"Yes, there is something I need to go over with you. The Miller fire was an arson, but not by the arsonist who set the first two. I suspected that from burn patterns I saw in the barn. Noah confessed that he set the blaze, and he asks for forgiveness."

They sat in silence until Bishop Esh's fist hit the table and rattled his sugar spoon against his coffee mug. The Amish men looked at one another, then at Nate. No explosions, no swearing, no name-calling or accusations. Finally, the bishop spoke. "He's paid a steep price for that sin, as all must for theirs."

"At least he's confessing," Reuben said. "It was an old tinderbox of a barn. He must have hoped for help rebuilding."

"That," Nate said, "and he thought another barn fire while his buddy Jacob was in jail would get him freed. Like others I spoke with, Noah believes however distraught Jacob was, he would not burn barns. Noah had no idea that Jacob was locked up on other charges. But the circumstances of this third fire make Jacob's guilt possible again, and Sheriff Freeman says he will probably be released on bail soon."

"Government law is sometimes not God's laws," Ben Kauffman said. "Will you, Nate, as the government's official here, charge Noah Miller with arson, even if he's not the arsonist we really want to stop? Just to be clear, he isn't, is he, maybe working with Jacob Yoder?"

"After interviewing him, I believe it was a naive attempt at what we call a copycat crime. Since I've returned from Cleveland, I've checked out Noah's alibis for the other two fires and he was not involved. When I told his parents what he'd done, they, of course, refused to bring charges. I'm willing to let your church deal with him. Under the circumstances, I can't see prosecuting him, if you'll handle things. He's already facing years of pain and rehab and may be crippled the rest of his life. Besides, prosecuting Noah would distract, in town and in the local paper, from finding the one we still need to capture. But can we agree to set a trap for the other arsonist?"

"Would you mind stepping into the living room for a minute or two?" Bishop Esh asked. "This won't take long."

"Sure. I understand," Nate said, and went into the neat, sparsely furnished living room. He could hear their low voices, but of course, they were speaking in German now. Looking out the window toward the road, he wished he could see how Sarah was doing from here.

He began to pace back and forth across the hardwood floor. Mark Lincoln trusted him to handle this delicate investigation. Nate had broken a minor rule or two, like hauling civilians around in VERA while heading for a fire. He was about to break a bigger one if he didn't arrest Noah. But the Amish had to be handled differently, didn't they, or was that wrong, too? His offer to let Noah Miller off scot-free from prosecution was a breach of ethics, but worldly ones. This was a different world here, and the Amish would see that Noah was punished and rehabilitated. But the worst—and, somehow, the best—thing he'd done here was falling in love with his Amish aide.

He stopped pacing and shook his head. He was sweating but a shiver snaked up his spine. In love? Was he crazy? In eight days he was in love and with an Amish woman? No way. He was just grateful to her, fascinated by her and under such pressure he wasn't thinking straight when he absolutely needed to.

"You can come in now, Nate," Ben Kauffman said, interrupting his thoughts. He went back to the kitchen and sat down at the table again.

"About your deal that we should set a trap for the arsonist, we don't make deals with the government," Reuben said. "Whatever the crime, is entrapment of the criminal fair and moral?"

"The government has made deals with Amish ways before. You know that. Being able to run your own schools, for example," Nate argued, keeping his voice calm and leaning forward over his clasped hands on the table. "The fact the U.S. government agreed that the Amish need pay no Social Security taxes because you refuse to accept Social Security benefits. Again, I think we need to work together for the safety of your people. So let me explain my plan, and then we can all seek the advice and permission of a higher power to get it done."

"Can I see you in private, Ray-Lynn?" Jack asked as he stepped in the back door of the restaurant.

Why the back door? she thought. What was going on? It was nearly time to run home for a while, but she'd been so busy this morning she was thinking of skipping her break.

"Why sure. Can't you come in for a cup of cof—"

"Right now, out here, if you wouldn't mind."

She told Leah and Anna she'd be right back and went out the door he held for her. The sheriff's car was parked behind the restaurant. No one else was in sight.

Her heartbeat kicked up as he took her upper arm and steered her around to the other side of his car, almost as if he was going to put her in it, arrest her.

"So what is this ab—" she got out before he interrupted.

"I learned something yesterday that teed me off, Ray-Lynn. I was gonna let it slide, but I just can't. Our state fire marshal investigator and I had a debrief about first tier and second tier suspects for the arsons, and I recognized a name I knew real well on the second tier. Now why in Sam Hill didn't you tell me you were at the Esh barn right before it went up in flames?"

She'd sensed that question was coming, but it didn't help. Although her stomach twisted, she was angry, too. "Because I didn't see anything suspicious, as I hope Nate MacKenzie told you. And, with the restaurant and all—as a partner to a man who puts every ding-dang thing in the paper he can find and manages to make everyone look guilty—I didn't want to get involved!"

"Didn't want to get involved?" he exploded when he'd been almost whispering before. "You should have told me, told MacKenzie right away, at least. He got it out of some kid who spotted you and then you confessed! Not get involved? You and I are involved, aren't we? You should have told me so I knew, so I could question you—protect you if it came to that."

"Protect me? And no, we aren't involved in any way other than I bring your food and pour your coffee and provide a sympathetic ear once in a while. Is that your idea of involved?"

He looked shocked either at the fact she'd shouted back or just maybe, hopefully, at what she'd said.

"I thought we were…friends," he said, looking hurt,

almost like a little boy. Yet he was still Jack Freeman, former-marine hard-as-nails sheriff, standing there in that sharp uniform, six inches taller than her with his macho gun belt. He was a bright man but dumb as a doorknob when it came to soft feelings, to emotion. She had to keep remembering this was a man's man, her own Rhett Butler, not an Ashley Wilkes. But she was no Scarlett O'Hara, who didn't know what man she wanted.

Before she could stop herself, she blurted, "Us being just friends is for sissies, Sheriff, and I didn't think you were that. If I'm not under arrest for wanting more, I'm going back inside where I'm needed for something, at least."

She stomped away without looking around and slammed her own back door.

To Sarah's surprise, Nate was the last to leave the farmhouse after the others pulled away in their buggies. Perhaps he'd been speaking with her mother again. They seemed to get along pretty well.

He walked out slowly toward where she was stirring a can of marine-blue to paint the dark triangles she'd laid out on her chalk grid. Even before Sarah returned from the restaurant this morning, Cindee Kramer had been kind enough to drop off the last two cans of the lighter paint she'd need. Called Wedgwood blue, they were still in a sack just around the corner of the barn in the shade.

She turned to face Nate, hoping she didn't look as giddy to see him as she felt.

"So you've got the pattern all laid out," he said, looking at her instead of above. He crossed his arms and tucked his hands under his armpits. He looked like he was hugging himself.

"Did you get your plans settled, about how to trap the arsonist?" she asked, still holding her paint can between them. "Three fires, one in broad daylight, but then he picked a good time when everyone was busy, and probably just never figured Noah would be in there."

"Sarah, I don't want this to become public knowledge—or get in the paper for obvious reasons—but Noah intentionally set that fire."

She stopped stirring. "In his own barn? To draw attention to how much it needed to be rebuilt?"

"More or less. Also, he figured if a barn went up while Jacob was in jail…"

"In other words, Jacob could still be guilty of the other two arsons. I was so sure he'd never do something like that. I'm still positive about Hannah, though. Is Noah's guilt going to stay private information, or are you going to arrest him?"

"I'll have to eventually explain things to my boss, and it sure would go a long way if we can catch the serial arsonist. But I'm going to let the church leaders handle Noah—if we can keep Peter Clawson from discovering and printing it, like he does everything else. Just before our meeting broke up, Reuben Schrock showed us a copy of today's paper."

"I saw it, too. But as for your handling of Noah," she said, blinking back tears, "Nathan MacKenzie, we're rubbing off on you."

"Someone is," he said with such an intense look she was glad she held the paint can between them—or maybe not. "So did the church leaders say you could try to trap the real arsonist?"

"I think we've come to an agreement. Stan Comstock, the state fire marshal supervisor for this region of Ohio, is back from his daughter's wedding. I'm going to bring him up to speed on everything and have him stationed in the Hostetler house with night goggles to watch their barn, while I camp out here with the same gear."

"But the first two fires happened when no one was home."

"Here's the way I explained it to the elders. I think the arsonist is feeling invincible, wanting to up his game. He's had two successful fires, and it hasn't been announced that the Miller fire wasn't set by the same person. He probably wants to reestablish himself. About now, serial arsonists get not only bold but careless. And how better to prove what they think is their brilliance and power than by a barn fire when the people are at home? It's the ultimate challenge, even if word may have gotten out that someone might be inside the barn or house on guard. Besides, I don't think this particular arsonist would fall for it if we put out the word your family or the Hostetlers were leaving their houses and would be back late. From my experience interviewing other serial arsonists and studying this one, I think we've got a good chance at this."

"But you and Mr. Comstock will stand out among us."

"We're going to dress Amish, try to blend in, and our vehicles won't be anywhere in sight. Your father has given me permission to use both your farmhouse and *grossdaadi haus,* since views from those windows will cover your entire barn."

"The *grossdaadi haus,* too? It will upset my grand-mother to have you around."

"I think your mother's going to move her to a bed-room in the farmhouse—you and Martha, too. Your part in this will be to keep painting that square. I would hate to have it be a target, but my goal is to save it, the barns—and get whoever tries to harm it or the Hostetlers' quilt square."

"I want to help. You can't be two places at once here. I could be in whichever place you're not at night. You'll need to sleep sometimes."

"We'll see. By the way, I guess they're going to get my Amish clothes from Lizzie's husband, Sam. I haven't met him yet."

"He's sinewy like you, but you're taller. I bet his trousers come above your ankles."

"Sinewy, huh? So anyway, what I actually came over here to ask is, do you still want your sketchbook back?"

"I can't stand to look at it. But yes, I do."

"The blood is type AB. Do you know what your grandmother's is?"

"No, but I can probably have my mother find out the next time *Grossmamm* sees her doctor."

"How about you get me the doctor's name and number, and I'll check it out?"

He walked to VERA and came back with the sketch-book. As if it were evidence, he had it in a clear plastic envelope. "Did you dust it for prints?" she asked.

He grinned. "No, but I tried to remove the blood from the last page in the book, and it smeared your lines, so I quit trying. I just wanted you to know that was me and not someone else tampering with it. And about my putting my hands all over you last night…"

"Yes?"

"I'm apologizing for doing that during your weak and emotional time. That's what I feel around you, too, weak and emotional. But an apology in this case doesn't mean I'm sorry."

He handed her the sketchbook; their fingers touched. She would have sworn a lightning strike crackled along her arm and ended up in the pit of her stomach. Despite his heartfelt admission just now, she wondered, with this other investigator coming in and with all the group activities and planning, would they ever really have the chance to touch again? She sensed that Nate was taking a huge risk, even needed courage, to admit deep feelings for her. Weak and emotional—not what a strong, take-charge man like him would easily admit.

In the moment of awkward silence, he thrust his hands in the pockets of his jeans, then said, "By the way, I also got permission to help with the Esh barn raising on Saturday. I hope we'll be celebrating the arrest of the arsonist by then. Word's going out about the raising. I can't believe how quickly everything came together for it, but the timber was all ordered already and partly donated. They say workers will show up in droves."

"But as soon as you catch the arsonist, you'll be leaving. If there's ever any need for a fire marshal here again, it will be Stan Comstock."

She felt her lower lip quiver. Surely, she wasn't going to cry.

"I'm planning to bring my foster mother to see Amish country," he told her. "I'll stop in here, show her this quilt square and the one on Hostetlers' barn. She'd love to meet you and your family."

"Sure. That will be real nice."

"Sarah, I want to grab you again, press you up against that wall or carry you into that barn and make love to you. But what would that get us except more pain—and trouble? We need the goodwill of your family and your people. I just can't see any way—"

"Neither can I," she said, turning away from him and climbing the ladder with her paint can. "Better take your VERA back to the pond and go swimming with her!"

The second it was out of her mouth, she was ashamed of such nonsense. It sounded like she was jealous of that truck. She was acting like a spoiled child, not a mature and proper Amish *maidal*. But this man did strange things to her.

Muttering under his breath, Nate walked away and drove off toward his usual parking spot.

Once Sarah had the marine-blue paint on one triangle, she knew she didn't like it, didn't like anything right now. Why did Nate have to come and ruin things for her here in the first place? It was bad enough she was tempted to take Ray-Lynn's offer to consider painting entire pictures. Truth was, she wanted to paint people's faces, too, and that was one step more *verboten* than painting just for pretty. And why did that Stan Comstock's daughter have to get married right now so it wasn't him who came to solve the arsons? Once Nate left, even if Sarah eventually wed, she knew she'd never quite be content anymore, not with memories of him, not here in Amish country, however much she loved the place and her people. It was a big, fat lie that it was better to have loved and lost than never to have loved at all!

Deciding to mix this dark paint with a bit of the lighter shade Cindee had dropped off, she hustled back down the ladder. It would take more time, but it would please her more—if anything could right now.

She set her can of paint down and went around the side of the barn and lifted the sack with the two cans of Wedgwood blue. She saw there was a receipt for it inside or maybe a note from Cindee. Putting the sack down, she reached in and pulled out the letter-size piece of paper and gasped. In big, bold, familiar print, it read: "He performs great signs, so that he even makes fire come down from heaven on the earth in the sight of men. What a revelation! Unlucky 13:13."

Unlucky 13:13? Nate was right. The arsonist was getting bolder, even adding things to the note that weren't from the Bible. She read it again, then, lifting the cans from the sack, dropped the paper back in it and ran down the back lane to show Nate.

20

Sarah saw Nate was swimming in the pond. She could tell from the waves that he had just dived in. Out of breath, she ran closer. He saw her coming and waved.

"You're going to take me up on the swim?" he shouted.

"A third note! Someone left a third note in the sack with the paint Cindee Kramer dropped off for me early this morning. It was sitting out by the barn! I just looked inside it."

He swam over to the edge where he'd left his shoes, shirt and jeans. Bare-chested, he got out, wearing nothing but his underwear, dark green-and-blue plaid, which clung to him. She knew she should turn away but she moved closer, extending the sack.

"Except for the second note," he said, "they seem to be coming to you, and I don't like that. But the fact this one was in that sack doesn't mean Cindee or Mike left the note, not if it was sitting outside for a while."

"I agree. Mike and Cindee wouldn't be this obvious," she told him. "Maybe someone wants us to think it's them or else just dropped it in a place I'd find it without knowing Cindee left the sack."

"Can you read it to me without touching it again?" He used the T-shirt he'd dropped on the bank to dry his face and upper body. Black, curly chest hair tapered down over his stomach and pointed below his navel. His hair was plastered tight to his head.

Grateful to have a chance to look away, she tipped the sack so that the printing on the note was visible without pulling the paper out. "It's in that same printing again," she told him. "It's a quote from the Bible, the Book of the Revelation. I'm pretty sure this section is about the beast, the evil one who serves the Antichrist. So here it is— 'He performs great signs, so that he even makes fire come down from heaven on the earth in the sight of men. What a revelation! Unlucky 13:13.'"

"'What a revelation' and 'Unlucky 13:13' is not in the Bible, is it?"

"No. So our beast is adding things, making a joke about his own revelation. Do you think the fact it says *he* makes fire means the arsonist is a man?"

"Not if he or she is just picking Bible quotes about fire. Let's check it out online—on the laptop."

"The Bible is in there, too?"

He nodded as he sat on the grass, struggling into his jeans, which stuck to his wet legs. "This means the writer of the Bible notes," he said, "who is probably the arsonist, is starting to get cute, sarcastic, maybe frustrated. That's what I was hoping for. He's itching to burn another barn and he's going to get careless. I hope he or she resents that we're holding the other notes without publishing them. You know thirteen is supposed to be an unlucky number, right?"

"Superstition, yes, but I'll bet that's the chapter and verse of the quote, too."

"Let's look it up," he said, pulling on his bright blue shirt without putting his wadded, wet T-shirt back on.

In VERA, he slid the paper out of the sack onto the narrow table, then, with a quick glance at the sack, set it carefully aside. He leaned stiff-armed over the writing, studying it from every angle, then turned on what he called his laptop. It sat on the countertop in a little frame, probably so it didn't slide around when he drove. She watched, wide-eyed, as he hit keys to bring up different screens, and there it was, the Holy Bible, then the Book of the Revelation, then the exact verse, 13:13.

"So tell me more of what you know about this section of Revelation," he said as he intently scanned the surrounding words.

"This part is prophecy about the coming of the Antichrist, the ultimate evil, Satan's tool. And, in turn, there are two so-called beasts who serve the Antichrist." She leaned close to him to skim the section from the note.

"It says this second beast who uses fire rises up, and people worship him. In this case, the arsonist probably means people are in awe of the fires. Most arsonists are egomaniacs—extremely prideful—one way or the other," Nate said.

"See where he makes war with the saints?" she asked, pointing to the screen.

"In the arsonist's perverted mind that could mean his battle with the Amish. It also says that he persecutes God's people during a time of tribulation. Sarah, this is someone who knows the Bible and hates the Amish—but that doesn't mean he or she is not Amish."

"But you just proved anyone can look it up," she

challenged. "Is there a way to somehow search to find a word like *fire,* or would the person who wrote the note have to have read and know the entire book?"

"You're right—as usual. It's easy to do such a search. I guess I'm remembering only the comforting parts in the Bible, not scary stuff like this."

"At least Jacob's not the one who sent it, since he's in jail."

"He isn't," Nate said, straightening. But just as she was starting to feel relieved that at last he believed her, at least about Jacob if not Hannah, he added, "I mean he isn't in jail. His parents somehow raised bail money for him. But the sheriff called me to say an *Englische* friend picked him up in a car about an hour ago. Legally, Sheriff Freeman couldn't hold him if we didn't formally charge him with the arsons, and we don't have enough evidence for that. I'm hoping, if we give him some rope, he may hang—or at least snag—himself."

"Oh," she said, feeling deflated.

"You still care for him?"

"Not that way. I told you, I just don't want it to be someone Amish."

He took her hand and they both stared down at the paper on the table, then at each other. "These notes I've tried to keep secret," he said, "are like a ticking bomb. Since Peter Clawson knows about only one of the three, I've made a deal with him that, if he doesn't print it, I'll give him some early, exclusive information when we catch the arsonist. I've told my boss about the notes. But now, not releasing the information—I'm not sure. I don't want to cause more panic than there already is, however your people accept the Lord's hand in what is happening. It's touchy when pacifist civilians start guarding their barns with hunting rifles. This has to end soon."

"I think you're right that releasing these notes would only foster fear."

"Speaking of which, I'm also starting to worry it could be someone random, someone we don't know. It's happened with serial murderers—serial arsonists, too. Peter Clawson may be right that it could be a hate crime against the Amish. Someone who resents Amish ways or beliefs—I don't know. But I do know you've been invaluable to me in all this, whatever happens. Wait—did you hear that?" he said, cocking his head. He dropped her hand and moved toward the open back doors.

"Sounds like Gabe's voice," she said. "I just ran off, so maybe they're worried."

"Good. I hope they keep an eye on you if I can't. Don't you laugh at me tomorrow when I turn Amish for a couple of days. Yeah, it's Gabe," he said, and stepped out and waved to him.

"She's here, going over evidence with me!" Nate called to him. "Sarah," he added, speaking quickly as he climbed back inside, "when you drop off the half-moon pies at the restaurant tomorrow morning, I'd like to ride back to your house in your buggy—hidden. I'm going to put the word out I've gone back to Columbus for something, then try to look Amish with your dad's help and live undercover that way at your house for a couple of days. Your father's going to explain everything to your family tonight."

She stood, amazed at all Nate, her father and the church leaders had agreed on. *"Ya,"* she said, "I can bring you back from town. I think *Grossmamm* will like you much more dressed Amish, but I kind of like you in green-and-blue plaid."

Just before Gabe popped around and peered up into VERA at them, Nate whispered, "Sarah Kauffman, you are a tease."

The next morning, Nate drove VERA to the sheriff's house—a nice brick ranch two miles east of town—and parked in his double garage, which the sheriff closed and locked. Hoping he didn't need more than the communication equipment he'd put in a pack with some personal items, Nate got on the floor in the back of the sheriff's car and rode into town with him. When the sheriff gave him the okay, Nate got out behind the office. After hiding his backpack behind the Dutch Farm Table under a bush, he walked around to the front door of the restaurant and went in to sit at the counter.

"What will it be?" Ray-Lynn greeted him. "Breakfast or more cleverly worded accusations?"

"Not much time for either today," he said, glancing down at his watch. "I'm heading back to Columbus for a couple of days—lab work, debriefing, but I'll be back in time for the barn raising."

"I'm sure someone around here will miss you," she said, her tone tart.

It was interesting, he thought, that she'd turned so cold to him when he thought they'd parted amiably after he'd questioned her. He'd figured that, no matter how upset she was, she'd be charming at the restaurant. The flip tone of "What a revelation!" in the note danced through his mind. Sarah had said that Ray-Lynn was raised a Southern Baptist. If anyone knew the Bible, they did.

"I had to tell our mutual friend, if that's what you're upset about," he told Ray-Lynn when she glared at him.

"If either of you really think I could be behind something like that, you can just eat elsewhere, both of you," she muttered, and flounced away.

One of the Amish waitresses came up, poured him coffee and took his order. Peter Clawson ambled in, looking rumpled and sleepless, like some absentminded professor, but Nate knew he was hardly that. Those comments on the last note—"What a revelation!" and "Unlucky 13:13"—sounded like something Peter would say. Of everyone he knew around here, Peter fit the egomaniac description best, but what would be the motive? Increased paper sales? That Pulitzer Prize? But then, why would Peter have cooperated with and even agreed not to publish evidence at the request of an arson investigator? Naw, this guy was pompous but he only had time to cover the arsons, not start them.

"Nate, my man," Peter said, and plopped down on the next stool. "How's Noah Miller?"

"Good news for you to print for once. Despite facing a long, hard haul, he's going to make it."

"I called the Cleveland Clinic, but they read me the patient privacy act. How in the world did the arsonist start that fire with the boy in the barn?"

"Noah was trying to repair the hole in the loft, which he then fell through and was trapped. I haven't had time—nor have the charred remains cooled-off enough yet—to confirm evidence. Meanwhile, I'm heading to Columbus until Saturday morning, but I'll be back for the Esh barn raising."

"While the cat's away, the mice will play."

"Isn't that a cliché?" he tweaked him.

"One that's apropos. Doesn't it worry you to be leaving right now?"

"Sheriff Freeman's on alert, and the Amish are much more aware now. Speaking of the Amish, I wish you'd quit featuring Sarah Kauffman in the paper. You know they don't like their faces photographed—or to have a public focus on them."

"She's a huge part of this story. Besides, Ray-Lynn is really impressed by her art, thinks she could have a good career in the big, bad world. I'm just giving that a boost. Besides, I think she's covering for a close contact, and I want to shake them both up."

Nate's head jerked up. "Jacob Yoder?"

"You're the investigator here. Let me just say I'm sure I saw Hannah Esh standing a ways back in the newly planted field between the Esh and Kauffman farms, watching that first fire—her family's barn."

Nate's stomach knotted. He stopped pouring maple syrup and looked at Peter. The man didn't blink but added, "Here comes another cliché, but they were thick as thieves, Sarah, Hannah and Ella Lantz. It's obvious Sarah is willing to buck the Amish establishment to a certain point with her art. I know, the bishop et al finally approved it, but only those copy-the-quilt-design paintings, when Ray-Lynn says she can do so much more. But I think Sarah would defend Hannah at any cost. Again, not to turn a cliché on its head, but I hope you're not so enamored with one particular tree that you're missing the entire forest. And one more thing. I'm going to have to print what was in that note dropped off at the paper. I can't sit on that anymore. The public has a right to know."

Though he was still trying to process Peter's information about seeing Hannah at the fire—why didn't he share that before?—Nate said, "I thought we had a deal on your holding that."

"It's too important to let slide. Besides, it might give you a lead if someone comes forward with info on it. It's a unique note with the threat, the Bible language. I intend to print it in full in the issue that covers the barn raising unless there's a reason to do another special edition first. If you're going to Columbus in the midst of all this mess, check out the paper's website to keep up with things."

Did Peter smell a rat with his leaving at a time like this? "If you print that note," Nate said, intentionally filling his mouth with a three-tiered bite of pancakes and chewing slowly before he went on, "and it triggers another arson, I'll hold you accountable. And be sure to print that the state arson investigator mentioned another Bible quote, Exodus 22:6— 'He who makes fire shall surely make restitution.'"

Peter looked impressed, so Nate hoped he'd recalled that right. After Sarah had left with Gabe yesterday, he'd done the obvious, searching the entire Bible online for quotes about fire.

He and Peter ate side by side, not saying much more, while Ray-Lynn went past, glaring darts at both of them, though Nate had no idea why she was ticked off at Peter. He saw Sarah come in and tried to ignore her. She sat in the rear booth where Ray-Lynn flitted back to talk to her now and then. He had to make his move now.

Nate said he'd see Peter on Saturday at the barn raising, paid his bill and, when he saw Mike Getz come in, chatted with him and just happened to mention he was leaving for a few days. Before Peter could pay and catch up, Nate walked down the street and ducked back behind the buildings. He retrieved his backpack and, looking both ways, tried to get himself settled in the narrow, short space behind the driver's seat of Sarah's buggy.

Lying down with his knees bent, he used his hard backpack for a pillow. Besides some personal items, it was jammed full with his satellite phone, three two-way radios—Sarah had lost his fourth one in the ditch—and night goggles. Stan Comstock would supply anything else needed, and they'd use only dedicated channels to speak to each other. If something needed to be sent back and forth between the Kauffman and Hostetler farms, however much they prided themselves on being cutting-edge investigators, they would rely on Amish help with a horse and buggy.

As he tried again to get comfortable—where was that woman?—he shook the buggy. Sally merely snorted once, as if she expected strange things from him.

He figured it was about ten minutes later when Sarah came out. The buggy rocked under her weight as she settled in. "All set?" she whispered. "I've felt more worldly while you've been here, Nathan MacKenzie, and now, I guess, you're going to get a little taste of what it is to be Amish—at least wearing the clothes and walking in our shoes a bit."

She blew a kiss to Sally, and they pulled away. The clip-clops and the sway of the buggy could have lulled him if he wasn't so upset that Peter had claimed to see Hannah at the first fire and suggested that Sarah was probably covering for her. Of course, Sarah had defended her friend tooth and nail. Man, he wished

Hannah had a decent alibi for the two arsons. And she'd looked so shocked to hear about the Miller fire—as if it really annoyed her that someone else had dared to set one. Hannah knew the area. Like Sarah, she could easily walk the fields to get to barns she'd known all her life.

He tried to calm himself. Peter had withheld that information, so what else was he holding back on? "We're going to be passing other buggies so I'm not talking to you." Sarah interrupted his agonizing. "But it's okay if you talk to me."

"Maybe I'm taking a nap or just enjoying the view," he said. He reached out under the seat toward her ankle, but withdrew his hand before he touched her. He had to fight his need for her. The only thing he should be concentrating on, he told himself, was catching the arsonist before one more barn burned.

Sarah was moving *Grossmamm* and some of her things into the farmhouse when they crossed paths with Nate in the living room as he came down the stairs. That is, she met Amish Nate, dressed in her brother-in-law's trousers, white shirt and dark coat. Clean-shaven, he looked like an unwed Amish man except for his short hair, but the straw hat hid that.

Gabe and *Daad* were with him. They nodded and both patted Sarah's and *Grossmamm*'s shoulders and said their names, but they went to the kitchen, and she heard the screen door bang closed. For a moment, she stood in awe at Nate's transformation, but before she could figure out quite what to say, her grandmother asked him in German, "Are you Sarah's come-calling friend?"

At least, Sarah thought, stifling a laugh but turning bright red, the old woman wasn't afraid of him now. "This is Nate, *Grossmamm,* a friend of the whole family," Sarah said in English.

Switching to English, *Grossmamm* retorted, "Well, even if he's just one of the cousins from Pennsylvania come to help in the fields, he should be your come-calling friend. He's handsome. And," she said to Nate, "our Sarah is a lovely, loyal young woman. I'd miss her if you took her away, but she would make a good wife." Looking back at Sarah, she asked, "You never married that other one, did you?"

"Grossmamm," Sarah said, wishing she hadn't switched to English, "let's go upstairs."

"At least up there, it will be harder for that man in black to look in my window," the old woman said, not budging. "When I saw him outside, I pulled up the window and told him to get away. He terrified me, though, because I think he was one of them—the burners."

Sarah got goose bumps. When she should have just passed over it and gotten her grandmother settled to avoid upsetting her, she asked, "What did he say? What did he look like?"

"He said nothing. He knew I'd caught him. Or maybe it was a woman. I can only say the person looked like a demon with huge eyes that stuck out like a grasshopper's. I wasn't dreaming. I was right on my knees, looking out. I've always told the truth. I'd tell the truth even if they tortured or burned me like is happening now. And I didn't want him to come in and burn your *verboten* drawings, so I put bloody fire on them before he could...."

Sarah gasped, shocked at the demented twists in her *grossmamm*'s mind. But at least the arsonist hadn't targeted her sketchbook.

"Sorry, Nate," Sarah said, and put her sacks down to take *Grossmamm*'s elbow to lead her toward the stairs. "I shouldn't have asked her."

Nate picked up the sacks and followed them up the stairs. At the bedroom door where the old woman had slept for many years—*Mamm* and *Daad* were putting her in there since it faced the front and not the barn— Sarah thought she would balk. But entering her old room seemed to calm her. She went right in, then broke Sarah's heart when she said, "Your *grossdaad* will be back from the fields soon. You two just enjoy yourselves, and I'll be fine, just waiting for him here."

Sarah caught Nate's gaze. There were tears in his eyes, too.

21

"You ready to pull an all-nighter?" Sheriff Freeman asked over the satellite phone Nate had provided for him.

"Hope I can stay awake after the supper they fed me here. Between the Amish and Ray-Lynn's restaurant, Jack, I'm tanking weight on."

"Yeah, it's all good home cooking from scratch," Jack said with a sigh. "I should appreciate it more than I have."

From the darkened room, Nate glanced out the upstairs bedroom window toward the Kauffman barn. Sarah had a good start on her quilt square. He hoped, if that "beast" of an arsonist was targeting this barn next, he or she wouldn't wait until the painting was completely done. If the arsonist wanted to burn a completed one, then Stan and the Hostetlers would have to be the ones to react.

Though it was barely dusk, Nate had stationed himself at the back window of the big bedroom he had learned Lizzie, Sarah and Martha had shared when they

were younger. Now that Lizzie lived nearby, it belonged
to the two younger Kauffman daughters, though they
usually alternated nights with their *grossmamm* in the
grossdaadi haus. It felt strange to be setting up a stake-
out in Sarah's bedroom, and, if he took a break for a
catnap, that it could be in her bed.

"Ray-Lynn's really mad at me for mentioning her
visit to the Esh barn to you," he told Jack.

"At you? Wouldn't be real surprised if she starts sea-
soning my food with arsenic."

Nate arranged his gear on the floor around his chair
while they talked. He had borrowed Ben Kauffman's
binoculars and would soon don his own night goggles.
Ben was stationed in the *grossdaadi haus* tonight, since
it would be better for him than for Nate to be seen tra-
versing the yard between there and the farmhouse if
necessary. Gabe and Sarah would take short shifts here
at this window to give him some breaks, and Martha
was out with her father. Mrs. Kauffman was in the
master bedroom with her mother-in-law.

"I just talked to Stan Comstock," Jack went on, "so
his satellite phone's working, too. First hint of trouble,
you call me."

"Copy that. But we need to be sure we have the arsonist here before the Jack Freeman cavalry comes
charging in. We don't want to spook him."

"He is like a spook, isn't he—or she? Like a specter
that comes and goes at will, but we're gonna nail the
bastard. Listen, I'll be moving around some tonight, not
just sitting in this office, not going home right away, but
I'll keep this phone with me. I'm gonna check out the
ruins of the Miller barn, be sure no one's around there
admiring his or her fine work."

"Jack, one more thing—and I'm trusting you with this, trusting you to understand why I did it and to keep it quiet, especially from Peter Clawson."

"I don't like the sound of that. You did what?"

"Kept something secret, with the agreement of the Amish leadership. The Miller barn was an arson fire, but not by *the* arsonist."

"Say again."

"The Amish are going to handle this just the way you handled Jacob Yoder at first, in an understanding and humanitarian way."

"What? Besides, that blew up in my face."

"Noah Miller lit that fire hoping to get his dad a new barn and show us his old buddy Jacob wasn't the arsonist. He's confessed, and the Amish are going to deal with him."

The curse out of Jack's mouth did the ex-marine proud. Nate realized he'd given up swearing since he'd been here. In Amish country, a *yes* or a *no* were emphatic answers that didn't need any kind of dramatic emphasis. He steeled himself for an argument or attack from the sheriff.

"So you got the idea from the way I handled Jacob at first?" Jack asked. He sounded touched, almost wistful. "I agonized over that, but it was worth a try to help a kid and the Amish. Living here for a while, when guys like us are used to hardened criminals, is a real revelation, isn't it?"

The word *revelation* jolted Nate more than Jack's surprising reaction did. It was, no doubt, just chance that he said it that way, but could he be behind those threatening notes? He didn't sound or act as if he had some serious grudge against the Amish. Although they tolerated professional soldiers and government law enforcement, their mistrust of officers was well-known, so did he secretly resent that? Jack had freedom of movement, access to information, probably knew who was away from their homes and barns....

No, there he went again, acting paranoid, Nate scolded himself. Pretty soon he'd be thinking Martha or Gabe was the arsonist.

"Are you managing to stay awake?" Sarah asked Nate as she came quietly into the room around midnight. "I'm going to take the first watch for you, then Gabe will be in about 3:00 a.m."

"I'm drinking a lot of coffee, but that means trips to the bathroom, so I'm glad you're here. You remember how to put these night goggles on?"

"I remember how strange everything looks through them, like swimming underwater."

"They're invaluable here," he said as he got out of his chair and she sat in it. He helped her adjust the goggles. "In the first place," he told her, "to us worldly moderns, it's strange to see an area so dark at night. No interior glowing electrical or digital gadgets, no exterior house lights, streetlights, city lights."

"Moonlight isn't much tonight, but at least we have the stars outside."

"I haven't been star-gazing in years. Be right back."

He hurried to use the toilet and wash his hands. A shower would feel really good right now, but then it might make him sleepier, too. He was usually good with just several hours of sleep, but, despite chasing an arsonist here, it seemed as if his interior clock had slowed down in Amish country. Besides, he hadn't done an all-night sting operation in a long time. He wiped his hands and face with one of the fluffy towels Mrs. Kauffman had laid out for him. He was still amazed by the modern look of the bathroom with all the amenities and had scolded himself for thinking it would be primitive. Even the kerosene lantern hissing gently on a small table gave enough light to see everything and probably had a calming effect—but not tonight.

He should have splashed his face with cold water, but he went back and stood behind Sarah's chair in the dark room instead of stretching out on the bed.

"So," he said, "do you miss this room, staying out in the *grossdaadi haus* so much?"

"Strangely, except for the comfort of the bed, which you'd better try out," she said, without turning her face away from the window, "I don't. I guess when a woman gets to a certain age, she's ready to move out, move on, have her own home."

"I can understand that. So you've considered that, too. Ever thought of living with Hannah for a while?"

"Not that. No goth friends who talk music all day long for me. I'd have a place with a room to paint, one sunlit in the morning."

"Sarah, can't you have that here? If everyone could see some of your sketches—new ones, so vibrant with Amish life—"

"You're starting to sound like Ray-Lynn."

"On that, I agree with Ray-Lynn. Surely, your family and your people care about you enough to give you a chance to try painting more than birdhouses and barns."

"It's a different world here, Nate. You've seen that. I'd have to leave them, leave the church, move away to the modern world. It would be too individual, too

prideful, considered too 'just for pretty.' I'd be painting images of people and that's *verboten*. Yes, they love
me and that's why they'd shun me. That's the real decision I would need to make, if it's worth leaving what I
know and dearly love to follow my dreams at the cost
of being shunned. Individual dreams aren't important
here, community, sharing—that's reality."

"Jack Freeman and I were talking about Noah possibly being shunned. Can you explain it to me? I can
sit back down there with the goggles while you talk if
they bother you."

"All right," she said. "Then, I'll take them back while
you get some rest."

He helped her take them off. The strap snagged in her
prayer cap and pulled it off, freeing the heavy pinned-up
braid that fell across his arm and down her back. The
fact she didn't try to fix either was strangely moving.
He sat down and put the goggles on, wishing he could
see her instead, though she'd just given him a glimpse
into her heart.

"Okay," she said, sitting on the floor beside his chair
with her back to the wall, "our words for what is commonly known as shunning are the *meidung* or the *bann*.
Believe it or not, it usually works to bring the erring or
sinning person back into fellowship."

Nate heard the bedroom door creak. Maybe Sarah's
mother was bringing more coffee or Gabe was here
already. He turned away from the window for a quick
look.

A woman screamed. Sarah scrambled up beside him.

"That's him! That's him!" Sarah's grandmother
shrilled, pointing at Nate in the goggles. "The barn
and people burner, the man in black with the big eyes!"

* * *

"Am I formally under arrest this time?" Ray-Lynn asked as she answered her front door and saw Jack standing there, hat in hand.

"I just wanted to talk, and I was afraid if I called ahead you'd tell me not to come."

"Very astute. Talk about what?"

"I'd like to step in just for a few minutes, as I'm making rounds. I want to apologize."

Not knowing what to say and feeling she was all out of sass, she moved aside and let him in. She wished she hadn't changed her clothes after work. She'd washed off her makeup and thrown on a comfy pair of jeans and a sweatshirt. Her hair was a tousled mess. And the way he was looking at her right now, half whipped puppy and half hungry wolf, really sapped what strength she had left.

"Please sit down," she said, leading him into the living room and gesturing toward the couch. He sat on its far end, turned toward her as she settled on the other end, tucking one leg up under herself. When he dropped his hat on the coffee table, he just missed her bobblehead Scarlett O'Hara who nodded at him. "Go ahead," Ray-Lynn said. "This is your party."

"Wish it was. I just want to say I know I overreacted to you not telling me you were at the Esh place the night of the first fire. But you should have told me, told me why and that would have been fine. Topic number two, I know you're gung ho about helping Sarah Kauffman paint more than geometric designs on old barn wood, but you better lay off. Not only because you'll upset the Amish community, but because she seems to be the focus of our arsonist."

"You want the truth? So far, this sounds like true confessions, so here goes. Yes, I want to help Sarah. And on a practical level, she'd be able to pour money into this economically hurting community, hurting at least until this big bump in visitors we've had from the arsons. But I want to help her for myself, too, partly because it would give me great satisfaction to bring her talent to others, partly because if I could act as her agent, maybe I could dig my way out from under my partnership with Peter Clawson. He owns seventy percent of my business, not fifty, like most people think."

He turned more toward her. "That right? Maybe you could get some local investors, buy out his share."

"No one I know has that kind of money, especially in these tough times, and he'd refuse unless I took him to court—where he'd defend himself brilliantly. I just don't like him telling me what to do, thinking he can control me in other ways."

"What other ways?" Jack demanded, leaning forward and frowning. "He been coming on to you in ways he shouldn't? Making passes?"

"Not for a while. Not since I told him off. You know, like in the old days, 'Unhand me, you cad!' and 'I'm not that kind of girl'?"

Jack threw one arm on the back of the couch and leaned toward her. "Ray-Lynn, you just say the word, and I'll see he never so much as orders anything at the restaurant again, let alone orders you around."

"And then you'll do what when he fires me? Technically, he can. Besides, he already resents you because you're the other big man on campus around here, not counting our fire marshal boy wonder."

"Nate's a good man for this job."

"I know he is, and I think he's a sort of silent partner on my side about Sarah daring to take control of
her life and talent. Now, please, don't you go roughing
up Peter, either verbally or physically, because it will
all come back on me. I don't want to get you involved,
but, I swear, I'd do about anything to get that man off
my back!"

"So how much money's involved for you to buy him
out?"

"I don't think he'd let me buy him out. Jack, I'm
sorry I've been so rude and inhospitable," she rushed
on. "Every proper Southern lady I ever knew is spinning
in her grave because I haven't offered you something
to drink or eat and here we are in food-for-all Amish
country."

She got up and started toward the kitchen, but he
snagged her wrist in his big hand and pulled her down,
close to him on the couch. "Ray-Lynn, listen. I meant
to say this the minute I stepped through the door, but I
figured you might brain me with one of those painted
china plates if I didn't work up to it. I'm not real good at
soft or sweet words, but since you're a Southern girl—
lady—let me put it this way, then you can toss me out
on my tail if you want."

Her eyes widened and her lower lip dropped. She
forgot to breathe.

"I'd like—I want," he stammered, "well, to court
you, date you, see you, if you could just put up with a
guy who's loved only once, ended up with a wife divorc-
ing me. I've lived alone too long, married to my job, and
I'm so upset about these arsons I can't see straight."

For the first time in her life, Ray-Lynn Logan could
not find her voice. So she nodded, kept nodding, until

she realized she must look like her Scarlett O'Hara bobblehead doll. She gave him a hard hug.

Sarah tried to calm *Grossmamm*. Her *mamm* ran
into the room. Since it was so dark with only wan hall
light reflecting here, Sarah's first instinct was to get
a lamp so the distraught woman could see it was just
Nate. But they didn't want light here so that someone
outside could see in.

Nate had turned back toward the window obviously
not wanting to stop looking out or else to help calm
Grossmamm.

"She was just sitting in the rocking chair," *Mamm*
told them. "I just stepped out for a second. Come with
me," she crooned in German to *Grossmamm,* taking the
old woman's arm. She didn't budge. "Sarah, help me,"
Mamm said.

They tried to move the old woman out into the hall,
but she kept shouting, "Burner! Burner! Leave my
people alone!"

"Those are just special glasses so Nate can see in
the dark," Sarah said, though she should have known it
was foolish to try to reason with her. She turned *Grossmamm* toward her and held her cold, fragile hands between her own. "That's our friend you met downstairs,
remember?"

"But he's been sneaking around in the dark. Have
you been meeting him secretly outside?"

Finally, Sarah and *Mamm* managed to get *Grossmamm* back in the front bedroom and settled. *Mamm*
kept talking to her quietly, got her going in the rocking
chair, which usually calmed her, while Sarah waited a

moment in the doorway, hastily pinning up her braid and putting her *kapp* back on.

"I'm surprised all that shouting didn't bring your father or Gabe running," *Mamm* said over her shoulder, "but the window was closed."

"Don't you believe me?" *Grossmamm* said. "That is the man I saw from my window at the *grossdaadi haus*."

Sarah hurried to her and knelt by the rocking chair. "I believe that you saw someone in night goggles like Nate is wearing," Sarah said. "But it surely wasn't Nate. He's our friend."

"That is how they used to arrest us, send a spy, someone trusted who told them where we were hiding. Then the torment, the ax and the fire."

"Go tell Nate we're sorry, Sarah," *Mamm* said, putting her hand on her shoulder. "You and Martha—I didn't really know how much you do out there at night. Go tell him. I'll be fine."

Sarah closed the door behind her and hurried across the hall and into her bedroom. How unreal it felt to have Nate sitting there in the window. After this was all over and he went home, she would always picture him there, not looking out but in.

He turned his head as she sat down on the floor again, her legs stretched out next to his chair, her back to the wall near the window. "*Mamm* says to tell you she's sorry that happened."

"It's all right, except I regret your *grossmamm* is haunted by a past she didn't even live through. But she gave us a piece of information I should have figured out on my own when she said the person in black had eyes like a grasshopper. She saw someone sneaking around the barn with night goggles, probably the same person who left that first note on the *grossdaadi haus* door. Probably the beast of an arsonist."

"But who would have access to night goggles? Didn't you say they are for soldiers and law officers? What about someone like the sheriff?"

"Anyone could buy them if they knew the right place, including online."

"*Ya,* it seems everything's online, from Grandma Moses paintings to the entire Bible. Being online is *verboten* to my people without permission, and yet those things are good. You—you still want to hear about shunning? I'm afraid you're not getting enough sleep."

"Now you sound like my foster mother, M.E."

"Is her real name Emma and you just call her Emmy?"

"It's an *M* and an *E,* my nickname for Mary Ellen. I know she would have loved for me to call her Mom, but after losing mine—and so close to where the Bosleys took me in—I just couldn't. That's what I mean about hauntings, like your grandmother suffers from. It was years ago, and I'm a grown man who's seen too many other arson scenes, but I can't bear to see that one."

"I understand. I'm sure M.E. will be glad to see you've put a little flesh on your bones here," she said, hoping that wasn't an obvious attempt to change the subject. The man suddenly looked shaky.

"Yeah, she's always asking me if I'm eating enough. The thing is, I'm not getting my jogging in here, where it would be a great place to run. But I am getting too much exercise lifting fork or spoon to mouth." He yawned. "Okay, tell me about the *meidung,* then I'll take a little nap while you keep watch."

"Shunning is a fearsome thing among our people, because it removes us from the community that is the bedrock of our being," she told him. "It means the one under the *bann* cannot eat with loved ones, or sleep with them, if it's a marriage partner. The Amish may do favors for the shunned one, but he or she cannot do acts of kindness or favors in return—and giving as well as receiving is also the foundation of our church and beliefs."

"But if you make confession and change the behavior in question—"

"The sin in your life."

"Right. Then you can be taken back?"

"With confession and a restoration process. There is so much joy when a lost soul returns to the flock, the prodigal son or daughter."

"What are some of the things deemed shunnable?"

"Well, of course, aiding and abetting a car theft ring—that could have sent Jacob to prison. Adultery, of course. Premarital relations—which does happen, though usually the couple makes confession and weds and is taken back in good faith. We're not saints. That's a wrong idea *ausländers* have of us sometimes. Also, cheating in a business transaction, using banned technology without permission, marriage outside the faith, owning a car, flying in an airplane—anything that is jumping the fence of our *ordnung,* the rules."

"But Mrs. Miller won't be banned for going with Noah in the medical chopper?"

"No. The *ordnung* might sound strict, but it is open to interpretation, and mercy rules judgment at times, like with Noah. He might be banned for a while but when he's taken back, he'll be stronger for the separation."

"Isn't there any hope against shunning for someone who decided to pursue her artistic talent to paint pictures and then sell them?"

She hesitated a moment. "There is an Amish artist in Pennsylvania, Susie Riehl, but she does mostly still life, quilts or buildings and, if she does a person, she makes him or her faceless. And she stays at home, never goes to shows of her work or promotes her own work. Considering the challenge I had just getting permission to paint quilt squares, my guess is that the *meidung* would be pronounced on me. Nate," she said, her voice trembling and hurried, "I'd have to go live in the world, and that would mean shunning, too. It's almost like being dead to your family and friends—to be dreaded as much as…as much as being burned."

"Don't talk like that. You sound like your *grossmamm*. I believe your artistic talent is a God-given gift and shouldn't be hidden or stifled. Just remember that, if your own people ever try to bring you up on *meidung* charges."

Sarah had to smile at the way he'd put that, law officer that he was. He still could not grasp the impact of an Amish person being cut off. Good old American individualism and independence made it so hard for the *Englische* to really grasp their ways. She let him help her get the night goggles adjusted once again and settled in the chair. Without turning her head, she knew he lay down on her bed. But then—

Her heart almost leaped into her throat. A man out there! A man walking past the barn, looking up at it.…

She saw it was *Daad,* coming back into the house for something, not hurrying. It must not be an emergency. It didn't seem as if he had seen anyone. If only one of them had seen who put that last note in the sack with the paint, but she'd asked the whole family. It would be pointless to ask Cindee. If she and Mike Getz wrote the note, she'd deny it. If they had nothing to do with it, the cat—like the note—would be out of the bag.

Grateful she hadn't scared Nate with a false alarm, Sarah leaned her elbows on the windowsill and stared into the darkness outside and that within.

22

"This bad weather is going to ruin your surveillance plan tonight," Sarah told Nate the second night of their vigil.

They stood inside the screened door of the farmhouse, watching the rain slant sideways so heavy they couldn't see the barn. The wind howled, and trees thrashed in the gusts. It was coming from the other direction, or they would have been soaked with just the screen between them and the force of the storm. But Sarah was so aware of another force of nature standing behind her, close but not touching her. She wanted to lean back against him but she stayed rigidly where she was.

"Bad weather is God's will, right?" he asked. "Maybe He thinks I need more than three hours' sleep, but I can't imagine sleeping during this."

"It's a good thing I didn't paint more today, or it might have washed away or been peeled off," she told him, hoping he realized she was joking.

She hadn't admitted that she was really torn about

working on her quilt square. The more progress she made, the more she felt she was endangering her family's barn, and yet they wanted to lure the arsonist out in the open. But on a night like this, they'd never even see him, let alone catch him.

"How do your people prepare for a weather emergency, if they don't know it's coming?" he asked. "No internet, no TV…"

"Sometimes word of mouth, but mostly battery-operated radios for weather emergencies. *Daad* has one upstairs, so I suppose that's where he's been since the others are in the living room."

Sarah knew Nate had been talking on the satellite phone to the fire marshal supervisor, Stan Comstock. From him, Nate had learned the storm was widespread.

They both jerked as a flash of lightning blinded them and a horrific boom of thunder resounded somewhere close. He put his hands on her shoulders, tight.

"All we need is lightning hitting the barn tonight," he said. "It's a good thing some of the trees by the pond are tall, because maybe they'd draw the strike. Stan says there are tornado warnings south of here, too, but you never know where those might hit."

"And that's why—" *Daad*'s voice came from behind them "—we trust in the Lord who giveth and taketh away. But I still agree we can call the arsonist the Beast now, since that last threatening note. You two get out of the doorway, 'cause I'm going to have to go on out to the barn and look around after that strike. Nate, you want to come with me?"

"Sure. With this storm, no one's going to start a barn fire tonight."

Although lately they had kept the horses in the fields

in case the arsonist struck, they had been forced to move the four big plow team Percherons and the three buggy horses inside. Not only did the animals get nervous outside, but they could be struck by lightning or hit with flying debris.

"Daad," Sarah said, "you know Sally always gets off her bean over thunder. I'll go, too."

"You've changed, my girl," *Daad* told her. "Just two weeks ago, you would have *asked* if you could go along."

Nate had taken his hands from her shoulders the minute they heard *Daad*'s voice. Her father looked at her, then at Nate. He turned and went into the living room. Sarah assumed he was talking to her mother there. When he came back, he carried three coats and two large flashlights, one of which he handed to Nate. Nate had to fuss with the backpack he wore. Since Amish clothes had no pockets, he carried his satellite and cell phones in there. Even if they'd had an umbrella, Sarah thought as they stepped out, it would be turned inside out or ripped away.

On the porch, they waited for a slight lull in the rain. Finally, after *Mamm* came into the kitchen to see if they had gone, *Daad* led the way out.

The wind hit them hard, ripping at their clothes and hair, whipping leaves and grit against their skin. They squinted their eyes almost closed and stumbled along through puddles. Nate pulled her to his side, and they bent into the blast together right behind her father.

"Forty, fifty miles per hour," Sarah thought Nate said, but she wasn't sure in the shriek of the wind. In the leeward shelter of the barn, under her partly painted quilt square, *Daad* and Nate worked together to slide the door open enough that they could dart in, then slide it closed behind them.

Within was a cove of quiet; however, the wind howled outside. Each rumble of thunder made Sarah think this vast building was clearing its throat or its belly was rumbling, giant that it was with them inside. In the drafts and wind, the entire barn seemed to gasp for air. It looked so different at night without the wan, golden glow of a lantern or two. The depths of darkness seemed to swallow their flashlight beams. As silly as it was of her, she almost felt she'd never been here before. How did the arsonist feel when he decided to murder a barn?

Nate and *Daad* played their beams along the floor so they could see as they made their way toward the snorting, stomping horses in their stalls at the back. Something was creaking, something else was banging, just as that day during a lighter rain in the Miller barn before it was burned.

Daad went to pat and talk in German to his work team, big, blond babies that they were. Sally tossed her head and showed the whites of her eyes in the reflected light of the flashlight Nate held.

"Will she be okay in the dark with you?" Nate asked as Sarah petted and crooned to the mare. "I'd like to go up in the loft and check around the interior perimeter—see and smell if that lightning strike hit anything. Something like that can smolder for a long time before bursting into flames."

Their gazes snagged and held. When he looked at her like that she could almost feel heat between them.

"Sure, we'll be fine. Won't we, girl?" Sarah said, and looked away.

Soon she could tell that her father also walked around
the barn, darting a beam of light into corners. Sarah in-
haled deeply, hoping she didn't smell smoke. No. She
was just imagining things, letting the sounds outside
shake her up as much as they had Sally.

It seemed an eternity before Nate and *Daad* came
back to her. When they held their flashlights low, the
shadows on their features made them look scary.

"Until it lets up a bit, I'm gonna stay out here. Nate,
you want to go back to the house or the *grossdaadi
haus?*" *Daad* said.

"I don't think any of us could so much as see the
barn tonight from outside of it. We've learned the Beast
is clever, so he or she must know it would be crazy to
try an arson tonight. You want me to get Sarah in the
house, then come on back? She can tell them what we're
doing."

"How about bringing out some coffee and cookies
or half-moon pies?" *Daad* said, and turned back toward
the horses.

Sarah wanted to stay, too, and tend her horse, but
since her father had made that earlier comment about
her not asking for permission, she kept quiet. Besides,
she still felt more skittish out here than poor Sally.

She and Nate waited for another little lull and, holding hands, made a dash for it toward the porch of the
house. When they almost slipped in a mud puddle, she
held him up better than he did her. She wanted to cry,
to laugh. She wanted all the dangers to go away so she
could just be here on a calm early June night with Nate.
She wished he'd come calling, wished he was Amish—
but then he wouldn't be Nate.

"*Mamm,*" Sarah called when she saw her mother's

silhouette behind the screen door, "*Daad* and Nate are going to stay in the barn for a while, but can you put some coffee in a thermos and pack some snacks for them?"

Without a word, *Mamm* turned away. "You should get some dry clothes," Sarah told Nate as they stood on the porch. Hers stuck close to her skin, and, after she took off her jacket and shook it out, Nate kept looking her over.

"I only have one outfit—one chance to be Amish," he told her. "You tell everyone not to worry about your dad and me out there tonight."

He tugged her away from the door. Between it and the window, he pulled her to him, holding her tight. They pressed together knees to foreheads in a hard hug. They didn't kiss, just held each other up in the sweep of the storm, but it sent her head spinning as if he'd kissed her silly. And she had the strangest thought. Although Nate was the outsider here, she suddenly felt she was, too. At that moment she felt closer to him than to her family or her friends and community.

They jumped apart when they heard *Mamm*'s quick footsteps in the kitchen, then her voice, "Here, double-bagged."

"Get some sleep," Nate said, talking to both of them.

"As if, in this noise," Sarah told him.

He waited on the porch a moment, picking his time, then darted into the wet, devouring night.

Mamm held the door for her, and Sarah stepped inside, dripping wet. "We have to be strong," *Mamm* said, and put her arm around Sarah's wet shoulders, "but then not be too bold, either. Keeping on the straight and narrow, that works the best."

"Maybe so," Sarah said, "but that's pretty hard in a big storm, one I didn't ask for, one I can't see through." Did her mother know she was talking about Nate? That's what *Mamm* had meant, hadn't she?

Mamm looked like she'd say more. Little worry lines like birds' feet crowded the corners of her eyes. "Nate's a good *Englische* man, and I like him," *Mamm* said. "But he can't be for you, Sarah. I'd burn that barn myself and confess to the other burnings if it would make him leave," she blurted, and then fled the kitchen.

"I can see you and Sarah are getting close," Ben Kauffman told Nate as they sat on hay bales in the barn. The lightning and thunder were getting more distant, but now this—a talk Nate did not want to have.

"She's been a tremendous help. Because of her barn paintings, finding the arsonist is personal to her, too."

"But you two been getting that way—personal."

Ben's voice was not raised. It was barely discernible above the rain on the roof. Nate knew the Amish man would not confront him in a worldly way. Somehow, that made it harder than if they could argue or fight it out. He didn't even know how to confront himself about his feelings for Sarah.

"She's a very special woman," Nate said. "Bright and talented."

"And tempted by things she can't have, a worldly art career and an outsider, however kind a man he is."

"Her God-given talents to draw and paint—why can't she have that? Some Amish build barns, some quilt, some grow and sell lavender, some bake, some build birdhouses and gazebos and farm, too."

"I was hoping you could understand what keeps the

Plain People going after all these years is unity of purpose, tradition and beliefs."

"I see that. But individual differences within the
group are to be cherished and encouraged, too, aren't
they?"

The older man took a gulp of coffee. He leaned over
and put his hand on Nate's shoulder. "Once you've found
the barn burner, we want you to leave with good memories of the Home Valley and the Kauffman family,
Nathan MacKenzie. But we don't want you to leave
with our Sarah."

"If she leaves, it would be her decision, not mine.
That much I can promise you. You've let me put a lie
out to the community that I'm not here right now and
for a good purpose. But I can't lie to someone who has
been such a good host as you, Mr. Kauffman. I care
deeply for Sarah and can promise only to support her
decisions as best I can, whatever she does or doesn't
do."

"Then let's agree the decisions will be hers."

"Fine. But if not mine, not her parents' decisions,
either. Hers alone."

Ben Kauffman nodded, and they shook hands. It was
quiet between them after that and not because of the
whine of the wind and roar of the rain.

"You didn't have to stay at the restaurant until I
closed up," Ray-Lynn told Jack as he walked her to
her car. She didn't see his, so it still must be parked
at the police station. "I've driven home in bad storms
before, and the worst seems over. It's barely sprinkling
right now. It sure smells fresh and clean out tonight,
doesn't it?"

"You get free bodyguard protection, you better take it, Ray-Lynn. This isn't exactly a mecca for crime, except for our arsonist, but you can't be too careful going to your car at night. Unfortunately, the evils of society are creeping out of the city and into the country more and more. Here, let me hold that umbrella over both of us. You want to take a little stroll?"

"Sure. It'll be like that old movie, *Singing in the Rain*. We'll splash in the puddles and dance."

"We could go dancing some night if you want."

She took his arm, and he held it tight to his side. "You do a great job around here, Jack, but I can't believe Nate's left this all to you right now. He hasn't called from Columbus, has he? Shouldn't he be here, keeping an eye on things?"

It seemed to her he was going to say something, then thought the better of it. "He'll be back for the barn raising Saturday," he told her.

"I hope he's got some evidence or at least a good lead. Do you think he does?"

"Just don't you worry yourself about any of that. Now, if you would have gotten that quilt square painting of Sarah's done on the front of the restaurant or even a mural inside, I might have told you different. We can't tell if the arsonist is targeting barns of Amish church leaders or her art."

"I wonder if Nate knows about the storm, at least. I actually saw some of Peter's precious newspapers being swept down the street as if they were tissues. He'd have a conniption if he looked up from his work long enough to see it, and now he'll have to cover the weather as well as the arsons and the barn raising."

"Like I said, he so much as hassles you over his

coffee getting cold, you let me know. Hey, see the light on in the hardware store? It's gonna do a land office business selling chain saws and such tomorrow to cut up fallen limbs. I wonder if Mr. Baughman's getting ready for the onslaught," he said, "'cause it looks like they stayed open late. For once, not just Peter's office but the hardware store's all lit up."

"But it's usually brighter than that when they have the store lights on," Ray-Lynn said.

"Good observation. That light's pretty dim. Mr. Baughman should have told me if he decided to start leaving a safety light on. I'm gonna get you back in your car and go check it out."

"Not when we're almost there, you're not. You just go peek in, and I'll wait here."

She stayed in front of the Amish Antiques Shop— some of their stock wasn't Amish and some wasn't antique—while Jack strode across the street. On the far edge of town she could see the lights from the McDonald's and the Wendy's that she once feared would ruin her business. Lately, they hadn't made a dent. Except for locals, the non-Amish eating places held little allure.

But she was starting to feel Jack's allure—no, not starting. For some reason, the man had gotten to her from the first, and it wasn't just the masculine marine aura or the spiffy police uniform. Maybe it was his deep aloneness, a soft side he tried so hard to hide.

She edged a bit closer to the hardware store. With all the visitors and strangers in town lately, she could see why Mr. Baughman would want it lit at night. Jack was right about crime creeping into rural areas, though that car theft ring Jacob Yoder got involved with was about the worst scandal they'd had in Home Valley—before the clever arsonist took to lighting barns.

She watched Jack peek in the corner of the front window of the store, then jump back. What? Surely not a robbery in progress? She pressed herself against the front of the Hair Port Barber Shop. She slid along past the Hole in the Wall—the pizza and subs shop.

If Jack was into something dangerous across the street, would he be all right?

She moved along until she could see inside the hardware store, which abutted the Homestead Pharmacy and Kwik Shop. Gazing into the store where Jack had gone was like looking at a distant, dim TV picture.

She gasped. Jack was inside with his gun drawn!

Figuring that Stan Comstock was calling to report in, Nate grabbed his satellite phone when it sounded. Caller ID showed it was the sheriff. Nate kept petting Sarah's horse as he talked.

"Nate here."

"I'm at the station. I just arrested and booked Mike Getz and Cindee Kramer for B and E, even though she had a key—and for attempted larceny. I surprised them as they were loading up his truck with some stock items from the hardware store, which I think she was juggling in the store records. They probably thought the storm would keep folks off the streets so no one would notice."

"Good work! So instead of Jacob, we have another suspect off the streets and out of the fields and barns."

"Right. But let me tell you what they had loaded up. Some tools and camping equipment, including a package of artificial fireplace logs, like you said ignited the Schrock barn. But here's the kicker. They took a dual-burner Coleman stove and two cylinders of liquid propane to fuel it—or to burn something else."

"Bingo! The arsonist has been using a different incendiary device for each burn so far, and propane would sure do the trick. Be careful with it because even the slightest spill can give human skin severe frostbite."

"Frostbite? And it ignites fires? So anyway, you want to have a chat with one or both in the morning?"

"I'll come into town in the back of Sarah's buggy when she delivers Ray-Lynn's half-moon pies. Let's hope Getz is our man. I hope I can question him quietly so people don't know I'm back."

"You want me to have a go at him first? I didn't trust the guy from the git-go, always in the right place at the right time to play the hero."

"If it's okay with you, I still think I'd better do it, since we want to tie him to the arsons. With the fireplace logs and propane—you know in law enforcement coincidences usually aren't. After I question them, I'll have you get me back here, let me out somewhere near Kauffman's and I'll walk back in. I'm looking pretty Amish these days. But I'll bring my civilian clothes along for their interrogation. Those two aren't locked up together, are they?"

"So they can think up a cover story? No way. I had to put Getz in the storage room."

"Thanks for the good work. This may be the break we need. See you in the morning, and I hope they don't lawyer up."

"Haven't so far. It's gonna be a long night without a deputy here right now, but I can't see having one drive in from Wooster with debris all over the roads until tomorrow. See ya."

A Coleman stove and propane, Nate thought as he punched in Stan Comstock's number. Then he'd call Mark Lincoln in Columbus. Yeah, that propane in Getz's possession could have burned Hostetlers' or this beautiful barn into oblivion.

23

The morning after the storm, Sarah had to guide Sally around broken tree limbs and piles of windswept litter on the roads to get to the Dutch Farm Table with the half-moon pies—and get Nate to the sheriff's office. She had him hidden again, dressed Amish, but with his own clothes in his backpack. She'd been surprised that her parents had let her take him into town since it was obvious they realized how much she cared for him. Well, they were hardly going to elope in a horse and buggy. Or ever. Above all, *Mamm* and *Daad* wanted the arsonist caught, so Nate could leave.

At least Nate now had another strong lead, not Jacob, and, thank the Lord, not Hannah. Sarah hoped the sheriff's prisoners might be the guilty ones, even if she felt real bad for Cindee to have picked the wrong man to fall in love with.

Nate seemed all business now, so she concentrated not only on safety but speed. She let him out behind the sheriff's office before heading for the restaurant. She had wanted to say so much that wasn't arson talk. She sensed that he had, too.

Ordinarily, she thought as she headed for the alley behind the restaurant, a big storm would be the topic of conversation for days around here, but it would probably still take second place to arson talk. And word would soon be all over town that Mike Getz and Cindee Kramer were under arrest. Still, Nate had said, if they didn't confess, he wanted to keep what he called a sting going at her house.

"Oh, good, you're here," Ray-Lynn greeted her as she came in the back door. "I should have known that neither rain nor snow nor sleet nor gloom of night—that's a post office slogan, I guess, but it suits you and your people, too. I know about Mike and Cindee's arrest," she said, whispering now and leaning closer. "It's not common knowledge yet. I was with the sheriff last night when he spotted them in the hardware store. We were walking in the rain. And the night before last, Jack more or less asked me out. I meant to tell you yesterday when you were here but I was so busy."

"Oh, Ray-Lynn, that's great, on both counts—them getting caught and maybe Jack, too. So your hard-to-get plan worked."

"Something did, my friend," she said with a glint in her eyes and a funny wiggle of her eyebrows. "I only hope and pray our intrepid arson-fighting duo have the right suspects. Here, I saved the back booth for you because I want you to meet someone who came in from Columbus."

"Nate's boss?" she blurted, afraid he might have come to tell Nate he was recalling him.

"The state fire marshal? Why would he come here if

Nate's not around? No, just a sec. Oh, here's the money for your mother and sister," she added, digging in one apron pocket and then the other. "Drat—it's still in the cash register. Be right back," she said over her shoulder as she broke into a half run around the counter.

Sarah sighed. She was happy for Ray-Lynn, the sheriff, too. But that just made her sadder about Nate, so close but yet so far. After the way *Daad* had given her his I-won't-say-it-because-you're-old-enough-to-know-better look and after what *Mamm* had blurted out last night that Nate was not for her, she felt all the air had gone out of her.

Ray-Lynn appeared, bringing a nice-looking *Englische* couple with her. She slipped Sarah the money and whispered, "These people could pay you a hundred times that every week."

So, Sarah wondered, was Ray-Lynn promoting *Mamm* and Lizzie's pastries to restaurant owners in Columbus? That probably wouldn't work since the pies needed to be fresh, and they'd have to pay someone to deliver them daily.

"So this is the quilt square artist," the woman said with a warm smile. She had smooth, copper-colored hair that looked great, not crimson and spiky like Hannah's, but not so natural as Ray-Lynn's, either. It blended beautifully with her creamy complexion, sharp brown eyes and the russet-and-olive outfit she wore. "We're honored to meet someone so talented and so modest about it," the woman added. "Most of the artists we deal with are overly entranced by themselves."

Uh-oh, Sarah thought as Ray-Lynn made the proper introductions of Ginger and Geoff Markwood.

"We've seen your barn paintings in the papers and in

person—the Hostetler barn one," Geoff Markwood said. He was quite a big man, but not fat. Like Mike Getz, he was bald but he had an earring in one lobe. "Ginger's the eyes and brain, and I'm just the moneyman," he said with a smile. "We both like your abstract work very much and hear you do primitive realism, also."

When Sarah simply nodded, Ray-Lynn said, "It must be great to have a marriage and a business partnership, even steven, like you two do. Sarah, Ginger and I were sorority sisters years ago in Georgia, and now here we both are, living in Ohio."

"Ray-Lynn has said you also do panorama work—scenes with Amish people and places," Ginger said. Sarah knew she had to say something. She didn't want them to think she was tongue-tied or dense.

"Only in sketches so far. The colors that would go with them are in my head."

"We'd love to see any sketches you could share with us," Ginger said. "We specialize in developing and launching emergent talent through our gallery New Horizons in Columbus, but we have a large online presence, also."

"Why don't we sit down here? I've been fixin' to get you all together for a long time," Ray-Lynn said, sounding more Southern than usual when Ginger didn't one bit. Ray-Lynn eased them into the booth across from Sarah, then squeezed in next to Sarah so she was blocked in.

"I have no sketches to share at this time," Sarah said, ignoring the fact Ray-Lynn gave her a little kick under the table. "My sketchbook's been damaged."

"Really?" Ray-Lynn asked. "What happened?"

"It's a long story. It was very nice to meet both of

you, especially since you're Ray-Lynn's friends, but I really need to be getting back home."

"Oh," Ray-Lynn said, looking upset when Sarah thought she was the one who'd been penned in here without warning. Nate might call this a sting.

"Of course, we understand," Ginger said. "We hope you won't object if we drive past the painting you're doing now, and please keep us in mind at New Horizons if you do decide to look for funding to paint or need a studio space or a gallery outlet."

"Thank you. I sure will, and Ray-Lynn will remind me if I don't."

Sarah bumped hips with Ray-Lynn to make her scoot out of the booth. At the back door, Ray-Lynn caught up with her. "Sarah—"

"You set that up when you know temptations like that can cause me all kinds of problems."

"I didn't set it up," she insisted as she followed Sarah outside to her buggy. "They just appeared today, surprised me, and I couldn't pass up the chance to introduce you. Sarah, I promise I won't bug you again, but you know your painting career would make you happy and help your people. Your profits could rebuild a lot of barns, pay for a lot of hospital bills...."

"We do that as a group, Ray-Lynn."

"Oh, right. All for one and one for all. I'm sorry, but I think you're making a big mistake."

"I've made them before. But I hope not to make ones to lose me everything—including someone I've considered a trusted friend."

She climbed into the buggy and snapped the reins to make Sally move. Weak rebel that she was—yes, rebel, because she wanted to run back there and promise to paint for them right now at their place called New Horizons, because she longed for new horizons of her own—she began to cry. She dared not strike out on her own and she was going to lose not only that chance but Nate, as well.

Nate emerged from a two-hour interrogation of Mike Getz and a half-hour one with Cindee Kramer, feeling like a failure. The guy hadn't budged from the claim that—yes, he'd been "borrowing" a few things from the Homestead Hardware Store since Cindee began working there two years ago, but he didn't have anything to do with burning barns. Oh, no, he was a hero in that regard, always on Nate's side.

It was just, Mike had explained, that Mr. Baughman who owned the hardware store, didn't pay Cindee enough. They liked to save money on firewood in the winter, and they liked to go camping. So the logs and the Coleman stove and propane would be well used.

The fact they'd taken the camping stove as well as the propane made Nate half believe the guy, even though he wanted to throw the book at him. In a way, it was Jacob Yoder all over again. A criminal was under arrest but maybe not for the arsons.

And Cindee? She'd done nothing but sob and say how much she loved Mike. She knew nothing about a note in the sack of paint she'd left by the Kauffman barn for Sarah, and she and Mike knew next to nothing about the Bible. Even though they'd been read their Miranda rights, neither of them had asked for a lawyer. And wouldn't they have done that, Nate thought, if they were guilty of arson?

"So, you still think we don't have our man?" Jack

asked as Nate almost collapsed in the chair on the other side of his desk.

"Or woman. Probably not."

They both sat silent for a moment before Jack spoke.

"Happy to say, I've got another woman, though, and I'm not talking arson. I believe Ray-Lynn's explanation of her being at the Esh barn the night of the first fire. But, on a personal note, I made up with her, too."

Nate glared at him. "Did you ever try to find out if she had an alibi for the Schrock fire like you said you'd do?"

"I said I believe her. You're getting punch-drunk, man. Go get some sleep. I'd arrest Bishop Esh—or Sarah Kauffman—before I'd think it was Ray-Lynn!"

Nate didn't want to get the man more upset than he already was. As soon as the rent-a-deputy got here from Wooster, Nate wanted Jack to drop him off near the Kauffman farm so he could hike back in as Amish. But he didn't know how long this charade would last. One person he wasn't fooling was himself. He wasn't Amish and yet he was falling in love with an Amish woman. She wasn't worldly and wasn't leaving her people. And he'd failed to solve an arson case he'd thought at first would be so simple.

The rest of that day did nothing to make Nate feel better. After the sheriff dropped him off near the cemetery and he hiked back to the farm, it was even more obvious that Sarah's parents were keeping her away from him. That evening, they insisted Sarah and Martha take care of their grandmother back out in the *grossdaadi haus* and keep watch on the barn from there.

Gabe stayed in the barn while Nate had Ben with him in Sarah's bedroom.

Out by the front of the barn, absolutely nothing had changed, except that Sarah's painting was growing larger. He had stared at it so long that it actually looked to him as if the multicolored ocean waves were moving, cresting, breaking on the dark wooden sea of the barn. He recalled how Sarah had told him she and Hannah had rescued Ella from drowning in the pond years ago, how there was some cold current deep down that tried to pull them under. He felt like that was happening to him.

On Friday morning, the day before the barn raising, Nate helped Ben and Gabe haul chairs and tables over to the Esh property. They even let him drive the big team on the road between the two farms.

Meanwhile, Mrs. Kauffman and Lizzie baked half-moon pies for the Dutch Farm Table and the barn raising. Outside, Sarah kept painting the quilt square. Back in the Kauffman kitchen for noontime dinner, Nate stared at the battery-operated clock on the wall. He heard his own clock ticking, his thudding heartbeat. He had to catch the barn burner. His boss had to have VERA back soon. Sarah—would he get some time with her to even say goodbye? He'd found the woman he wanted and he could not have her without destroying her. The Bible notes he'd kept secret were more than a ticking clock. They were a time bomb in Peter Clawson's hands. Nate could be accused of secrecy, of betrayal. He'd blown this case, his first failure on the job he used to be more passionate about than anything else—before Sarah.

He almost refused to eat dinner with the family, but

where else would he go without a car? He didn't want
to insult them, but he couldn't bear to see Sarah across
the table, because she might as well be across the continent. Once he was called back to Columbus and this
continuing investigation was turned over to Stan Comstock—however much the man had hinted he wanted
to retire—he'd never see her again. In this world, one
just didn't text or call or pick up an Amish woman for
a date. He was sure she cared for him, too, but that
made everything worse. So when the family bent their
heads before the noon meal and prayed silently as was
their custom, he asked the Lord for help to know what
to do—to stop the arsonist, to not have to give up the
woman he loved.

Right after the meal, when Ben and Gabe had gone
next door to help Bishop Esh with a big delivery of
timber for the new barn, Ray-Lynn called Nate on the
cell number Jack had given her. M.E. was at the restaurant with two of her friends to see Amish country and
she wanted to see him, too, because "she knew very well
he wasn't in Columbus like this nice lady who runs the
restaurant said."

"I don't like being misled or strung along by you or
Jack," Ray-Lynn told Nate over the phone, her voice
sharp. "He figured he had to tell me you've been around
here the whole time despite what you told me. Trying
to trap me, Nate? And Jack went along with it, so he
doesn't trust me, either. If you're still looking at me as
a suspect, then the kind, sweet woman sitting in booth
twelve did a lousy job of raising you! Jack said to tell
you if you need to get VERA, he'll unlock his garage
door. So if you're going to turn back into Superman
instead of being Clark Kent again, you just stay away

from Sarah because neither you nor Jack deserve either of us!" She hung up.

Nate explained to the Kauffman women that his cover was blown. "With Ray-Lynn and anyone in ear-shot of the restaurant, I'll have to give up the ruse of not being here and get to VERA so I can go see my foster mother. I'll let the word out that I've returned for the barn raising. I'll come back and park at the pond later, if it's all right with Mr. Kauffman, but it ruins my pre-tending I'm not here. Still, I'd like to help keep an eye on things around here tonight."

"Sarah, with us so busy," her mother said matter-of-factly, "you'll have to buggy Nate to get his VERA." Mrs. Kauffman and Lizzie were rolling out more balls of pastry dough for their second big batch of half-moon pies that kept coming out of the oven like a production line. "Then you come right back so you can finish the painting like you wanted." Mrs. Kauffman gave Nate a narrow-eyed look as if to say, *You behave now.*

He'd felt furious that M.E. had just shown up and ruined things. But had she? He'd wanted a chance to talk to Sarah, though he had not one clue what to say, and he'd been close to tongue-tied when she'd taken him into the sheriff's this morning because he couldn't bear to say a private goodbye, or any goodbye to her.

Sarah pulled the buggy out of the farm lane onto the road, heading for Sheriff Freeman's garage so Nate could get VERA and change his clothes before he headed into town. She knew he was real down about the arson case, and she wished she knew what to say to comfort him. In case this was their last time alone, she wanted to say so much, but Nate spoke first. "I don't like riding around hunched down like this—except for the view," he told her.

"How can you see where we're going down there at all? Oh, you mean—"

He put a hand under the seat, gently grasped her right ankle, then took it back. She fought to keep her hands steady, but she jolted so hard she could have steered Sally right off the road.

"We never got our swim in the pond together," she blurted. "The twelve days you've been here have gone pretty fast."

"Sarah, I think I'm going to be recalled to Columbus and Stan Comstock will take over here."

"I was afraid of that."

"Being here with you, your family and the community has given me a lot to think about. My nightmare of losing my parents in the fire my father set—I realize in a way I've resented M.E. as much as I've been grateful to her. She could never be my mother, so I shouldn't have punished her for that. I was afraid to really let her in my life, to really love her, as if I'd betray my own mother that way."

"You just put it really well how I feel about my parents. I love them, respect them, but I'm resenting the ties that bind me to them. I feel like I'd be betraying them if I tried to paint these places and these people for a career, so that takes a lot of soul-searching and courage. Ray-Lynn introduced me to the Columbus people with the art gallery this morning at the restaurant. I practically ran away from them when I really didn't want to. Now I'm going to kind of run away from us, too."

"Your father talked to me during the storm about not getting more personal with you. I don't want to alienate them, but you and I have had something going from the first—curiosity, sure, but a powerful attraction. You've really changed me in a short time. I feel deeply for you. If you ever do decide to leave here, I could help. Loan you some money, get you a place to stay while you paint."

"I just don't know. It would be worse for my people than when Hannah left. She wasn't shunned because she was never baptized in the church, but I was—I would be put under the *meidung*."

"I'd like you to meet M.E. After you let me out, will you buggy to the restaurant on your way home? I'll catch up with you and introduce you. I know your mother said to come back to the farm fast, but it would mean a lot to me if you'd come in to meet her."

"I'd have to face Ray-Lynn after how I ran from her friends, then argued with her this morning."

"You could wait out back. She's mad at the sheriff and me, too, for lying to her about where I really was. And right after she and Jack were flying high."

"Flying high—that's a good one. Not very Amish, at least if it means an airplane. Now if it's a bird—"

"Or a woman at the top of the ladder, reaching up to paint the ocean or the sky…"

Sarah didn't say so, but she didn't like that picture in her head of herself at the top of a ladder. The nightmare of being tied to one and burned still haunted her really badly. But she realized she was trying to change the subject now. She was afraid of her emotions, of having to meet Nate's foster mother, of being without him. Even of having the arsonist still on the loose. She pictured a farewell kiss coming when she let Nate out of the buggy, but Sheriff Freeman was home and came out to meet them by his garage.

Well, Sarah thought, perhaps it was all for the best. She'd break into a million pieces if she had to say a final goodbye to Nathan MacKenzie.

Nate parked VERA in the front of the restaurant—had to take a parking spot and a half—but figured he might as well let everyone know he was back. Had he actually cooked up the sting operation, he asked himself, just to be able to stay at Sarah's house for a while? No, it had been a viable idea, at least for someone who was desperate to catch an arsonist.

He hadn't passed her on the road into town after he'd changed his clothes and talked to Jack, who was fuming at Ray-Lynn for cutting him off after they'd just come to some kind of an understanding. "Women! Can't do with 'em or without 'em," Jack groused.

Nate could only hope Sarah had not gone right back to the farm but was parked behind the restaurant as he'd suggested. The only thing Ray-Lynn said to him when he walked in the front door was, "I'm not sure you deserve a mother—foster or step or whatever—as nice as that woman. Nice friends, too."

"Have you seen Sarah?"

"I told you to leave her alone. Yes, she's out back, although I warned her to leave you alone, too."

"Thanks, Ray-Lynn. I'm sorry and Jack is, too, but—"

She spun away and filled someone's coffee cup. He saw a lot of empty booths, but it was midafternoon. He hurried back to where he saw M.E. Silver-haired and slender, she was sitting with two chunky blondes, both on the far side of seventy. M.E.'s hair was straight and sleek with bangs that almost hid her eyebrows. She had a pug nose and pert smile.

"Nathan!" she greeted him, and stood for a hug. "You made Amish country sound so lovely that when I talked about it to Claire and Janet, we just had to come. I hear there's a big barn raising tomorrow, but we've got hospital volunteer work then."

He knew both of the other women, had for years, so he accepted their hugs, then perched on the edge of the booth beside M.E.

"Nathan," she whispered, "what's this about you being in Columbus when you really weren't?"

"I'll have to explain all that later. If you ladies wouldn't mind my taking M.E. away for a minute, there's someone I'd like her to meet. It's Sarah Kauffman, M.E., the Amish woman who's helped me here."

"Oh, well, yes, of course. I'd be honored to meet anyone important to you."

"It's not like you're thinking," he told her as he escorted her toward the back of the restaurant. She'd been matchmaking for years. But actually, he scolded himself, it *was* what she was thinking—only impossible.

"You don't know what I'm thinking, except that you look tired but a whole lot more healthy with a little more meat on your bones. And Ray-Lynn's food is rather filling, isn't it? Tasty, too, though I'm thinking Amish fare may be a little too heavy on the salt and sugar."

He opened the back door and escorted M.E. out into the alley. Sarah climbed down from the buggy, smiling but looking almost as shaky as he felt.

"M.E., this is my friend Sarah Kauffman, who's been such a help here."

"We're still not sure Nate has the arsonist under arrest," Sarah said, "but he's been a big help to us, too."

"I'm glad to hear that. I'd love to stay for the barn raising tomorrow, but my friends and I do volunteer work on Saturdays. The house feels a bit empty since my husband passed away and Nathan moved out and is so busy. You just come and visit me sometime, won't you, Sarah—I mean not by buggy, but somehow? You are always welcome."

"I've never been to Columbus—Cleveland, though. I'd like to take you up on that, but I just don't know."

Was she actually wavering about leaving here? Nate wondered. If she came to Columbus maybe M.E. could take her in. But then, to visit Sarah, he'd have to go past the barren lot where what some neighbors still called "the death house" had stood.

He gave Sarah a hand up into the buggy, though he knew she didn't need it, probably, in the long run, didn't need him. He realized she was in a hurry to get back to the farm and her family, her real life.

M.E. waved as Sarah blew a kiss to Sally and headed out. Like some kind of adolescent, Nate pretended she'd blown the kiss to him.

24

"Why does that woman keep looking out the window?" *Grossmamm* asked Martha, as if Sarah were not in the room and she didn't know who she was. Recognizing people came and went, but their grandmother had been pretty good lately on that. It was after dark, and the three of them had moved back to the *grossdaadi haus*. They had not lit a lantern so Sarah could watch the barn and not be on display herself.

"Just thinking about her quilt square she finished today, I guess," Martha answered with a helpless shake of her head when Sarah glanced their way. Martha, like Ella, was a stickler for not even telling what the world called little white lies, but she knew not to get *Grossmamm* upset again about barn burnings.

"When I was the age of you two," the old woman told them as she rocked in *grossdaad*'s old chair, "I was stitching entire quilts, not just one square."

"Let's go in the bathroom where there's a lantern, *Grossmamm*. You can get ready for bed, then I'll read to you from the *Budget* again," Martha said.

"I always did the family budget, especially the egg money," she told them, and got up with Martha's help. "I don't know why your father decided not to keep those good laying hens when we moved to this little place."

Well, at least she had those details right, Sarah thought. Things from the past seemed to stick if not the present. Still keeping an eye outside, she darted up from her chair and gave *Grossmamm* a quick good-night kiss on her paper-smooth, cool cheek, then hurried back to the window. Barely a moon tonight, just rising, but to eyes adjusted to the dark, it made enough light to watch the barn without the night goggles Nate was using. She pictured him sitting in her bedroom window, looking out with *Daad* right behind him.

She'd told Nate that she was ready to move on from that bedroom, but was she also ready to move on from this farm, this way of life? Ray-Lynn was right that painting made her happy and was purposeful. But would it be enough to carry her through if she lost everything here she had loved since she could remember?

Besides, Nate would haunt her heart everywhere she worked around here, everywhere she went after he was gone. At the Dutch Farm Table where she wanted to paint a mural for Ray-Lynn or a quilt square outside on the street. The pond—she'd always see him swimming there—the spot where he'd parked VERA. In the barn, the house, her own room and window and bed...

Something moved outside! Someone in black. Sarah shoved her chair aside, knelt by the window, hunched down. Someone carrying binoculars—*Grossmamm*'s grasshopper eyes! Could Nate see the man and would he come running? Her pulse pounded so hard she heard drumming in her ears.

She saw the intruder carried something. A sack? A
sack with what kind of incendiary device this time? Because *Daad* was not a church leader, the arsonist must
be targeting her paintings. Someone wanted her either
to stop doing the quilt squares or to draw attention to
them in the most horrible way.

She gripped her flashlight so hard her fingers went
numb. Don't startle the intruder, she told herself. Wait.
Wait. But don't let him run.

Maybe Gabe would spot him from the barn. Nate
had given him the extra phone. She'd wondered if it
was because she'd lost the other one in the ditch when
Jacob hit her buggy or just because Nate could keep
an eye on the *grossdaadi haus* but not the inside of the
barn. If the intruder started toward the barn, she would
have to confront him, then shout for Gabe and Nate. If
a fire started, she could not let Gabe be trapped like
Noah Miller.

Instinctively, she blinked and ducked as gravel hit
the window.

Hannah? Could that be Hannah? The form seemed
so shapeless she wasn't sure. She'd been relying on the
fact that someone else—whoever had left that first Bible
note—knew that signal would draw her out. Still, she
wasn't stepping outside unless she saw Hannah's face.
She'd trust her then, of course she would. None of this
horror could be her fault.

When the person threw a handful of gravel at the
window again, Sarah saw it was Hannah, the silhouette
of spiky hair, the shape of the pale face. Still she hesitated, then started to open the window sash to speak
before going outside.

But as she did, a second form appeared. Nate! He

grabbed Hannah, forced her to the ground as Sarah opened the window just in time to hear the confrontation.

"Ow! What? Lemme go!"

"Hannah? It's Nate MacKenzie. Just lie still."

Sarah rushed outside. Nate held one of Hannah's hands behind her back and had her face down in the grass. He was patting her all over as if she was hiding a gun—or a wick and matches.

"Nate, she was just throwing gravel against the window," Sarah protested. "That's how she always got me out to talk at night!"

"She's real good at night appearances near endangered or burned barns, isn't she?" he muttered, coming up with her car keys, which he dropped on the ground next to her bag.

"That's right," Hannah cried. "I just came to see Sarah."

With his night goggles still around his neck, Nate shone his flashlight first on Sarah's binoculars, then inside her bag.

"Amish clothes," he said, dumping the contents on the grass. "For an incognito getaway? And those are really big binoculars. Great for watching barn fires from nearby fields, I bet."

Sarah shivered. That person she'd seen in the field at the Schrock fire—she hadn't been able to tell if it was male or female, but in black… No, she knew Hannah as well as she knew herself. It could not have been her.

"I borrowed them," Hannah muttered. "You're hurting me."

Nate ignored that and kept pawing through the things

he'd spilled on the ground. *Daad* and *Mamm* came out of the house, and Gabe came running.

"Gabe, get back in the barn," Nate ordered. "Mr. Kauffman, can you go with him? She could be working with someone. This could be a distraction, a diversion, while someone else torches the barn."

"I'm not working with anyone! You're crazy!" Hannah insisted.

As the men left again—looking reluctant but alarmed—Nate got up, pulled out handcuffs and put them on Hannah behind her back. He lifted her to a sitting position. She looked horrible, Sarah thought— stunned, furious, frightened, her heavily made-up face dirty. Her skin was ashen, a shocking contrast to her dark mascara running from tears. She almost looked demonic. Surely, Hannah was not the Beast who had written those threatening notes. For a moment Sarah wavered. No, she still had faith her longtime friend would not burn barns.

Nate was looking more frustrated as he kept playing his light over the items from the paper bag. As far as Sarah could see, besides Amish garments, the pile included a big bottle of water and snack bars. Nate looked hesitant, puzzled.

"Hannah, if I search the grounds near the barn, am I going to find something to light a fire?" he asked, his voice quieter now. He knelt beside her, looking closely into her belligerent face. Sarah sat down beside her and *Mamm* hovered over them. Sarah saw that Martha stood now on the other side of the *grossdaadi haus* window, but she didn't come out. Only her white *kapp* and apron showed, ghostlike.

"I have no idea what might be near the barn," Hannah

said. "If you find something bad—incriminating—it's not mine."

"Let's hear why you're sneaking around here in the dark," Nate said with a frown at Sarah that clearly said, *Keep your mouth shut.* "This seems to be a habit with you—all the wrong barns, too."

"I know my family's barn raising is tomorrow," she said with a toss of her head. "Jacob told me."

Sarah let out a little gasp. She felt sick to her stomach at what might be coming next.

"I guess misery—and revenge—loves company," Nate said. "Nice of Jacob to keep tabs on the barns for both of you, but then you've been doing that for yourself, too, hanging around in dark nearby fields, right? Go ahead."

"I was going to ask Sarah if I could secretly watch the raising from the loft window of this barn, that's all. With the binoculars, I could see pretty well across the field. I know everyone will be there tomorrow at the crack of dawn and no way I was going over there to see it. You know I gave some money toward it, Mr. MacKenzie. I still can't—won't—go home, but I wanted to be near for this, at least. That stuff in the sack is the last of my Amish things, and I thought Sarah could use them—plus, some things for my breakfast if they let me stay here."

"Of course," *Mamm* said. "You can stay here, and we'll fix you breakfast, too."

"Mrs. Kauffman," Nate cut in, "Hannah Esh is only staying here tonight if she's under lock and key and if I don't find anything she brought to burn your barn around here or in her car."

"You're arresting her?" Sarah blurted.

"I'll tell you what. Since you're evidently so certain
she isn't involved in the barn burnings, even though
she's demonstrated an amazing amount of guilt over
her parents' barn, let's just—"

"Of course she shows guilt for that," Sarah argued,
"for leaving them. She's torn about that, not about
arsons she didn't commit."

"Sarah, I'm not reading her her Miranda rights or
calling the sheriff in—yet. How about you stop playing
defense lawyer and let me handle this?"

"*Mamm* and I know her better than you do, that's
all."

"Hannah," Nate said, "I have a witness who spotted
you in the field watching your family's barn burn."

Hannah gasped for air like a beached fish while
Sarah insisted, "I didn't say I saw Hannah through your
night goggles that night!"

"Not you. Keep quiet or go back inside the *grossdaadi haus!*"

"It wasn't me!" Hannah cried. "Someone's mistaken
or lying."

"Then that's enough from all of you right now,"
Nate said. "Here's the deal. Hannah agrees to stay in
the house—handcuffed to you, Sarah—while I search
the grounds and her car. Is it at the cemetery again,
Hannah?"

She nodded.

"Do I have your permission to search it? If not, I'll
get a search warrant."

"Yes, I don't care. Look, I can understand it looks
bad. I know you've been bugged by my lack of alibis,
but I did not harm our barn or any other, let alone watch
them burn. I did not!"

He unlocked one of her cuffs and, without asking for Sarah's permission, snapped it on her wrist. "Let's go inside the farmhouse," he said, putting Hannah's things back in her bag and handing it to *Mamm* while Sarah and Hannah got to their feet, not only cuffed together but holding hands. "Mr. Kauffman and I have a lot of ground to cover out here in the dark," he said as they all trudged toward the farmhouse.

"Don't waste your time," Hannah told him. Her voice had slowly come to sound like her again, almost defiant.

"You going to tell me where your stash of fire starters is, then?" Nate challenged when Sarah had thought he might be softening.

"I've done a lot wrong in my life, Mr. MacKenzie," Hannah said, turning to face him on the back porch, so that Sarah's hand was yanked around and she faced Nate, too. "But you're the one who's wrong about this. Dead wrong."

It was nearly dawn when Nate finally had to admit he'd found nothing to incriminate Hannah Esh. A few cigarette butts in the ashtray of her car was the closest he and Ben Kauffman could get to anything having to do with fire, though the interior of the old compact model smelled of smoke—incense, Sarah had said once—the same scent on Hannah's clothes and in her hair. He could not see hauling her into the same small jail cell that held Cindee Kramer, because that would make three suspects locked up, none of whom he could prove were guilty of arson.

"Hard to believe anyone Amish or former Amish would do it, anyway, Nate," Ben said as they dragged themselves into the farmhouse just before dawn and slumped at the kitchen table. "We know how precious the barns are. In the old days, folks would build a decent barn before they built themselves a good house."

Mrs. Kauffman poured them both coffee and, without a word, pointed to her husband's grimy hands. He and Nate got up to wash at the sink while she got bacon and eggs going on the stove.

"I haven't heard a peep out of the girls for a couple of hours," she told them. "But I heard them talking for a long time last night, not what they said, though. Always tight friends, those two, and Ella Lantz, they sure were."

"I'd better go up and unlock their handcuffs," Nate said. "I can't see grounds for holding Hannah."

"Her watching the raising will hold her here today," Mrs. Kauffman said. "It's fine with us if she watches from the barn window. I'm going to take your *mamm* over with us, Ben. I think it will do her good, but if it disturbs her, I'll bring her back. She keeps muttering about burnings, so seeing the *sheierufschlagge* up close will do her good. As for Hannah, I'm just praying that Sarah will convince her to come home for good—and not the other way around."

Taking a quick swig of his coffee, then pausing at the kitchen door, Nate said, "Sarah told me she'd never go to live with Hannah."

Both of the Kauffmans looked at him. The silence, but for sizzling bacon, screamed at him. Were they still afraid he would take Sarah with him?

"I'm leaving after the barn raising," he told them. "VERA's needed in Columbus for other cases, and Stan Comstock's back now. I apologize to you and your

people for stirring the waters without forcing the arsonist to the surface."

"We'll still be watching the barn today," Ben said.
"Gabe and I will be taking turns, and we're real glad
you're staying for the raising."

Nate nodded and went upstairs. He knocked on
Sarah's bedroom door. "It's Nate." Like Siamese twins,
bound together, when the door opened, both Hannah
and Sarah stood there, looking tousled and bleary-eyed,
still in the clothes they'd worn last night. Sarah wore no
prayer *kapp* or bonnet, of course. Her long, thick hair
spilled over her shoulders.

"Nothing was found," he informed them, "so either
I owe Hannah an apology or I missed the other sack."

"There was no other sack," Hannah said. Her face
looked ravaged by tears. Sarah, too, looked as if she'd
been crying.

He unlocked their handcuffs. "The Kauffmans say
you can stay in the barn during the raising," he told
Hannah. "Either Gabe or Mr. Kauffman will be back
and forth, and I might be, too. It's my last day here, and
I'm honored to help rebuild your family's barn."

"I know you need to do your job," Hannah said, rubbing her wrist with her other hand. "I want whoever
burned the barn found and stopped. Sarah tells me
you're to be trusted."

Nate's stare slammed into Sarah's, just as it had that
first time they'd met at the ruins of the Esh arson. "It's
because I'm *trying* to be worthy of trust that I'll be leaving the Home Valley tonight."

He wanted to say much more, but it was best that
he didn't. He hustled downstairs to eat breakfast with
Sarah's parents, planning to head for a swim in the

pond, then get over to the barn raising as fast as he could.

A new barn in a day—amazing but doable. Catching the barn-burning arsonist—difficult beyond belief. Forgetting the unique woman he'd come to love—mission impossible.

25

Like most Amish endeavors, barn building was a community event—a miracle of cooperation and coordination. Just after dawn, Nate stood in awe at the number of people who appeared at the site of the old Esh barn. They kept arriving through the morning mist in an army of buggies, and some *Englische* neighbors came in cars. Vehicles filled the Esh side lot, lined the driveway and one side of the road, clear to the Kauffman farm. Peter Clawson was everywhere, taking notes and pictures, toting a big camera bag around.

The women watched the children and kept busy in and out of the Esh farmhouse, fixing what would be a big noon meal. Nate noticed that the older women either sat outside to watch or set the long tables that had appeared from wagons and buggies. Sarah's *grossmamm* sat among them, seeming subdued today.

"Can you handle a drill?" Ben Kauffman asked Nate, and thrust a battery-operated one into his hands before he could answer. "Over there, holes in the boards we'll pound foot-long pegs through to hold things together later. Just follow what the others do, teamwork."

Nate nodded and bent to his task. Eli Hostetler seemed to be the crew boss for this swarm of laborers. He recognized several of the other Amish men. They all seemed to accept him with a nod or a brief word. When directions were given—perhaps for his sake— men spoke in English.

Nate looked up now and then, keeping an eye on the Kauffman barn and Sarah, but also just trying to cherish the moment, the feeling of acceptance, of working together. He wished—he prayed—he hadn't failed them. Maybe when the arsonist saw how the so-called Plain People accepted tragedy and rebuilt from it, he or she would stop or move on to someplace else. But he'd give almost anything to get his hands on whoever burned the barns.

Later, he saw Sarah move among the men with a tray of water in plastic cups. It was still early morning—coffee time—but this was heavy, hot work, and water was best for that. Besides, Mrs. Kauffman had fed them well this morning, and her coffee was great. Sarah had come in partway through breakfast after delivering half-moon pies to the restaurant. Before that, Nate had been forced to try to make conversation with Hannah, and they had gotten along pretty well. As for Gabe, as ever, he had hung on Nate's every word.

"Thank you," Nate told Sarah when she extended the cup of water to him. "Thank you for everything."

"You too, *ausländer,*" she whispered.

She moved on with a smile and a nod, blinking back tears. *Ausländer,* outsider. Was he an outsider here but also in his own world, not wanting to ever go near where his childhood home burned? Never letting M.E. and Jim Bosley adopt him or even get as close to him as they would have liked? To be so driven by his dedication to fighting arsons that he hadn't taken time for a wife and family?

His thoughts were nearly drowned out by the banging of hammers, the sound of saws. He watched men drive joining pegs with their big wooden mallets into the holes he'd helped make. The tall wooden framing pieces for the barn, called bents, were secured to the foundation. The sides of the barn now lay on the ground in sections, being formed before they would be lifted into place. Nate sensed the unity of the effort; they were raising a barn, but everyone's spirits, too.

How she would love to paint all this activity, Sarah thought, to capture the strength of her people, working together, separate lives, yet united. *All for one and one for all,* Ray-Lynn had called it the other day when they argued. Ray-Lynn was her dearest *Englische* friend— before Nate, anyway—and Sarah felt bad to disagree with her. Actually, she didn't disagree, if she could just find the backbone, a sturdy one, like the beams of this barn, to go out on her own to paint precious scenes like this one.

She went inside to help peel potatoes, standing next to Ella. She longed to tell her that Hannah was home, at least as far as the next barn, but she'd promised to keep it a secret.

"I miss you," Ella told her. "You come over sometime soon, *ya?*"

"I will. Just like old times, right?" Sarah said, but she knew that old times could never quite be captured again. How had the three of them grown apart? Ella had never forgiven Hannah for taking off, so what if Sarah decided to do something more radical than painting on barns someday? They bent to their work, only talking of distant cousins and other *maidals'* autumn weddings.

When other women had the potatoes boiling in big kettles on the stove, Sarah went outside and checked on *Grossmamm* again. She seemed to be entranced by the builders, but that was better than living her nightmares.

A sudden hush descended on the rumble of men's voices, then came the cry they all awaited from the master builder, Seth Lantz. "Take 'er up! Take 'er up!"

The women in the kitchen rushed outside to see the moment this big construction job was named for. Almost sixty pairs of hands seized one massive side section of the barn. It began to rise. Muscles strained, men grunted as it was lifted, first by hands, then by long poles while men sitting on the beams high above waited to secure the pieces and begin pounding them into place. Sarah's heart lifted, too, when she saw Nate among the men. She hoped Mr. Clawson would put a picture of him among the Amish brethren in the paper, because she would cut it out and cherish it forever.

Like the huge beams Nate had helped to lift earlier, shoulder to shoulder with the Amish men, the weight of the sides of the barn was tremendous, yet up they went. He got splinters in his hands, but he had splinters in his heart from loving—yes, loving—then losing Sarah, having to leave her behind so he would not hurt her, hurt these people.

Again, behind them, came the men with long, spike-tipped poles to push each section higher into the blue sky. Men with ropes pulled them upright, a span of eight-inch-square timbers and two-by-fours. Four times they groaned, lifted, pushed and pulled so that the men aloft, straddling the sections, could connect the entire frame by the hand-hewn joints and wooden pegs.

"Everything will fit perfectly." Peter's voice behind Nate emerged from the cacophony of other sounds. "Quite amazing. Plan and cut ahead and everything comes out *magnifico!*"

"You mind if I email you later for some of the photos?" Nate asked.

"Pushing your luck, asking for favors, aren't you? I'm still holding the story on that hellfire-and-damnation note, and you promised me some inside scoops I don't see coming my way. Not about Jacob Yoder this time, but about Getz and his girl's arrest."

"Once again, they aren't under arrest for ar—"

"Right, not for arson. Oh, there's Ray-Lynn. I was hoping she could get away for a while."

Nate watched Peter head straight for her, toting his camera bag and equipment. She was taking big coolers out of her trunk and clear plastic jugs of something pale like lemonade. Nate recalled that Jack had said she might start putting arsenic in his food. He hoped Jack and Ray-Lynn could patch things up.

As ever, Nate kept a good eye on the Kauffman barn whenever he looked up. He thought about Hannah over there, in self-made exile from all she loved, longing to come back, but unwilling or unable to. As much as he wanted to take Sarah away with him, he'd never put her through that. He also noted that every two hours, Gabe and Ben changed positions between guarding their barn and building this one. More than once, he saw Sarah glance over at their barn, too. At least with buggies parked as far as their property, a lot of eyes would be on that barn today as well as on this one. He'd heard her people admiring—or at least remarking on—the bold, newly painted quilt square there.

When the dinner bell rang, Nate was swept along with the men and wedged in at a long oilcloth-covered table—actually, several picnic tables shoved together—while the women served. It turned into a real gabfest with news of families, jobs, marriages and distant kinfolk the topics of conversations in both German and English. People kindly included him from time to time, but no one asked him how the case was going, maybe because they knew it wasn't going anywhere. He didn't see his replacement, Stan Comstock, though he said he'd try to come. Did Stan like the Amish as much as he did? At least he'd never been nuts enough to fall for one of their women.

Pulled pork sandwiches, roast beef, chicken and too many side dishes to count went by, served by the women or just passed down the table. There was coleslaw, beet salad, chowchow, casseroles of corn and green beans, bean and fruit salads, homemade bread and rolls with a peanut-butter-marshmallow spread he'd come to like and, later, about ten kinds of pies and cakes. With bittersweet feelings, Nate tucked in to what he figured would be for him the Amish equivalent of the last supper.

After the men had gone back to work and the women had eaten, they cleaned up. So many hands made light work, so Sarah went out to check on *Mamm* and *Grossmamm* again. She need not have worried that her grandmother would be tired or upset, because she was asleep in her chair under the shade of a red maple tree. *Mamm* was nearby, sitting with others, a quilt stretched between them on separate hoops, stitching and chattering away.

Leaning against the tree trunk, Sarah watched the raising of the roof rafters while other men swarmed around the foundation, nailing on the wooden siding. The din was almost deafening, yet it was a good sound, steady and strong. Amazingly, it did not wake the babies or the older women who were nodding off in the early-afternoon sun. Such a perfect day for the barn raising, a beautiful day for most things, except saying goodbye.

That reminded her of Hannah again. Though Hannah denied it, Sarah had a theory that she would have tried coming back home except for Seth. Hannah's come-calling friend had gotten another girl pregnant, then married her. Sarah could see him among those straddling the peak of the roof, a big, muscular blond, hammering away. He was a widower now, but that hadn't softened Hannah's anger at him. Seth and Hannah, Sarah and Jacob—how had things changed so much? With her binoculars, could Hannah pick Seth out, too? Now that Sarah had come to love and want Nate—now that he was leaving, though he hadn't let her down like Seth had Hannah—she understood Hannah's rebellion even more. Because today, more than ever, even amid this huge, happy community effort, Sarah had to admit that she herself felt like an *ausländer*.

Last night, Sarah had made Hannah promise that when she was ready to leave today, she'd hang the apron she had brought for Sarah in the loft window of the barn. Though Sarah hadn't said so, when she saw it, she planned to rush over to say goodbye. Too many goodbyes...

"Hey," Ray-Lynn said, startling her. "Sorry I upset you the other day."

"Forgiven if not forgotten," Sarah told her as she accepted a paper cup of lemonade from Ray-Lynn's tray. "It's my heart's desire to paint, but I'm needed here, too."

"I understand," her friend said. A long pause stretched between them. "I hear Nate's leaving."

"After this, heading back. His boss needs VERA and Nate."

"Not just a painting career awaits you in Columbus, but him, too."

Sarah sighed. "I do intend to do some drawings of this barn raising. I'm taking it all in. But don't mention that to anyone unless I decide it's time to."

"I've overheard a lot of talk about the new quilt square on your barn."

"Not all of it good."

"If they're not impressed by it, and still think it's like a worldly decoration, that's their problem. It stands out so you can see it from the road, the fields and hills. It's great."

Ray-Lynn bustled off, but her words snagged in Sarah's soul. Not only *it's great* but *it stands out.* That had probably been her problem from the beginning. Things she did stood out; she stood out, didn't fit the pattern, the people. *It stands out,* and she wanted it to. She longed to draw and paint pictures where individuals stood out and yet were part of the Plain People. She hated to be a fence jumper, but she had to admit that she wanted her art to reach out to others, *to stand out.*

And then she saw the small white square in the loft window of their barn. Hannah was going away, not coming home.

"*Mamm,* I'm going to say goodbye to our guest," Sarah told her, leaning over her mother's shoulder as she ran a line of even, tiny stitches through pale blue cotton, her hand amid the others working on the quilt, a Sunshine and Shadows pattern.

"Your *daad* came back from there, so it will be just Gabe and our guest. If you catch her, you remind her she can visit us whenever she wants, and we'll keep her secret she's been there today," she went on, whispering. "But she needs to think about coming home, all the way home."

"*Danki, Mamm,*" Sarah said, and squeezed her shoulder before turning away. She skimmed the crowd for Nate as she walked toward the field. She finally spotted him up on a tall ladder, pounding nails into the siding over the barn doors. It looked to be the ladder from VERA, the one he'd loaned to her for the painting and had just taken back. Would Bishop Esh ever dare to ask her to paint another quilt square there where Nate was working?

The workers started nailing down the sheet-iron roofing. If the siding made a din, this was a clamor. Surely that would wake the sleepers. Sarah could hardly think, and the sound seemed to echo off her own barn as she hurried toward it.

Tempted to put her hands over her ears, she picked up her pace through the field she'd run across the night of the Esh fire. Only two weeks ago, but so much had happened. At least Hannah's name had been temporarily cleared, she thought, even if Jacob's hadn't. She

watched where she stepped because their plow team
and buggy horses were grazing here today. It wouldn't
be good to be tracking horse apples around. She barely
broke stride to pat Sally as she came up to nuzzle her
and walked along for a minute before stopping to graze
again on the fringe of the field.

Sarah looked back at the new Esh barn. That gentle
slope of land where it had been burned had seemed so
naked without it, but there the new one stood, almost
identical. The men atop and around it in their black
trousers and white shirts with so many moving and
bobbing straw hats made the barn look like a living
creature now, a benign beast.

She rounded the corner of their barn and glanced up
at her new quilt square in satisfaction. Not in pride or
hochmut, not because it was "just for pretty," because
it wasn't. It was a sign of Amish gifts to the world, a
sign that the Home Valley was a good place to be, bad
publicity of barn burnings or not.

The sliding door to the barn stood about three feet
ajar. Gabe probably wanted the light and air inside.
"Gabe, it's Sarah!" she called out as she stepped in.
"Hannah, you still here?"

The distant hammering seemed muted inside the
cool vastness. No air stirred and silence engulfed her.
"Gabe! Hannah!"

Maybe one or both had gone into the house or *grossdaadi haus* to use the bathroom or get something to eat
or drink, but Gabe should not have left the barn open.
Even in broad daylight, it was dark in here with just the
light from the loft window, muted by Hannah's apron,
and the single shaft of light from the barn door.

And then, behind her, the door rolled shut and

slammed, plunging the barn into deeper darkness. Sarah spun to stare in the direction of the door, but her eyes still had not adjusted.

"Gabe Kauffman!" she said. "This isn't funny!"

Something shuffled through the straw, across the wooden floor. She could hear it, feel it—something alien and evil. Instinct, self-preservation, fought with rising fear as she felt the hair on the back of her neck prickle. Whoever now stood in the corner of the barn near the door, behind the grain bin, was breathing heavily, even as Sarah was from her dash across the field. She had to make a run for the door. One more step back, around to the side, not straight for it.

She tried to tiptoe but a board creaked. Fear careered through her. Was there a beast, some sort of demon? Human, of course. Her heart nearly thudded out of her chest. Even if she escaped and screamed for Nate, for the others, they would never hear her with their noise. She had to make a break for it, run all the way back to her people.

But as she took another sideways step, she tripped over something and fell to her knees over it. In the darkness, she sensed more by touch than sight.

A body!

"Gabe?"

No answer came but the sound of someone's breathing and the muted din of pounding, pounding. *Ya,* it was Gabe! He lay unmoving, sprawled facedown, his hair and the floor sticky with wetness.

"Hannah! Hannah, are you still here?" Sarah screamed.

"She left," a whispery voice said. "Though she'll be blamed for this barn going up in the flames of hell."

26

Was it Jacob in the darkness? Surely he hadn't been working with Hannah. Or was she here somewhere unconscious, too? But something about the voice—she was sure it wasn't Jacob.

She heard footsteps coming closer and backed away, hitting the ladder that led to the loft. Slowly, her eyes adjusted to the dim depths of the barn she knew so well. A form emerged to become the shape of a man holding two weapons. No, a canister with a spout was in his hands and a camera on a strap was slung over his shoulder.

For one moment she thought to play dumb, ask him to take pictures of the scene so the sheriff could find clues to learn who had hurt Gabe. But she knew the truth now.

"Nate MacKenzie is meeting me here in about two minutes," she lied, amazed that the words came out of her mouth before she could form a plan.

Peter Clawson laughed. "I knew you two were an item, and if I printed a scandal sheet, I'd lead with that story," he said, his voice taunting. "I have no doubt he'll be here, but too bad, too late. He's still pounding away over at the Esh place. This barn burning is my pièce de résistance, my masterpiece—you know, like a fine painting."

She made a move to bolt past him, but in one quick blast he shot fire from the canister in front of her feet. She gasped and jumped back.

"'He even makes fire come down from heaven on the earth in the sight of men'—women, too," he said, and she knew he was quoting from his own threatening notes. The flames scorched the barn floor but did not ignite the wood. Still she had no doubt what that fire thrower could do to the rest of the barn and to her.

She needed to talk to him, stall him. Obviously, this was a man prideful at his own cleverness. Since she and maybe Gabe knew who the arsonist was, he must intend to burn them with the barn. He might not have meant to at first, but he would have to now. If she played on his weakness, it might give someone time to come. Hannah might have second thoughts and return, Gabe would wake up—or, dear Lord in heaven, wouldn't someone notice she was gone or taking a long time and come help? No, no, she'd told *Mamm* where she was going, and she'd only been here a few minutes.

"But why burn our barns and my paintings?" she asked Peter, her voice quavering. "Just to get good stories?"

"Partly, but that's too obvious and shallow a motive. Ah, my dear, let me count the reasons. I need to keep Ray-Lynn in my control, and she has some wild idea of repping you to her artist friends and leaving me in her dust, so I was hoping to warn you off further painting.

She'll come around, though, admit she belongs to me. Eventually, I'll find a way to get rid of the sheriff—make a fool of him as I have your gung-ho fire investigator MacKenzie."

Her mind raced. His words barely made a dent in her frenzy. She knew she had to try to escape soon, even if he shot that fire at her. Her skirts would catch. They would flame, and she would be burned like poor Noah. But if she could get outside, someone across the field might see her. Surely, Nate and *Daad* were keeping an eye on this barn, too.

"Why do you hate the Amish?" she asked. "Without us, what would make your paper special?"

"I would!" he shouted. "You could put me in the middle of a field, and I'd find something exciting to write about even if I had to create it. The *Budget*—that gossipy, amateur Amish paper you all read—is nothing compared to mine, and these barn burnings have proved that, so—"

She ran. She leaped past him and made for the door, but something hard hit her head from behind, and the world went black.

Nate scanned the crowd of women, searching for a glimpse of Sarah. When they all wore their bonnets and prayer caps, many looked alike, though he could distinguish the women he knew—and he was good at picking out Sarah. He could spot her mother and grandmother, her sisters, too, but saw no sign of Sarah. With all the clatter and pounding around and over him, he couldn't hear himself think.

He climbed down his ladder and moved it closer to the corner so he could help to nail the next sec-

tion. He walked over to the trough filled with nails
and stuffed more into the canvas work apron he'd been
loaned before he climbed up again. Shading his eyes,
he looked across the field toward the Kauffman barn.
Everything looked normal, except for a white something
in the single, high loft window. Hannah must have covered it for some reason. Maybe she'd done it to just look
through a slit so no one would see her there. Or it could
be the glint of sun off the windowpanes at this angle.
Despite the fact there seemed to be a separation of the
sexes here today, he headed down the ladder again and
walked into the throng of women and bent to speak with
Mrs. Kauffman.

"There's a white cloth in your barn loft window," he
told her as some of the women turned their heads his
way, lifting their eyes from the quilting.

"Oh, *ya,* I know," she said, and stood to walk away
from the quilting circle with him. "Hannah told Sarah
she'd put an apron there when she was ready to leave,
so Sarah ran over to say goodbye. Gabe's there, too.
Don't worry."

"I didn't see her go."

"I know you watch her good."

Their eyes met and held. A frown furrowed her brow.
This woman—all the Amish—seemed to have a talent
for saying so much with few words.

"Don't you worry about her," she repeated. "It's nice
you are helping here."

In Amish-mother-speak, Nate thought, that meant
don't go over there where you could have time to talk
to Sarah alone, especially right before you are supposed to leave. He excused himself and went back to
his ladder, wishing like a fool that he and Sarah had

planned that she'd put a white flag of surrender in the window if she'd leave with him today.

Sarah regained consciousness in a haze of crushing pain. She tried to move her arms and legs. Could but just a bit. Couldn't talk, couldn't cry. Was she dead? Something in her mouth—gagged. Tied.

It all came back in a rush. The Beast was going to burn the barn.

She forced her eyelids open and saw she was tied to the ladder that went up to the loft. The dreadful nightmare of being burned with the Amish martyrs hit her hard. They tied her to a ladder and were going to tilt her into the flames. They had ripped her bonnet and prayer *kapp* off. She was going to die. The crowd was screaming for blood—no, that was the distant din of the pounding at the Esh barn. She was so woozy, but she heard a voice in her head, "For wickedness burns as the fire! Burn them! Burn them for the fires of hell!"

"I was hoping you would not wake up again, Sarah—really," Peter called to her, dragging her from her half-waking dream. He was quickly and methodically going around the edges of the barn floor, shooting flames from his canister until he had a ring of fire burning everywhere but near the front doors. Each blast of flame he threw illuminated his face as if he were one of those fright masks in the store windows at Halloween. Where straw or hay caught, flames leaped and smoke began to billow.

"Since you have such an inquiring mind," he went on, his words more muffled as he lit the empty horse stalls, "I'll tell you that my incendiary device of choice this time is a drip torch, used by men fighting forest fires for controlled burns. Controlled burns—that's one of my many talents."

It didn't matter what he said anymore. She had to get loose, get out. Gabe still lay sprawled on the floor, unmoving, almost at her feet. At least the outer walls of the barn would burn first. But then the flames would get to Gabe; though he was low enough the smoke would choke him after her, that smothering stench of this sick man's hatred and pride. She half prayed, half tried to send Nate a mental message. *Barn burning! Come now!* That other nightmare was nothing next to this, for this was real.

"Parting is such sweet sorrow," Peter called through the smoke and flames. "I'm sorry, Sarah, really. I didn't know either of you would be here but it's too late now. And Hannah's being here, then leaving—how perfect. I'll do all I can to see that she is prosecuted as the Amish barn arsonist. Now won't that be a fine series of articles? I can see the headline now Rebellious Amish Woman Turns Against Her Own People. Well, back to the barn raising. I'd better return before anyone notices I'm missing."

He coughed in the thickening smoke. She heard the barn door slide open, then shut, and the outer latch bang down.

The man was everywhere with his camera so no one would suspect him, blame him.... The Beast would no doubt just blend back into the crowd as he always did, or if found here, say he was taking pictures of her painting. Hannah...poor Hannah would be blamed. She had to stop him, to save Gabe.

The smoke thickened; the flames crackled. The gag in her mouth made her want to throw up. Surely someone across the field—anyone!—would see smoke or flames soon. But it was a wide field, and it would take time for the firefighters to come. All their worst fears, their premonition that this barn could burn... Coming true... Nate's VERA was still back at the pond, so his suit he'd rescued Noah in was out of his reach....

She began to cough. Her eyes stung with smoke. As she pulled against her ties, she saw they were reins for the plow team. Peter had tied them around her and the ladder but not tightly, maybe because she was a sagging deadweight in her unconscious state or he was in a hurry. If she could just get up a step, slide her backside and her bonds upward against the ladder, maybe she could reach the loft, break the window, get out, wave the apron. Maybe she could slide herself right off the top of the ladder. She had to get down to the ground, then back in the barn to try to get to Gabe.

Breathing through her nose only, gagging on whatever was in her mouth, trying not to take in smoke, she managed to slide the reins from around her thighs up enough that she could lift one foot, then the other. Yes, her knees could bend now. Lift one leg, get her heel on the next rung, then the other leg. It was so hard, grueling. If she could only scream Gabe's name again, try to wake him. Gagging, gasping, sweating, up another step, inching the cords around her upper arms up, too, then straining to take another step.

It seemed a climb up a mountain, higher, higher. But the smoke was thickening, and this took so much strength, so much time. This barn, her family's barn, was burning, dying. And she and Gabe were, too.

* * *

Nate kept watching the field, waiting for Sarah to return. She'd talked to Hannah all last night, so did she have to take so long? He didn't like it that she wasn't here when things were winding down. He couldn't bear to leave if he couldn't say goodbye to her, even if the entire Amish and *Englische* community was watching. Or was it her plan to stay away while he left so they would not have to say goodbye?

"Hey, Nate!" Mr. Kauffman called down to him from the roof. "Want to come up and see the view from here before you go?"

Before you go—another kindly worded hint, Nate thought. "Sure," he said, though he realized his ladder was not tall enough to get him up there. "But I've got to check something out first."

"How about me?" Peter Clawson called out from below. "Nate, can you at least take my camera up there for a shot of the crowd?"

Nate saw Peter was sweating and out of breath, but then he was lugging the camera and a big equipment bag. Before Nate could answer, Jack approached Peter and started jawing with him about something.

And then Nate smelled the faintest whiff of smoke. No barbecues here today. No bonfires for trash. Surely, no one was smoking. But that wasn't cigarette or cigar smoke.

He didn't even wait to assess the situation or go for the binoculars he'd brought, thinking he might just end up watching the action today. "Jack, with me!" he shouted, ignoring Peter's snatching at his arm. He broke into a run across the field with the sheriff right behind.

He wasn't even halfway across when he knew. The

Kauffman barn had smoke seeping out under the front doors. It was ready to break into a blaze.

Sarah slid herself—torso, then legs—off the top of the ladder. The worst of this backward climb had been getting past where the ladder leaned against the edge of the loft, but she'd found the strength—the desperation—to drag the back of her bonds through that snag. Now, unable to break her fall, tipped backward, she fell about four feet to the loft floor where Hannah had been looking out today. Her eyes streaming tears, her hands still tied but with more leeway now, she scrambled to her knees, pulled her arms around in front and picked up the feed trough from *Grossmamm*'s old chicken coop. In a burst of panic, she rammed it into the window.

Nothing. She was too weak. No air. She felt faint. If she broke the glass, it would feed the flames below. No choice, no choice. But she did have a choice about painting what she longed to, about who she loved. She desperately wanted to live to make those choices.

She hooked the part of the gag that protruded from her mouth onto a nail sticking out of the loft wall and it snagged. She managed to pull it out of her mouth. It was her wadded-up prayer cap. Coughing as she sucked in air and smoke, she yanked the apron off the glass and hit at the window again with the old trough, wood against bare glass. Two panes shattered outward. Smoke seemed to grab at her, but she broke out the rest, both glass and wood.

She sucked in fresh air even as the smoke rushed past her. Then, through the gray-white haze, she saw salvation coming from across the field—Nate, the sheriff, others. She seized Hannah's apron and tried to flap it out the window.

Wreathed with smoke, she stuck her head out. Nate was below her, shouting, "Stay put. I'll get a ladder!"

"No— Gabe's lying on the floor of the barn! Help him!" In case she didn't make it, they had to know who did this. "Peter Clawson's the arsonist!" she shouted down, still coughing. She watched as Nate, the sheriff and her father raced around to the front of the barn.

Her eyes and nose were running. She wiped at them with her sooty sleeve and realized she was not burned.

Her mother and Martha emerged from the growing crowd, Lizzie and her husband, too. Ray-Lynn stood there, wringing her hands. "Get my paint ladder!" she shouted, and her sisters ran for it. She heard voices below her in the barn. She wanted to scream down to ask if Gabe was all right, but her throat was raw.

With Ray-Lynn's help, Lizzie and Martha banged their father's ladder up under the loft window. It didn't reach, but Sarah didn't care. She was getting out.

She would have to dangle her feet to reach the top rung, but she knew this ladder, the feel of the rungs, how far it could tip. She saw that she would cut her hands hanging from the broken window, her artist hands, so she covered the jagged glass at the bottom with Hannah's apron, folded over. She hung there, smoke streaming past, clinging to her, billowing out. But just when she knew she'd have to let go, Nate was scrambling up her ladder to the very top, shouting.

"Hang on! I'll grab your legs and you can fall back on me!" She felt him grab her ankle, both ankles. It felt so good. So strong and safe.

"Gabe?"

"Alive but still out. Help is coming. I've got you! Let go! Trust me!"

His words pounded in her head. She did trust him. And she was going to have to learn to let go.

She fell against Nate and the ladder. Somehow he held on to her as the women below gasped, then cheered. Nate held her to him against the ladder. She put her arms around him and held on, even as he guided her down. She saw more of her people streaming across the field to help.

"Did you hear me say Peter Clawson?" she asked, coughing, her voice rough. It hurt to talk, but she had to.

"The bastard dared to show up first over at Eshes', then here, just business as usual—arson. I tackled him and Sheriff Freeman arrested him—with a drip torch in his bag."

"I'll testify," she insisted, hacking. "It would be wrong not to. I'm going to have to go against my people on that—on other things. Oh, Nate, *Daad,* not our barn, too!" she sobbed as he handed her down the ladder to her father.

They heard the shriek of the approaching siren. They wanted her to lie down but, holding on to both Nate and her father's arms, with trembling legs she walked around to the front of the burning barn. The scene reminded her of the night they saved Noah from the Miller barn as her mother knelt over Gabe's prone form.

Coughing up gray mucus, sucking in air, then breathing pure oxygen from a mask while the firemen and Nate fought the fire, Sarah sat by her brother, too. In the end, they saved only the front wall and doors of the barn, where Peter Clawson had not used the drip torch, no doubt so that he could escape, but he'd never escape justice now.

In the midst of praying women, Gabe regained consciousness and moaned. The ambulance came to take him to the Wooster hospital with *Mamm* going along. With her sisters by her side—someone, blessedly, must have kept *Grossmamm* over at the Eshes'—Sarah looked up at her quilt square painting. It was sooty, charred at the edges; some of the color had crackled and blistered, but it was pretty much intact. It had come through the flames, just like her.

She glanced over at Nate again, still busy with the firemen, then back up at her painting. Instead of an abstract pattern, she pictured there a panorama of a barn raising with the Amish brethren lifting the wooden sections toward the heavens, and the women bustling around the long tables to feed everyone, and the hills of the Home Valley under a brilliant sky with puffy clouds but no smoke—and, like the golden sun, with lots of love shining over everything.

27

One month later

It was worse than when she told her family she was
going to testify against Peter Clawson in a Cleveland
courtroom. Now Sarah looked at the dumbstruck faces
of each of her loved ones around the breakfast table. She
had waited until they were all together. Gabe was home
from the hospital and had started to grow his hair out
where they'd shaved his head to put in stitches. Plans
were set to rebuild the barn. But she wouldn't be here.
She'd just told them she was leaving for Columbus.

"Just for a visit?" *Grossmamm* inquired in the
stunned silence. "That will be nice."

"Staying where?" Martha asked breathlessly. *Daad*'s
fork had clunked down on his plate, and *Mamm*'s eyes
swam with tears. Sarah knew it was what they'd been
dreading.

"Staying with Nate's foster mother, Mary Ellen
Bosley," she told them, gripping her hands in her lap
so they couldn't see how scared she was. She'd ago-

nized over this ever since the barn burnings had been solved. "She's a widow and has a spare bedroom and a nice glassed-in sunroom I can use to paint. I *have* to paint. It's part of me."

"And we aren't?" *Mamm* blurted. "You'll be put under the *meidung!*"

"I know. I've thought it all through."

"If you could paint here, more than decorations," *Daad* asked, his voice very quiet, "would you stay, or is there another reason you are going to Columbus?"

"I need to find out if there's another reason. Yes, I think there is, but I need to give that time, a chance."

"A chance?" *Mamm* jumped back in. "We don't live our lives by chance. And how will you get a hundred miles to the big city of your dreams?"

Sarah blinked back tears. She'd steeled herself for this, rehearsed it over and over, but she felt as if she was being ripped apart.

"I hired a car, the same driver we used when we went to see Lake Erie. Ray-Lynn offered to drive me there, her art gallery friends offered, Nate and his foster mother offered, Hannah offered, but—"

"All those people knew before us?" *Mamm* cried. "And Hannah? Her rebellion gave you this idea!"

"No, my own head and heart and hands gave me this idea," Sarah said, fighting to keep her voice under control. "I am so sorry that what I need to do cannot be accepted here. I know our people strive to keep the community and our traditions honored and preserved. By painting precious scenes from our lives, I'll preserve all that in a new way, and I'm sure it will send more tourists here."

She stood. Her chair scraped back much too loud. "I

regret I will not be here to help with *Grossmamm,*" she
added, "especially now that Martha will have to take
the half-moon pies into the Dutch Farm Table. Martha,
I'm leaving you my buggy and Sally, and I know you'll
take good care of both."

"I'll help more with *Grossmamm,*" *Mamm* said, snif-
fling. "I didn't realize how much you two did there, and
I'm grateful." Sarah wasn't expecting that kindness. She
couldn't hold back her tears.

"I am, too," *Grossmamm* piped up. "But I want both
of you girls—Gabe, too, when his bean heals—to meet
someone you can marry, get a come-calling friend."

Sarah could feel everyone's eyes on her, even as
Grossmamm went on about "frolics in the good old
days."

"I'm not running away to be with Nate," Sarah told
them, "although I respect and—and love him. I'll be
leaving late this afternoon. I can pack everything by
then. I deeply regret that this decision cuts me off from
the people I love, those I will paint with great affection,
and that all of you will suffer as I will by our separation. But I have to do this. It's not the accepted thing
but it's the right thing."

She turned and ran, thudding up the stairs. Later, as
she packed her things in large shopping bags, including the new sketchbook she had almost filled, Martha
came in to help and Gabe poked his head in the door,
as if to flaunt his twenty scalp stitches as he had in the
hospital.

"I think Nate's a great guy," he whispered. "He likes
the Amish—maybe he could come live here instead."

"It wouldn't work that way," she told him, hurrying

to the door to hug him before he got away. "It has to be like this."

He hugged her back hard and fled.

She left her home and family and people at one-thirty that afternoon, trying not to look back at the Home Valley as her hired car sped away and turned south on the highway. Everyone had embraced her in the kitchen, but no one had helped to carry her things to the car.

"I hope you will feel at home, but I'm sure it will take a while," M.E. said as she and Sarah sat over lemonade and gingersnap cookies later that day in the sunroom where Sarah would paint when she purchased her supplies. An easel Nate had bought for her stood waiting to be used. She and M.E. were both watching the clock. Nate was on assignment in Southern Ohio with VERA but he said he'd be here about 6:00 p.m. For once, M.E. had refused to meet him somewhere so he could avoid coming down the street past the place where his parents had died.

"You've been wonderful, you and Nate both," Sarah said. She was without her bonnet and prayer cap and wore her hair down her back in a loose braid. She figured she'd cut some of it soon, maybe to shoulder length, because, for the first time in her life, it felt too heavy. She also wanted to get some other clothes, conservative ones, but not Amish. Today, she'd borrowed a long denim skirt and long-sleeved blouse from M.E. She was only Amish inside now, not outside, since she'd taken this big step, she kept telling herself.

"And a phone call from home already!" M.E. said. "So how is our friend Ray-Lynn? She said she had a surprise for you that you'd tell me."

"Her good news is that Peter Clawson is going to have to spend so much money for his legal defense that he agreed to let her buy out his share of the restaurant."

"I thought she didn't have the money."

"She doesn't, but Sheriff Freeman does."

"So he's back in her good graces?"

"I wouldn't count on it, not the way she operates. But I still hope she'll partner with me to get my work sold in the Homestead area. M.E., if you don't mind, I'd like to walk down the street to meet Nate. I know he hates to go by the lot where he lost his family, and I thought maybe I could help him through that."

"I've tried, but not with the same skill set you have, my dear." She walked Sarah to the front door with her arm around her shoulders and gently closed the door behind her.

It was a lovely but humid early July day. Several people had their sprinklers twirling water on the lawns they had cut with loud mowers. Kids played in the end of the court, just like Nate probably did when he was young. No sidewalks here, yet there was too much concrete and noise. Well, she'd get used to all that.

She walked briskly to stand in front of the empty, overgrown lot where Nate's parents had died. She could see a ragged concrete foundation amid the weeds and wildflowers. The city owned the land now, but evidently no one had wanted to buy and build here. She was standing about ten feet from the curb in the tall grass when she saw a car turn into the court. It was Nate. No VERA, but he had to give his partner back at night when he was here in Columbus.

She wondered if he'd drive on by, not recognizing her or refusing to stop, but he didn't. Frowning, yet looking relieved to see her, he turned off the engine and got out, slamming the car door. But he didn't budge from the curb.

"Thank God you're here," he said, "but why *here?*"

"So we can put our pasts to rest and go on. Outsiders—we've both been that in a way. We've both lost our families, but—I think—we still have each other."

He nodded but did not advance to where she stood her ground—the ground, she knew, he had not so much as looked at, let alone walked on, for many years.

"You won't believe what happened today," he said, still not moving. "Stan Comstock is retiring in six months, and the state fire marshal has offered me his northeast Ohio supervisor job. If I take it, I'll be stationed not far from Homestead."

"Oh!" she said. "That's wonderful, and my peop—the Amish—will love you."

"But will you love me? If so, I think that move is something we should decide together."

"Yes, I do and will love you, Nathan MacKenzie, and I'm not even jealous of VERA anymore."

He didn't laugh, though his blue eyes lit up. He strode across the wild-grass space between them, lifted her and held her tight.

"Then, wherever we are together—in Amish country or even here on this sad spot," he said, tears in his eyes, "I'm home."

"*Ya*—yes—me, too!"

* * * * *

Author's Note

Each time I visit Amish country now, I see it with new eyes. To write about something, for me, is to become part of it. Unlike most writers who begin with plot or character, I almost always start with a place that intrigues me.

Special thanks to the Amish of Holmes County at such places as the Berlin Helping Hands Quilt Shop and other venues who answered questions. Ray-Lynn's restaurant is partly based on Grandma's Homestead Restaurant in Charm, Ohio, and partly on the various Ohio-based Dutch Kitchen restaurants. I am especially grateful to the Amish who were kind enough to let me visit their barns and to the Amish barn builder, or timber framer, who sketched various styles of barns for me. And I appreciate the interview I had with Shasta Mast, Executive Director of the Holmes County Chamber of Commerce and Tourism Bureau. Her insights were very helpful.

Quilt square paintings on barns are becoming popular in the Midwest. One place to view these online iswww.monroecountyohio.net/tourism/barns. Interesting articles about Amish life are available at an excellent website at www.amishnews.com/amishseries.html. Clinton County in Ohio has an excellent Barn Quilt Trail for tourists to enjoy. For information on that, contact Barn Quilts, 2846 Starbuck Road, Wilmington, OH 43177.

Anyone interested in learning more about the Amish book, the *Martyrs Mirror,* in an English translation, can enter in Google "The Martyrs Mirror" + "English translation." Some of the woodcuts and etchings of that book inspired Sarah's nightmares about people being burned tied to ladders—the tragedy of the Amish past when they were persecuted in Europe for being Anabaptists.

The Amish, like many Americans, have been hit hard by the national and global recession. Melvin Troyer, an Ohio craftsman who makes Amish furniture, has said they've been marking items down to "rock bottom" to keep more members of the Amish community earning a living.

Special thanks to Meredith Bair, LPN and Hyperbaric Technician, for her information on burn victims and their treatment at the Cleveland Clinic.

VERA is very much based on the specialized vehicle of the office of the state fire marshal of Ohio; however, it is called MIRV for Major Incident Response Vehicle. I have, however, fictionalized the state fire marshal's name and staff. Any mistakes in investigating techniques are my error, not theirs.

Of course, one of the joys of visiting Amish country

is the delicious, homemade food. This story mentions different, favorite dishes, but the half-moon pies were the main focus. A recipe for these can be found online at such charming sites as www.anniesrecipes.com. These pies—which I also see are called preaching pies sometimes, probably because they are good ones to take for individual people at church—are also similar to the popular Amish fry pies.

The other books in the *Home Valley Amish* Trilogy will focus on new main characters—next time Hannah Esh gets center stage—but Sarah and Nate will also return. Happy reading, quilting and eating—and just appreciating life day by day.

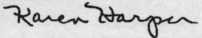

REQUEST YOUR
FREE BOOKS!

2 FREE NOVELS
FROM THE SUSPENSE COLLECTION
PLUS 2 FREE GIFTS!

SUS11